MW01006938

System of Controls

System of Controls

IT's Guide to Managing Cyber Risk

William D. Reed

Vision Park Media

Dedication

This book is dedicated to all the IT professionals who design, build, operate, and defend the digital infrastructure that makes the modern global economy possible.

Table of Contents

Preface

Smart IT is an approach to getting the important things done by transforming the way traditional IT thinks, works, and leads. It supports the disruption of the status quo, simplifies the complex, and mitigates risk. This is the next generation of information technology.

This approach models a different way of thinking by framing principles on how we work. It is much more than a play on the mnemonic of SMART goals. It goes beyond a sense of natural intelligence or being good in school. It's a way of thinking and working that is open to everyone in IT.

This Smart approach to IT is a construct for the profession of information technology. It frames the conceptual aspects of thinking about one's role in the larger organization and the nature of the work itself. It illuminates the larger forces shaping the drivers of the challenges we face and the creation of new opportunities. This is a guide to inspiring the change that is needed in our professional world.

Smart IT is a way of working and being. It is about being conscious of our environments, new enablers, and opportunities to help our organizations.

Teams work differently, maintain their relevance, and provide more value to their organizations than traditional IT. Smart IT allows a business to maintain pace with the market. As in life, we want to hire smart people, send kids to school to become smart, and make smart decisions to have fulfilling lives. The same goes for business—we want IT professionals to embody the principles of SMART goals, an especially useful tool for attaining what you want.

Teams leverage this framework to see useful information other people can't see or don't notice. They then draw accurate, useful conclusions from that information. Thirdly, these teams design useful goals that take advantage of the information. Finally, they create an efficient and effective plan of action to attain these goals.

They take pride in great work honed over the years in hands-on experience, professional training, established norms, and integrity.

At the macro level, these teams work at fitting the nature of a given technology with the underpinnings of the global economy. They drive organizational success. There are several characteristics of Smart IT. The first thing to emphasize is that this approach is purposeful. We are not relying on hope or luck to be successful, but rather explicitly going after our objectives. We choose real-world, proven problem-solving methods combined with an open mind to trying new solutions to produce successful outcomes. We use the resources currently at hand to apply the right leverage at influence points to overcome the sometimes seemingly insurmountable obstacles of complex systems. In this way, the impact of our daily work is multiplied. Even the smallest work efforts applied at the right points of our organization's value chain can create the outcomes our business needs. Smart IT makes use of wise leverage to create needed impacts. Recognizing the mission of our work, we acknowledge this is an infinite endeavor with infinite players. IT is a multiplayer effort. We only succeed when teammates play the same game according to well-respected rules. This game we play is infinite. The journey may bring multiple waypoints we could not see earlier, but we work together to travel through them.

Smart IT is inspirational. It inspires others to join the cause, including internal customers across the business. They see what we do and how we do it. It's our job to build the respect and resulting cooperation that gets the IT job done. We undertake our work through deep focus. Like a laser beam on a target, our focus on the most important work that benefits our business allows us to improve situations with steady attention. When we encounter difficulties, we are very resilient. We persevere to achieve our goals no matter the trials and tribulations.

Smart IT is empathetic. We observe our environment to discern both the problems and the solutions. We tune in to the human needs behind our services both inside and outside our organizations. That is how we identify the jobs to be done. We prioritize our daily work by the wants of both internal end users and external consumers. For example, if an end user wants access to certain information on her mobile phone while on the road, she doesn't care about the app itself. The job to be done is getting her the data she needs when she pushes a button. For an external customer who wants to buy and pay for a product, the job to be done is presenting items for sale and arranging for safe payment.

We understand that because we operate within a complex web of systems, we need to have a multicausal perspective. Complex adaptive systems have multicausal problems. Smart IT recognizes this and decomposes problems to surface their root causes and target fixes for them.

This approach encourages distributed decision-making. Understanding that the entire organization can't be centrally controlled, we push authority and decision-making down to the edges of the organization. We consider scalability limitations and inefficiencies so we can solve the problem. Many times, this will entail problem reframing. We don't just accept the problem as it first comes in. Instead, we dig deeper to identify what needs to happen to solve a problem or make an organizational improvement. We find new opportunities and alternative actions.

Smart IT is resilient, agile, and thoughtful. Smart IT can be viewed from the perspective of four dimensions: purpose, development, intentionality, and realization.

Purpose

"The purpose of life is to live it, to taste experience to the utmost, to reach out eagerly and without fear for newer and richer experience." [1]
—Eleanor Roosevelt, former first lady of the United States

Purpose denotes relevance, professional pride, or perhaps a higher calling. Purpose answers the questions of why you do what you do and why you think in the way you do. When you go to work, what is it that drives your actions during the day? Why do you do or create or use certain things? What's your intended result or goal?

The purpose of Smart IT is clear: support the disruption of the status quo, simplify the complex, and mitigate risk.

Purpose separates viable decision paths from the sea of noise. When your goals, strategies, and principles are clear, your methods and technology become clear too. Does this action or that policy match your purpose, or is it a warning light?

IT has traditionally focused resources and budget on operational activities such as maintaining infrastructure and keeping the lights on. But today, IT must enable transformation. IT has become a strategic differentiator, changing how companies market and position their products and services.

As we improve IT agility, we improve business value. Simply put, Smart IT is the shift from how IT does technology to how businesses use IT in the marketplace. At the macro workflow level, every IT group is a service provider. All technology projects are business projects.

IT is the master orchestrator of each consumer/provider ecosystem. High-performance IT teams make new technological advancements available to larger organizations. We are the vital link between new technology and business use.

Smart IT can empower organizations to say yes, to be nimble, and to be resilient. We can help design and empower business initiatives.

You can see the relevance of IT through the lens of real-time factors. Our business is our internal customer. The consequence of not delivering a product or service in time could result in the words we never want to hear: *"We will get it elsewhere."*

We must be the department of *yes.* We need our businesses' external customers to have choices. If we don't deliver, the business doesn't deliver. Our customers then get their goods and services elsewhere.

Patterns of IT success include not waiting for the end user to complain, adjusting with plenty of time to spare, measuring to understand and improve, embracing new consumption models, and valuing finite resources.

When you fear being bypassed, keep in mind that not every IT service can be found outside. While business units may bypass IT for a time, they may come back to IT looking for help to integrate the new solution with existing infrastructure to get the full return on investment. So be ready.

Don't try to boil the ocean. Instead, discern where to apply your brilliance. Time, people, and money are finite. Find what draws your organization out of the shadows and into the light.

It is one thing to technically be able to do something; it's quite another for your organization to capitalize upon that possibility. You can equip your organization to know the secret sauce and execute the actions that profit from it.

IT must view the world from the perspective of business thinkers. Business leaders innovate and transform their business models. IT supports digital transformation efforts. This means we must be masters of the technology systems complexity that enables more options for these leaders. We must show agility.

And finally, IT must provide probabilities that support our businesses in winning even amidst market disruptions. It is our job to make the uncertain certain.

Again, the purpose is clear: support the disruption of the status quo, simplify the complex, and mitigate risk.

Development

"Working life has extended so much in the last fifty years that it exceeds life expectancy of even the most successful businesses. Very few businesses are successful for more than 25 or 30 years. And yet most educated people who go to work in their early twenties will keep working until they are 70. And so they had better be prepared for a second career whether it's in another organization where they are doing what they have been doing or in a new line of work. They must be prepared to learn again. They must be prepared to position themselves. They must be prepared to want to learn—to see it not as something they need to do, but as something they enjoy doing. They will have to learn how to learn." [2] —Peter Drucker, management consultant and author, whose writings contributed to the philosophical and practical foundations of modern corporations

Enter development, the process of attaining and improving your professional and interpersonal skills. This lifelong skill set means you can be ready when an opportunity presents itself. Education is the gateway to developing yourself so you can succeed at both work and life. T.D. Jakes, bishop and author, says, *"The world is a university and everyone in it is a teacher. Make sure when you wake up in the morning, you go to school."* [3]

The IT workforce of tomorrow will need a well-rounded set of professional skills to thrive. Job titles that don't exist now will pop up, requiring a combination of business, social, and technical know-how. Ten core professional skill sets, broken down into the following four levels, are vital to IT professionals to be successful in their future work, no matter their job title.

Level 1 - Fluency. Develop these two foundational skills.

Business literacy. IT professionals thrive with a working knowledge of business. This includes the general structure of a business as well as global market principles. Seek to understand operations as well as the financial elements of revenue, expenses, and profits.

Know how your organization's financial goals and objectives are measured. Look at your company's organizational structure to understand the various team roles, responsibilities, and decision-making processes. Embrace the concept of customer value. Study how your organization makes money.

Be a teammate. Find out how your work relates to the larger organization as well as to individuals. See and understand the business context to imagine how technology could help your organization.

Digital fluency. To fully participate in a knowledge society powered by digital infrastructure, grow your digital fluency. This includes knowledge, skills, and behaviors that use digital services. Digital fluency uses technologies to create, explore, and share in both personal and professional contexts.

Understand how your organization is currently using technology to run its operation. Be mindful of how others in the market are leveraging new technologies that you could introduce to your company's business model.

As IT is the interface for new technology usage, we are the bridge for making IT accessible and usable for our colleagues in other departments. You'll have greater success as you understand each colleague's experience and needs related to all things digital.

Level 2 - Expanded thinking. Focus on what's most likely to happen.

Systems thinking. Systems thinking allows us to see both the system (i.e., forest) and the individual components (i.e., trees). Understanding how both interact together and the patterns of behavior that emerge matter to IT success. Learning how the individual components of a system interact enables one to better manage their environment.

Systems thinking allows you to see underlying structural patterns of relationships instead of focusing in on seemingly unrelated parts. The benefit of these archetypes is that they allow learning across a wide variety of system behaviors for different situations.

The more you understand system behavior, the more you can anticipate individual behavior and work within systems to make improvements and stave off problems. Systems thinking gives you the patience to understand that cause and effect in a system are often separated in time and space. Systems thinking reveals what actions reinforce or counterbalance each other.

Analysis. Learn how to explore components in more depth. Analysis is the process of unpacking a situation, problem, or potential opportunity. This involves decomposing factors, making observations, making inferences, capturing comparisons, and finding meaning in situations and data. All of this facilitates decision-making.

Analysis guides you to make sense of a situation or of data. This covers ad hoc back-of-the-napkin type ideation, formula calculations in spreadsheets, and model simulations in advanced analytical platforms to crunch data.

You'll make better decisions as you become more proficient in analysis. You can break apart a problem, understand it more deeply, troubleshoot it, and develop responses.

Probability theory. Probability management allows for the measurement of uncertainties and calculates the likelihood of something happening. This skill set increases your ability to look at possibilities, understand the uncertainties, and improve your decision-making in all areas of work. The possibilities for risk management can be infinite; focus on the probable.

As a probability theorist, answer questions your business leaders need, such as whether a project will complete on time, which threat scenarios are the most dangerous, and what information is still needed for a decision analysis.

Level 3 - People-first focus. Notice what people need, then instruct machines to aid human efforts.

Human-centered design. This approach puts the focus on people's needs. By putting human requirements at the center of any solution, you increase the chances of solving actual problems. Adoption will be higher.

Human-centered design uses an outside-in perspective. This type of design approach is helpful for improving processes, experiences, and products. Empathy for the users you serve provides an edge in meeting their needs.

Human-centered design encompasses how something looks and works. This tangible and experiential approach to problem-solving can guide enterprise architecture choices and improve users' experiences with the systems we build.

Coding. Humans communicate with machines via coding. Technology works because humans instruct machines what to do, how to do it, and when to do it. Program your machines by writing instructions in human language and then translating them into machine-executable language. From desktop applications to mobile apps to software that runs middleware, IT spends significant time creating and managing code. You also need coding for installing, updating, and troubleshooting digital infrastructure. Use coding to speed up the process of building and deploying software into production.

Coding is a fundamental skill alongside math and reading. Coding drives innovation. Coding gives machines their instructions. If you want to off-load manual and repetitive tasks, then code. Scale your work efforts with coding.

Level 4 - Engagement. Encourage shared goals in the people around you.

Leadership. Leaders set the direction, build an inspiring vision, and create something new. You will need the abilities to inspire others for common causes and create change.

Grow your ability to get yourself out of the way while you're guiding other individuals, teams, or entire organizations. Help others do the right things for the right reasons. Provide guardrails on action.

Communication. You are responsible to ensure the message you want to get across is received and understood. Communication is the exchange of information through the use of symbols, signs, words, or behavior.

Team cohesion depends on you facilitating good communication. Breakdown in good communication is a common obstacle to work productivity. While work is being done, make sure your communication is two-way for consistent and fast feedback. Communicate as tasks are handed off from one person or group to the next.

Team building. Little of consequence gets done with individual efforts alone. Build teams that draw upon one another's strengths and help with each other's weaknesses. Working as a team builds morale, motivation, and productivity. Team building includes a collection of actions that enhance the trust and familiarity of individual workers as they collaborate to get things done.

Team building is not touchy-feely exercises. It's an ongoing factor associated with a company's success in the marketplace. Team building gets people together to get things done.

How work gets done is critical as it directly affects the speed and impact of those efforts. You get much more done with teaming.

These ten skill sets make for a well-rounded IT professional who can keep pace with the dynamic requirements of the digital workforce.

Armed with your *why* and having put in the effort and time to prepare yourself by developing your skills, it is time to focus time, effort, and resources on the objective(s) at hand. It is time to be intentional.

Intentionality

"Without a solid, realistic, and detailed plan, the goal is nothing more than a pipe dream. And without the commitment to follow through on that plan and put forth the necessary effort, the dream is nothing more than a good intention."[4] —Les Brown.

IT professionals clearly identify goals and the actions needed to accomplish them, and they set out every day to get there.

Successful intentionality is at the center of our interest. We lock into the task at hand. We become deliberate. Intentionality is a mental state that represents a commitment to carrying out an action or actions. Intentionality involves mental activities including both planning and forethought. We will be part of teams that have seemingly unlimited possibilities to accomplish our goals.

To be intentional, we can leverage five widely known requirements of SMART goals (highlighted at the beginning of this book): specific, measurable, achievable, relevant, and time-bound.

Specific. What precisely do we want to accomplish? Specificity answers the who, what, where, and why. Specificity includes context. If our goals are too broad, the daily activities we undertake can meander because we lack clarity on what to do right now, or what can wait until tomorrow or next week. Be too vague, and we fog up concrete actions. For example, if our goal is to make it easier for users to use our systems, what does *easier* mean? Which users? Which systems? Which functions? How will we do that? Directions should be very clear to accomplish specific actions. Accept no ambiguity around what we are trying to do.

Measurable. We started somewhere and want to get somewhere else. Measuring tells us when we're done. Measuring communicates that we're on schedule. It alerts us if we won't be done on time. Measuring shows progress. Measuring provides critical visibility. Measuring lets us know if adaptation is required in processes or goals. If our goal is to reduce the time to repair our systems, we measure how long it takes now. Then we determine how changes will be measured. We will know when we have accomplished what we have set out to get done.

Achievable. Think big and out of the box, but not beyond reality. Set goals that can be done with current constraints, resources, abilities, and influence. A common cause of failure is reaching past realistic capabilities or timelines. For example, if we don't control the factors that influence our systems, including the monitoring of and access to logs that we need, all the dedication in the world can't help us achieve what we hope for.

Relevant. The question is, should you be doing this task or work in the first place? Answering this validates how you spend your time. For example, why try to improve a new mobile app whose division is about to stop that service? Whether or not it should be done should tie into your larger initiatives and align with their objectives. Does it make sense to undertake it after considering timing and payoff? How does this compare to more relevant or less relevant endeavors?

Time-bound. Time is a finite resource. Use it well, or time will make your effort irrelevant. You must discover what will be done by your specified time, which includes both target milestones and finish dates. All things are bound by time. The amount of progress that can be made is unlimited when not bound. In reality, there is always a time limit for when the goal must be reached. It is the same with achievability and relevance—for example, when target completion is at the end of the quarter, yet everyone knows that this is unachievable.

Without these SMART criteria, our daily actions tend to conflict with our stated goals. They are too generic, impossible to measure, often unrealistic, not relevant to creating value, and open-ended. We must work differently to have not only a smooth flow, but an effective one.

SMART criteria matter to individuals and IT groups. The criteria matter to technology and systems. They apply to strategies, tactics, goals, and activities. SMART criteria are where the rubber meets the road to do certain things to make your goals a reality.

Realization

"Some people want it to happen, some wish it would happen, others make it happen."[5] —Michael Jordan.

The Nike saying is *"Just Do It."* Getting things done is the hallmark of organizational, and IT, success, but this takes much more than simply deciding to do something. Making it happen is Smart IT's role in organizational success. We use realization to do this. Realization makes real something imagined or planned. Realization fulfills or accomplishes the tasks, goals, or mission. Making it real requires the three critical work actions of model, sprint, and adapt.

Model. Modeling forms a virtual pattern of where we're headed. Modeling shows what the future state looks like—in the mind for thinking, on paper for qualitative exploration, or on a spreadsheet for quantitative analysis. Modeling allows for evaluation, planning, and achievement. Modeling is a detailed representation of how to get from the current reality to the desired future state.

With all the talk about business transformation to counter market disruptions, IT must embark on and be successful in new endeavors.

How do we make our systems more resilient? How do we reduce security incidents? How do we speed up our value delivery to our businesses? We model every task and process, such as migrating to the cloud, developing new apps, and supporting teleworkers. After that, we can transition to the *doing* of those actionable tasks, sequenced in a way the model directs.

Sprint. It is time to translate models into action. How do we get past the distractions of myriad IT tasks? We work in bite-size chunks that are focused on scope. Sprints explicitly break a task into units of progress that lend themselves to faster feedback and adjustments. Each team member knows what to do at what time and with which tools to get the model into reality. Rather than falling into analysis paralysis, start faster, fail faster, and move to the adapt phase faster. Think of sprints as bursts of activities.

Obstacles and roadblocks are everywhere. If work were easy, it would already be done. Breaking tasks into smaller chunks helps. For example, for an enterprise rollout of a new application, upgrade 10 percent of hosts in the sales department, then migrate the data, update the forms, build a basic mobile app that replicates paper forms, update the flow, and then update the interface. Then we can move on to the next 10 percent and follow a similar breakdown of tasks inside that smaller sub-set of user population. Before you know it, you will be at 100 percent complete.

Adapt. Sometimes the smaller chunks of work strung together in sprints need review and changes. Build adaptation into the process. Modify or change your plans in response to new conditions, such as an unexpected roadblock or unfamiliar terrain. When the project is veer-ing off into a ditch, adjust the friction, other vehicles, weather, troop-ers, or whatever else is needed to get the project back on the road.

Adaptation may be the most critical work style change for IT. When the iceberg is melting, we must react in time. Our job is to serve the needs of the business and add value. We do this with technology and a digital interface.

Specific adaptations include bypassing organizational friction with an executive push, reducing the size of a sprint team, changing work times and deliverables, and updating modeling constructs. Adaptation will be important later in this book, in the discussion on multi-dimensional thinking. These insights into how teams traditionally operate will ex-plain the reasons for difficulties in being successful—and how to move past those difficulties to become successful.

In this book, we will explore the Smart IT approach and principles that will guide traditional IT towards the next generation.

Introduction

Every frustration opens the door of opportunity for someone to leverage technology to fulfill the unmet needs in the global marketplace.

There are so many technological marvels of our age. We have more computing power in our smartphones than NASA had when it sent men to the moon. We have connectivity to billions of people, visibility into the causes of our problems, and a collective knowledge base unrivaled in known human history. Technology has dominated every market vertical and industry. It's embedded in most business processes and market supply chains in the modern world.

Driven by fundamental advances in technology, widespread connectivity, and start-up thinking, the conventional ways of doing business and working are being disrupted. What is possible for each of us today is incredible!

This is the time for all of us—organizations, governments, individuals, customers, and professionals—to make a difference by embracing the rapid pace of change and the climate of uncertainty in order to capitalize on new opportunities. In this time, we have the potential to reimagine the way we work and create new careers, start from scratch in our garages, and enter new markets.

We are living in an age of rapid disruption, complexity, and risk. The global economy is undergoing massive changes. Today, businesses that have stuck with the status quo for too long are losing market share and being confronted with shrinking profit margins. The outcomes of yesterday are not enough for an economy undergoing transformative change in value proposition and consumer demands. However, for those who think differently, work smarter, and are ready to lead, there are opportunities to thrive.

The world of modern IT is not your father's IT. Today it is possible for the chief executive officer and chief information officer to be fired because of a cyber breach. A lawyer might approach the email administrator to retrieve old emails from a user for a court case. Executives could approach the CIO about the soundness of another company's IT assets and process maturity prior to an acquisition. The board of directors could wonder if its company will see their next security incident on the nightly news. IT might be asked for progress on a digital transformation initiative to gauge if the company will survive tomorrow's competitive pressures.

Today's IT is different—more business requests and higher stakes. Yesterday's nice-to-have services are today's critical systems, with the mantra of "always on, from anywhere, in lightning-fast time." Our businesses want speed, choice, and freedom. The pressure, frustrations, and constant changes in the environment make for a challenging time. IT is at a crossroads. Either continue on the same path or substantially change how we think about the work we do.

That change will require taking the viewpoint of the challenges our businesses face from disruption, complexity, and risk. For the purposes of this book, we will view those three terms as follows.

Disruption is the interruption of the status quo. In these times, disruption is happening very rapidly. Major change will be required for your company to continue to be in business. "By some estimates, 40 percent of companies today might not exist in ten years," remarked John Chambers, former CEO and chairman of the board for Cisco Systems.[6] He went on to explain that companies must disrupt themselves or risk being disrupted by the competition.

Complexity is the state of being woven together. This is people, things, process, and technologies woven together and working together and among each other in systems that operate within other systems. The digital world we live in is too large, fast, and complex for any of us to keep up with in our heads. As the business world continues to embed more technology into processes, services, and products, a "complexity trap" masks dependencies and exceeds most people's comprehension. When sprung, this complexity trap keeps a company from getting ahead of a situation. It makes managing the environment more challenging and diagnosing problems more difficult. Many team members understand only pieces of this digital world.

Risk is something bad that could happen. Risk can be epitomized by these five words by Michael Lynton, former CEO of Sony Pictures Entertainment: *"They burned the house down."*[7] He was describing the November 2014 cyber-attack that leaked confidential corporate data to the public. This attack destroyed data, made thousands of workstations unusable, and effectively shut down Sony's network. Risks from technology breaches run the gamut from monetary losses to stock price decreases, market positioning slippage, opportunity losses, loss of relevance, and bankruptcy in extreme cases. The risks further extend to delayed services or broken customer-facing operations.

This approach to understanding disruption, complexity, and risk lays the groundwork for the men and women who operate digital infrastructure that drives our modern world.

Information Technology

Global market changes, powered by new technology, transform how we work, live, and play. IT plays a crucial role in making technology useful and usable. They are composed of talented workers across a wide spectrum. IT teams combine internal employees, third-party contractors, consultants, technology integrators, vendors, and cloud providers. These professionals design, build, operate, and defend the technology infrastructure that makes our modern digital economy possible, including running the service desk, supporting user devices, managing infrastructure, writing code, and engaging the C-suite in planning and strategy.

Business and end users may see IT as a monolithic entity that either helps or gets in the way of productivity. But IT equips users to do their daily work and make their big decisions. IT touches almost every aspect of business operations today.

IT professionals are under unprecedented pressure to deliver for their businesses. IT is no longer simply who workers call when their computers crash. IT is needed upfront to help directly engage the customers and drive business growth.

Technology is the engine, software code is the brains, and data is the fuel in the digital economy. IT should move to the front seat to enable new market value, help confront increasingly dangerous cyber threats, and navigate uncertain roads ahead. Organizations need IT more than ever before.

But for too many teams in too many industries, IT is distracted fighting preventable fires. The speed to deliver business value is slowed by manual tasks, countless handoffs, endless meetings, decision overload, and too much finger pointing. IT is pulled in too many directions by the constant business changes caused by market disruptions. IT is too mired in the complexity of its own technology to power new business initiatives. IT is stuck running inside, around, and between silos.

As if these market and organizational challenges are not enough, IT is also under extreme pressure to avoid unwanted damage from cyber-attacks. As IT battles to keep pace, it is confronted by criminals, nation-states, and terrorists using the same technology and infrastructure to carry out their acts.

So how can we stop this hamster wheel and free IT to help businesses win? I'm glad you asked.

IT professionals want to protect their organizations' brands, keeping their systems not just operating, but bypassing the competition. IT can assist their organizations' experiments with new ideas to stay competitive. IT wants to be active participants in their organizations' missions. IT wants (and needs) to be trusted, to be relevant, and to make a difference. IT wants to say "Yes!" to business requests. IT wants to be ready when called upon.

IT wants to bring more to the table to help lead the way forward in this age of disruption, complexity, and risk.

We Can Do Better

IT can do better for its organizations. You as an individual contributor can do better. The current way of doing things is not safe. IT can either become the linchpin of our organizations' transformation efforts or the constraint that holds them back. When the rubber hits the road, businesses often find out the hard way that IT does more than just provisioning hardware and servicing tickets. Businesses lose sight of the full IT value stack.

We have a responsibility to display our full value. Our slowness to adapt and grow has at times left our businesses in the dark. Even when internal IT has what the business needs, IT often does a poor job of packaging and branding it. Any user can go to a website, take out a corporate card, and presto, services on demand. Contrast this with some standard IT processes that make it difficult to use new technology or services.

We must become better if we want to stay relevant. We must become what today's businesses need. Otherwise, the risks will overwhelm our businesses. We must intervene to tame the risks that slow business growth, increase operating costs, and increase opportunity losses. We must grasp the strategies to deal with technical operations. We must provide the time, space, and legitimacy to impact the business bottom line.

It's no small task to see possibilities through the noise of compliance, security fears, vendor hyperbole, and endless requests from our businesses. We must develop the appropriate culture, frameworks, and approaches to thrive in these challenging times.

Tactics are critical to the execution of any strategy. No advancements happen without details. If we don't do our jobs, the cloud will come knocking. If our businesses go to the cloud without IT, they take on unnecessary risk.

Today's business landscape sees large, established companies attempting to hold out against new upstarts. These young upstarts challenge—sometimes rightly—existing business models. Our businesses need quick, nimble, and relevant IT teams to support new initiatives. Prominent in this competitive environment is the need for speed. The tools, knowledge, and expertise to succeed are in our reach. And with all of that, we can do better by thinking and working smarter.

The IT Value Proposition

When you embody something of value, people value you more. They are more apt to be led and to join your cause. When leaders across the organization work in concert as a winning team, IT can elevate its relevance. The value proposition is that IT helps the business win in the marketplace.

IT brings new customer value by building new code, deploying new technology, and mitigating risks enough to allow us to operate effectively everywhere and at any time. We collect raw data, refine it, and make it available to the business, often out of sight of end users but visible to those we lead.

Different business users will ask different questions of the same underlying data. For example, there are overlaps in the data needed by the marketing department (to understand how customers are making use of the products), by plant facilities (to optimize floor equipment), and by a security operations center (to determine if a breach has occurred).

All rely heavily on IT to serve up the actionable data that directs their work. IT has the advantage of seeing different teams work across multiple facets of the organization.

While there are many possible outcomes in business, IT can tip the scales in favor of positive outcomes for the organization. One of the ways to showcase our value and understanding of business imperatives is to make sure we are always delivering value. The markets and industries we operate in are wide and diverse. The value we bring will be specific to our businesses. With the power tools discussed previously, we can engage the business to answer the questions that matter most to the stakeholders, focusing on what they value and where we can make a difference.

We must ensure that we value the money and time the business entrusts us with. Often, we can leverage what's free, simple, and fast to make an impact. Ask yourself if you are leveraging all the features, capabilities, and benefits you already have. Do the board, assembly line manager, and CEO view your group as one that values a dollar? Do they value you as one that gets more done in less time? Educate the board on a regular basis. Market your wins to the business in their own language. Spread the word on new features and capabilities. Show the C-suite or the line managers how you are making use of the tools you already have at your disposal.

Rather than hoard what IT knows, provide avenues of training, and share the knowledge held in the IT department. Most of the C-suite is inundated with technology in their personal lives—so extend a helpful hand. How simple can this be? Consider these examples:

- Does everyone use the basic features of Microsoft Excel? Could someone in sales pull relevant data points from your data sources to use in an existing formula to provide more timely outputs?

- Do you advertise what you have accomplished? Did an upgrade on your wireless network enable support for anyone using Apple Bonjour to print from an iPad to that nice, shiny color laser printer down the hall?

- Did one of your developers add a new lookup feature on the product web portal for historical order listings that saves time?

- Did you finish deploying new scripts that automate loading truck routes over cellular networks to the drivers in the field?

Make a list of the major IT projects completed over the last year; then map those to digital enablement initiatives, business priorities, and pain points. Communicate the successes. Upstream or downstream, someone is benefiting from your work. Think about it. Then communicate it.

IT can do more to help the business make decisions in the land of uncertainty. And when some of the outcomes could involve a loss, injury, or catastrophe, or are simply undesirable, IT can do better at managing the risks with true quantitative alternatives and rational changes.

IT is the champion of mining data and processing information—the virtual oil that deals with uncertainty in business operations and decision-making. The CIO or other leader helps the organization analyze data. IT builds the systems that provide the CIO with plans, tools, and procedures for collecting, displaying, analyzing, and interpreting data. Together, IT helps the business operate and win.

IT understands how to increase profits by using its digital and human assets while simultaneously holding down operating costs and limiting the likelihood and potential impact of unwanted outcomes. IT can share new applications of technology and their associated risk factors with the business.

IT is at the apex of business—in the effects of technology, in strategy, and in communication matters. IT is vital in driving productivity across the organization. The next generation of IT will work with principles such as agility, simplicity, standardization, predictability, efficiency, resiliency, and service orientation. We are that next generation.

IT imagines, reimagines, dares, innovates, and takes chances. IT is informative, helpful, collaborative, Lean, Agile, and fast. Our businesses depend on what we do in IT. Our success depends on it.

The first time we encounter a problem, we are surprised. The second time, we learn. The third time, we adapt. We in IT champion our people, our services, our value, and our results. We measure, we experiment, we fail, and we learn from failure. We give and receive feedback. We incorporate the feedback in a timely fashion into our decision-making process and that of our business leaders.

IT must build a culture that is more impactful than strategy. We need a strategy that challenges today's realities and whose outcome is a high-performing organization. It takes more than writing checks, approving projects, hiring more talent, and doing more training to build a culture of success. IT is an integral part of improving the culture.

IT is responsible for the technology needed for growth, productivity, efficiency, innovation, and improved customer experiences. IT keeps the line operating. IT helps the website attract and sell to customers. IT equips the C-suite with the tools needed to adapt the operations of their business. IT should be leading technology-driven business innovation, not be mired in daily firefighting.

The manifesto for IT could read as the following:

- Seek to understand the landscape and context to see the possibilities.
- Understand the constraints and risks.

- Observe, learn, focus, act, and improve.

- Lead.

Smart IT supports disruption. Smart IT does what it needs to do to get the job done. Smart IT designs, builds, supports, and protects the organization's digital realm. Smart IT enables whatever technology the business needs at just the right time. As the business pushes into new areas to compete in the marketplace, IT is able and ready to respond. Armed with a dynamic, always-changing mentality, IT embraces adaptation.

Smart IT simplifies the complex. One of the greatest values IT gives the business is ease of use. IT marvels proudly at the months of effort leading to push-of-a-button use. IT provides messaging around new capabilities and features in ways that are intuitive to end users. IT provides workable alternatives and cost flexibility.

All of this leads to the business feeling good about having IT as a real partner.

Smart IT reduces uncertainty and mitigates risks. IT equips the business to operate in tough and uncertain areas. As such, Smart IT approaches all the services it provides in a manner that reduces confusion and unwanted outcomes.

Smart IT does these things natively. These are natural ways of being and working.

Opportunity Never Sleeps

An *opportunity* is a time, condition, or situation favorable for a change in circumstance or standing. Each new day has the potential for us to learn something new, to improve something, or to make a difference.

IT has countless possibilities to reimagine how our world works, lives, and plays. The opportunity of our modern lifestyle and the resources and advancements in this digital age afford doors and pathways not available to those who came before us.

IT gets to do work that is humane, purposeful, and fulfilling while building a life in which we all thrive.

IT has the opportunity to do better individually and lead the changes needed. We see, understand, and empathize with the effects of our actions. We empathize with our fellow humans.

If there is one thing you take away from this book, let it be to map out your opportunities. What are your challenges and obstacles? What are the risks of inaction and staying with the way things are today? How will you focus your team's collective efforts to confront complexity?

The pathway to Smart IT is available for those who see the light. The road is filled with hints, guidelines, and contexts that allow IT to navigate it and get around the potholes, congestion, and detours. Load up your bus and set off on the path! Bring about the change IT needs to take advantage of new opportunities, to focus, to align, and to execute!

Analyze, synthesize, show, inspire, teach, and lead change to a new state.

On your map, identify the current state. Observe the actual way things are, not the reality you imagine or want. Visualize the current state that includes the individual factors and relationships. Visualize your future state and the gap that needs to be closed.

Journey with milestones, feedback loops, and metrics. Celebrate the wins, learn from the failures, and enjoy the journey. Be explicit in your intentions, actions, thoughts, and work. Once you inform yourself, everything changes. You are on the hook.

Will you know opportunity when you see it? When you look more closely at the things that matter most to you, your teammates, and your organization, you find opportunity. When you feel the challenges are not bringing out the best in everyone, you find more opportunity.

When something bad happens, identify which conditions may lead you down a better path the next time, conditions that challenge your thinking.

If the tension between what we say we want to accomplish and how we currently approach our challenges does not match our intent, focus, capability, and applied effort, then we have an opportunity to fix that.

We must apply our knowledge and experience to reduce unwanted outcomes for the business. We have the opportunity to reduce business risk in its many forms by helping our organizations deal with market disruptions and technology complexities. The author of the blog *Philosoblog* explains:

> Most people expect opportunity to knock on their door from time to time. But what do you expect to see when one opens the door? Many expect to see opportunity dressed in a suit, holding a bouquet of balloons and a very large check. Unfortunately, that's not what opportunity is, at least for 99.9% of us. Opportunity is just that, an opening, a chance to apply yourself and make something happen. Opportunity, when it knocks on your door, is usually a chance to work your butt off for a significant amount of time with the hope for a great reward at the end (if everything goes well). Here, when I say hard work, I mean work of a non-trivial level of effort over a non-trivial period of time. Hard work is the opposite of feather dusting the coffee table. And I don't just mean physical work. Planning, organizing, putting something together, that can be hard work for the brain.[8]

We are no strangers to working over a non-trivial amount of time. We know that we create success through repeated coding, persistent testing, and other repeated efforts. When finite time is broken up with time set aside for maintenance, learning, thinking, and sharing, then IT puts in the work necessary to capitalize on opportunities to help our organizations.

IT help can come in any form—don't limit how you believe it should look. Visualize the opportunities before IT. We need to create a map of the opportunities to inspire us to detect what others don't see yet. That gives us visibility into what should garner our greatest attention.

Up Next

You are IT—this could be your moment. How is your organization doing? If not great, why not? If not okay, why not? What are you prepared to do about it?

If things need to change, is there anyone leading the charge on that front? Is that someone you? Is the last IT transformation effort stuck in the ditch? Are you the change agent who can start reimagining IT to help your business navigate market disruptions, technology complexities, and risks?

So, what are you going to do? IT is made up of individual people, and you are one of those people. IT changes because the individuals change. It may be your time to decide.

If your organization believes it is doing everything possible to maintain market share, and you have evidence this is incorrect, how will you change your actions tomorrow to help others see the possibilities?

If the organization is assuming an unnecessary level of risk because of a lack of awareness, what are you going to do to enlighten them on the true state?

Don't fall into the trap of believing any action is too small. Someone down the hall could benefit from something as simple as creating a spreadsheet formula, building a different type of report, updating the layout of an app, or allowing users in the field the ability to connect remotely to fill out paperwork.

Market share, revenue performance, and business goal attainment all hinge on capitalizing on opportunities and mitigating risks. What role will you play in making this possible?

It is time for IT to enable change. When the current situation is no longer working, it's time for you to lead the change needed. To do that, you should be the one to disrupt how things currently stand, to master the complexity, and to embrace the uncertainty.

Embrace the opportunity of the Smart IT approach to getting things done by transforming the way IT thinks, works, and leads in the face of mounting challenges. Support the organization's ability to disrupt the status quo. Simplify the complex to make using technology easier. Embrace mitigating risk.

For IT, the opportunity is to reimagine itself, to make technology work. IT responds to what matters to your organization when, where, and how it is needed to power new opportunities.

Opportunity leads to different outputs, which leads to different outcomes.

Each day we awaken is a blessing, another opportunity. Do you have your leadership badge on? Are you ready to reimagine leadership itself? Are you ready to lead?

You are a part of enabling a new IT. The time has come for you to make it happen. Enable the new functionality that your organization needs. Be more explicit in mitigating risks. Enable transformation of existing business models.

This is not an overnight change. This is a journey, one that won't be easy or quick. But it is possible. Everyone must put in the work. Things we need to do differently won't happen by themselves. We have to put in the work to adapt ourselves in order to enable our organizations to leverage new technology. Let's put in the work smartly and give the business the tools it needs to be successful.

Thomas Edison is believed to have said, "Opportunity is missed by most people because it is dressed in overalls and looks like work."[9] We must pave the way ahead and enable what the business needs.

Overview of the Book

This book will guide you to understand how the digital world works and how the challenge of managing our complex digital infrastructure threatens to hinder business progress. Technology is both an enabler of business operations and a tool to solve both. You can use technology for a competitive advantage. Getting our technology houses in order allows us to assist our businesses more effectively.

You will learn how to forecast new opportunities and hold off avoidable risks to productivity, revenue, and brand reputation.

You will deliver IT services to the business world in record speed in such areas as digital storefronts, back-end integration of new systems with legacy systems, new mobile apps, and data collection through smart devices on the front line. All of this happens by using new ways of thinking and interacting with customers.

You can use new systems of engagement to leverage the investment in systems of record. IT needs a way to think about, talk about, and approach the new opportunities to support our organization's business model transformation efforts and the myriad of challenges to being successful.

Audience

The target audience for this book is IT professionals. IT includes individuals such as chief information officer, chief information security officer, chief technology officer, IT director, business analyst, project manager, server administrator, network administrator, storage administrator, messaging administrator, mainframe admin, service desk technician, help desk technician, information security analyst, incident responder, application developer, quality assurance specialist, desktop support technician, enterprise architect, team lead, and many others.

What do IT professionals do? We write software code that runs the internet. We manage the software that runs the data centers that process the digital economy. We take calls from end users when they have problems with their computers. We design, install, configure, and operate the routers, switches, load balancers, servers, hypervisors, mainframes, and storage area networks. We support the infrastructure that makes it possible to send and receive email, to take orders from a website, and to find something by typing a web address instead of an IP address. We present to the board of directors and interact with the CEO and VP of divisions on new initiatives. We work on both the back end in operations and the front end with our business's interactions with customers.

IT professionals work in a large and diverse collection of organizations; profit and nonprofit companies, companies of different sizes, and companies in almost every industry. These industries include retail, government, finance, healthcare, oil and gas, construction. Some companies are public, some are private, and some are subject to regulatory and compliance requirements. All these organizations have different business priorities, cultures, and business models.

While there are many differences, fundamental principles allow IT to thrive in this disruptive landscape.

Let's start bringing clarity to our new world by understanding its complexities and opportunities. We must first understand ourselves, the market, and the disruptors well enough to be relevant. And to do that, we need to be sure we understand the rapid changes in our work landscape. That includes the software that's pervasive in running our digital infrastructure, the convergence in technology stacks and architectures, and the new technology capabilities that can increase our ability to make better decisions faster. We need to continually learn to overcome new skills gaps. We need to see how our careers and roles could evolve in the next few years and make the necessary changes to stay relevant.

Book Layout

Throughout this book you will learn how to make IT leaner, faster, and smarter, moving at the speed of business needs and adapting as needed. We must make decisions faster.

To do this, our decision-making framework should be built to support decisions with analytics. We need to speak in the languages of our businesses to learn, inform, and provide feedback. We will explore the mindsets, frameworks, and terminology of business operations.

Part 1, *Understand*, takes a macro look at gaining a better appreciation of risk and an organization's response to managing it.

Chapter 1 covers various concepts of Value at Risk. At the intersection of producer supply and customer demand lies value. And that value is increasingly at risk. The failure to get our hands around the business risks introduced by technology has led to misguided priorities, wasted resources, and the illusion of improvement in risk management. We will set the table for IT on the context for the work we do in helping our organizations manage risk.

Chapter 2 discusses scenario analysis, a fundamental building block of all risk management. IT owes stakeholders the confidence to make sound risk mitigation decisions by being realistic about their organization's current ability to avoid potential losses in technology and cyber risk. IT needs to analyze scenarios with a holistic scope and measure the consequences on those events of concern to your organization.

Chapter 3 examines the support our organizations need to make risk-informed business decisions at scale and with speed, helping our businesses improve their decision-making skills and improve operational execution. Decision support needs guidance from scenario analysis. We use it as inputs to the decision-making process in support of the large number of decisions that we must make. These are decisions that various teams across the organization must make every day, ranging from big decisions to small decisions and everything in between.

Part 2, *Align*, addresses how a deeper integration with the business should shape how we approach our work by taking into consideration the other aspects of our organizations and technology.

Chapter 4 discusses guiding our efforts in the context of the business. IT works inside businesses, which operate inside of markets. Businesses provide value on the market to customers in exchange for value (money). The disruption that impacts IT emerges from the larger market environment. To work with the changes this causes, we must look at the effect technologies, innovators, and inventions have on the market. IT responds to the business, which responds to the market forces and the players inside it. This drives changes to how technology is consumed by organizations.

Chapter 5 takes us to a high-level view of the board room and C-suites to see risk from the perspective of those who have liability when things go wrong. Enterprise risk management must account for all sources of risk to the businesses. Risk never sleeps for the boardroom as cybersecurity adds to the long list of concerns that must be managed. As the list of concerns continues to mount for the board, cyber risks are getting more attention. IT must align their security function with their organization's risk management efforts.

Chapter 6 discusses the context of the technology use of the business. The world in a state of many components woven together leads to more complexity. No simplicity can happen on the front end without complexity in the back end. IT can understand and manage the fundamental complexity challenges. IT takes on this complexity to enable the business.

Part 3, *Manage*, is how IT can reimagine how to approach security.

Chapter 7 looks at supporting enterprise risk management for the cyber realm by running a robust security program that is business-aligned and risk-based. IT's goal is the same as that of every other group within an organization to maximize value and minimize cost. IT cuts through all the noise and explicitly understands how losses occur and properly frames the business context to mitigate risks. Our operation of a mature security program is what allows us to manage cyber risk.

Chapter 8 discusses the power of designing a mitigation system to keep cyber risk in check. A series of controls working together to accomplish the organization's defined risk management objectives. A system on controls that coordinates the resources to properly defend an organization and mitigate cyber risk. The aim is to maintain an acceptable level of frequency and magnitude of losses. This is managed by the security team to organize overall organizational efforts for cyber risk management.

Chapter 9 looks at variance in the factors that make up the loss scenarios of concerns for our organizations. All value in risk management is the ability to sustain mitigation efforts over time. As the business and technology environments change, how threats affect our organizations will continue to be dynamic. A security program must be dynamic just as well to keep pace with risk management needs of the organization.

The efficacy of our security efforts will have variance from day to day. Nothing stays the same as risk factors are dynamic. The factors that drive risk are dynamic and IT must be persistent.

Call to Action

We will pave the way to success by thinking differently, working smarter, and leading change. The call to action is for us in IT to commit to continuous upskilling and applying new ways of thinking to our organization mission. Let us do more than survive the day; let us thrive. Let us embrace the uncertainty and risks and do amazing things, for opportunity never sleeps. Let's go on this journey together. Let us learn, explore, and grow together.

Please use this book as a framework for discussion, to lay the groundwork on how to approach the major challenges ahead and capture the opportunities. When the status quo is no longer working for us, change is needed. IT should lead it.

All of this begins with a change in our thinking. Let us explore the landscape that awaits IT. We need the right perspective. We need a perspective of our world.

Part 1 – Understand

Gain a systemic perspective of your cyber risk environment.

Chapter 1
Value at Risk

At the intersection of producer supply and customer demand lies value. At the intersection of innovation, capability, and opportunity lies risk. Risk is an uncertain situation with the existence of at least one possibility that is unwanted. Good outcomes could happen, but bad outcomes could too. The failure to get our hands around the business risks introduced by technology has led to misguided priorities, wasted resources, and the illusion of improvement in risk management.

In a work environment with high uncertainty, where the options, details, and results are not known, the potential of unwanted outcomes increases. People and entities frequently have different perspectives on how negative an outcome must be in order to be considered risky. Stakeholders are many and diverse, each with their own appetites and tolerance levels for risk. When they can't come to a consensus on the appropriate level of acceptable risks, the mitigation efforts can be suboptimal. Be it cyber-crime, catastrophe, injury, monetary loss, or reputational loss, the bottom line is that something bad could happen. Whether from the perspective of the individual, department, or group, risk is in the eyes of the beholder.

IT can use the challenges of uncertainty as opportunities to clarify the potential impacts and likelihood of a given occurrence. In the age of this rapid disruption and increasing levels of complexity, uncertainty and risks are increasing as well. Even more importantly, IT can become more valuable in showing the business how to avoid or lessen those risks. IT's assessment of the probability of an unwanted outcome is ever occurring. IT's help in the mitigation of risks can lead to an organization-level competitive advantage when new areas of innovation can be explored.

Risk is not new to business, just potentially more uncertain than in the past. Risk analysis feeds the decision-making processes for organizations, informing decision makers so they can optimize their actions. Organizations that mitigate the impacts and probabilities of unwanted outcomes build the opportunity to be more aggressive in finding new market advantages.

Many organizations have struggled or failed to adapt their thinking on risk assessment. As new technology and new ways of working disrupt traditional risk factors, organizations may be operating at higher levels of risk than they realize. In essence, there are blind spots created by a lack of awareness. IT becomes valuable by bringing these to the table and explaining how to manage them.

It should be considered a fantastic accomplishment for IT to both efficiently operate the technology (keep the lights on) and actively help the business contain costs, grow, and innovate. It should be more than enough. But we all know that is not the end of our duties.

The benefits our advanced technology has brought are available to anyone. But these business and societal benefits now amplify the threats all too common in human history. In some respects, this should not come as a surprise. But when our society becomes accustomed to historical risks, sometimes we lose track of just how much we have learned to live with, including the increased costs, delays, and inconveniences. Those who thought the digital world provided cost-free, easy, and risk-free benefits are finding out they were mistaken.

There are several common challenges for IT in the area of risk management. IT may not know the business it works for well enough. The team may not understand at their core why the business exists, how it makes money and competes in the marketplace, and the extreme pressures business stakeholders are under. They are at risk of being disrupted out of business.

One of the most common challenges for business leaders is trying to recognize the market threats of disruption fueled by new technology fast enough—and making the necessary changes in time to make a difference. IT could compound these challenges by deploying controls that create too much friction for business operations, resulting in decreased productivity. Or they could fail to support decision makers in the new realms of cyber warfare, crime, and activism, opening the business to new loss scenarios.

In the following sections, we will explore missed opportunities, operational disruptions, and digital threats.

Missed Opportunities

"Nothing is more expensive than a missed opportunity," observed author H. Jackson Brown, Jr.[10] Opportunity loss is an important concept to understand. IT failures, such as stalled or canceled projects, cybersecurity breaches, or antiquated systems that hinder productivity, have direct consequences for businesses. The goal is to have the agility to not just survive but ultimately to thrive in the marketplace. Imagine the following scenario where the business needed IT to deliver:

> *"The ACME project will not be ready on schedule,"* said IT to the business unit as part of an update for a new project the business hoped would save it from competitive decline. This project was massive and involved scaling multiple teams, allocating a multi-million-dollar budget, and committing to a multiyear effort. The project touched legacy systems, integrated with a new, modern, service-oriented architecture, involved a homegrown middle-ware app, and reached out to third-party services for lookups, all while integrating in-store POS systems with marketing and customer membership sites. Also involved were financing, shipping, the back-office inventory system, and some mobile app telemetry.

This massive undertaking had been brought forward by new executive leadership. This project was born to save the company. Unfortunately, this IT team was not ready for the challenge. Granted, this was not all IT's fault. They had been dragged down after years of just keeping the lights on. The team was underfunded, suffered from low headcount growth, and was expected to provide faster delivery, all while functioning in an increasingly complex and interdependent environment. IT was under extreme pressure to perform.

But IT was responsible to communicate its role. Instead of "The ACME project will not be ready on schedule," they needed to say, "Here are the factors that would help ACME not only be ready on schedule but beat the timeline." And then they needed to garner respect by presenting well-crafted specifics.

Yes, IT's role in a business is often misunderstood. Yes, IT is too often viewed as a cost center only. And yes, IT is pressured to fight fires with all-nighters to get situations fixed. But the fact remains that IT needs to deliver.

Even in a case with plenty of technical domain experts, great software developers, consolidated and virtualized data centers, an all-new, modern infrastructure, and all the latest endpoint devices, IT must still deliver on time and take advantage of opportunities. IT must become part of the team.

When transformation is required, we must understand and provide the scope of the opportunity. To see the possibilities, we must explore what competitors are doing and what the marketplace offers. We must also look at the challenges, constraints, and risks of bringing change into being. In order to be successful, we will need to lean on our strengths, expertise, and wisdom. This is the digital world, and we were born for this.

The question becomes, how fast does IT need to be to stay relevant? The answer is as fast as is needed to keep up with the business's demands.

We should ask ourselves if we are taking advantage of all that is new and possible out there. We must ask ourselves if we are confronting the challenges or merely trying to get around them.

Can IT strategically manage the risks associated with our organization's transformation initiatives while dealing with compliance, governance, and the security associated with new projects? IT must answer that question with a resounding yes.

If the controls we put in place to mitigate identified risks impede the organization's ability to conduct business and compete, then we will have been the cause of our organization's lost opportunity. In a similar fashion, if we are not ready to make the needed risk mitigation changes in a timely fashion, that can be problematic for the business.

IT can influence the risk appetite of its organization. The real risk for today's businesses is not taking enough calculated risks because of internal constraints, lack of knowledge, or lack of imagination. The more risks a business needs to take to leapfrog competitors, the more it comes to lean on technology and IT.

Many companies today will not exist in ten years. This is a sobering reality of our challenging market conditions. The impact is real. IT may be limited in what it can do to prevent that, but one thing is certain. We want to make sure that IT is not the reason the business loses. IT needs to do all it can to make business operations as efficient as possible while supporting growth and innovation initiatives. At the same time, it is imperative that we do our part in mitigating business risks from cyber threats.

Market Losses

Risk from market losses is top of mind for management. The challenges our organizations face are formidable. Disruption in the market is eating away at corporations' profits. A new upstart that is operating 100 percent in the cloud and with a workforce of fewer than one hundred people competes with established brands for market share. The incumbents are in danger of being "Uber-ed."

Amidst all of this, a new chief digital officer might be far enough along with his new initiatives to vastly improve his company's systems of engagement to capture the mindshare of its customers. But another challenge arises when four months into the project, the Hadoop cluster is still in its shipping boxes due to the lack of power in the data center to bring it up. IT struggles to identify which of its overprovisioned systems can be turned off to make room on the uninterruptable power supply system for the new gear. When those systems are identified, yet other challenges arise with moving workload around.

But those are the easy challenges. Enter a new problem. Consultants had subcontracted software developers to write new code to integrate all the company's systems and provide an automated workflow and an improved customer experience. No one had told IT early on, as the in-house developers had tried to communicate requirements for integration into the legacy systems. The storage team tried to communicate the capacity and performance issues. The security team had tried to communicate the issues with opening APIs to mission-critical and sensitive systems to third-party vendors. But with only loose coordination between business stakeholders, the contractors, and IT, the pressure of the deadline to complete the project mounted. So, the contractors had just gone off on their own to get started working.

The head of marketing is left explaining to the board of directors why the plan to just use the cloud to bypass the slowness of IT is not working.

This scenario illustrates the challenges all of us in IT face. Businesses with failed or slow service delivery models are the most exposed to competitive forces. Changes in how goods are consumed, such as moving from DVD movie rentals to streaming subscription models, can put your business model in jeopardy if you don't have enough of a mix of existing and new buying mechanisms. The speed at which the market shifts makes standing still risky.

This was the case with Blockbuster and their decision to pass on the opportunity to purchase Netflix years ago. A decade later, Blockbuster filed for bankruptcy while competitors using alternative delivery systems took their market. A lot happened in that span of a decade. What seems obvious looking back today did not necessarily seem so back then.

Delivering movies over digital infrastructure has saved the customer from traveling to the local store. Leveraging the digital infrastructure with high-speed broadband access and sharing the same wires for web browsing and reading email has revolutionized the entertainment industry. But IT had to be involved to make that a reality.

IT now needs a different IT model, a new delivery model enabled by technology. The next time our businesses are looking at what they can do to compete—to be a Netflix rather than a Blockbuster—we have an opportunity to help them think beyond what they're doing today to make possibilities the reality.

Future Losses

Losses that have yet to materialize occupy the minds of executives. Losses that have yet to materialize can come from various sources. These sources include technical leapfrogs, slow market delivery, or resistance to change. They could be supply chain structure or contractual constraints—or stalled transformation initiatives or foreign competitors who steal intellectual property.

Wealth transfer via espionage has a painful impact. Economic espionage represents *"the greatest transfer of wealth in history,"* said General Keith Alexander, NSA director and commander of the US Cyber Command, at the American Enterprise Institute in 2012.[11] BlackOps Partners Corporation, which does counterintelligence and protection of trade secrets and competitive advantages for Fortune 500 companies, estimates that $500 billion in raw innovation is stolen from US companies each year. This innovation includes trade secrets, research and development, market intelligence, and product information. Casey Fleming, CEO of BlackOps Partners Corporation, remarked: *"When this innovation is meant to drive revenue, profit, and jobs for at least 10 years, we are losing the equivalent of $5 trillion out of the U.S. economy every year to economic espionage. To put it into perspective, the U.S. will take in $1.5 trillion in income taxes and $2.7 trillion in all taxes in 2013."*[12]

What happens when your company's breach doesn't get detected or make it to the headlines? While the headlines are screaming about breaches in credit cards, medical records, or personal information, this attention can hide the fact that many intellectual property breaches will not make the news.

Many breach reports focus on data record leakage and quantify the effect with the number of records lost. But this narrow focus loses sight of some of the bigger impacts of data loss. Individual organizations use sensitive and valuable data to drive their businesses. They are at risk of losing market advantages when someone steals it.

Businesses undertake great efforts to keep trade secrets out of competitors' view. These include confidentiality agreements, stringent data handling policies, data loss prevention controls, and data access governance.

When the threat actor behind these cyber breaches happens to be from other countries, the stakes can be even higher. News reports highlight cases of nation-state espionage. The most reported country involved in these cases is China, a country of over one billion people and a government dedicated to ensuring a very aggressive growth in GDP every year. China's turn to capitalism has created a spiraling growth to meet the burgeoning demands of a growing population. But China's innovations and intellectual property designs have not kept pace with the Western world. Therefore, the Chinese government has sponsored a state strategy of corporate nation-state espionage with the express purpose of helping Chinese industries keep pace. The FBI has reported that US jobs are lost through these intellectual property-stealing efforts.

In addition, businesses are at risk of strategy errors when decisions are not properly risk informed. Mergers and acquisitions are another common way for business leaders to respond to market risks and new opportunities. Some businesses must guard against being cannibalized, while others eagerly consolidate.

During upfront accounting for the costs of merging organizations and their cost structures, the last thing the CEO wants is to blow through cash to integrate technology infrastructure. But this cash *must* be spent for IT to preserve the expected payoffs of the merger.

When it comes to integration challenges, IT and the disparate systems of the two companies are at the top of the list in terms of difficulty and cost. Hugo Sarrazin and Andy West said in "Understanding the strategic value of IT in M&A":

> We've all heard about deals where the stars seemed aligned but synergies remained elusive. In these cases, the acquirer and target may have had complementary strategies and finances, but the integration of technology and operations often proved difficult, usually because it didn't receive adequate consideration during due diligence.[13]

IT must be persistent in protecting good ideas from being stolen and prevent strategic decisions from ignoring risk factors that lead to future losses.

Lagging Value Delivery

When the delivery of value lags, businesses are at risk. A business with lagging innovation loses opportunities to maintain market position, grow revenue, and capture new market share. Sometimes, the task of infusing the organization with new ideas falls on IT, such as when success is dependent on new technology use.

Technology speeds up tasks, organizes information, and automates processes. But people, from the secretary to the CEO, are who make a business succeed or fail. We in IT are part of that people group. We must excel in the parts of success that we can influence or control.

When workers need to get things done, the last thing they want to do is wait. And why should they? Yes, budget and time constraints exist. But why can't we work together to put more resources—people and time and money—into helping our businesses earn back more than what's invested?

If professional pride doesn't inspire us to do this, another motivation waits in the wings—shadow IT. These shadow IT options promise faster, cheaper, better service to work around the shortcomings of central IT. Let's be an IT group that is engaged and aware.

We need to make ourselves nimble and communicative to show business leaders how well we spend budget dollars and how much we earn back for the company. Otherwise, our businesses may not even ask us for our advice on big decisions, and instead reduce our role.

It is salt in the wounds for IT to be pitched by third parties. The individual employee is becoming the main consumer and target for product and software design. As such, the end user heavily influences what they use inside their businesses. This is a big contrast to the traditional model of corporate-issued and -managed devices, apps, and services. This disruption is forcing businesses and IT to evolve how they procure and manage technology assets.

Into the Shadows

In the shadows lurks a challenge for IT that is a risk for the business. IT must be careful to maintain relevance to the business. In the past, there were fewer alternative sources of technology for business users. Corporate IT was it. If you needed a laptop, email address, file storage, or customer database, you had to go to IT. But today, cloud providers and value-added resellers compete intensely for the same internal users. Having shown their chops with the consumer market, these productivity marvels that have sprung up are in reach of corporate users as well. Managed services across the IT technology stack have become available. From data centers to user endpoints to phones on desks, there's a treasure trove of options.

All lines of businesses must prove their relevance on a day-to-day basis to prove to the CEO, and ultimately the board, that their money is spent well. IT is no different.

We can build trust or let trust break down. As trust breaks down, business users go into the shadows. How should IT view shadow IT? Maybe as the potentially unauthorized use of third-party systems that compromises security.

Perhaps it should be viewed as an opportunity. Shadow IT could be viewed as honest feedback from users and the business, amounting to a wake-up call. By looking at it as a signal for areas to improve, we can view it as a positive. We can work with the business to take advantage of the situation. IT should consider shadow IT as an opportunity for collaboration. Technical advancements have made possible the quick, fast, and efficient lower barrier to new technology services.

From file sharing and video collaboration to workflow analysis and many other services traditionally deployed internally, IT can work together with the lines of business to provide the right mix of internal and external services in a unified service delivery front.

IT can reduce friction in technology consumption for the end users. At the end of the day, internal IT needs to be involved to reduce organizational risks by providing governance, compliance, security, performance, and resiliency for all technology systems supporting our businesses.

Far too often businesses are bypassing IT and later regretting their decision. Common results are compliance violations, security breaches, and incompatibility with existing systems. In instances where a business unit uses an unapproved third-party platform, integrations costs can get out of control.

If IT took inventory of all of accounting's expenses, corporate credit cards might be shown to be a surprising drain of resources. The practice of expensing systems can open a business to too many risks. The CEO and board of directors are often not aware of these risks.

To combat these risks, IT must first be quick enough to deliver the services it is capable of, using existing technologies and personnel. Second, IT must collaborate with third parties on the services it can't provide. IT must use its experience and brilliance to make workable solutions for both the business and IT. This two-pronged approach is win-win, providing governance, compliance, and risk mitigation.

Shadow IT is in part the result of a loss of trust in IT. Shadow IT is also in part the result of the reality that new services and choices have emerged that businesses require (or want) but that IT can't provide. In the latter case, the business has no choice but to go around IT to third parties.

It's ironic that in some cases the problem is not in functionality but in packaging. IT has not traditionally been in the customer experience business that third parties specialize in. IT builds systems with business functionality. Branding these new services is an opportunity.

The consumption model has changed. IT can work with third parties to create a hybrid service model, finding the best of what both parties do and providing a seamless integration plan for the business. IT is uniquely qualified to do this as well as to provide the governance for it. IT therefore becomes a huge benefit to a business that doesn't have domain expertise necessary to safely choose third parties. And by "safety" I mean choosing providers at the right cost. The business doesn't want to find out later that the control they invested money in is of no use because the sensitive data now lives somewhere else. Ease of use now can cost the business time and money later.

Loss of governance can lead to an increased likelihood of sensitive data being leaked, expenses being higher than needed, an under-utilization of invested solutions, more difficult collaboration, or potential blind spots on new customer insights. In the end, we need to head these outcomes off and facilitate the functionality the business needs.

Operational Disruptions

Stopped work, lost productivity, and lost revenue mean discouraged workers, frustrated customers, and unhappy stakeholders. As businesses have increasingly leveraged technology to operate, improve, and grow their operations, their level of dependency on technology has increased exponentially. No modern economy in the world can operate today in the absence of pervasive technology.

Major advancements over the last couple of decades have driven our use of ever-advancing technologies. From hardware and software to network connectivity, all aspects of modern life on earth depend on the functioning operations of our digital infrastructure. And when these systems fail, the impacts are noticed.

System Failures

Previously, the internet being down meant only a small inconvenience. You went about doing other things with little worry when it would come back up. Now, it means interruptions in the abilities to access a financial report, view surveillance footage of the parking lot, or signal a programmable logic controller to close the valve to a pipe. IT must revisit the designs of our systems and redundancy strategies.

"Always on, always available" is not just preferable, but critical for a business to move forward. With the number and types of systems sharing a common infrastructure increasing, common mode failure analysis is becoming a more critical process.

Common mode failures occur when a single fault causes failures in multiple other parts of a system. An example is when all the telecom carrier equipment is in one room and connected to the same UPS. If the UPS fails, then all the connectivity will fail at once, rendering redundant circuits moot. Another example is a business application that has redundant resources, but they are only using a single availability zone from a cloud provider. A failure in that zone can cause all resources to be unavailable and knock out the service.

Like a common mode failure, a common mode *vulnerability* also has the potential to multiply impact. A single vulnerability in a single component could become a vulnerability of the many systems behind it.

As controls often rely on location, a weakness in a firewall could potentially expose thousands of systems behind it to the public internet. A problem at a load balancer could affect all the services behind it; a failure in a redundant heartbeat could render a firewall pair inoperable. An outage in one cloud provider region could render a business application unreachable if it is not designed to also be in a different region.

IT has the huge job of keeping vulnerabilities from becoming failures and failures from being lengthy. Businesses' dependency on IT operations and fulfillment has evolved from "It would be nice to have this" to "We can't work without this."

And then there's communication. Take for example an organization facing its largest business initiative to date. All the pertinent parties had met to discuss the scope of the project, including costs, risks, and expected goals. The VPs of marketing, sales, and product development, along with the third-party vendor and implementation consultants, hammered out the details. In short order, hardware was ordered to support the project. A project manager was assigned, contracts were signed, and money was allocated.

Everyone was in sync on this initiative to drive growth in a competitive market landscape. Everyone except IT. No one from IT had been invited to any of the planning or implementation meetings. The first sign something was going on was the arrival at the primary data center of a new million-dollar Hadoop cluster in a rack. The delivery people asked the IT folks at the data center where they should put it. Shrugged shoulders and blank stares over something they knew nothing of led to rushed and poorly planned changes to the infrastructure, which led to future system failures.

Unintentional Intent

Risk can be driven by unintentional intent. In another example, one by one, as employees came through the door, they were not greeted with a hello but by a large sign in the lobby that read, *"The network is down."* Employees searched for other tasks to work on while they waited to learn the fate of the thousands of hours of work that lived on the single server that housed all the firm's data—data that could no longer be accessed because of a failed hard drive. Months of work stored in digital format were unavailable. There was no backup in place! The culprit was maintenance work that had been done to increase storage capacity for future work. Nobody meant for this to happen, but everyone was affected.

In another story across town, there's a paper company. In its production plant, reams of newly minted paper were traveling station to station on an assembly line. Various workers on the line completed their tasks at their control stations. Outside the noise of the line, an IT contractor was in the main lobby waiting to gain access to the server room. He was there to upgrade their existing control system software—one that runs applications on a Windows server and connects to a local SQL instance. This system was one of three primary apps that controlled various processes on the assembly line.

The contractor was ready to apply the needed changes to the server. As he did his work, one of the managers on the line noticed a problem with the next job scheduled to run. His screen had locked up. As the previous job made its way through to the end, it was time for the next one to be moved from the queue to the active state. Minutes later, there was a commotion in the hallways and alerts went off—the production line had stopped. The manager shouted for an explanation: "*What is going on?*"

As IT investigated the problem, the familiar "Starting Windows" screen indicated a server was booting up. It seemed the contractor had applied the changes and rebooted the same server that housed the production line app—the same server running SQL that hosted the databases for all the applications. After the server made it back up and the databases had reconnected to the applications, the job queue got moving again. This was more than an "oops!" It kept teams from meeting that day's customer orders.

Elsewhere, at an e-commerce firm, when the primary website went down, it created millions of dollars in losses. In a normal week, the orders would come in, products would move across different categories, users would browse the product pages on the site, and the purchase numbers on the organizational dashboard would be looking fabulous. However, things turned gloomy very quickly one day as the number of purchases started to decline—after an 8 percent increase every minute in the previous hour. The number of new orders was slowing down, yet the number of new visitors to the site was not plummeting—they just couldn't get in.

A frantic call was put into the help desk asking *"Is anything wrong with the system? Is the site up?"* The help desk tracked down the server administrator on duty. Then that administrator got calls from several business leaders looking for an explanation. After making the rounds, the service desk manager called the user back and indicated everything was okay. Eight hours later, an irate and unhappy CEO called the CIO, questioning if IT was on top of the problem. IT's response of "nothing is wrong with the systems" led to all-hands-on-deck.

An engineer checked the file server at the hosting site for the application, and the developers said they rechecked the main database server five times yesterday, but it turned out the actual business service used nineteen different servers and five databases spread out across three data centers—some in the AWS cloud—and five third-party partners. This company's e-commerce site was not a single server; it was an entire business service.

In the end, the developer indicated he didn't have access to the production logs to investigate further. Not all the server logs were available, and some of the systems were not reachable due to a DMZ firewall. Hours turned into days, with sales pressing for answers. IT did not know the service chain, know the technology dependencies, or have visibility. IT failed its main customer—the business.

Modern companies run on technology. And when the unintentional happens, when something goes wrong, *"What's going on here*?" can be heard.

In more painful real-world examples, when mainstay economic activity involves mass transit such as air travel, the disruption is widely impactful. Traveling business passengers rely on a sophisticated air traffic system.

Delta Airlines experienced the biggest disruption to its operations since the terror attacks of 9/11 over a computer glitch, affecting over 4,000 flights. The airline took days to recover.[14] The impact on passengers was immeasurable.

A computer system failure at Southwest Airlines resulted in the cancelation or delay of more than 2,000 flights. This potentially cost the airline between $54 million and $82 million in lost revenue and increased costs, as well as a 0.5 percent drop in its unit revenues during one of its reporting quarters.[15] This revenue loss included direct and indirect costs, including the inability to accept new reservations.

Airlines aren't the only ones that rely on complex infrastructure. According to *The Wall Street Journal,* in July 2015, a software glitch caused a nearly four-hour outage at the New York Stock Exchange.[16]

Hospitals up the ante in the need for reliable computer systems because people's lives depend on them. Hospitals rely on many sophisticated machines for patient diagnostic and care functions. A person in need of emergency medical assistance and transport to a hospital could have their care negatively impacted due to a technology mishap. In a real-world example, after a network infrastructure upgrade, hospital technicians could not restart the MRI systems. The hospital's emergency room service had to be put on standby and could not accept ambulances. Typically, an ambulance routes to the closest, most appropriate facility to handle the situation, but in this case the ambulances had to go elsewhere.

In retrospect, the cause was a misunderstanding of the infrastructure network changes being made during the upgrade maintenance window, which triggered the reboot of hospital equipment. With a little documented knowledge of how to properly bring these systems back up, critical systems needed for patient care would have become available much more quickly. IT owned the technical infrastructure, but not the medical gear that the hospital relied on to operate. IT was responsible for pieces of the value chain. But once again, the needs of the organization require the whole system to be managed.

Malicious Intent

Risk can be driven by malicious intent. Unintentional disruptions are bad enough. When the intent is malicious, the negative impacts can be not only disruptive but also dangerous. In one city, no court cases were heard for four days because their system was down due to a computer virus. Those awaiting trials may have been in town just for their case but were turned away. Could this virus have been from someone the courts had convicted? Multiple systems across the network were disabled when the antivirus control system could not detect this virus. IT had to call a third party to assist with the identification of the virus and to assist with the plan to clean out the machines.

When the computer-based monitoring system in a pediatric intensive care unit went offline, a frantic call was made to off-duty pediatric nurses to return to the hospital to monitor the children. The cause was simple. A virus had spread around the network that disrupted computer systems. But the result was anything but simple. Very sick children were put in unnecessary danger.

In this hospital, the monitoring technology had been implemented to reduce the number of people required to monitor children in the ICU ward and increase the children's safety. Sadly, the IT team did not have answers, and technicians went from room to room to see if a computer was infected. This was like having third-party, value-added resellers going door-to-door, trying to clean machines with three-and-a-half-inch floppy disks. Some of those computers had been sitting there for over a decade, victims of poor inventory records. Elsewhere, computer failures affected work shifts and workflow.

These operational disruptions were not caused by accidents or happenstance. They were the side effects of threat actors operating in cyberspace. Cyber threats pose a complex and dynamic risk factor in the digital and physical world and deserve special attention.

Digital Threats

A digital threat, commonly referred to as a *cyber threat*, is an entity or agent that intentionally compromises the confidentiality, integrity, availability, safety, or privacy of technology systems.

Cybersecurity is more than a technical problem. The first rule of cybersecurity is to acknowledge the business implication. To drive home the point, when Verizon Communications Inc. acquired Yahoo in 2017, it did so at a $350 million discount off the original agreed price. The reason was the effects of two cyber breaches at Yahoo in previous years. The sale was delayed, the price was cut, and now Verizon will inherit the future ongoing legal responsibilities.[17]

Stakeholders and policymakers sometimes miss the long-term pervasiveness of cyber threats. They limit cyber threats to a temporary technology problem that IT will handle. Yes, IT will handle certain aspects, but the handling happens much more effectively on the front end with wise decision-making.

Newsworthy cyber-attacks spur executive attention in all industries. But when the news returns to other stories and breach fatigue sets in, executives turn their focus to other concerns.

When the board asks how much time and money they must spend on the cyber threat, IT can respond. Until crime and war no longer inhabit our society, Cyber threats are a permanent part of our digital world. These threats are an extension of the dangers in the real world. Like in the real work world, there is no end in sight to the need for law enforcement and armies to provide risk mitigation. Cyber defenses are needed as long as police, fire, and military services are needed. We'll need protection as long as we need smoke detectors, door locks, fences, alarm systems, and sprinkler systems in buildings.

Disruption and complexity provide the context for cyber threats to reign. IT is at a crossroads. Many IT departments are starved for budget, with business leadership assuming they'll never become headline breach news. But government regulations do compel more spending. As a result, we must advocate for larger budgets and more personnel.

Businesses at the macro level have seldom come to grips with the nature or risk of cyber threats. The risk is persistent due to our always-on dependence on technology. As a society, this active embedding of technology into our cars, houses, and bodies puts our freedom, work lives, and existence at stake.

Cyber threats have the potential to thwart not only daily activities but also economic stability and growth. Cyber threats target personal freedom and privacy. Cyber threats stymie organizational advantages from innovation.

The board of directors and C-suite don't tune in to the details of cyber threats. The plant foreman knows that when his people hit that button over there, the factory works. That's okay. That's what businesses hire IT for. But IT must communicate the security protections for technical systems that keep the line moving, why those protections are needed, and how to execute those protections.

Recent business disruptions have wooed the population toward a free-and-easy mentality. The danger is that nothing is free. Businesses that offer "free" services use them to gather data or otherwise gain from the not-so-free gift. Cyber-attackers use the lack of protection in shareware to steal money or control.

With the powerful luring the unaware toward the cheap and free, IT must develop new governance and control models. Headlines and compliance rules aren't enough to sway those with budget and power.

IT is in danger of being relegated to constant blame if it fails to understand real business risks, to teach stakeholders about the organizational impacts of cyber threats, and to lead users toward fast and safe computing use. IT is tasked with knowing and managing how these systems work. Sadly, systems that are running amok become noticeable only when something breaks. IT needs to get out in front.

Challenges for IT in protecting an organization's digital assets and services include a borderless perimeter, an increasingly mobile workforce, an influx of employee-owned devices and applications not under IT control, and stolen assets that are copied but not removed, making it harder to detect a breach.

Rather than focus on the increased attacks, IT must focus on the opportunity. How? By becoming the go-to for enabling new technology services. The primary purpose of all of this technology is enablement. IT is responsible for the connectivity, speed, and software that are designed to enable work and innovation.

The costs a business incurs for cybersecurity is the expense of doing business. Armies, police, guns, insurance, and fences are all costs and are not core desires; they are add-ons to enable the economies and workings of human endeavors.

There are many threats to your organization, your nation, and the underlying infrastructure of the global digital economy. But IT can provide the metaphorical armies, police, weapons, insurance, and fences to keep business moving forward.

Speed kills, and ours is a world of fast compromise. Internal detection by IT is often slow and notification is often provided by third parties. The FBI ranks cyber threats above terrorism as a threat to national security.

Threat Landscape

Threat landscape is vast and dangerous, filled by people, groups, and things likely to cause damage or danger. The features of a digital infrastructure and its complex systems connect the elements of value, threats, and mitigations. It is this threat environment that drives cybersecurity.

Cybersecurity has gone from a niche for IT to a boardroom priority. The global security spend is in the hundreds of billions. When large companies get breached, they can end drastically increasing they security spend to address the challenge. There is real money being redirected from other areas of the business.

The number of industries coming under attack is increasing. More companies are reporting breaches to the public, partly because of legal requirements for companies that lose credit card data and personally identifiable information (PII). Politicians and a wary public are increasingly asking who the people are behind these attacks, how they got in, and what was stolen.

Who are the bad guys, and what are they after? Individual criminals, organized criminal organizations, and armies have expanded into the digital space. Bad guys are reaping the benefits of ubiquitous connectivity, speed, and access to global resources.

There is crime in the world, both physical and cyber. There are nation-state military operations both in the physical and cyber realms.

The biggest gap in our collective mindset is the lack of appreciation of the fact that that criminal and military activity happens via the same digital infrastructure we businesses and society use daily to great benefit. This has led to our collective response being haphazard and scattered.

We need to map threats from criminals and nations onto the digital world to ascertain the needed adjustments to our thinking, strategies, and defenses. In the past (although it still occurs), the bad guy had to physically drive down to a bank to perform a stickup to steal money. Today, criminals steal behind laptops located around the world. There is no longer a moat helping to protect your assets. Criminals break into virtual safes behind virtual walls. The benefits of connectivity from anywhere in the world also provide a new avenue of attack, a new *attack surface*. This allows an even greater number of people to steal from you.

The digital world also affords the bad guys anonymity. Whereas great physical harm can come to one who must physically come to your bank to rob it, hiding behind the internet provides a comfort level for criminals and other threat actors.

Truth be told, we should not be shocked to know that just as much crime is happening in cyberspace as in the physical world.

We'll now describe the threat landscape with examples from various perspectives, including global security, terrorism, and social media attacks.

Global Security

Security is global. The principle of collective defense is at the very heart of the North Atlantic Treaty Organization's (NATO) founding treaty. Collective defense commit members to protect each other from attack. An attack against one member is considered an attack against all members. NATO officially recognizes cyberspace as the fifth domain of warfare. The implication is that conventional weapons can be used in response to a cyber-attack against a member.

The domain of cyber space is now in scope for nation-states to pursue their interests. That puts the domain that IT operates under extreme pressures for well-resourced and persistent threat actors.

Most critical infrastructure companies are owned by private entities. Attacking via the digital infrastructure increases the attack surface and lowers the barriers to entry. An attack on the digital infrastructure itself is an attack on our economy, and an attack on the digital infrastructure with the purpose of physical impact is warfare.

From Target to Sony, Home Depot to Anthem, Ashley Madison to the United States Office of Personnel Management (OPM), boards are paying more attention to headline news. Articles on cybersecurity are a mainstay in *The Wall Street Journal*, prompting more questions from stakeholders to IT about the relevancy to their organizations.

"Cybersecurity is the biggest risk facing the financial system," said Jo White, the chair of the US Securities and Exchange Commission (SEC) at an interview at the Reuters Financial Regulation Summit in Washington, DC, on May 17, 2016. This was in the context of the Bangladesh central bank, which had just suffered an $81 million cyber theft.[18]

Social Media

In the realm of social media, Twitter found itself making news as a result of a cyber incident. At the axis of Twitter, the New York Stock Exchange, and hacktivism sits an interesting source of new threats:

> At 1:07 p.m. on a Tuesday, the official Twitter account of the Associated Press sent a tweet to its nearly two million followers that warned, "Breaking: Two Explosions in the White House and Barack Obama is injured." Some people who momentarily panicked were apparently on or near the trading floor of the New York Stock Exchange. At 1:08, the Dow began a perilous but short-lived nosedive dropping about 150 points, from 14697.15 to 14548.58, before stabilizing at 1:10 p.m., when news came that the tweet had been erroneous. By 1:13 p.m., the level had returned to 14690. During those three minutes, the "fake tweet erased $136 billion in equity market value," according to Bloomberg News' Nikolaj Gammeltoft.[19]

The market recovered quickly and later a hacker group out of Syria claimed responsibility. A little-told element of the story was the impact machines played in the rapid response to the false news—in particular, the algorithms, which handle much of actual trading on the stock exchange. The algorithms took in the fake Twitter info and automatically made trades in response. This wiped out $136.5 billion of the Standard & Poor's 500 Index's value.[20]

We are living in a new reality in which the number of news sources has exploded, there is less fact-checking, information is coming in faster, and there are more automatic responses. The barriers for putting false information out into the world have all but disappeared. New media models are in place, with less journalistic research and reporting.

Another emerging threat is the ability for stolen data to be altered and then put into the public space. Without the ability to validate it with established journalistic standards, public figures could be subjected to reputation smearing and slander, potentially causing embarrassment and, in some cases, altering their public careers.

Major US banks have received distributed denial-of-service (DDoS) attacks—to disrupt operations and, at times, to mask intrusion attempts. Considering the importance of online banking, this impact on the customer experience and the business bottom line is serious.

Nation-State Warfare

War activities among nation-state are real in cyberspace. Nation-states are using the digital world as an extension of the battlefield, triggering a race among nations to militarize cyberspace. No better example is what many believe was a state-sponsored cyber-attack from the government of North Korea against a private US company for political reasons. When Sony employees came into work on a Monday morning to log on to their computers, they were greeted by a message indicating they had been compromised. On reboot, every disk was wiped. Massive numbers of machines became inoperable. Emails between executives at the company were leaked online, showing embarrassing correspondence and inappropriate business language. Contracts and other legal info were also leaked.

Sony was forced to resort to fax machines and cellphones to do business. The replacement of 10,000 PCs caused an interruption in the normal delivery times for hard drives to reach customers. Threats made to the company about its business operations garnered the attention of the president of the United States, who would later sign a new national initiative giving the US the authority to respond to cyber-attacks with physical retaliation.

The profound implication of this is the potential for cyber-attacks to disrupt the infrastructure that underpins the digital economy. The scale of this risk, outside of nuclear warfare, has not been seen in human history.

The physical economy is also critically dependent on its underlying control systems, which are interconnected to an ecosystem of digital infrastructure. This makes fast, global, negative threats possible.

Nation-states with the largest economies in the world depend on this critical infrastructure. The other source of potential risk is the internal routing of traffic across the internet, leading to disruption, eavesdropping, or alteration. Our economy depends on the integrity and safety of network traffic.

An example of cyber nation-state military action being substituted for physical force is Stuxnet, a computer worm that many call the world's first digital weapon. Stuxnet was unlike any other virus or worm that came before it. Rather than simply hijack targeted computers or steal information from them, Stuxnet escaped the digital realm to wreak physical destruction on the equipment the computers controlled. It's widely believed that Stuxnet was created by the US and Israel to slow down Iran's nuclear weapons program, but one of its unfortunate side effects is that this advanced malware is now out in the wild, being reengineered and repurposed by others for future use.

Nation-state espionage has also been included in cyberspace. China is widely viewed as a source of espionage against US companies, stealing intellectual property and feeding it to their industries to compete. The FBI has said economic espionage is a problem that costs the American economy billions of dollars annually and puts our national security at risk. The number of billions is staggering. While the FBI has put the annual cost of economic espionage at approximately $13 billion, that only reflects cases the bureau has actually handled. The Commission on the Theft of American Intellectual Property has estimated total losses, including jobs, competitiveness, stock value, market share, and so on, to reach into the hundreds of billions.[21]

In the political realm, the news is full of reports of nation-states using the digital space to supplement geopolitical tactics, including influencing elections and destabilizing governments. Even before the headline news of Russian interference in the 2016 US presidential election, cybersecurity experts discussed the potential future threats of stolen digital data to influence the public sphere.

Terrorism

In the world of terrorism, hacking can get you targeted by the US military. According to news reports, a cyber hacker affiliated with the Islamic State Hacking Division was responsible for exposing the personal information of hundreds of US military and government personnel.

The US infrastructure remains a top target for threats and is essential for the functioning of our society and economy. We know this infrastructure as the power we use at homes and work, the water we drink, the transportation that moves us, the stores we shop at, and the communication systems we rely on, as well as the computers we use for work and recreation.

The Department of Homeland Security (DHS) identifies sixteen critical infrastructure sectors that have assets, systems, and networks that are considered so vital to the United States that if they were incapacitated or destroyed, it would have a massive and debilitating effect on the nation.[22]

Most of our nation's critical infrastructure is privately owned and operated. This means technical controls that protect this infrastructure (and consequently, the US's ability to operate) are vital. In addition, there are serious consequences of disruptions, like those caused by DDoS attacks. Many organizations run their businesses on the public internet infrastructure—everything from remote offices and teleworker connectivity to IoT devices and digital storefronts.

Extortion

Extortion by means of holding data hostage or threat of public release of sensitive information. Crime pays, so criminals have expanded operations into cyberspace. Some organizations have been victimized by extortion by means of ransomware. Attackers lock machines and encrypt data, demanding payment to get the decryption key. A variation of this attack is to threaten to release data online to the public if the attackers are not paid. Criminals often attack those who can least afford to be down or lose data. They also attack those who may not have the budget for sophisticated defense, such as hospitals, municipalities, and cities.

The Path Ahead

The path ahead requires a mindset of putting hands on keyboards and battling other humans. Threats in cyberspace and the physical world have the commonality of *people* behind each. A tagline from CrowdStrike, a leader in the cybersecurity field, stated: *"You don't have a malware problem, you have an adversary problem."* [23]

The threat actors operating in this dynamic threat landscape include insiders, criminal organizations, competitors, nation-states, and hacktivists. As mentioned earlier, the digital space often gives anonymity that allows anyone to hide more easily.

Adversary methods include nuisance (including botnets and spam), data theft (for economic or political advantage), cyber-crime (for financial gain), hacktivism (for defamation, publicity, and policy changes), and destructive attacks (to disrupt operations).

How do these threat actors go about their attacks? Let's look at their tactics, techniques, and procedures (TTPs). Threat actors travel a well-worn path of gathering information, enumerating systems, determining targets, exploiting weaknesses, pivoting from one system to another, and remaining persistent as needed.

These methods exploit users through phishing, compromising credentials, installing malware, living off the native host tools, and taking advantage of flat networks for lateral movement. The methods are tried and true. Patience, persistence, and ingenuity are the hallmarks of attackers.

Prominent in the digital threat landscape are the challenges IT confronts in cyber defense. Unfortunately, in today's digital world, most organizations only rely on an external breach incident notification system. This lets the company know someone has compromised data from its systems. Getting a system like this up and running is not intrusive to business operations because it has zero cost to deploy, needs no training, and requires no lengthy implementation time. This notification system is the FBI, Brian Krebs, or your customers!

When the bad guys breach security controls and successfully extract data, make it available in the criminal underworld, and then actually attempt to leverage it for criminal activities like identity theft or fraud, this external system detects it and the business is informed. You may have noticed this notification system in use while monitoring public news reports.

But this is not the way it should work. IT must be first to notify stakeholders.

Many boards of directors show concern about two kinds of risks. One is reputational risk, which could ultimately impact the bottom line. The other is the risk of the business being disrupted, such as by a start-up company that alters the revenue stream of the current business model.

Both kinds of risk impact income. Ways to lose money include loss of income, loss of potential income, loss of future income, and increasing expenses.

The most pertinent fact about financial losses for a business is the focus on why the loss happened and how it can be prevented in the future.

In the end, from a business standpoint, it does not matter why the loss occurred. But for IT, that *why* helps us head it off in the future. IT must stay focused on their organization's most relevant business risks.

It makes no difference if the inventory worth millions of dollars is burned up in a fire or if the theft of intellectual property results in a million-dollar profit loss. The adverse effects can be accidental or intentional. They can be caused by an insider or an outsider. They can be natural or unnatural occurrences. IT works to mitigate whatever the adverse effects may be.

Therefore, you will see organizations bringing cybersecurity under the umbrella of enterprise risk management. The particulars are important in mitigation efforts and in figuring out who might be responsible for a breach, but at the end of the day, a $5 million expense is an undesirable outcome. IT as the defender of cyberspace is the expectation our organizations hold. Threat actors are active in all areas of life and across most industries, performing attacks and presenting defenders with many dilemmas.

Defenders Dilemma

Cyber defenders have a defense dilemma. IT is charged with helping mitigate business risks in all their forms—all while running the technology the business runs on. IT can run behind on standard maintenance and basic security hygiene due to having to keep up with new business demands and service availability requirements.

Many risk factors surface when assessing the probabilities of a successful cyber-attack against your organization. Often these risk factors will be elusive to the security team and to the larger IT team. The challenge is often seen when outside security teams are brought in to assess the threats and risks of an organization's cyber defenses against current cyber-attacks. Time after time, whether it's a vulnerability assessment, a penetration test, or some type of compliance or regulatory statute, the recommendations will be sidelined rather than executed. The reasons for this tend to be based on a combination of lack of budget, lack of know-how, or lack of time.

As in the past, talent continues to be the most critical tool IT possesses. The cybersecurity talent market is heating up, with open positions going unfilled for long periods. This is especially noticeable in analyst roles in security operations and incident response. In trying to keep up with the cybersecurity skill shortage and headcount limitations, IT must continually attract qualified talent while keeping existing staff happy. When the budget for salaries and IT processes is constrained, people with the right skill mix will go elsewhere.

Many organizations are saddled with fragile infrastructures. It doesn't take much to break business-impacting services. IT can design them to be resilient, but due to time or budget constraints, these systems often are characterized as single points of failure. In addition, poor documentation is often the norm, with a high dependency on the knowledge of one fallible engineer who set up the system. Even for internal recommendations, lag time happens between fixes and actual patches. A majority of attacks are successful because of a small number of vulnerabilities that have had patches available for many years prior.

The attack surface is growing, with software code running all things. And all code can contain vulnerabilities. All code is susceptible to bugs.

With code existing everywhere technology lives, the attack surface that needs to be protected is very large. It is not enough for IT defenders to use controls to mitigate cyber threats. The controls as well as the systems themselves process services and hold data. We must address the very code itself to make an impact on safety. Any-to-any connections, some on corporate-issued endpoints and some on personal devices, bring great benefits to the workflow and the workplace. Information sharing is currently too slow. IT needs to have an open line of communications with business stakeholders to manage the new risk factors, including architectural, structural, and mindset adjustments.

IT must overcome the tendency to speak in code, which is understandable only to other techies. The board of directors, the C-suite, and other stakeholders are at a loss for what we are talking about. The risks, threats, opportunities, and cost justifications are a mystery to them because we don't speak their language. We have an opportunity to improve this situation, and we must speak their language if we want real solutions. We can and must encode technology jargon into business language.

The nature of work is changing, and this affects the risk landscape in a major way. Most current controls were built, designed, and tested for the physical world. For example, a corporate or branch office was protected by locks and fences. As the workforce has continually moved outside that perimeter, we now live and work in borderless environments.

A challenge of sharing cyber-attack knowledge with the larger community is the legal constraints and corporate restrictions on what a company can report. This can lead to sub-optimal outcomes because the cyber criminal's TTPs are kept obscured rather than disseminated. This limits overall learning that would improve our defenses. Various laws exist that curtail what can be reported publicly. And a lack of clear standards often prevents quickly sharing threat intelligence among our industry peers. The result is that cyber criminals have an open lane to reuse the same TTPs against thousands of organizations.

Security budgets too seldom assess real risk. Not enough business is basing their level of security spending on sound risk analysis. Many use a percentage of total technology spend or industry benchmarks. However, that does not adequately answer the question of whether that amount is enough. It also does not provide confidence that these security investments are in the right areas and provide the best return.

Complexity and fragmentation slow down IT's ability to execute protection strategies. As we look to adjust to this new threat landscape, we can expect to experience challenges, constraints, and risks along our path.

Systems designed for ease of use tend to be more challenging to control. Ease of use is good, but businesses must mitigate associated risks. Ease of use helps customer acceptance but could hurt those customers when vulnerabilities in the software are exploited by cyber-attackers.

Take the Microsoft Windows operating system, for example. It is designed for functionality across the widest audience and the broadest set of software and device support. It is designed for ease of use to a consumer market. It offers a broad platform for applications written for business. However, other design choices also reflect these priorities. Many consider the Linux platform to be more secure, but it just does not have nearly the user popularity on the desktop front. Microsoft's popularity with users and application developers also makes it an attractive target for attackers. With this base operating system supporting both Fortune 500 companies and your home PC, Microsoft must balance functionality and security.

In addition to platform and server, infrastructure gear favors functionality. The priority for IT and end users alike is to get gear up, get it running faster, and make it easier to use. IT can and should account for enterprise-wide risk management when balancing functionality and security.

The technology underlying our infrastructure may live in silos. Hidden silo costs happen when research into the technology choices is limited during the product procurement process. Key features, functionality, and support costs are not always fully explored prior to purchase.

Seeking the most bang for your buck is certainly wise, but we must be certain the value continues. For example, consider the problem of a new, secure mobile solution from a vendor that does not support a wireless infrastructure. This mobile solution may have trouble integrating with a local area network in corporate offices, forcing IT to have two network vendors, one for wireless and one for wired. This is the opposite of the most bang for your buck.

Some vendors are attempting to unify solution sets to make things easier. IT must be wary of architectural solutions like this. IT must make sure vendors provide integration capabilities, that the vendor's product provides information to other products, and that the product can take the information from other products into its core. Only then can a product deliver actionable controls.

In addition to silo problems, there are the vendors themselves. Vendors frequently only add transformational functionality or deeper integration when they are pressured to do so. Vendors only put direction and effort into a transformational product if it will grow revenue or protect existing market competitiveness. A vendor's failure to transform the underlying principles of its product development drives weaknesses across the technology stack, and that makes the efficacy of our collective defenses against cyber threats more challenging.

Some industries are agile. Others are saddled with legacy systems that are extremely difficult to upgrade. Vendors need to make changes to how they develop their products to stay relevant.

Niche players are increasing innovation to improve their control sets. Some traditional infrastructure vendors and software players are trying to break into security. Some traditional security vendors are integrating new technologies. Companies turn to new approaches like machine learning, threat intelligence, and automation to keep up. The primary example of this is antivirus companies whose solutions now have improved abilities to stop advanced malware from running and better detection of attacker activities on the endpoint.

Non-niche players are attempting to acquire niche players to integrate their technologies, or to have add-ons. Integration can be slow and clunky, and it takes time to see how all the integrated pieces will work together.

In any case, an IT group putting together a long-range plan for the next three to five years will find it challenging to find vendors, niche or otherwise. This can make budgeting more challenging, especially when IT needs to come to the business and ask for money upfront that would normally be stretched across multiple years.

For all the systems and software that IT manages, they all need to be kept up to date. That requires finding the time to get all the maintenance windows scheduled and approved by the business to do all the patching. We must be diligent as well, as it is not always about the pace of patching. Think again of the Verizon breaches, where patches available for ten years would have prevented disaster.

Cost models are not in our favor. It is now cheap for the bad guys to run attacks but expensive, time-consuming, and sometimes disruptive for IT to implement defense strategies. IT's main purpose is to run a business.

Right now, our cybersecurity cost model is broken. Criminals can often use the same attack against thousands of entities. It's cheap for them to use the same tool and keep trying until they succeed.

We in IT must be continually on the lookout for transformative approaches, techniques, and models that change the game so that mitigating unwanted outcomes becomes the most attractive business option.

A Full Plate

Cyber defenders have a full plate. Our organizations must respond to market pressures with innovation, agility, and speed. If you were to study companies that have been disrupted in the marketplace, you would see how their value streams were changed to add more value to their customers. The goal is to find competitive advantages.

If our organizations don't innovate, there will be negative marketplace implications. By using new technologies to enhance their business models, organizations are finding ways to win. This is where IT can shine—clearing the path for new uses of technology. But make no mistake, there is a lot on IT's plate. Myriad challenges with systemic roots make any type of change that IT undertakes to better deal with all these risks hard. There is a lot at stake for our organizations. The complexity of the systems IT cares for must be agile enough to keep pace with market demands. A lot can go wrong. The biggest risk is our businesses losing in the marketplace or failing. Every day brings new risks.

To understand what we must do to help our organizations win, we must have a firm grasp of the underlying technology capabilities needed by our businesses to execute their go-forward market strategy. IT must take a systematic approach to tackling the status quo. This approach entails assembling a team that's built to leverage different working agreements and tools to prevail against the inevitable roadblocks. We must develop agility and resiliency.

With a firm grasp of this construct called "value" in the light of threats to business objectives, we now can dive into the specifics of how something bad could and might happen. And if it did, how bad might it be? IT needs to get into the weeds of the details of potential future losses.

Chapter 2
Scenario Analysis

IT needs to instill in stakeholders the confidence to make sound risk mitigation decisions by being realistic about their organization's current ability to avoid potential losses caused by cyber risk. IT needs to analyze scenarios. Organizations are concerned by the threat to business value from cyber-attacks. Everyone needs to see a picture of what bad looks like if realized. We need to create the scenes. We need to start by setting the scene. You need to look out and see what's in front of you for the workday, identifying who and what are involved, the timeline when this occurs, where it occurs, how much is involved, how it occurs, and why it occurs. Identify how high up the management chain this should reach. The place where an incident in real life or fiction occurs or occurred. A sequence of events and activities of interest that play out over a period of time; in our case a cyber-attack from beginning to potential breach. Decompose, to separate into constituent parts or elements or into simpler compounds. To break up into constituent parts as if by a chemical process. Unpack, to analyze something into its component elements.

Scenario analysis is a detailed examination of what could possibly happen to understand its nature or to determine its essential features. It is an essential input into the decision-making process across all aspects of organizations.

A scenario is a series of events that follow logically within a causal frame of reference. It is a potential future sequence or development of events. It describes what could possibly happen. It is an account or synopsis of a possible course of action or events. It could be an imagined or projected sequence of events, especially any of several detailed plans or possibilities.

Analysis is a detailed examination of anything complex to understand its nature or to determine its essential features. A detailed examination of the elements or structure of something. Analysis is the process of breaking a complex topic or substance into smaller parts to gain a better understanding of it. The technique has been applied in the study of many fields. It is a careful study of something to learn about its parts, what they do, and how they are related to each other. Also known as an explanation of the nature and meaning of something. A thorough study. Separation of a whole into its component parts. The identification or separation of component parts.

The value of scenario analysis is that it provides the necessary guidelines and constraints at work. From design build to run of infrastructure and securing of access to that infrastructure, the insights in detail are provided by scenario analysis to approach their tasks. Those who design, build, operate, defend, and support can all leverage the results of this type of analysis.

When you can describe in detail the scenario, you can be intentional in your work. The intentionality is the hallmark of a great security program that delivers for the business the true value of risk management that is optimized to meet organizational objectives.

A scenario is an imagined or projected sequence of events, especially any of several detailed plans or possibilities; a postulated sequence or development of events.

Someone clicked on the link, and boom! All the data was stolen, and our company was in the headlines. So, what happened in between that initial click and the CEO in front of the cameras addressing the headlines of a breach? From those on the sidelines looking from afar, the headlines can be quite scary. For us in IT, we need many more details. So much more went on behind the scenes for that headline-grabbing event to occur. That thing that we fear might happen doesn't happen every day. Even though in general cyber events occur every day, the reality is they don't happen very often for most organizations.

So, with this new understanding of what value is of the construct and a new appreciation for assets, we see that there are a lot of risks in our landscape. All business runs with attention to detail. The governance structure that allows a business to operate day-to-day and make money to stay in business and be successful means there are a lot of people doing a lot of things right. And one of those things is taking in as much information that is available to make sound decisions. The business looks to IT to provide the necessary details on how a cyber event might occur, how bad it might be if it did occur, and potential ways to decrease the chances of it happening.

Before we get into the technical nuts and bolts of firewalls and anti-malware defense, we need to understand how bad cyber risk can be. There must be some type of unwanted impact to the business and the bottom line that makes it so important. Obviously, good actors are quite capable in the aggregate. Not every bad guy is out there looking at your organization day in and day out. You probably would not be in business today if that were the case. For perspective, it would not be believable to assume that your current home security system is the only reason a criminal has not stolen your TV.

So, our team must analyze what's likely with enough detail to be useful. This is where scenario analysis comes in. We must have the ability to unpack a scenario down to the individual characteristics that allow us to analyze all the components necessary for that one mouse click to get our organization into the headlines.

Scenario analysis is the process of examining possible future events, along with various possible outcomes, their impact, likelihood of occurrence, scope, and individual factors involved.

A common trait of threat actors is their ability to think creatively to accomplish their objectives. IT professionals need a creative and agile mind to think differently and perform useful scenario analysis.

Multi-dimensional Lens

Dimension is an aspect of a situation, problem, or thing. Multi-dimensional is a relating to multiple dimensions of those aspects. A lens is something that facilitates and influences perception, comprehension, or evaluation. An object that has more than one point of reference or aspect is multi-dimensional. A focused view from a specific perspective is a lens. A lens allows for zooming in to explore something of interest and zooming out to get a wider perspective. Together, a multi-dimensional lens is a powerful tool for seeing risk factors to model. A multi-dimensional lens helps us to see risk. At the most basic level, humans perceive risk in different contexts. These contexts can be seen through multiple lenses. A multi-dimensional lens provides different groups inside an organization the means to understand and process all forms of risk.

These actions allow you to structure your thinking around risk so you can identify, make, and support sound decisions in your organization. It is vital that IT understands that the domain of risk management is much more than an annual risk assessment. Risk impacts all aspects of our organizations daily.

IT must view security threats in terms of business risk. There are many vulnerabilities, flaws, and bugs in our technical infrastructures, software, and defenses; however, our focus needs to be on unwanted outcomes as defined by the business. This is a critical point. The business must define unwanted outcomes for us. IT can't do this for the business. The role of IT here is to facilitate the identification process and then to provide relevant, timely, and actionable information to the business.

IT needs to understand two dimensions of risk. The first is the frequency at which undesirable outcomes happen on an annual basis. The second is the business impact of those undesirable outcomes.

Let's talk about the business context. You cannot have a serious discussion about risk without explicitly defining the asset at risk. Otherwise, you're engaging in an exercise of infinite possibilities. You must have an asset mindset.

Risk mitigation is all about the value at risk, the corporate assets, and operations. This value includes reputation, brand, data, services, and experiences the business brings to the market that generate revenue. As such, asset value is business derived. IT does not need to attempt to protect against every technical attack, but instead, it needs to prioritize those threat actors and TTPs that pose a risk to business-defined assets.

If there is a measurable opportunity loss that would result from certain digital information being read or used by an attacker, then that should be further evaluated. The business and IT should map out threat models to identify what type of intellectual property could provide an advantage to a competitor. We need to differentiate the impacts of the various threat actors. But first we need to understand the point of view of our analysis.

It is important to understand how people see risk in your organization. At the most basic level, humans perceive risk and different contexts. These contexts can be seen through multiple lenses. A multi-dimensional lens provides IT, as well as the business, a way to look at all forms of risk so they can be understood and managed. We can gain understanding in spite of the fog of noise by the systematic analysis of risk. It starts with manifestation.

Everything has a point of view. How we think about our scenarios is informed by the various players involved. Risk has been said to exist primarily in the eyes of those with liability or have a stake in the outcome. How those in the board room view a particular scenario can be drastically different from how a security analyst views it.

For those building the scenario, you must be cognizant of the multiple dimensions of the points of view. Let's look at three top-line perspectives of the business, the IT, and the security team.

From the view of the business, executives and stakeholders focus on the financial bottom line. That involves increasing revenue, increasing profits, growing market share, and reducing costs. This could be from the view of a board director, CEO, line of business manager, or frontline worker.

From IT's view, their purpose is to support the business's money-making capabilities. This involves digital transformation, service availability, and new technology-enabled functionality. This includes people like enterprise architects, engineers, developers, and service desk analysts.

And from the security team's view, the focus is on limiting the loss of money through risk mitigation and operating a cost-effective security program. This includes people like CISOs, security architects, engineers, and analysts.

These different perspectives—business, IT, and security team—use a different lens for assessing risk. For example, new threat capabilities increasingly bypass traditional endpoint defenses, but maybe IT has just renewed with that endpoint-solution vendor for a three-year term. A valid question that should be asked is whether you should wait three years to go back to executives to ask for funding for a new endpoint solution. The answer depends on how you are informed on threat data. If you want to get that funding and take the sunk cost, then you should have the picture, data, and numbers you need to convince those who focus on cost-control and profit-making.

Ways of Thinking

IT needs different ways of thinking. As Albert Einstein remarked, *"We cannot solve our problems with the same thinking we used when we created them."*[24]

Multi-dimensional thinking, known hereafter as MDT, is the processing of human sensing of the world in a variety of different ways. MDT is the key to changing our circumstances. MDT applies to the four functions IT has:

- Design: reimagine architecture to support business transformation

- Implementation: deploy new technology into operations while keeping services active for the business

- Support: operate and maintain technology systems while maximizing availability

- Protection: maintain loss exposure within risk tolerance levels and actively defend against threats

MDT applies no matter our title: chief information officer (CIO), chief technical officer (CTO), chief marketing officer (CMO), chief information security officer (CISO), architect, engineer, operator, project manager, developer, service desk analyst, incident responder, etc.

To support organizational and team change, each of us needs to consider different perspectives. These perspectives must include our own, those of others in our company, and those of others in our industry. We must always come back to *why*, our purpose, to use as the anchor point. Then we can improve ourselves intentionally based on that insight, using both personal and professional development. We can work with the higher-level purpose in mind.

We must go out there and execute on a strategy to make the desired future state a reality.

The business perspective of new technology and emerging risk factors all play into the act of making changes that can help our organizations. What is IT enabling for the business and why? In the digital realm, how do we make changes happen while giving users a way to interact? What digital functionality creates new risk factors that need to be mitigated?

In MDT, there are multiple ways the human mind can be applied to solution development and problem solving. There are various dimensions of thinking that can be brought to bear to specific challenges. First, second, third, and higher dimensions of thinking are possible. This thinking process acknowledges that the current level and type of thinking is not enough for the challenges that await us. The right combination of thinking levels expands our beliefs and expectations of what our world should look like.

Nth levels include temporal implications. Time is often considered a third dimension of thinking. Time influences the context of the thought at hand, including both current and historical timeframes. The historical context can be particularly significant in properly framing problems, opportunities, and risks.

The features of any issue can necessitate more dimensions. As we capture the proper essence of a current state, we typically find more than initially meets the eyes. MDT is the most effective way of approaching and seeing problems, seeing a problem's underlying structure, or seeing hints of problems.

To outthink our challenges, obstacles, and problems, we need MDT. Nth level thinking about our new world allows us to consider opportunities not imagined before. Nth level thinking makes it possible to illuminate a path ahead and to undertake the desired transformation in the organization. This kind of thinking reveals elements and factors not obvious with simpler thinking approaches.

Think differently on different levels to excel at the design, build, operate, and protect functions. Disruption, complexity, and risk take on new meaning when our thinking is more expansive.

MDT equips us to reimagine our problem space. An idea, problem, or situation is doomed to stay misunderstood unless we unpack it. Be open to coloring outside the lines to find an unexpected solution to a tough problem.

Necessity is the mother of invention, so change it up. Change your route. Change the way you do other little things. Gain a new perspective on the old. Turn the problem upside-down and inside-out. Take it apart and look at the individual parts. Change aspects of the problem.

If you still have difficulties, you may not have gone far enough or visited enough parts. Try the "5 Whys" problem-solving approach to pinpoint the root cause of any problem. Simply described, this technique asks "Why?" of every *why*. For example, *Why is this client unhappy with the mobile app we just rolled out?* The company's provisioning portal has been sluggish and some sales orders were delayed. *Why was this the cause?* And so on, to dig more deeply and explore more widely. [25]

Stubborn and recurring problems are often symptoms of deeper issues. This means we need to think more expansively. Quick fixes may seem convenient, but they typically add inconvenience down the road. Quick fixes tend to solve only the surface issues rather than the real, underlying causes. They waste resources that could otherwise create processes that prevent stubborn problems from resurfacing. By taking the time to develop a quality problem description, we increase the chance of a finding a quality solution.

Ensure all the people working on the same problem make their assumptions explicit, break down the problem's elements into more manageable chunks, and visualize the stated end state. It is important to think about the "thinking mind."

The Thinking Mind

A mind that applies itself in different ways to tackle problems is a powerful tool in making change be successful. We can look at three types of thinking dichotomies to help us understand different ways of thinking: System 1 and System 2; left brain and right brain; and convergent and divergent thinking.

Beyond outthinking the challenges, take advantage of how the brain works. The human brain uses two systems (system 1 and system 2). Daniel Kahneman, a psychologist and economist, explains the advantages and disadvantages of each in his book *Thinking, Fast and Slow*:

> System 1 and System 2 are two distinct modes of decision-making. System 1 is an automatic, fast, and often unconscious way of thinking. It is autonomous and efficient, requiring little energy or attention, but is prone to biases and systematic errors. System 2 is an effortful, slow, and controlled way of thinking. It requires energy and can't work without attention but, once engaged, it has the ability to filter the instincts of System 1.[26]

The autonomic system, called System 1, operates automatically and quickly with little or no effort and no sense of voluntary control. Breathing and heartbeats are autonomic processes.

System 2 allocates attention to effortful mental activities. Complex computations and deciding where to walk next are System 2 processes. The operations of System 2 include agency, choice, and concentration.

Systems 1 and 2, widely referenced in psychology, work in tandem to solve problems. For example, we use System 2 agency to create endurance, such as what develops through regular gym sessions. Rather than reverting to our old ways of not exercising, our repeated System 2 choices develop new habits that give us perseverance over longer periods. At that point, we establish a System 1 autonomic system that we don't even have to think about. We rise, we exercise, and we go to work.

System 2 thinking helps us create similar systematic responses in IT— responses that become autonomic and thereby create an ongoing solution.

Knowing how each set of thinking works helps us use each one to help the other. Errors in our judgments can be overcome by engaging in more System 2 thinking. Long-term solutions can happen by putting System 1 processes into place until they become habits. We can leverage the way System 2 thinking works to influence our daily work practice.

Another example of dichotomic thinking is the left and right brain, also known as one's analytical and creative sides. The left side of our brain does more verbal, analytical, and orderly processes than the right brain. The left brain is sometimes called the digital brain. It's better at functions like reading, writing, computations, logic, sequencing, linear thinking, mathematics, facts, and thinking in words. The right brain provides complementary approaches that are more visual and intuitive. The right brain is sometimes referred to as the analog brain. It has a more creative way of thinking, specializing in imagination, holistic thinking, rhythm, nonverbal cues, feelings, visualization, and daydreaming.[27]

We can consider how each way of thinking generates solutions in our work, as well as how each one can help the other. We can choose one over the other to focus on.

The third dichotomy in thinking is convergent versus divergent. This has also been described as "zoom in" and "zoom out." Convergent thinking (zoom in) uses logical approaches such as critical or analytical thinking. Convergence presumes facts lead to an answer.

The complement to convergent thinking is finding multiple options and possibilities. This divergent (zoom out) thinking is also called horizontal thinking, creative thinking, or brainstorming. One question leads to multiple ideas, options, and possibilities. Divergent thinking can lead to solution integration because the many ideas spotlight the strongest path. With divergent thinking, IT might decide which project to tackle at the beginning of the year, or whether to cancel some projects, scale back others, or do more with them.

Like the other dichotomies, convergent and divergent thinking generate stronger ideas when used in conjunction with each other.

Ultimately, we are attempting to broaden, deepen, and shift our thinking. Jeff B.R. Gaspersz, professor of innovation at Nyenrode Business Universiteit (Netherlands) explains these three ideas in more detail in research: *broaden*, the search for a range of characteristics and angles related to a certain problem; *deepen*, detect and describe a problem's underlying concepts and assumptions; and *shift*, view the problem in a context that is completely different from the one in which it originated.[28]

Other Types of Thinking

There are other types of thinking as well. They include critical thinking, lateral thinking, liminal thinking, and multi-order thinking. Bringing the powerful capability of the mind to think in multiple ways supercharges IT's ability to outthink its problems.

Critical thinking is not about fussing but rather thinking systematically. Critical thinking is an excellent process well worth cultivating. Critical thinking is the intellectually disciplined process of actively and skillfully conceptualizing, applying, analyzing, synthesizing, and/or evaluating information gathered from, or generated by, observation, experience, reflection, reasoning, or communication, as a guide to belief and action.[29]

We should use critical thinking on issues both small and big, important steps, and critical decisions. Do not hesitate to use critical thinking on design and support matters.

In contrast to critical thinking, lateral thinking focuses on new and atypical ideas. These ideas add to the traditional solutions people already use. You'll find lateral thinking used in fun puzzles that confound people with brain-twisting challenges. Lateral thinking frees the mind to go where it doesn't normally go to discover never-before-discovered solutions.

Lateral thinking is creativity in problem-solving. Lateral thinking uses reasoning to find solutions that are not immediately obvious. Here's a frequently used example of a lateral thinking puzzle. A man lives on the top floor of a very tall building. Every day he takes the elevator down to the ground floor to leave the building to go to work. Upon returning from work, though, he only travels halfway up the elevator and walks the rest of the way. If it's raining, he rides all the way to the top. Why? The man is only tall enough to reach halfway up the elevator buttons! However, if it is raining then he will have his umbrella with him to press the higher buttons.

In liminal thinking, liminal means threshold, border, boundary, or edge—a marginal, in-between space that defines two things while at the same time being neither one nor the other.[30] Dave Gray, founder of XPLANE, describes liminal thinking as "the art of creating change by understanding, shaping, and reframing beliefs."[31] He explains: "*Change happens at the boundaries of things: the boundary between the known and the unknown, the familiar and the different, between the old way and the new way, the past and the future.*"[32]

Use liminal thinking to bring change to an underlying IT belief system that may no longer accomplish its purpose. This type of thinking generates breakthrough insights. With liminal thinking, you can find and create new doorways to possibilities, doorways that may be invisible to others. Others on your team might find doorways you did not see. Gray lays out key principles for understanding beliefs, paraphrased here:

- Beliefs are models. Beliefs seem like perfect representations of the world, but, in fact, they are imperfect models for navigating a complex, multi-dimensional, unknowable reality.

- Beliefs are created. Beliefs are constructed hierarchically, using theories and judgments, which are based on selected facts and personal, subjective experiences.

- Beliefs create a shared world. Beliefs are the psychological material we use to co-create a shared world, so we can live, work, and do things together. Changing a shared world requires changing its underlying beliefs.

- Beliefs create blind spots. Beliefs are tools for thinking and provide rules for action, but they can also create artificial constraints that blind you to valid possibilities.

- Beliefs defend themselves. Beliefs are unconsciously defended by a bubble of self-sealing logic, which maintains them even when they are invalid, to protect personal identity and self-worth.

- Beliefs are tied to identity. Governing beliefs, which form the basis for other beliefs, are the most difficult to change because they are tied to personal identity and feelings of self-worth. You can't change your governing beliefs without changing yourself.[33]

Your IT teammates may be the ones who hold and live by these beliefs, or the customers may be the believers. With all the thinking approaches in this section, we can find solutions that may have eluded us before.

Liminal thinking allows us to shift, rethink, reframe, and reorganize beliefs. We can move from autopilot beliefs to solutions that fit the current state. We're at the threshold. Navigate both sides of the boundaries rather than staying outside.

For multi-order thinking, there are first and second orders, two levels of thinking that give a more complete picture of a situation. First order thinking considers the intended implication of an action. The immediate results of the action are in sight, as they often can be observed in a short period of time. Second order thinking considers the implication of the first order action. Unraveling the implications of those first order actions that have unintended or unknow effects downstream. Second order thinking is harder to do, it takes more time, and it is more complex. Many do not go that far. But second order thinking starts with what first order thinking discovers. First order thinking operates in shorter time horizons for potential effects. If those effects are farther in distance or downstream, many can't or won't look that far.

Decisions can be made faster with little consideration for tomorrow's effects. But only second order thinking will get us to decisions that solve the problem.

Mindful Thinking

What you focus on often shapes your reality. Reserve deep thinking for specific objectives that are relevant to your situation. Problem, meet solution. I would like to introduce you two. Insights to root causes and critical factors feed a plan of action. These insights enable workers to affect conditions on the ground where problems live.

We all need to focus on our areas of control, make improvements in our areas of influence, and make peace with the areas of concern. Control and influence are different and are the root of much frustration.

IT must be mindful of the specific actions that are needed to solve tough problems.

Are you in a downward spiral? If there's no time to read an email, respond to it, or think about the essence of the message, much less find the time to delegate the solutions, you are in a downward spiral.

If you're not comfortable saying *no*, you could be in a downward spiral.

Have you learned to clear your time? Can you create the space to think, analyze, and plan?

Start finding your way out of the spiral by eliminating the noise and focusing on the possible. To aid in this process, we need to understand the three important concepts of construct, context, and perspective.

There is construct. Teams, value, security, risks, the cloud, and infrastructure are all constructs. A construct is an idea, theory, or perceived understanding of our surrounding world and everything in it. A construct contains various conceptual elements. Typically, these are subjective and often used for social understanding that produces order.

Everything we humans know is an approximation of reality. The inputs to our senses are filtered to allow us to function. For example, the perception of day versus night, the twenty-four hours in a day, and the calendar are all constructs that we humans use to order our world.

We use constructs such as calling a room full of servers, storage, and networking equipment a *data center*. We use a construct called *the cloud* for paying to use other people's technology resources. Or there's the construct of security, which is not something that you can touch and say, "Aha! That is it." Constructs like those are from a point of view that is heavily influenced by context.

There is context. Context is composed of the circumstances that form the setting for an event, statement, or idea, in terms of *which* circumstances can be understood. The nature of *what* the situation or problem is depends on context.

To understand context, consider what we mean by these common phrases: "Too big." "Too small." "Too hard." "Everything is okay." "The process moves too slowly." "Who?" "What?" "Where?" "When?" "How?" "Why?"

Context informs us so we can determine if something matters and if so, how much. Context helps us determine importance. The system is down! In the context of *why*, IT is doing maintenance. In the context of *where*, a test environment is not being used. The system is slow! In the context of *when*, the perception of slow is the morning user logon storm versus off hours.

Ideas are contained in content, while context is king because it answers the question of why and how. Many speak of having an organizational structure that has the CISO report directly to the board at the same organization level as the CIO. But if you drill down, reporting and org structures are content. What is important is the context.

Focus on context, not content, to help your board get the message in a language they can understand. Then they can make informed decisions. It makes no sense for your CISO to speak technobabble that goes over the board's heads. Let the CISO communicate at the C-suite table with what the C-suite needs.

There is perspective. Context is further influenced by an individual's perception. Every person uses multiple filters to regard, understand, or interpret something. Some perceptions are accurate, and some are not. The latter can lead to a faulty path for IT's desired future state.

Sometimes thought of as a mental impression, reality is understood from the view of the current perception. Perception is affected by filters that humans see the world through. These filters alter how your mind processes new information. Details that align to our beliefs and experience are more likely to match the filters. The result is reduced objectively.

Your perception filter works in your unconscious mind. People are not aware it is at work. Perception filters may hinder your understanding of the reality of the actual current state. Working together as an IT team can help all of us see our context filters and tweak them to match reality. Then we can move forward to use analysis tools to assess and solve problems.

In an example of a person using a table, different perspectives can make perfect sense. From a child's perspective, the table could be too tall. From a rapidly growing teen's perspective, the table cramps his legs. Similarly, a perception that a project is progressing too slowly or progressing quite well arises from individual perspectives. From the perspective of a business user in the field trying to close new business, an interface is unusable while pecking on a small screen, while their colleague sitting at a desk with a large screen and keyboard finds the application very practical.

Misunderstandings make sense because people use imprecise communication and work from multiple perceptions. People operate in different contexts, with different job roles, bound by each person's understanding of the construct being discussed.

For example, coming into work in the morning on the northbound expressway, one may comment on the slow traffic. For another going in the opposite direction on the same expressway, one may say the traffic is moving fast. Who is right? Both, from their individual perspectives. Ask the same question on the way home, and the answers could be swapped based on traffic patterns at different times of day. Your perception can change based on the context.

Imprecise communication is often the result of trying to match multiple perceptions to different contexts.

So rather than bristle when you hear, "IT doesn't get it," "end users are at fault for the breach," or "the network is slow," take a step back and consider the perceptions, contexts, constructs, and beliefs. Use some MDT to guide the group to the goal that solves the problem in a way everybody can get behind.

MDT can be paired with applying problem understanding and solving to a variety of different audiences, with different objectives and needs, using different communication mediums. MDT needs to work through different lenses.

Mediums of Thoughts

Those lenses of thoughts need different mediums for expression. We need workspaces to think and collaborate as individuals and teams. Now that we are aware of the perspectives provided by a multi-dimensional lens, we can gather the IT team to flesh out scenarios of concern. We do this in different scales of the scope of the decision at hand; strategic, operational, and tactical needs.

There are three decision types we think about in a in sequence to analyze as individuals and teammates.

- Look at scenarios via a think space—the mind

- Orientate them on a dimensional scale via a whiteboard

- Explore context via the workspace of a spreadsheet

It is critical to have the manifestation of scenarios that clearly shows a sequence of events that fully describes in context the risks that are relevant to your organization. There are various ways to explore the analysis in the three contexts of where we can think about risks.

First it starts with the mind. Everything starts in the mind. The human mind is the element of a person that enables them to be aware of the world and their experiences, to think, and to feel; the faculty of consciousness and thought.

The mind is the set of cognitive faculties including consciousness, imagination, perception, thinking, judgement, language, and memory, which is housed in the brain.

Everyone is familiar with manifestation in one's mind of risk. It occurs in the mind every day, as one drives a car, navigates crossing the street, or engages in other common everyday tasks. Humans are always on the lookout for things that could cause it harm. Something falling from the sky will trigger it an instinctual response. That response has been learned and embedded inside the human response system. Its quick action realizes the complexity behind the modeling of the potential adverse effect that triggers the body into action.

IT often warns users about what they should click on in their emails on links, fearing the link may be malicious leading to the host machine or user credentials eventually be compromised. When a user receives a request to disclose information or transfer funds, they must make the decision within that context to determine if they suspect the ask is suspicious.

Two challenges exist that we need to be aware of. The individual is often not consistent in their thinking process and logic. Asking someone to repeat their responses consistently is difficult. In risk management that is a requirement. A lot of confusion occurs when individuals build loss scenarios in different ways on different days. Organizations require that there is consistency in how the scenarios are designed.

On to your colleagues and team. Unfortunately, there is no Ethernet Wi-Fi connection between IT, the security team, and the business. We have to do it the old-fashioned way. We must talk with each other. Everyone has different risk models in their mind. They have different pictures of risk factors—different people with different pictures of what's important, what is a threat, how likely our controls will be overcome. Everyone on the teams must have the same picture. IT's picture must be grounded by the business picture. The business picture must be grounded in the realities of true and relevant threats and their TTPs, the actual efficacy of current controls.

Secondly, it moved to the whiteboard. A whiteboard (also known by the terms marker board, dry-erase board, wipe board, dry-wipe board, and pen-board) is a glossy, usually white surface for nonpermanent markings. Whiteboards are analogous to blackboards, but with a smoother surface allowing rapid marking and erasing of markings on their surface. The popularity of whiteboards increased rapidly in the mid-1990s and they have become a fixture in many offices, meeting rooms, school classrooms, and other work environments.

The term whiteboard is also used metaphorically to refer to features of computer software applications that simulate whiteboards. Such "virtual tech whiteboards" allow one or more people to write or draw images on a simulated canvas. This is a common feature of many virtual meeting, collaboration, and instant messaging applications. The term whiteboard is also used to refer to interactive whiteboards.

The human mind loves to process visual input. In fact, we humans can consume much more visually than from hearing. Understanding topics, especially complex ones with lots of parts and connections, greatly benefit from "seeing" the scenarios of concern. It's time to take those conversations and written material to different medium. We must move on to manifesting our models onto the "board." Any in many cases, this may be an actual whiteboard, physical or virtual. A whiteboard is a space to work with ideas and concepts. This gives us a shared spaced to align what is in our individual heads, allowing us to identify the different factors and elements in play in a scenario or model. You can move elements around and see patterns and connections. We can resolve differences by working off the same picture. We can deal with qualifying low-hanging scenarios. Move beyond talking with our peers to visualize and share...to start to merge our collective minds. This is a medium that allows us to make sure that what you see in your mind squares with your colleagues. Up next is the need to take our pictures and translate them into numbers.

Thirdly, it moves to the spreadsheet. A spreadsheet is a computer application for organization, analysis, and storage of data in tabular form. Spreadsheets were developed as computerized analogs to the paper worksheets used in accounting. The program operates on data entered in cells of a table.

The worksheet, most famously with Microsoft Excel, is the workhouse of business decision-making. Before numbers get to an accounting or financial application, numbers are worked through on a worksheet. It is used for decisions such as staffing levels for teams and annual budgets for technology. To work through questions such as how much to spend on security, we need to measure to help in this determination of loss exposure. We can do these measurements by running simulations of potential outcomes. Performing cost-benefit analysis in spreadsheets is common in organizations. We must make sure the uncertainty around business initiatives is reflected in our numbers. As well as the potential downside to projects, if not, the business models will be incomplete and could potentially understate the risk impact. Annualized loss exposure joins the budgeting process. Use worksheets to do some heavy lifting. Everything from new business deal, cost analysis, investment, and security loss scenarios.

All forms of risk can be viewed and analyzed in a spreadsheet. It is a cross-org/domain think space. All divisions and groups can be compared. It is a common language for comparison. It is a framework for decision-making by the business. This work gets aggregated across the organization in various other tools and mediums.

At the heart of risk management in the digital realm is the measurement of risk for context. This reduces uncertainty and supports effective decision-making. There are some useful power tools often used in other professional fields to facilitate better observation, visualization, understanding, and sharing.

Qualifications

Setting the scene to determine if a scenario is a problem worth dealing with is at the core of managing risk. We need to define the qualifications for this determination. These qualifications help determine the triggers for scenarios worthy of management's attention and allocation of valuable resources to address. Business activities include the potential to cause some sort of unwanted outcome in the future. IT needs to assess the potential severity, scope, and implications. We need to define some criteria to use to qualify those potential issues, problems, dangers, or threats to organization mission. We must identify the assets that should be considered for the scenario. Also, we need to identify the current controls already in place and assess their effect on impact and likelihood; and determine which stakeholders would have interest in those unwanted outcomes. Qualifications help with the level of effort we should undertake in our analysis to make this determination. We may use some sort of scoring criteria to make the decision process faster. We can start by building scenes.

Scene Builder

Risk needs to be noticed, and we must become aware of the specific relevant scenario. As a collective we need to agree on those loss scenarios that we all believe to be relevant to our organization. The factors that comprise that scenario must resonate with the people who are performing the risk management function of the organization. It is often said that you will know it when you see it. Organizations need to have common language and framework to truly know business relevance to our organizations. After that first step it's now on to the next one of how to work through what we see.

It is only through the correct use of their scenario analysis that we can effectively intervene and reduce risk. To understand if a new control should be put in place, the type of controls, how they should be deployed, how they should be configured, how they should be managed, or how often to update them should be guided by the results of the analysis. The outputs of scenario analysis provide the key inputs for determining your risk responses, and those are a combination of different types of controls.

If one wants to know if a penetration test result is good or bad, one should compare it to the results of scenario analysis. This means that a good result from a penetration test might be good or bad depending on the context of the analysis. For example, if the scope of the penetration test was not guided by the analysis, the test may not be pertinent to this specific scenario. This means that the scenario of interest to stakeholders might not be matched by the way this test was scoped. The results could be answering a different question than asked. If what is driving higher loss scenarios of a particular type of attack against a specific type of asset, if a test is scoped in such a way that is testing different controls or perhaps different assets, we may not be getting the answers that we think we are. To understand any security assessment results, we must understand the context it is applied to from the output of the scenario analysis.

The implication of this is stark. To know that we are investing in the right resources in the right places, we need to be able to compare and grade ourselves against something beyond external regulations and industry frameworks. If something in the news is gaining a lot of attention from other companies, that does not necessarily mean it's also a higher priority to your organization. Your organization may have different business factors that make a particular type of external threat less severe or a non-factor.

One of the main causes of confusion on how to manage risk is the fact that everyone is using their own mental models of bad. Many organizations do not have a standardized way of looking at identifying risk. Across the organization, many have their own way of determining importance. This is a bad way to approach risk management as it leads to inconsistency in decision support. The business requires a defined process, defined models, useful data, and an established approach to clarify loss scenarios that are relevant to their organizations. It's time to set the scene for your environment.

To build a scene properly and with the right context for your organization, start identifying the assets at risk. You will know which assets to work with by working backwards from the value that is at risk. You can use the level of detail necessary for this scenario of interest to determine how granular to be with the asset identification. It could be as simple as a specific database or more widespread as sensitive research data stored in multiple locations.

Then you can start identifying the threat actors of most concern. Asking yourself questions about these threat actors' objectives, their motives, and their capabilities will be very useful in the latter parts of the analysis. There's a difference between a committed adversary and an opportunistic attacker. That has implications on whether you're going to be working throughout the night or if this will be one of these campaigns that your organization has to deal with on an ongoing basis.

Not all assets are in the crosshairs of a threat actor. We can start to think about how well current controls in our environment will perform against their attacks. Previous investments have been made in controls that will have various effects on the operations of our attackers. This will give us some idea about whether we think the likelihood of such an attack from these attackers may be successful against our systems. In some cases, the likelihood could be very high; others could be highly unlikely, depending on the nature of our assets, architecture design, and type of assets in play.

Then we can examine those occasions where the attacker is successful in bypassing our initial defenses. There is uncertainty about how far they get in their attack. It's unclear how long they might last in their campaign. There is a question of will they be limited by other controls downstream and how much data potentially could be stolen. For a ransomware attack, there is a chance that you might be forced to pay to retrieve access to your systems. And then the uncertainty around final effects to the business. It could be a small or large impact to our organization. Or it could be a run-of-the mill frequent event with limited effect that we see daily that did not make it up to the C-suite.

Analysis Focus Level

When creating a scene as part of the process we've been building, there are different levels of details and specificity in the exercise. There is the macro top-level view of the scenario. There are also more granular details that can continually be added to provide more context and details to the different elements of the scenario. We can go all the way down to the nitty-gritty details of the technical components. The level of detail needed at any one time is a function of the purpose out of the analysis. If you stay high level on the analysis, you should have the ability to drill down all the way to the technical level as needed. And it also works the other way as well, where you should be able to go from the granular detail level all the way back up to the higher abstract layer. Between the high and low resolution of details in the scenario analysis is the necessary context from the business and the technical teams.

The process itself of going back and forth on the detailed level among different stakeholders is extremely valuable. For many, just the process of building this scenario will be the first time that they will see such a comprehensive view of risk. If you find that you cannot connect the lower and higher levels, then you should revisit the nature of how you put this scenario together. The logic of the scenario should be clear to those in your organization. It should not require a lot of translation to understand it when looking at it. By connecting these different elements in the correct sequencing and showing the resulting impact, it allows everyone to be on the same page. It also lays the prerequisite to do further and more detailed financial analysis on impact and likelihood. The building blocks need to include a series of events, timeframe, probability, effect, business impact, value at risk, underlying asset(s) at risk, relevant threat actor(s), capabilities, motives, and current controls.

You need to know risk when you see it. We need to observe the factors that could indicate a risk, the factors that are of interest for the different stakeholders and teams. After identification of a relevant loss scenario, we need the ability to triage them. There are some risks that require immediate attention and action that must be taken care of right now. For others, there needs to be a prioritization method for the timing of addressing them. This is where we sort through them, make sense out of them, and aggregate common areas of concern. Determining which scenarios are urgent, what can be dealt with later, what are more longer-term concerns, and how we sort through that familiar long list helps us make sense of all the risks that are in play. These are all core tasks in risk management. These are not necessarily easy tasks. Many organizations struggle with risk identification, assessment, and response. IT can make use of "power tools" to help.

Power Tools

There are certain tools, used to carry out specific functions, that are or can be enhanced to produce exponential capabilities in output or efficiency. Like an electric drill to a screwdriver, a spreadsheet to a calculator, or binoculars to the naked human eye, "power tools" enhance, accelerate, and supercharge knowledge work.

Instead of limiting ourselves to guessing and analyzing a single scenario, we can run hundreds of thousands of simulations in minutes on a standard compute. Like the use of a nail gun to put up drywall in a home instead of the manual hammer and nails, tools that are powered by a wall outlet accelerate your time and improve your productivity. Both tools get the job done, but the powered one is more efficient in delivering value. In IT's case, the difference is between using a framework to guide decisions and making on-the-fly selections. These power tools help with IT's new opportunities for thinking, working, and leading.

Use serious introspection, careful thought, and a different way of looking at a problem, situation, or crisis. IT has access to decades of knowledge, models, and theories across many domains in business, economics, finance, communication, engineering, science, and mathematics. We understand organizational and employee needs and opportunities, and we need to leverage our knowledge to get our message across and inspire the change needed. It's time for IT to step up.

But before we do, we must remember economist and professor Theodore Levitt's observation, *"People don't want to buy a quarter-inch drill. They want a quarter-inch hole!"*[34] IT must focus on the outcome or experience, not necessarily the tool used to get there. You could also take that further by saying the hole is not the goal either, but rather the picture hanging on the wall.

We use tools to accomplish goals. In IT's case, many tasks, projects, and sprints could use some acceleration. Make use of the wide variety of power tools available to get the results you are looking for.

Tools have the characteristics of:

- Allowing us to see what was previously unseen
- Making it possible to find root causes of a problem
- Allowing us to see the interconnections of a system
- Accelerating our understanding

- Accelerating the transmission of relevant information and insights to others

End users see IT as superheroes when we fix their problems or roll out some cool new app or feature. Tools are like the capes that let us heroes fly. Get your tool belt ready to visualize, understand, learn, and share by leveraging Gemba walks, stories, maps, trees, models, frameworks, and statistics. Power tools can be viewed from the four actions of observe, visualize, understand, and share.

Observation helps us to perceive our environment, the people in it, the flow of work, and the interactions as inputs to thinking patterns. Observation drives your understanding of the current state.

IT is always in need of observing the people, processes, and technology of their organizations. Let's look at the survey, the *Gemba walk*, and the retrospective.

A survey focuses in on something of interest to know and understand it. To survey is to look carefully and thoroughly at people or things to appraise them. Surveying investigates the opinions or experiences of a group of people by asking them questions.

Some surveys appear on paper or online as a series of questions constructed to elicit responses.

A Gemba walks observes the work. Workers frequently discuss problems in emails. But at times, you need to leave your desk and go the front lines to see them firsthand. *Gemba* comes from a Japanese term meaning "the actual place or thing." A Gemba walk notices (1) the person doing the work, (2) the core principle of the tool they're using, and (3) the work where it is being done (as opposed to discussing a warehouse problem in a conference room).

Gemba walks interact with the people and processes in the spirit of changing them for the better. In his article "Why Management Should

Go to Gemba," Sam Grier writes, "*If you seek solutions to problems that need to be fixed, go to Gemba. If you want to see the work behind the reports, go to Gemba. If you want to show leadership, go to Gemba. Go to where the work is performed and observe and engage with those who do it.*"[35]

Go watch a security analyst work on an incident. Watch a service desk employee work on a ticket. Sit in on a project update with the application development team. Sit in on a change management meeting. Sit in on a sales call or marketing meeting. Visit a store, factory, or remote office. Go where the work is being done, while it is being done, by the people doing it. See your business colleagues in action. And do all of this with an attitude of help, not of catching someone doing things wrong.

Retrospectives allow a chance to identify opportunities to make improvements in the work. Promote a culture that seeks to learn from yesterday's mistakes to improve tomorrow. Retrospectives give teams the opportunity to reflect on how things have been going.

Such retrospectives need to be done frequently to feed improvement. Waite and Lyons recommend asking four questions: *what went well*; *what did not go so well*; *what have I learned*; *what still puzzles me?*

Ask retrospective questions when developing a new application, updating a new project, installing an enterprise resource planning (ERP) system, or installing data collection systems at remote locations. Ask to join in the conversations after work has been done.

Visualize the challenge of getting alignment in any area lies in the difficulty of seeing interdependencies across the organization. Each group or department may function fine on its own, but from the users' perspectives, the experience is a patchwork of interactions they navigate themselves. Visualizations help break down siloed thinking.

Pictures help others see what you see, and help you see what they see. Visualize your environment and current state to see what truly is there. Visualize new things to clarify the issue. In contrast to verbal communication, which is frequently linear, visual communication is spatial and can contain a higher amount of information at one time.

Visualization of data is the creation and study of the visual representation of data. When implemented properly, it succeeds in communicating complex ideas and processes with clarity, precision, and efficiency. Visualization can tell a story or help the target audience digest the information and insights you are trying to highlight.

Consider that the transmission speed of the optic nerve has been estimated to rival that of early versions of Ethernet networking, comparable to fast image processing.

This makes our eyes good for pattern matching and edge detection. It also means our eyes can interpret a massive amount of information packed into a small space—hence the power of visualization.

Visualization takes advantage of the brain's ability to recognize patterns, find trends, and consume a much larger amount of data in a given timeframe compared to written or oral formats.

Don't limit visualization to PowerPoint. Slides are not an end goal in and of themselves. PowerPoint is one tool that empowers you to change the way you encode a message, but it's not the only one

Don't discredit PowerPoint either. Many people have a negative view of it, often blaming bad meetings on the tool. You have probably heard of "death by PowerPoint." As a result, people are looking more at whiteboarding to solve their problems. But is PowerPoint really the problem?

When the message leads the presentation, this tool works just fine. It's supposed bad traits are often due to design choices by the creator, not a requirement or constraint enforced by the application itself. When you have something you want to say, time must be spent upfront to craft the correct message framework for PowerPoint to present the message effectively. Move beyond the pre-packaged templates.

We are now going to look at three concepts that aid visualization: maps, boards, and trees.

Maps for spatial representation view of the scene. There are several types of maps, including process, value stream, service, and empathy.

A map depicts and highlights relationships between elements such as objects, regions, and themes. Maps can be static, two-dimensional, geometrically accurate, or approximations of three-dimensional space. Maps can be dynamic and interactive. Maps commonly depict geography, work processes, and thinking.

If you want to see the flow of work, use a *process map*. Process mapping visually maps a work process as it exists today. It provides an opportunity to see work duplication, delays, reworks, and other non-value-added activities. When a team maps, it can see both upstream and downstream, it can clarify the flow of work, and it can identify ways to provide improvement.

A value stream map includes additional information and is often used in agile processes to find waste and identify value. A value stream map also puts a spotlight on potential opportunities.

Risks are everywhere. So are possibilities. How do you transform a possibility into an opportunity? You must see how things work.

Value stream maps are one way to do this. IT should construct value stream maps for all the services it is responsible for managing. This provides documentation and team-wide acknowledgement of the stated flow. Value stream maps are a tool to highlight improvement in velocity, waste reduction, and delivery times.

It's hard to improve on something difficult to see. The value stream map gives a level of system-wide visibility to the entire team. This includes the business stakeholders, DevOps, security team, and the service desk.

Value stream maps are great at painting a complete story for individual team members who are accustomed to silos. The ultimate business goals can be highlighted to remind everyone of the business's overall purpose. By having the stakeholders periodically review the value streams with the technical teams, the business/IT relationship will be strengthened. Handoffs between teams will become much clearer.

When the business wants to know the underlying inputs to service delivery times, IT has them already documented through value stream maps. Going through each task in the stream and having each team validate its role benefits the entire team.

You want all the assumptions of the design, implementation, and support aspects of our systems to be clear across the board. For example, the service team may find a value stream map instructive in improving its assistance to end users, as it has a picture of the flow and where potential problems may be.

The security team members can be on the lookout for potential threats by understanding flows. Developers will have a better appreciation of what operations is going through to deploy and support its apps. Security teams can better understand the design implications of dual-homed servers, with one interface in the DMZ and another on the internal network. Security teams can also gain more insights on the implications of virtualization of physical compute nodes and its impact on control enforcement areas.

IT should use another kind of map, a *service map*, to produce a top-down view of a system or process. The team should review this map regularly. In reviewing key business services, the team can look for time traps, areas suitable for automation, or potential risks, and opportunities for optimizing or transforming the business service delivery.

IT should perform this internally, with a technology-focused review, and branch out and do the same with business groups, stakeholders, and executive teams. Each group will improve the understanding of business operations.

Gathering business input should be considered part of normal IT operations. For example, when reviewing the value stream map for a store, a review done by customer support reps handling incoming calls may reveal the potential to bring down call hold times and add a new feature to the CRM software.

How do the people you interact with feel about the services you build and support? Discover this with an empathy map. With this collaborative tool, teams can gain deeper insight into their customers. Much like a user persona, an empathy map can represent a group of users, such as a customer segment.

Position elements of a scene on a board. A board is a spot on the wall that displays a bird's-eye view of something to aid humans with processes and systems. Boards make work visible.

A kanban is one effective board tool for monitoring work flowing through the system. In Japanese, kanban means visual signal. Each task is represented on some type of card. Each card is placed on a board in columns labeled for status. Three common labels to the columns are: to do, in progress, and done. At a glance, everyone can see the flow of work and its current status.

Another board tool, and currently the most popular one, is the dashboard. It provides at-a-glance views of key performance indicators relevant to a particular objective, as well as operational or business processes. In network operations centers, we often use dashboards to monitor system health. At the service desk, the call queue's status is often shown on a dashboard.

Visualize scene elements in the form of a tree. Now, let's look at fault and attack trees to showcase connections. In systems, connections are vital.

To understand how something might fail, use a fault tree. IT uses fault trees as a power tool in risk mitigation, detecting infrastructure design flaws, software bugs, policy gaps, and the like. Fault trees have proven useful in common mode failures where the complexity of an infrastructure makes it difficult to account for all dependencies.

One good fault tree application would be to aid in analysis during the introduction of a business-critical process at a branch location that has not had its infrastructure updated to account for the new service-level agreement (SLA) and other factors. If cost pressures have limited the level of system redundancies at remote locations, initial design considerations and assumptions must be revisited. Fault tree analysis is an effective tool for this review.

In nature, trees have roots in the ground that support branches, stems, and leaves above the ground. Fault trees use similar constructs. For example, fault trees analyze undesired states or outcomes to identify ways to mitigate the possibilities. Using the undesired state at the root of the tree, we work backward through Boolean logic—the idea that all values are either true or false—to determine different ways they could occur.

Attack trees are conceptual diagrams that show how an asset or target might be attacked. Use them for threat modeling and determining appropriate security controls needed to mitigate risk.

For example, understanding the TTPs used against mobile workers can give insight into the best way to approach the question of bring-your-own-device (BYOD) policies. The right approach can only be properly addressed by analyzing the actual technical domain of the issue. Bruce Schneier, cryptographer and computer security professional, explains how attack trees are used:

> [Attack trees] have been used in a variety of applications. In the field of information technology, they have been used to describe threats on computer systems and possible attacks to realize those threats. However, their use is not restricted to the analysis of conventional information systems. They are widely used in the fields of defense and aerospace for the analysis of threats against tamper-resistant electronics systems (e.g., avionics on military aircraft). Attack trees are increasingly being applied to computer control systems (especially relating to the electric power grid). Attack trees have also been used to understand threats to physical systems. [36]

Additional tools that are useful include loss flow diagrams, attack chains, and bowtie diagrams.

These different views help us as we seek better understanding of scenes.

Don't let mysteries, knowledge gaps, and unexplained occurrences exist for too long. IT comprehends and makes sense of complex systems. Cut through noise and distractions with constructs. We will look at several tools we can use for these processes.

We need to frame our thought processing. This will allow us to improve our understanding of a subject area and improve communication among teams.

We leverage taxonomies. This involves ordering objects of interest into categories or groupings. Taxonomy provides a means of classification, making it easier to reference and work from these groupings. In biology, taxonomy is the classification of organisms by shared characteristics. Similarly, some IT teams use technology business management

(TBM) as a taxonomy to promote alignment between IT, finance, and business unit leaders.[37]

TBM provides a standard taxonomy to describe cost sources, technologies, IT resources, applications, and services. It provides a generally accepted way of categorizing and reporting IT costs and other metrics. It classifies and shows hierarchy.

We leverage ontologies. Ontologies are an expansion of taxonomies, focusing on relationships. A set of domains whose individual properties have a relationship between them. Ontologies show how things work together and affect each other. A popular example is the Factor Analysis of Information Risk (FAIR). This structured framework for thinking about risk is defined as the probable frequency and probable magnitude of future loss. FAIR breaks down the factors that make up risk and shows the relationships between them. Jack Jones, creator of FAIR, developed this ontology to support risk quantification and provide a framework for thinking about risk and the factors involved.

We use frameworks. A very common concept is the framework, a basic structure underlying a system. Frameworks improve one's knowledge and challenge one's assumptions. Frameworks take different approaches to gaining understanding about a topic, whether it be a system or the cause of a failure.

We use methodology. This is a system of methods used in an activity. IT frames the approach, steps, and general course of action when undertaking a specific activity. An example is the Waterfall approach to software development, a linear approach that defines a goal and goes from one gated phase to the next until completion. In a true Waterfall development project, each gated phase represents a distinct stage of software development, and each stage generally finishes before the next one can begin. Waterfall typically places a stage gate between each. For example, requirements must be reviewed and approved by the customer before design can begin. Agile is an alternative method-ology that is now driving the DevOps movement.

We can leverage causal loop diagrams. To go beyond seeing a system is to understand it. To do this, IT makes use of a causal loop diagram. This diagram visualizes variables and connections in a system. The dia-gram makes use of nodes and links. Nodes represent variables and edges represent connections. By showing these relationships, cause and effect in systems can be examined. Causal loop diagrams are indis-pensable when troubleshooting complex systems.

We can use descriptive statistics. Next up, it's time to get into some math. Descriptive statistics are numbers that describe data. In a world deluged with data, we need a way to present a summary of the raw data to allow for interpretation by the audience. IT will often use de-scriptive statistics to support its case for a new budget, as justification for necessary changes, or simply to persuade. For example, IT might be required to summarize how its systems are used, instead of guessing. This leads to more questions, such as: Exactly how many users use per-sonal devices? How often do users go to dangerous sites? How much time do they spend looking for information on data share?

We can use inferential statistics. Inferential statistics use a random sample of data taken from a population to make predictions and infer-ences about the population. Inferential statistics are particularly useful when it is not practical to look at all the targets of interest. For example, if you want to get a better understanding of the strength of your organ-ization's education campaign, you can leverage selected surveys to guide future investment needs.

We can leverage regression analysis. When IT wants to analyze, IT turns to regression analysis. Regression analysis is a powerful statistical method that examines the relationship between two or more variables of interest. At their core, these analyses examine the influence of one or more independent variables on a dependent variable. For example, a performance analysis of our teams happens to determine if training and skill set development is working, or if outside influences drive results.

We can make use of cost-benefit analysis. IT uses a cost-benefit analysis to systematically estimate the strengths and weaknesses of several options. IT uses this kind of analysis to determine which options provide the best approach to achieve benefits while preserving savings, making it perfect for the business justification process.

We can make use of the value of information. The value of information (VOI) tool is incredibly powerful in aiding IT decision-making. VOI indicates the highest amount a decision maker would be willing to pay for information prior to deciding. VOI is calculated as the difference in economic value between the best courses of action, with and without the information.

For example, when should a CIO reach out and bring in an outside consultant for help? Should he or she be willing to pay that consultant $100k for an assessment? How about $250k? Is there a way to determine if it's worth that much? Yes, by using the VIO analysis. When uncertainty is high in a business decision and the internal resources can't reduce that uncertainty themselves, an assessment from outside experts can help reduce the uncertainty to improve the odds of making the right decision. The VOI can be used in a decision model to improve the potential outcomes.

We can leverage a SWOT analysis. IT uses this to evaluate strengths, weaknesses, opportunities, and threats (SWOT). This strategic planning technique helps a person or organization identify the key areas related to business competition or project planning. It is intended to specify the objectives of a venture or project and identify the internal and external factors that are favorable and unfavorable in achieving those objectives. Users of a SWOT analysis strategically ask and answer questions to generate meaningful information and identify their competitive advantage.

We can do decomposition. Next up is a deeper dive into components. Decomposition separates components into simpler constituents. Often referred to as *unpacking*, decomposition helps with the analysis of problem resolutions. Decomposition makes understanding more manageable by focusing in on smaller parts of the whole.

We can use experimentation. When IT wants to explore further, IT runs experiments. Experiments verify, refute, or establish the validity of a hypothesis. Experiments provide valuable insight into cause and effect by manipulating different factors and observing the outcomes. Experiments vary greatly in both goal and scale, but a key characteristic of true experiments is their reliance on repeatable procedures and logical analyses of the results.

Experimentation should follow the scientific method, a powerful methodology whose impact cannot be underestimated. Used in all major technological, scientific, and mechanical advancements of our modern society, the scientific method allows IT to explore observations and answer questions in our search for cause and effect. Experiment to know if a plan is going to work, to validate a vendor's claim, or to test an internally held belief with big implications.

Better understanding leads to sharing our new insights.

To evaluate what tools to use, consider what tools you use today and how they help you. These types of tools can assist you in the process of modeling risk in a complicated and noisy world.

The tools help IT with business relevancy of our loss scenarios. With the context from the business, IT can chase its own version of reality. Stakeholders are not concerned with threat events—they care about loss events. You need to be able to help answer the question of if a *"high risk"* is high or a rounding error in the context of the business.

Risk

Risk is about impact for stakeholders and the measure of likelihood bad things will occur. Think and act on it in the same manner businesspeople do.

Cybersecurity's primary objective is mitigating business risk. In concert with the business, IT should be operating mitigation strategies in line with agreed-upon identification, categorization, and prioritization of business assets, priorities, and operations—the guiding principle when actively defending the organization. This will include upstream and downstream partners, industry competitors, and your customers. You need predefined scenarios that are relevant for your organization, inside your industry, and within your current culture and setup.

Once the scope of business interests is defined, relevant threats are monitored, and the organization's appetite for risk is agreed upon, IT can confidently and actively pursue activities to accomplish its mitigation goals.

What is the business's risk appetite and tolerance? When a security control cannot be applied because of its business context, IT must identify the business risk factors. Some of these might sound familiar: *"Our system was too old to upgrade to a newer model which supported encryption." "The vendor won't allow us to patch it." "The support contract will be broken." "This version doesn't have third-party radius support."*

Not all bad things are equal. We must move toward a common language for what is bad for us. There is a distinct difference between incident, intrusion, and breach.

In the digital world, copying data is stealing. Many metrics count cost per record, like credit card and health and data records. That is just a subset of important and valuable digital assets being actively "stolen" across industries.

We are only capable of reporting breaches we know about, or a third party tells us about. If we don't know, we can't report.

There is also the consideration of the nature and scope of the intrusion. Having non-regulated data stolen may not be reportable. Having non-sensitive data leaked is different than intellectual properly falling into the hands of a competitor. To be a relevant loss, the intrusion has to have specific effects to be relevant.

For example, POS malware running on a thousand of your stores that does not transmit credit card data has not technically caused a reporting event. If IT blocks the transfer of the credit card data from the jump station out of your network, what is the reportable event? Conversely, persistent malware that does not access any of your defined critical systems or data may not rise to board-level conversation. It remains a potential threat that could cause an unwanted outcome but has not yet. The business can influence what impact a successful exfiltration has. If the business is unable to map out a negative outcome, loss of revenue, expenses paid out, or loss of productivity, then from its perspective, there was no risk. IT can influence what systems and data are susceptible to exfiltration. IT needs to work off a framework aligned with business operations and designed to aid its cyber defense efforts.

If our architecture is flawed, the stakeholders are not informed, the business is blocking efforts to apply controls, and IT is not following design and operational best practices, then we as a group have failed the minimum standard of care. The bad guys are repeatedly fielding similar tactics, tools, and procedures. It is time we joined the fight through stakeholder education, quantifiable analysis of risk factors, formation of risk mitigation strategy, and accountability by all.

When discussing the risk in the business landscape, cybersecurity is vital to discuss. First things first. IT must have the correct mind-set to think about cybersecurity and risk in the business landscape. A bad outcome commonly impacts the bottom line, and a cash outlay is an adverse effect the business wishes to avoid. Any technology-related issue that causes the company to lose money or force a payout is a risk. IT needs to help the business mitigate against this as much as possible.

Before our digital economy took off, IT had a pretty good handle on the controls necessary to keep the business relatively safe. The boundaries of assets that needed to be protected were clearly defined. Endpoints were desktops and maybe a handful of laptops that were all corporately owned and IT managed, but most endpoints were all behind the firewall, providing a clear boundary between us and them. Remote locations all connected back to headquarters, with no direct connection to the internet. This clear boundary made it relatively easy to deal with the threats coming our way.

In fact, IT had been doing a pretty good job of preventing threats from outside, providing great protection at the boundaries, hardening our publicly facing endpoints, reducing vulnerabilities on Web servers, and closing off avenues of access. IT had done a pretty good job of frustrating attackers trying to get inside the network. That was then.

Now the landscape has changed, and it's not something IT brought on or something attackers came up with. It was a result of a change in business models. It was a change in mind-set from the end users driven by an onslaught of the consumerization of IT—the cloud, mobile, and bring your own device (BYOD).

Bad guys are well-known in the physical world. For some reason, their presence in the digital world is viewed by many as different. However, it should come as no surprise that crime, war, and political activism existing in the physical world would also operate in the digital one.

Not all organization views risk the same way. Every organization has a different appetite for risk and is subject to different laws and regulations, and IT's use of technology varies widely. You must ensure your stakeholders are informed on the cyber threat landscape, your current defense disposition, and the gaps. Use a variety of responses including process changes, user education, infrastructure enhancements, cyber insurance, faster mean time to recover, and improved operational visibility.

The impact of attacks can really be minimized. Traditionally, business impact analysis (BIA) has been performed to prepare disaster recovery and business continuity plans. We must ensure this process captures the complexity of systemic dependencies of business services to the underlying infrastructure. It is becoming beyond the scope of people to maintain and watch manually. The point is that a list of impacts that ignores true dependencies will underestimate actual risks.

For example, many IT budgets are trimmed for financial reasons, and some of those line items comprise critical components to maintaining a resilient infrastructure. This is a team effort. The security team has domain-level expertise in cybersecurity; however, the actual factors to determine levels of risk are a function of factors from across the entire IT team and, indeed, across the entire business. We must be vigilant in conveying this concept to the business, which has too often believed security was an issue just for one group, such as the way the accounting department takes care of payroll.

One main example of an unwanted outcome for the CIO is losing his or her job. The CIO has a vast number of responsibilities and must carry out numerous roles, and as such, the risks are vast. A cyber breach that makes headlines could result in blame being affixed to individuals, and the firing squad is called to aim at the CIO.

A key perspective in BIA is understanding the amount of loss magnitude, as many technical losses are minuscule compared to those at the business level. Be sure to focus on business risk and don't delineate cyber from business.

In the case of the big names in cyber breaches, many of them are still in business. What helps to explain that? The impact of the breach involves the various forms of losses, and the mitigations put into place in response combine to make for a more complicated answer. Beyond the headline, months and even years later, you should analyze using a more structured approach if you want to better understand the impact to your specific organization.

What are the effects from cyber incidents? There can be various ones. There can be multiples of them. Taken together they can add up. To understand the impact of cyber incidents, let's start at various effects from the original CIA triad and add on to it.

Threat Effects

The threat effect of a bad scenario can be viewed through the five lenses of confidentiality, integrity, availability, privacy, and safety. These lenses also apply to loss scenarios and together feed the primary financial health of our organizations. Threat effects decrease revenue and profits while increasing costs.

- **Confidentiality.** In this context, confidentiality is a set of rules that limits access to information. Confidential items are kept secret, based on a need to know. Authorized user access only. Payroll, employee evaluations, strategic plans, personally identifiable information, and intellectual property are types of information that should be kept confidential, requiring governance on who should have access.

- **Integrity.** Integrity ensures that the information is trustworthy and accurate. Data must not change in transit and must be protected from alteration by unauthorized parties. IT ensures that infrastructure, code, and data is as we left it.

- **Availability.** This guarantees reliable access to the information by authorized people. The pressure for continuous availability is intense.

- **Privacy.** This is similar to confidentiality, but instead, it means something is for certain eyes only. That includes users and consumers' rights to their own data. Regulations such as GDPR and the CCPA were designed specifically for this area. Privacy could be an offshoot of confidentiality but consider its unique aspects such as demand driven by consumer rights, questions of data ownership, increasing regulatory oversight and financial penalties, user rights to data, and consumers' right to be forgotten.

- **Safety.** This could be an offshoot of integrity but includes unique aspects that make it more useful to separate it. With the internet of things (IoT), new elements in the physical world are controlled by digital technology. These include activity trackers, refrigerators, desktop printers, and dozens more. IT must therefore contribute to a culture of safety in digital systems that interoperate with physical entities. The safety of people is increasingly reliant on automated systems connected to other networks, which are accessible by third parties to provide support. The IoT also includes factories, plants, and smart buildings, all run by code. Lives depend on the bad guys not hacking into the integrity of digitally controlled physical things.

So what? When something bad happens, how bad? Loss of life. Business. Financial? How much? The effects that inform the business impact can have real consequences. The one consequence of most important to business is a financial loss. Financial loss in this sense is money paid out. Money that is no longer available to support business operation, objective, and initiatives.

We need to use risk modeling to answer this question. First, though, what is the likelihood of this scenario playing out in the future?

Probability, Likelihood, Odds

IT needs to pay more attention to the probability of occurrence. The reason for this is that likelihood, at its core, is about probabilities. The security industry has gained a lot of its fear tactics reputation from not properly framing the actual likelihood of these bad outcomes occurring. Problem framing where all bad things could happen, with no thought about the likelihood of them happening to your organization, is an unaffordable proposition for most businesses. This runs counter to how business and the wider world works. No one would or could buy insurance that tried to cover all losses for everything.

Likelihood is probability, which is in the knowledge domains of statistics and probability management. We are getting into the chance of rolling a six on any roll of the dice, the chance of heads or tails on the flip of the coin, and the chance a criminal organization will target our organization using existing weaknesses in our controls.

Many options and strategies about mitigating risk are thoughtless. We need to step back and look at the risk formula again, focusing on which assets we are trying to protect. We can avoid something bad happening when we take the time to define what the impact of the adverse effect will be.

Risk can be expressed in monetary terms. Back to our example involving houses. If it costs X amount of dollars if our house burns down, then we can buy a certain level of property insurance to protect us from a large out-of-pocket expense. Organizations will conduct a BIA to identify its assets and assess the business impacts of damage. As part of a BIA, the team works with the business owners and the stakeholders with liability for the company to determine an inventory of all the critical assets, both physical and digital. From there they develop a list of scenarios for bad things that could occur to these assets, and then assign a monetary value to each one. IT can help the stakeholders understand the changing landscape and what assets mean in a digital world.

IT will also need to educate others on the technical dependencies of operating in a digital economy so their input in the BIA process is relevant.

That's one aspect of risk. The other main aspect IT focuses on is the actual likelihood or chance that something adverse will happen to the business or a particular asset. Or put another way, what is the probability my digital assets—for example, intellectual property or IP—will be compromised or that my main competitor will gain a copy of this intellectual property, thus allowing the competition to leapfrog us in the market?

If the probability is low, that fact can have a large impact on what you do to mitigate against this risk. It is of high impact to have your competitor gain access to your research and development (R&D) data, but you can consider it a low probability because of the controls IT has put in place. Conversely, it might be that you think the probability is high because you're not exactly sure of how well your controls are working.

The probability is critical to the process of managing risk. Traditionally, the impact has been more known in the physical world—however, in today's digital world we must make sure we adequately prepare ourselves for defending digital assets. The likelihood or probability numbers that IT often presents to the business could use more work. There are many security impacts that could involve many bad things. The severity of the impact and dollar amounts are incomplete without quantifying or expressing how probable it is that this "thing" could happen. In a world of finite resources and a lot of uncertainty, one cannot mitigate against all potential risks, but making the calculation of probabilities is a critical step in managing risk in business.

We need to think in terms of systems. When we do, we will greatly help our organizations win! If we're too slow to respond, the business fails, IT fails, and security fails. Unfortunately, the impact must sometimes be big and painful to force change.

There are many dangers that lurk within that include the assets we protect, the threats that challenge us, and the infrastructure we depend on. This awareness is now getting board-level visibility. The question is how risks from technology threats can impact the business's bottom line. Failure is no longer confined to a help desk ticket.

As to the industrialization of hacking, keep in mind these are not your father's hackers. It's important to set our terminology to facilitate a useful discussion on this. We have been approaching security all wrong!

We must strive to close the gap between our dependency and our effectiveness as quickly as possible in protecting our digital infrastructure. Our continued benefits and return on investments depend on the gap closing. It is a challenge to mitigate risks and improve our defenses while simultaneously not breaking things or disrupting business operations. After sitting through another third party's assessment report and list of recommendations recently, many of the conclusions were familiar to IT. Many of the remediation items were things they had wanted to do in the past. However, budget constraints, technical challenges, and integration difficulties made it extremely difficult, or sometimes even impossible, to get them implemented.

We see this caused by restrictions from third-party vendors who threaten to invalidate support contracts if their systems are updated, from business units who forbid their data from being shared with other groups, or from hardware limitations or licensing problems that will not allow for completion of the work. When operating under the constraints of just keeping the lights on, it's often more problematic to make the Center for Internet Security's Critical Security Controls a reality. When the big cyber breaches disappear off the front pages of newspapers, the attackers work once again in the background, where they stay quiet.

With many attackers out of sight and running quietly, coupled with the urgency of *now*, stakeholders will shift their attention back to the pressing issues of competing in the disruptive marketplace. This is normal human behavior. To make the point poignant, consider this example. Many people live with high risk factors and go against their doctor's recommendations. It is often an emergency trip to the hospital that brings the problem back to the forefront. Many people allow illnesses and health issues to grow over time, failing to address them early when indicators hint at future problems. If you could act today to reduce a problem tomorrow, how many would see that as an opportunity?

With potential impact and odds, how do we get more details? How do we get a better understanding beyond our intuitive nature and experience? We need to model.

Risk Modelling

Models are useful for understanding our environment and how it changes with modifications to certain variables. A model is a mathematical, economic, or statistical representation of relationships that determines the probable future consequences of decision choices. Models investigate, test, and discuss a situation. Models demonstrate our options, our constraints, and how to optimize our decisions. It is important in models that the inputs and assumptions are understood by all so the results are transparent. IT uses models for everything from budgeting and security to root cause analysis and capacity planning.

By its very nature, modeling, in all its forms, is often done unconsciously; but we need to do it purposely, with focus, and in a timely manner. Modeling happens in context—the circumstances that form the setting for the risk outcome, and the terms by which to assess it.

Risk has been called *"something that never sleeps."* Risk lives and exists in all domains of life and business, such as financial, legal, operational, project, reputational, market, credit, digital, and cyber—are all fair game for risk. Each domain has internal experts who are tasked with thinking about how risk management impacts them. IT is tasked with digital and cyber risks. Regardless of the domain of interest, the concern is the same.

The *"So what?"* question can ultimately be expressed as the hit to the bottom line in dollars and cents. It is the nature of business that stakeholders have the ultimate responsibility for all risks across all domains—and that means the bottom line is of top concern, no matter the area or domain.

IT's role is to help stakeholders understand the probable risks, risk landscape, organizational context, and circumstances that form a relevant loss scenario. IT must do all of this in language that the C-suite can understand and assess.

IT understands the context of digital and cyber risk by modeling this space. IT begins with building a virtual representation of loss scenarios to determine the assets at risk and the value they provide to the organization. Any value to the organization is an enticement for bad actors. Bad guys want to take value that benefits them. These threat agents are part of a threat community with a multitude of motives, means, and TTPs. IT stands between them and the business's assets. IT deploys myriad controls to counter these threats. These are part of the security program, whose overarching purpose meets the business need for mitigation against these cyber risks.

The difficulties of addressing an ever-expanding list of threat actors, attack methods, and large attack surface are compounded by shorter response time requirements. But IT still has the tools and methods that will work.

Yes, it's challenging to arrive at clear and focused decisions. But the good news is no one starts from scratch. Mitigations are typically already in play, many of them provided by other groups within the organization. What's more, each mitigation addresses many risks. Businesses provide many external mitigation factors. But it's up to IT to guide all these efforts. Modeling gives IT the proper context and decision guidance.

IT explicitly models loss scenarios to understand when, why, how, or even *if* something bad is likely to happen. IT models risk to identify all relevant factors to allow for analysis, understanding, and context to support decision-making. This is a team effort, where the model accurately reflects the security team, IT, and the business's shared concerns about the risk factors in play. Modeling provides the technical-to-operational and operational-to-strategic business mappings necessary to speak the multiple languages of all parties involved in risk management.

A vital aspect of risk modeling is calculating the threshold at which threat events become loss events. Near misses are important not only because they are a signal for intervention, but also because they help us update our models' probabilities of future occurrences.

Indeed, even a somewhat faulty model that exposes assets to unnecessary risk has the potential to provide an opening to create better protection. Let us stay fully aware of and responsive to our surroundings. Let's exploit lessons learned from previous incidents.

Why use models to assess risk and set our security program? To distinguish between possibility and probability. Models help IT answer the ultimate business questions:

- What are the chances a bad thing will happen?

- If that bad thing happens, how bad will it be?

- How much will it cost?

- What should we do about it?

- How much will doing something cost us compared to what we could lose if we don't do it?

This paradigm supports an explicit form of enterprise risk management. This management starts with stakeholders, assisted by IT and security team, and encompasses everything from risk target ranges all the way to controls that determine proactive risk posture.

If security teams use modeling purposely, with focus, and in a timely manner to drive risk management, the result is a program that embodies the following:

- Reduced waste of resources through cost-effective risk mitigation efforts.

- Minimized control friction, which would otherwise interfere with and slow down the business.

- Stakeholders who have information and advice to support their decision-making responsibilities.

- An organization-level annual loss exposure that's in line with stakeholder tolerance levels.

System Lens

The benefit of modeling is the ability to handle complexity and systems. A traditional linear analysis that assumes static factors in only a singular sequencing becomes limited when confronted with the realities of our business world. Our scenarios taken together need to be analyzed in a dynamic environment with lots of uncertainty. The identification of risk and its significance needs a certain type of approach. One that can see through complexity and identify potentially larger negative business consequences. That means being able to string together individual scenarios, from different risk areas, and sense the interdependencies among them.

Scenario analysis needs a systems lens that models can handle. Loss scenarios are a collection of elements that are connected in ways that lend themselves to systems view. These can be natural in origin or human constructed. The human ones can be intentionally created or by happenstance. They are varied in the types of elements, meaning they could be any combination of objects, people, or things; tangible or abstract. Systems tend to have the ability to surprise us in their behavior. Looking at just the elements won't give you an accurate picture of its functions or projected impacts on the world. Systems have feedback loops, where elements can respond to the actions of other elements inside the system and potentially change this behavior. The actions of elements can also influence other elements to reinforce a looping type of behavior. Also, the action of one element could produce a balancing loop, in the example of element #1 producing more action from element #2. Predicting all the behavior of the system is not easy. Many times, the system in question is not under our total control. But for scenario analysis to be useful for decision-making support, we need to at least be aware of what the system impact is on this scenario under analysis. We also must be aware of system of systems, where there are many systems that are interacting with each other, influencing, and responding to each other.

Systems by their very nature are complex and dynamic. If a risk response that we take to an analysis we have done does not produce the expected results, remember it might not be a problem with our analysis or our actions; we must be more aware of the underlining systemic elements and behaviors.

Measurement

Risk comes in many flavors. Beyond qualifying potential losses, we need to go a step further to provide management with better context to understand how much risk there is. The good news is organizations are already there. That is how businesses operate. It is time for IT to catch up. Money is the best known and used reference for business context.

Business management tracks costs (money that goes out the door) and benefits (money received from revenue). Realized losses from risk can increase cost and decrease revenue. As a result, risk analysis is fundamental to cost-benefit analysis. All we have seen focused on risk analysis for cyber and digital threats, the loss events that create monetary outflow in all those scenarios, is also applicable inside of a business opportunity. This cost-benefit analysis must take in consideration risk considerations because the cost can go up and the benefit can go down.

This mean that in effect all business decisions that involve costs and/or benefits have the potential to be adversely affected by unmitigated risk. The qualification process takes risk factors into consideration for a critical input for both costs and benefits. The additional insights into the financial impact of scenarios make it extremely useful for decision analysis.

Businesses run off numbers, and everything that management uses to run their operations can be digested into the numbers. Financial modeling is the process of creating a summary of a company's earnings and expenses that can be used to calculate the impact of a future event or decision. It is a representation in numbers of some aspects of a company's current or future operations. A scenario that management is concerned with that includes unplanned expenses stemming from a cyber loss scenario is a top concern. Every dollar spent attempting to avoid such expenses or recovery from an incident is a dollar not spent elsewhere for the business. All cybersecurity-related spend is reflected on the balance sheet. All potential future losses are reflected in future business performance. The ability for IT to report to financial leaders is crucial. We already make our asks in monetary terms. So let us also express the potential loss exposure in monetary terms as well to make a clear business impact.

Our digital world rarely gives complete certainty for decision makers. Instead, we need to measure uncertainty, especially where there exists more than one possibility. Business leaders are accustomed to uncertainty, but in an era of disruptions and complexity, the level of uncertainty has never been higher. The speed of change is so fast that even experienced decision makers may be overwhelmed with keeping pace and staying relevant. Uncertainty is not the lack of knowledge or data to decide. Uncertainty means the impossibility of exactly describing the existing state and future outcome or outcomes. To manage the effects of these uncertainties on decision-making, we measure. Measurement of risk shows us the size of a potential loss.

Risk modeling helps with this by specifying and managing potentially bad outcomes. Something bad might happen, which leads to the question of how likely it is to occur. How often might it happen in each timeframe? And, if it does occur, how bad might it be financially?

The uncertainty of risk can be quantified statistically to approximate potential future loss. According to the World Economic Forum report, Partnering for Cyber Resilience: Towards the Quantification of Cyber Threats, *"The concept of cyber value-at-risk is based on the notion of value at risk, widely used in the financial services industry."* The report goes on to state that value-at-risk (VaR) is a measure of risk defined as a threshold loss value for a given portfolio with a given time horizon.[38] The value of such an approach is to bridge the gap between technical cybersecurity from IT with the language of business—dollars and cents. Once risks from cyber threats are encoded in financial terms, true reduction of business risk will be achievable. IT will then be able to effectively optimize its recommendations for controls—any person, process, policy, or technology that reduces the probability of a loss event or the magnitude of the loss.

Risk analysis in some form is part of every decision we make. We are constantly faced with uncertainty, ambiguity, and variability. And even though we have unprecedented access to information, we can't accurately predict the future.

Modeling risk involves dealing with lack of certainty about potentially bad outcomes. Measurement is to assist with decision-making. To help with design and build. Measurement reduces uncertainty. In risk management, we need to identify the relevant risk factors that make each risk unique. With those risk factors, we increase our level of understanding at hand to support good decision-making with the best information at hand at the time.

Loss types, their event frequency, loss magnitude, and loss exposure. It is time to do the math. Taking the measurement, reducing uncertainty. The quantification of cyber risk involves taking the identified elements of a scenario and expressing your current level of information about each. Where before there was intuitive understanding between teams on what a high risk meant, quantification puts that out for all to see in a shared language. One million dollars is much clearer than high. And when we are unsure the amount is exactly $1 million, we can instead express that uncertainty with a range, for example $750,000 to $1,500,000. This means the loss of concern could fall within that range, but we are not sure. But that is okay. Contrast with the specific number of $1 million that suggests a high confidence in that number. The more uncertain we are about the exact number, the larger the range we can make it. If we find that that range is too large to help support a meaningful decision, then we can seek to add additional information and clarity to shorten that range.

So, where do we get these numbers from? We get them from people, such as subject matter experts in the relevant fields and domains. In this case the subject matter experts are like a measurement tool, such as a thermometer, and as with all measurement tools we need to be aware that they need to be calibrated to ensure that they produce consistent types of inputs. One way to calibrate subject matter experts is to take them through a process of calibration to help improve their estimation and become consistent in the way they provide those. Consistency in the way those inputs are provided is critical, and it will be used later in the decision-making process to compare the current state versus the future state with additional controls in place. Subject matter expertise elicited from those can provide information on the value at risk, the underlying at risk, the nature of the threat actors in their objectives, and the current control state.

How likely is it that this scenario will happen? If you invest in your new control, what will that probability of occurrence look like? Realm of probability. Probability. *Probability* is the measurement of the likelihood of an event occurring. Frequency. In addition to the likelihood of an event occurring, we also need to know its frequency. Frequency refers to how often an event occurs within a given period. It is the number of occurrences of a repeating event per a defined unit of time. Over a specific timeframe, what is the frequency?

Note that if you stand still, your impact and frequency could go up. Think inflation for money. Sitting in a standard checking account over the years, you could lose value of the money as inflation eats into it. It is common to move that money into other investment tools that return a higher return to keep ahead of inflation. If the efficacy of a security control goes down because of a newly discovered flaw, then you can run the same type of simulation of the model to show the business why you are asking for this level of new spending. Increased spending, more mature security, and better technology has closed off lots of attack vectors. As expected, threat actors continue to adapt. That is what they do; that is their job. That mitigation cost could include a new head count to operate a new technical control.

IT needs to communicate its value and concerns to the business in a language they can understand, money. Risk is expressed as loss exposure. To match budgets and financial reporting requirements, the annualized loss exposure (ALE) is a key result from quantitative analysis. Loss exposure is how we can communicate risk. Performing the math on frequency and magnitude of future loss allows us to calculate loss exposure. For example, 6 loss events per year x $10,000 per event loss = an ALE of $60,000. Or 1 event every 4 years x $800,000 per event = an ALE of $200,000. This allows for cost comparisons between different loss scenarios and feeds the decision process on what to tackle first.

Cyber risk matters to the business the same reason other types of risk do. It could cost the business money. Impact expressed in dollars and cents is what management needs to efficiently manage all types of risk. There is a lot of attention paid to the early parts of a scenario, where we talk about what the attackers are doing. We see lots of headlines with big numbers thrown around. For your organization, you need specifics in your scenarios for what that impact of the cyber incident caused.

Loss can take various forms of financial impact. One form is direct economic loss from the inability to conduct operations or delivery services. This is dollars your organization is not collecting from your customers. Other forms of financial impact include:

- expenses incurred to pay for an external assistant responding to an incident
- breach response, legal, public relations, etc.
- having to replace personnel or equipment
- direct costs from legal judgments and/or fines
- marketplace competitive levels changing with loss of intellectual property either falling into the hands of a competitor or loss of access to use it
- effects on cost of capital or change in market share

Simulation

We need a way to take the potential range of losses, aggregated across the potential various loss forms, to look at what potential exposure looks like from likely ranges of possible financial impact. We need a way to look at multiple potential futures; we need to run simulations. A simulation is the imitation of the operation of a real-world system over a defined period of time. Simulations require the use of models. Risk models represent key characteristics of a system of interest, whereas the simulation represents the evolution of the model over time. A risk model is a representation of a system where the outcome is uncertain and at least some of them are unwanted. Conceptually it helps people to better know and understand the possibilities of the future.

A Monte Carlo simulation is a model used to predict the probability of different outcomes when the intervention of random variables is present. Monte Carlo is a method for analyzing data that has significant uncertainty. Perform repeated random sampling to obtain numerical results. The output used in risk analysis is shown as probability distributions. The primary advantage is the ability of the method to perform thousands of calculations on random samples, allowing analysts to create a more accurate and defensible depiction of probability given the uncertainty of the inputs. The outputs are distributions, owning to the expression of uncertainty. If using a PERT distribution, you will get a minimum, maximum, most likely, and confidence level.

When IT creates models and wants to explore many scenarios with uncertain variables, IT uses simulations. Simulations provide a way to improve decision-making under uncertainty by looping through many different possible outcomes. It uses mathematical and statistical modeling. Monte Carlo iterates through multiple variables across different spaces and aspects to come up with different outcomes available from the input. IT can then apply these statistical analyses to systems of control, interest, influence, and concern, better determining the probability of success for a project or quantifying the current level of loss exposure.

Monte Carlo's computerized and mathematical technique is used by professionals in such widely disparate fields as finance, project management, energy, manufacturing, engineering, R&D, insurance, oil and gas, and transportation. The technique was first used by scientists working on the atom bomb during World War II. It was named for Monte Carlo, the Monaco resort town renowned for its casinos.[39]

Running simulations opens the door for discovering some interesting insights on scenarios. High probability tends to lend itself to high frequency. Low probability tends to lend itself to lower frequency. A high frequency of low-impact events can equal or exceed a single low-probability, high-impact event. High-impact events are influenceable by controls to reduce to lesser impact. Low-impact events can be a problem with high frequency. The final costs of an incident are heavily dependent on the chance secondary stakeholders are affected and act up an organization. Most cyber incidents don't involve them. The costs are contained as response expenses. How high the impact of an event will be influenced by the smarter use of controls; for example, ensuring that backups of systems are not compromised during an incident to allow for relatively fast recovery that mitigates the impact.

These types of differences in outcomes can be explored in depth with modeling to support our analysis. It is to our advantage to build and use explicit risk models tailored for our specific organizations. It allows for that critically important technical-to-business mapping. A model is a system or thing used as an example to follow or imitate. A risk model is a system used as an example to illustrate something bad that might happen. It allows all interested persons to have visibility, provide their unique perspective, and come to a shared understanding of loss scenarios. It can be represented mathematically. Modeling helps the decision-making process for the security team, IT, and the business.

In all its form, modeling is always used. However, it is often done unconsciously. It is often influenced, directed, or mandated from outside the organization, resulting in an indirect form of risk management. This leads to a reactive security posture that focuses too much on meeting the minimum compliance requirements. Modeling is used in both simple and complex tasks, by everyone. But it needs to be done purposely, with focus, and in a timely manner. For the security team to be effective in its job, risk modeling needs to be explicit. Modeling should be considered a prerequisite for running an effective security program. Risk is a fundamental aspect of all things driven by uncertainty. All endeavors are surrounded by risk. As such, identifying and managing risk is a fundamental component of decision-making that comes up daily. It provides the necessary context for everything we do.

Why use models to guide our security program? To distinguish between possibility and probability. To answer the ultimate business question of what are the chances that a bad thing will happen. If that bad thing happens, how bad? How bad in financial terms? This supports an explicit form of risk management, which stems from stakeholders. In the case of technology, they will be assisted by IT and the security team.

Our call to action then is to purposely model risk. When we want to understand when, why, or could something bad happen, IT needs to capture the factors, inputs, and outputs, to allow for analysis, understanding, and context to support decision-making. This is a team effort, where the model accurately reflects the security team, IT, and the business's shared concerns with the risk factors in play.

Everyone needs to be using the same mental model of bad things that could happen and respond accordingly. Test your assumption by analyzing your relevant scenarios. Stress test the models you use. Often gaps and deficiencies in your security program is a result of flaws in your model that produced the organization response to a loss scenario. You should have gated translators between the security team, IT, and the business. All models begin with an organization's value at risk. Models assist in providing visibility into the funding requirements for risk mitigation efforts.

Performing scenario analysis well is a prerequisite for an effective cybersecurity program. Modeling risk is a prerequisite for designing, building, and running a cost-effective security program. Models allow us to mitigate risks properly by accurately focusing on those that are relevant to our organizations. All modeling is designed to provide support for future decisions. We gather the appropriate inputs to process to provide context for the questions at hand. From identifying risks, to qualifying significance, to quantifying the issue, to provide needed insights to make informed decisions. Modeling is the critical step in taking control of all the chaos in the risk landscape.

Explicitly modeling risk informs the development of an effective security program. Design, build, and operate a security program that keeps an organization's annual loss exposure in line with stakeholder tolerance levels.

Scenario analysis is applicable to our work that is actionable for risk responses in tactical, operational, and strategic dimensions.

You should structure your thinking around risk so you can identify, make, and support sound decision-making in your organizations. It is vital that we understand that the domain of risk management is much more than an annual, long-risk assessment engagement. Risk impacts our organizations.

Now what? Now it's time to inform the organization. Informed decision makers are in a better position to determine what is most important, to understand high probability and large-magnitude loss scenarios compared to highly frequent, low-magnitude scenarios. Now that we have the means to fully form the scenarios of concern for our organizations, know all the known factors, and have measured impact and likelihood, we have the insightful inputs necessary to support cost-efficient and smart decisions at all levels on needs. With the proper people informed, we can turn our attention to supporting those who have to take action.

Chapter 3
Decision Support

So, what are we going to do with the results of all our scenario analyses? We use it as inputs to the large number of decisions that we must make. These are decisions that we must make every day. Decisions from various teams across the organization. Big decisions, small decisions, and everything in between. The decision-making process needs to have rigor. Building relevant and complete scenarios and analyzing them is in support of this process. A common challenge with cyber security programs is mis-prioritized activity and investments due to inconsistent risk analysis, which has hindered this process, obscuring real issues that go unaddressed. There is also the challenge of the decision process itself. Even if scenario analysis is done well, if the decision process is ad-hoc, broken, or non-business aligned, then the organization is being done a disservice.

Scenario analysis helps with the identification and further understanding of risk. Now the output of their analysis can be used as input to the decision process. The decision process must be structured in a way to be able to handle this input to understand how to process it and make informed options for the business. We must know the optimal responses to the loss scenarios that could potentially happen in the future. The maturity of an organization's decision-making process is critical as it is a leading factor in the quality of risk response recommendations for action. A major cause of failures in business is poor decision-making and inadequate risk management. In a sense, the board of directors and the C-suite have been operating with blind spots from it. They must manage their decisions.

A decision is a conclusion reached after consideration. All of us are involved in making decisions many times a day. Inside of organizations, it happens hundreds of thousands of times a day. All around the world, the biggest decisions are made. The difference between a good decision and a bad decision could be bad luck. But business is run with more intention behind stacking the odds in favor of good decisions, leading to good outcomes for their organizations. Security programs often do not take in consideration decision management. Organizations need to have a well-defined management system around decision-making. That decision-making needs to be organized around documented processes and established approaches to produce consistently good decisions at all levels. The age of gut-level decision-making for a few at the top of the organizational struggle are over. There is too much at stake to leave important decisions to chance.

You need to identify the components needed to make a sound decision. Under the hood for decision-making, there are minimum requirements for a decision. This includes alternative options for a decision and organization preference for those options that are influenced by appetite for risk taking.

An alternative is one or more things, propositions, or courses of actions that can be chosen; one of two or more available possibilities. If your organization's governance, culture, or constraints make it only one course of action, then you don't have a decision. For preferences, in relation to choosing between alternatives; someone prefers red over yellow or blue over brown. If your organization's governance, culture, or constraints don't provide any preference between the alternatives, then you could just randomly make the decision. There would be only one course of action and you don't have a decision. The decision makers have preferences, such as familiarly with a platform or pricing. It would be a rarity to say for IAAS that there was no preference for IT to go with Azure, AWS, or GCP. Information can be thought of as the resolution of uncertainty; it is that which answers the question of "what an entity is" and thus defines both its essence and nature of its characteristics. The concept of information has different meanings in different contexts. The acquisition of information on features, interoperability, security features, usability, pricing, implementation, etc., are all relevant. If you could not go out and gather any information, then that would starve the decision-making process of thought.

Be careful of a false decision, where time and effort are being spent on a situation that does not involve an actual decision. When a manager predetermines option number one as the only option, it is more likely a case where the actual decision is how to execute on that choice versus should we do it at all.

We need a way to frame the decisions at hand and in the future. What are the decisions at hand? Knowing that one scenario is a higher priority than the other does not mean that it should be addressed first. Why? We must decide how our risk management structures will be designed and operated across our organizations. The decision at hand guides the level of scenario analysis, the details, the scope, and how much. There are core mitigation responses that are part of enabling a new businesses capability. As a result, the cost of those controls is part of the total cost of ownership leading to sub-optimal risk/rewards decisions.

Many controls gaps are overdue based on functional enterprise architecture capabilities needed for modern digital infrastructure. You are ready to address a specific scenario but know that the internal resources needed to be successful are not available at this time. Other projects are ready and able to be initiative now. Risk management itself needs decision support to be effective.

We need to have structure in our decision-making process. The larger organization does a good job on their side of the house. They successfully are in business providing to customers willing to pay. They need IT's help in matters of continually making using of technology for business value. As the use of technology attracts various cyber-attacks, they need advice and guidance on cost-effective mitigation. And IT needs guidance on our side in deploying new technology and protecting it.

Decision criteria need to be defined. That can be supported by using decision trees and matrices. Those will have defined decision points to highlight if there is a decision that needs to be made and the known options.

Decision-making requires information. We must be informed on the current situation and possible choices when a decision needs to be made. IT provides underlying technology, support tools, user interfaces, and collections of vast amounts of data every day from the front lines and from interactions across the organization. IT provides the analytical crunching of the raw data into useable formats for consumption to drive operations and support decision-making.

Which way? How far? When? Making decisions is what workers do every day. Our outcomes and experiences are influenced by how we make those decisions. Many of us strive to always get better at it.

As IT professionals, we must make the most effective use of our finite resources and maximize the available business opportunities to make these decisions faster. With the right approach, framework, culture, and technology, we can start anywhere along the problem spectrum and still beat competitors in the marketplace, many of whom are still relying on hunches.

A massive amount of effort is being directed at supporting our businesses' need to make better decisions, resulting in more important consequences, and at a faster pace; but the number of decisions made daily can lead to decision fatigue. This can lead to bad outcomes. IT can help with this.

A business runs on decision-making, so how good is your organization at making great decisions? Could your decision-making process be leaving money on the table? Could it be adding extra percentage points of cost to your current operations? Could it be sabotaging your organization's future earning potential?

Decision-making, whether good or bad, should be measured. If the ultimate success or failure of the organization hinges on outpacing the market, it behooves everyone to ensure the decision-making process is producing optimal outcomes.

It is critical we make good decisions to improve the condition of our businesses. It is a hallmark of great leadership to assess the situation, be guided by good data, analyze that data, and then execute. Optimizing decision-making is vital to business strategy, decisions, and operations.

IT can help facilitate the decision-making process by bringing together stakeholders and providing them with a useful framework that structures the relevant data in a consumable manner.

The fundamental aspect of decision-making is to decide. Merge, acquire, increase production, reduce prices, or run a sale. Migrate to the cloud, stay on-premises, go with vendor *X* or vendor *Y*, let users bring their own devices or issue them, upgrade the system of record, or migrate to a new platform, and so on. Countless decisions put together can make or break a company. IT provides both alternatives and information for these decisions.

To accomplish any of the goals we've studied in this book, we must look at the decision-making process. Decision-making is a key component and key skill for IT to improve upon. Transformative decision-making affects every aspect of what's been previously discussed.

Decision-making ties into how to procure services, how to choose a vendor, how much to pay for services, how to make recommendations, and how to assess security risks every day. IT must make decisions, and the business must make decisions. IT can improve business decision-making by leveraging new tools and analytic processes available today.

Decision-making needs to occur in a wide variety of contexts, such as strategic planning, real-time process support, and critical operations. Some decisions occur in a process that could take months and involve extensive data gathering and detailed analyses. Multiple stakeholders could be involved in the ultimate decision. A consensus may need to be reached to make the most beneficial decision for the business. In this context, IT is supporting the business by providing the relevant data fabric necessary. Also, IT has its own strategic decisions it must make on an ongoing basis.

In other contexts, decision-making could mean making near real-time decisions in operations: Where data and analysis are automatic, inform the decision maker in a relatively short period of time, and mitigate risks. Decisions often need to be made on the front lines in business settings. This is a critical place for wise decision-making to occur for operational relevancy to be maintained.

To support differentiated needs for decision-making data and analytics, we must distinguish the various data needs of the organization.

Unwise decision-making can have bad consequences, which affect us all as individuals, employees, governments, organizations, and IT. Bad decisions can result in negative outcomes in market competitiveness by causing us to be late in responding to customer needs; to waste finite time, money, and effort; and to needlessly expose our organizations to risk.

When we decide wisely and rightly, secure operations become table stakes. Considering how poorly the industry is doing, it is critical for IT to get protection, detection, and response right. Making bad decisions can cost our company big-time. It could result in our companies going out of business.

IT needs a framework in place that enables good decision-making that goes beyond hunches and good luck. A good number of companies may not be in existence in the next decade because they decided poorly amidst disruption by a competitor. Or they were weakened due to shifting market needs and wants. In these arenas IT can help itself, individual employees, and its organization. Businesses strive to make good decisions. IT supports the decision-making process of business. Let us not forget what the *I* in IT stands for.

Business Transformation

At the heart of all advancements in the daily lives of billions of people on this planet is *innovation*—something new. Innovation is a new idea, service, or product, or a new way of doing things, engaging your customer, or thinking.

Innovation tackles pressing challenges to market viability, competitiveness, and continued customer relevance. As such, including innovation is necessary for an organization's survival in a world of rapid disruption, complexity, and risk. IT must help bear the weight of the organization's innovative efforts. IT's assistance is not only valuable but critical.

IT enables better solutions to meet new requirements, unarticulated needs, and existing market needs.

If a business is to remain agile, it must care about ongoing transformation in response to market conditions. This chapter will explore business models, digital enablement, and decision-making surrounding transformation.

Understanding today's business, technology, and risk landscape sets the foundation for identifying possible growth. Once the decision has been made to innovate, IT transforms at the business level while mitigating new cyber threats. Much is possible.

Is your company or industry in the news tonight? Is there some market shift, change, or disruption that affects your organization? If you are a publicly traded company, then stockholder pressure for ROI puts the pressure on for nonstop top-line growth and cost control. The stakeholders in your organization are also under extreme pressure. This is the framework from which IT operates.

IT does not panic about all of this but instead operates as an enabler of growth, an engine for innovation, and a protector of the business value stream. This encompasses helping our businesses see threats on the horizon, enabling digital transformation, supporting decision-making across the organization, and supporting business operational excellence.

IT needs to capitalize on what is possible. IT must see it, respond to it, adapt to it, and realize new opportunities as a result of it. Not all opportunities are in direct response to a problem; they can also arise from a change in thinking about how to approach how end users live, work, and play. IT doesn't directly handle the profits & loss statement, but it can support those who do.

Imagine that even if Blockbuster, under pressure from Netflix, had made an available deal to acquire them before being displaced by them, they would still be a dramatically different company, operating with a changed business model. Brick and mortar stores would still be closing. The consumption patterns are different today. Blockbuster would be in the content delivery business, not commercial retail.

What business is your organization in? Your stakeholders grapple with the answer to this question. The answer may change in a relatively short time. The book *Digital Vortex* explains:

> Understanding how customer value is created, the business models used to produce it, the competitive dynamics in play, and the strategic response options available to companies creates a north star for the journey of digital business transformation. There is no one-size-fits-all approach to transformation.[40]

All decisions are subject to constraints and tradeoffs. But IT has stepped up in its part to enable, support, target, and inspire transformation efforts that the business needs. IT is here to support both value creation and value protection.

The first step in helping the business enable transformation lies in understanding why our businesses exist—we must understand our organizations' business models.

Business Models

How your organization does its business, and what it delivers, can be viewed through its business model. A business model describes the rationale behind how an organization creates, delivers, and captures value. Business models are even more critical than the new technology itself. Great technologies are critical as they make it possible to build new offerings. An enabler to even allow for market success. However, the key is putting together all the pieces (great technology, timing, reach, etc.) in such a way to identify and address a fundamental customer problem that needed a solution.

IT's activities are focused on the three fundamental elements in a business structure of the back end, the value proposition, and the customer end.

The back end is the data center and can be likened to an engine room or kitchen. It is composed of key resources, activities, partnerships, and the cost structure.

The value proposition answers the *purpose* question of the reason a business is able to attract customers in the first place. It is composed of revenue streams.

The customer end is what users want. It is composed of customer segments, value propositions, channels, and customer relationships.

If your organization went out and asked people what they wanted, there is no guarantee their responses would be what they really seek. People didn't know to ask Henry Ford for automobiles, perhaps because most had never experienced one. Ford said, *"If I had asked people what they wanted, they would have said faster horses."*[41]

How we work, live, play, and travel are all up for disruption. This also includes how we teach and learn, how we fight and die, how we produce, and how we consume. It includes where we work, when we work, how we work, how we get news, and how we consume it.

Alexander Osterwalder and Yves Pigneur in their book *Business Model Generation* describe a business model through nine building blocks, which they refer to as the business model canvas, each of which represents a question:

- For whom is the business creating value?
- What value is delivered to customers?
- Through which channels are customers reached?
- What type of relationship does each of the customer segments expect from us?
- What value are customers willing to pay?
- What key resources do the value propositions require?
- What key activities do the value propositions require?
- Who are key partners and suppliers?
- What are the most important costs inherent in the business?[42]

At the nexus of those nine building blocks lie business opportunities fueled by new technology uses. From new payment methods to alternative delivery mechanisms, alternative subscription models, or an enhanced buying experience, new tech allows changes to all nine areas.

To innovate new business models that respond to market forces, we should think differently. To do that we should ask "What if?" questions as part of an ideation process. Questions enable us to challenge assumptions and reexamine constraints so we can break free from outdated ideas and imagine a new vehicle for customer value.

The business model canvas can assist the CIO and their team in understanding the nature of the organization in the market. This is an opportunity to better align IT thinking, strategy, and priorities with organizational dynamics.

The other benefit of the canvas is its ability to better forecast changes in business direction in response to market forces, from acquisitions and mergers to downsizing and new partnerships to reorganizations and growth.

Know why your business exists, how it competes, how it adapts, and most importantly, how it can be ready to help when needed. A business model is a blueprint for how to adapt IT's organization, skill sets, and strategies to maintain IT's value proposition.

You will be the answer to the question of what kind of IT your business needs. You will take part in informing the powers that be of what software applications are needed, the infrastructure needed to support it, and the security control requirements.

A better understanding of the *why* and *how* of your organization empowers your ability to evolve your thought processes, strategies, operations, and goal setting. By keeping pace with business demand, anticipating future needs, and guiding business growth and competitiveness via digital strategies, IT stays attuned to how the business is adapting to market conditions, which will be key to the success of new market opportunities.

Your business looks for ways to find new, alternative elements of their model for competitive reasons. Because there is uncertainty around what new element will work, flexibility is required. IT needs an open and fluidly thinking mind because of uncertainty. The three questions business innovators often ask are:

- From a technology standpoint, "Can you build it?"
- From a customer standpoint, "Do customers want it?"
- From a business standpoint, "Can you make money on it?"

Every day, businesses are experimenting with components of their business model. And as they do, IT can support those efforts at change. Let's look from the front, back, and aligned views.

From the view from the front, cooking transforms raw ingredients into the finished output of food for people to eat. Imagine IT as a restaurant, to orient your perspective. Restaurants include seating and tables, waiters, payment systems, etc. People could cook at home themselves, but there is value in having someone else do it for you. They can exchange value (money) to a second party (restaurant) for the value of saved time and effort. The complexity of the cooking process, from ingredient acquisition to prep to final plating, is hidden from sight.

When customers walk into a restaurant, they sit in the dining area, look at the menu, and order from their chairs. They interact with the waiter or waitress. At some point, food is brought to them. They eat, make their payment, and go.

Like the cook, IT transforms the raw ingredients of technology into the finished output of technology-enabled functionality. Most of this is hidden from view.

When you walk into a new business, you are often presented with new offerings and experiences. The customers view businesses from this front lens. They see what is available to buy and reveal how they feel in the interactions through their buying patterns.

Your business leaders are trying a wide variety of new things, and IT needs to be connected with the big picture of those initiatives. Many requests for changes from the top are driven by what is being experimented within the marketplace. The business needs to innovate by trying new ideas.

Mark Zuckerberg, founder and CEO of Facebook, said, "People think innovation is just having a good idea, but a lot of it is just about moving quickly and trying a lot of things."[43]

IT powers the back end and interfaces with new digital inputs on the front. When customers see the username/password prompt on a screen, they are presented with a customized front-end technology-enabled functionality.

From the view from the back, before a customer ever shows up at the restaurant, the staff is prepping for the daily opening—opening the doors to employees, cleaning up, receiving supplies, and cooking delectable dishes. After the doors open and customers start ordering food, requests make their way back to the kitchen.

A business model is made of distinct parts that can be identified, studied, and improved upon. The back end, the hidden kitchen, receives and manages rapid changes and pressures.

IT must build the technological capability to keep the lights on while adapting to what's coming at a faster rate. The capabilities of the existing infrastructure power the business's current model. When the C-suite explores alternative market options, data centers stay ready to adapt quickly. The constraints of current technology can limit the view from the front.

In the bowels of our organizations, we can become more intentional in our value activities to enable new business value upfront, such as opening additional customer channels, expanding customer segments, or changing resources and business activities. That's all part of keeping our customers coming back for good meals and keeping us in business. Think of a happy, effective restaurant kitchen as you manage all of the capabilities from your data center and cloud services like the cabling, network, wireless access points, and other elements of the infrastructure that business users don't see—all of the hectic work that IT has been doing for years behinds the scenes.

From the view from service, getting a meal served to a customer is a complex process, not to mention all of the subsystems of the global food supply chain, access to good workers, and the societal infrastructure that allows this to be a reality. Hundreds of components need to come together in a coordinated manner to deliver each meal.

Alignment in this context brings agreement between the customer and the business. Seamless interactions between the front and back ends are critical.

Track the interactions between front and back, and you will find new opportunities. This is the essence of the intersection between technology and service. Technology capabilities intersect with process, experience, and opportunity.

When IT is aware of its goals, tasks, and services, it can map them to customer-facing service offerings that connect to the underlying structure of the business model. Service alignment brings clarity to the tensions of the various demands on the technology and provides the necessary context to guide its approach to its work.

Technology-enabled functionality can take costs out of the back end, reduce friction on the front end, improve workflow efficiencies, enable new revenue streams, and protect existing ones.

Digital Transformation

Enabling digital capabilities in cyber space is a critical business driver. Hence, digital transformation has implications for both the back end and front end. Research from the Global Center for Digital Business Transformation, an IMD and Cisco initiative, explains:

> Digital business transformation is a journey to adopt and deploy digital technologies and business models to improve performance quantifiably. The first step of this journey is to grasp the need for change—an imperative driven by the inevitability of digital disruption. Digital disruption now has the potential to overturn incumbents and reshape markets faster than perhaps any force in history. Simply put, digital disruption is the effect of digital technologies and business models on a company's current value proposition, and its resulting market position.[44]

The theory and strategy of digital transformation sounds good and all, but unless IT can execute, IT is just wishing. The new standard response from IT must become, "Yes, it is possible, and this is how." For comprehensive decision-making, add to that: "This is how much it will cost, this is when it will be ready, and these are the levels of new business risk that will be introduced."

IT develops a digital strategy aligned with business challenges, priorities, and risks. In collaboration with the business, IT can jointly formulate and continue to refine strategies around ways to capitalize on the digital transformation that disrupts all markets.

The disruptor sets the new bar for what's better, faster, and more desirable in the market. Every day, someone or some company is trying to change the standards for excellence, redefine what is possible, and challenge how we do what we do.

Sleep too long on a problem, and the business across the street will take advantage of your slumber and leapfrog you. Technology-enabled business transformation is creating disruptions in all industries, even when you provide what the buyers want at a lower price. Things are different. And that's good. Those who win are the customers who use these new products and services. IT becomes a hero in this process.

We won or lost, we made our revenue numbers for the quarter, or we didn't; we delivered on time, or we didn't. Binary yes or no responses answer the question of whether the desired outcome was achieved. If my investment in a company delivered a return, I'd want to stay with them. If brand *X* is cheaper than brand *Y*, that factor may decide which one the end user purchases. Or, as in the case of Starbucks, some end users may purchase the more expensive option because of a value they perceive.

Another binary concept is *surviving* or *not*. This could refer to your company, the product, or your job. Outcome matters. Because of this, just showing up and delivering what is expected is not always enough. Customers want more. Outcomes only tell part of the story. The experience of the buying process and the consumption lifecycle dictate that the experience also matters. And that applies across all industries.

Customers can buy a myriad of things from many places. Job seekers can get work from many places. Companies can hire from many places. Sometimes price is the most important buying factor. But consumers also heed all types of criteria at different times and for different types of products and services.

When the consumer wants more, we must create a distinct experience if we want to compete. When we want more, our company must be different.

Your business is undergoing digital transformation not just to survive but also to grow revenue and market share. The customer experience is reimagined through digital transformation. *Experience* refers to how the customer feels about the brand, the company, the product, and the service, and not just at the beginning of the interaction but all the way through. Technology systems must engage the customer.

System of Engagements

Systems of engagement transition from current enterprise systems designed around discrete pieces of information (records) to systems that are more decentralized, incorporate technologies that encourage peer interaction, and often leverage cloud technologies to provide the capabilities to enable those interactions.

When you compare decentralized systems to systems of record, which are largely geared toward passively providing information to a company's workers, the differences and ramifications are motivating.

Systems of record serve some of our country's most critical systems, like banking and insurance. These are run on mainframes. As those industries transform to meet market demands, they are building new services with systems of engagement and innovation using newer technology, such as extended web services for mobile technology. In that, we see the old and the new working together, extending services with modern web architectures that work with legacy systems. Systems of engagement bring the business closer to its customers.

Another system that connects digital connectivity is the internet of things (IoT), a network of physical objects embedded with electronics, software, sensors, and network connectivity that collect and exchange data. The IoT allows objects to be sensed and controlled remotely across existing network infrastructure, creating opportunities for more direct integration between the physical world and computer-based systems. This gives improved efficiency, accuracy, and economic benefit.

When the IoT is augmented with sensors and actuators, the technology becomes a cyber-physical system that encompasses technologies such as smart grids, smart homes, intelligent transportation, and smart cities. Each thing is uniquely identifiable through its embedded computing system but interoperates within the existing internet infrastructure.

Having billions of things sensing, capturing, and controlling objects—and communicating with each other, other systems, and people—opens an enormous opportunity to transform growth and operations across all industries. This includes tackling operational challenges in the field, in inventory, in remote facility operations, and in end-user consumer experiences. The IoT gives feedback to determine when a robot needs to be serviced, where to improve traffic flow with traffic light control, how much medicine to administer via an IV pump, and even how to locate a wheelchair.

What does the IoT mean for IT? Before convergence, before the ubiquities of network connectivity, the advances in smaller electronics and distributed software were not within IT's scope. Now, IT's scope includes items like telephones, video cameras, wheelchairs, badge readers, and factory motors. Systems covering both the executive suite and the factory floor are involved, with thousands of dispersed systems now running on a common IP-based backbone. These systems run software code that needs to be maintained and generate massive amounts of data to be processed. This means more responsibility for IT but also more opportunities to help our organizations.

How many of your systems today have some IP connectivity that runs on your network and is the responsibility of someone else in your organization?

We must become aware of areas that now fall under our influence and begin to think about how they interact as systems that support the business—here we will find opportunities to help. This help can be embedded in business offerings through value platforms.

Value Platform

Today, most organizations rely on IT more than they know. Almost every commitment a company makes to the outside world, whether related to projects, operations, compliance, or financial reporting, requires IT. Yet many CEOs will still say, *"We're not Google or Microsoft. IT isn't a core competency. We can outsource this stuff."*

For most companies, IT functions as the nervous system of the organization. Many critical business functions are automated. Most innovation initiatives have technology components that require at least some level of change to existing digital infrastructure or IT processes.

Where do you find opportunities to help your organization? They can be found everywhere, every day, as they present themselves cloaked in problems, complaints, disruptions, threats, and the silent and unseen market needs.

Organizations that leverage their software developers to produce more embedded and impactful business process functionality, in both the front end and back end, position themselves to have the largest positive impact and contribution to the business.

To participate in business growth, IT can increase the value of its offerings by interfacing with other ecosystem partners to enhance the experience, improve the outcomes, and increase the touchpoints to drive bottom-line revenue growth and increase market share. We're all about speed to market and enhanced offerings a company cannot build on its own. We in IT need to connect with other technology geniuses to add more value and scale to what we provide. IT can leverage what we already have—including data stored in legacy systems—combine it with new sources of data, and connect it with third-party data sources and services. This will allow IT to bring new value to the marketplace.

Data fuels all these engagements, making them possible and allowing for improvement in the decisions a business makes at the point of customer interaction.

Everyone needs a support system (roles, authority, process, timely data, etc.) to make good decisions in their functions. The widespread disruptive market forces driving business transformation are leading to the need for more decision support for good and timely operational execution.

Operational Execution

Those who need to make decisions are widespread across the organization. In fact, all employees in an organization must make many daily decisions. At various levels decision-making is made at the board level, the C-suite, the line of business units, and the frontline workers. Risk management professionals, IT, and security teams are just some of the entities that make decisions every day. How these individual entities across their organizations make decisions directly impacts the odds of successful execution of a business strategy. Because of the very nature of the type of decisions that are made across the board, it can be overwhelming to find out where good decisions are being made and how to improve them in other areas. We must take consideration of the scale of the decision at hand, the time frame, and its relevance of importance compared to others.

What provides operational value is reducing uncertainty. When asking the business for more money, IT should embed qualitative features into the decision-making process. We need these to qualify our presentation of why it is in the company's best interest to do x, y, or z action. We can explain that we think project number five is better than project number four based on experience and facts.

Measurement requires a discovery process that surveys users for more information, runs experiments, creates models, and contextualizes what was captured beyond hunches. The goal is to find out exactly what a situation is. Does this line of business like this service we have been providing? If not, let us find out why and make a change. Which of a third party's features or benefits does the business unit like? What specific feature is used most often?

We can use surveying tools to find out exactly what is going on. When we bring as much clarity as possible to each component, we reduce uncertainty, thereby improving our overall chances of making better decisions.

In the absence of perfect knowledge of the future, decisions must be made under uncertainty. All the data in the world, no matter how good or easily accessible, can't substitute for the way you leverage data to support your decisions.

Making good decisions, big or small, is the difference between success and failure. The decisions being made every day could sabotage today's success and future market viability. Or they could secure them. That is why measurement is critical.

IT supports good decisions by reducing uncertainty and providing reliable data. IT chooses key business factors to discover data that enhances decision quality. The benefit is to reduce the chances better ideas are not identified and time is not wasted on the wrong actions.

It isn't easy to quickly determine the risks or rewards of a decision where there is no perfect information and uncertainty is a constant to be reckoned with. IT knows that reducing uncertainty to optimize the decision-making process is critical to reducing overall risk. IT can use measurements to gather data that grants an understanding of the real opportunities and risks. We need to ask questions about all this data pouring in to get answers around how we measure the intangibles inputs that would increase the chance of better outcomes; how we determine the intangibles we should measure and how do we do it; or how we recognize how to reliably reduce uncertainty about the decision.

Having data can now be considered a competitive advantage. The competitor who has the information first has the potential to take advantage of it first. In today's market, data is critical—it's a necessity to help give a return on investment, an opportunity to improve operational efficiency, and a chance to better mitigate risk.

Is your organization using its guts instead of the data? Consider the case of customer engagement. We can measure the very finest detail of user transactions. If we capture this, we can then feed pertinent information into our decision-making process. The digital world is observable and quantifiable. We are then using data instead of hunches to make decisions.

We have many decisions to make daily. Also, there are many things we do today that feed into decisions we must make tomorrow. In a complex landscape, the time to digest and process information can be very compressed. It is critical to have a methodology in place for framing the decision to be made, quickly getting the supporting data, and processing that data for decision analysis.

We don't necessarily need big data for decision analysis, but big data needs data science. We often have more data than we need. We must know how to frame our data to feed decisions more effectively.

We must be smart about data. Businesses run off clarity of data, answers, and insights. They journey from hypothesis to insight. Sometimes this happens in near real time. Information from IT is key to supporting this organizational endeavor.

Make sure you can track down answers to these types of questions such as, *"How long before a manager knows the lines are backing up?,"* *"How much extra gas is your truck fleet expending from using suboptimal routes?,"* or *"How long does a customer who walks into your store wait?"*

The number one way IT should support this process is by the effective refinement of raw data in a timely manner and the delivery of insights to those in the field to improve day-to-day business processes and operations. In doing so, IT supports decision-making through leveraging data in the daily operations of the business. Most organizations see unlimited uses for big data. Insights derived from this data can support strategic decisions made in the board room and operational decisions at point of customer interaction with your services. Big data can highlight the small clues to solving tough business problems.

The sheer volume and variety of new data generated worldwide are outstripping the current capability of organizations to manage, analyze, and act upon it. We in IT have an opportunity to tame these technical challenges. IT can extract the clear from the complex so businesses can focus on the insights and drive more customer value.

Business leaders trying to detect fraud, marketing directors looking for insights into customer buying patterns, salespersons trying to determine the next best strategy to increase profit, and the CEO determining the growth of the business as a whole all need to use data. IT itself is a consumer of information to optimize its operations.

We in IT understand that having data affords a business a tremendous opportunity, as it places it in a position to analyze and leverage its data to make operational intelligence possible. By using mathematics, data can be transformed into valuable insights.

Machine data is digital information, or raw data, created by the activity of digital nodes. Data science sorts through raw data to find relevant data that applies to specific decision-making processes. Machine data can be captured directly from devices, sent from a device to another node to be queried, or gathered from external observations of another node.

If the decision-making process is to improve, we first must understand the current process by which people are making their decisions. We need to know what is driving their choices. That can be a scary thing for some people, but it is in the best interest of the entire team to ensure decisions are based on the most relevant data at the time.

We are generally concerned about hunches. We don't want to stifle intuition-based decisions honed from years of experience, but when uncertainty can be reduced, incorrect hunches and bad assumptions can be minimized.

For example, a store manager may have a good feel for when to put more cashiers up front, a skill developed from experience. But if the extra cashiers are taken from their roles in the warehouse of unloading goods and shelving items, then that process could be starved of needed resources and ultimately frustrate shoppers looking at empty shelves. Every time the manager shifts personnel to the front, there could be a negative impact. If we can help inform the manager's decision with a combination of historical data on time to wait in line along with real-time tracking of the build-up of the lines, we may reveal a pattern that allows the manager to proactively schedule people in a way that optimizes both front-counter and back-end warehouse operations. This also has the benefit of giving other managers understanding regarding the underlying rationale for the manager's resource allocation, allowing the other store managers to potentially learn from this scenario.

A data-driven approach allows us to discover what we are doing wrong and right. It challenges some of our long-held assumptions and affirms other assumptions. We have many opinions that we sometimes treat as facts. Data can help when we don't necessarily know where we are wrong or only partly wrong. We need to start asking questions, having conversations, and learning from the data. When done right, data insights become a critical artifact of the decision-making process.

Scenario analysis feeds decision analysis, both for the business and for IT. How we make decisions is frequently as important as the decisions themselves. Every action, from whom to hire to what system to procure to whom to partner with for IT, is based on decisions. And there isn't just one way a business makes decisions. Choices of whether and how we should change our organizational structure, enter a new market, or change our strategy all utilize various methods for coming to these decisions.

Data science lends reliability to decisions. Data science doesn't disqualify intuition or wisdom. A data-driven culture is one in which personal experience, intuition, and data combine to give more a solid basis for choices. Hunches may work sometimes, but they can't be consistently counted on. They aren't based on enough information, context, and knowledge about a situation.

The purpose of data science is not to replace people but to aid them. The goal of data science is to inform the decision-making process, not to automate it. People can formulate good questions and use the principle of the scientific method to bring more rigor to the decision-making process.

Start leveraging the multiplying power of data-driven insights. Stop running your business on feelings and stale data. Instead of being prisoners to future certainty, we can let the data guide the way forward.

One concern that comes from too much uncertainty is decision overload. Complexity and speed force more decisions to be made and at a faster pace. When both the choices and outcomes are murky, the decision-making process can be even more difficult. The stakes can be very high, and if the outcome is negative, its impact can be devastating. With the number of decisions, from minor to life-altering, that come stream-ing in every day, business members can be overloaded.

IT can help with decision overload by sorting the data with data science.

Decisions affect the entire organization. In a digital world that promises everything with such ease, the choices put in front of us can seem sim-ilarly easy. They're not.

Making decisions on limited information with massive uncertainty can have negative consequences, depending on the context in which they are made. IT can transform at least some of the uncertainty into con-crete facts. Uncertainty can be the result of too many variables, many of which are out of our control. The first step in dealing with decision overload is to break up the problem into smaller bites or components and then determine which of the components are critical in choosing the direction to take or choice to make.

There are several questions IT needs to answer, such as:

- Is it cost-beneficial to move this to the cloud?
- How safe are we now?
- Is our competitor gaining on us? Should we outsource?
- Should we bring something back in-house?
- Should we upgrade?
- How can we break down the walls of our silos?
- How can we respond faster to the business's needs?

Decision overload can be stifling and produce sluggish business re-sponses because of analysis paralysis. IT can help.

Executing at a high level every day requires operational excellence. Every opportunity to improve the way your organization conducts busi-ness is an opportunity to save money, capture a new customer, and stave off the competition. High-performing organizations think differently to outpace their competitors.

At the heart of operational excellence are great processes. Healthy processes are the lifeblood of any organization. They impact everything from efficiency and quality to customer satisfaction and employee happiness. Even so, most companies lack healthy and effective processes.

Day-to-day information, visibility, and progress need to be readily available to frontline workers. Some of the features of improved frontline support for operational agility include:

- Distributed and secure communication
- Real-time data streams
- Visual process mapping
- Market intelligence
- Daily operations tracking
- A business response system

Too many businesses still operate in siloed information lanes where actionable information is slowed by organizational and operational friction. Management is tasked with dealing with all the components of a business, where the opportunities for improvement are, and where the threats lie. Management's purpose is to help your company gain system-wide, organizational visibility to become agile.

Another purpose of management is to remove friction from decision-making and response while painting a consolidated picture of current organizational health. In this case, management would include business process dashboards, visibility, alerting, and escalation processes. It would be accessible virtually, with secure communications to authorized employees and stakeholders. It would address the issues employees have keeping up with emails and voicemails.

The business would work with IT to build the relevant metrics, business rules, contexts, process assumptions, and operating methods. Then the data can be made available where needed, ensure system-level visibility, and greatly enhance the business's ability to adapt in real time to threats and opportunities.

This level of transparency can be scary for some—however, disruption, complexity, and risk require a level of agility that exceeds gut reaction, phone tag, email hell, wasted time in nonproductive meetings, and useless, out-of-date reports.

Operational feedback loops are important. All aspects of business operations can run better and, ultimately, positively affect the bottom line when everyone receives feedback on their daily activities. How well are we doing, where should we change course, and how close are we on target?

Organizations and their people must be ready to adapt. Be prepared, IT. When called upon to act, be ready to say *yes*.

Your organization's response to market threats can adapt in a variety of ways. Each response can trigger different downstream technology demands, changes, and new capabilities. This can happen by sensing the market shift early enough and making investments—to capitalize, make acquisitions, form strategic partnerships, develop tactical partnerships, use freelancers, implement a skunkworks project, or spin out talent in a start-up atmosphere. Here are just a few of the needs IT can respond to that you might overhear in the hallways:

- A security guard converses about a break-in at one of the warehouses, resulting in big financial losses. The IP surveillance cameras deployed at corporate last year were not extended out to remote locations because of the cost. He's asking if warehouse managers will be calling IT soon, and what new changes will be made to the infrastructure to accommodate surveillance across the business at more locations.

- Across the hallway, the VP of marketing is upset about her group's inability to locate the business's most common customers to direct a new campaign their way.

- Farther down the hallway, one of the truck drivers comes in and mentions the problems he is having with the routes he is being given; he thinks they are taking him a longer way.

- The manager of the call center mentions that her reps still can't pull up certain historical information when customers call in.

- A security analyst in the SOC remarks on the number of manual lookups across many disparate systems to resolve a single alert.

For IT, think of these as invaluable insights or opportunity signals—chances to improve a situation. Hanging around the business and looking to help is great. Be very aware of the context.

In the past, it was sufficient to receive a specific request—depending on what part of IT you were in. We did our part and moved on to the next task in the queue.

Today is a new day, a new age, when our impact on our organizations requires us to move further up the value creation stream. We see opportunities to partner more with the business for early indications of requirements, to ensure we have our bases covered. We are responsible for all technology-related code, hardware, and services that fuel the engine for business operations, innovation, and future growth.

Let us make sure we are ready, that we can deliver. Are we fit enough to keep pace with the business needs?

To be a driver in the transformation of a business, IT should work smarter so that that which needs to be done can be realized.

Decision Modeling

In the course of executing strategy and operating a business, risks are identified that need to be accounted for. Identified risk needs a response. There are various response options that an organization can take. Risk response is the planning that is part of the decision-making process to determine the best course of action in response to identified scenarios.

At the heart of business is the management of the decision-making process. Let's look at how technology is helping in the sports industry. The question of should a basketball coach rest their star player for an upcoming game is now a decision under consideration. A seemingly strange question years ago is common in today's game as it is believed to improve a team's chance of winning a championship. The team is leveraging analytics and smart devices to augment coaching staff observations of player health to inform the decision on whether a player should be held out of a game in a proactive move. Sports doctors surmise that wear and tear on basketball players' bodies leads to the increased probability of future injury. The hypothesis is you can head off potential injury by resting a player if you can get an indication of tiredness and undue wear on the joints of a player. Some teams have their players wear exercise sensors on their bodies during practices to help predict which player might be reaching exhaustion. If injuries to key players can be decreased, the chances of winning a championship can be increased.

That was an example of a decision that had meaning to that organization. For the thousands of decisions that are made every day across groups for big and small matters, it is useful to frame these various decisions to optimize the results. Successful businesses normally are disciplined about how they go about making decisions. One of the ways of improving the successful outcomes of decisions that businesses make is to create decision frameworks. These frameworks, designed and built from the inside, define decision criteria and process. This can be done for both decisions that need to be made every day and big consequential ones. They don't have to be complicated. The benefit is it makes clear who will make the final decision, who is involved, what the key elements are, and timelines. All decisions need information to help with the process. Sometimes that information is not readily available. When more information is needed, a useful tool to leverage is the value of information, which is the difference in economic value between the best courses of action with and without the additional information. The quality of your decisions can be improved by using the VOI. Our decision-making processes should leverage the VOI to make good use of our finite time and money in making decisions.

The value of information can be IT's best friend when making big decisions. It can help answer questions such as how much an outsider's help is worth when it can be handled inside your organization alone. For example, in the case of the pressure to "get it right," IT is navigating upcoming big decisions. Business is feeling market pressures. IT is feeling that pressure to deliver for their organizations.

Organizations have a portfolio of decisions that need to be made. The nature of the type of scenario analysis that we undertake as part of risk management is in support of various types of different decisions that need to be made. There are different types of tooling and approaches to structuring the process to optimize the time everyone spends making decisions. Ultimately, framing the decision process well improves the odds of a successful outcome. What kind of decisions are made that need support? There are various, crossing the spectrum between strategic, operational, and tactical dimensions or perspective. Scenario analysis feeds into various types of decision-making processes. And these various types occur on both the executive level and across different departments and groups spread across strategic, tactical, and operational decisions.

To reach organization goals, strategies are formulated that have longer-term plans. A strategy is an action plan that you will take in the future to achieve a defined goal—a plan of action designed to achieve a future goal. Strategic decision-making is a process of intentional management of actions and a series of plans to meet objectives, relating to the identification of long-term or overall aims and interests and the means of achieving them, and carefully designed or planned to serve the defined purpose. Strategic decisions are those that are more future-oriented and wider scale, relating to the identification of long-term or overall aims and interests along with the means of achieving them. This happens at the global level as well as in individual areas of the company. Examples include the implications of mergers and acquisitions, use of third-party vendors, and insuring against the downsides. Inside the cost structures of business activity are costs (expenses) and benefits (returns and revenue). To remain competitive and survive, organizations must make decisions that will maximize finite resources to meet their business objectives. Strategy is the action plan that takes you where you want to go. This plan must take into account the potential benefits and associated costs. Care must be given to foreseeable expenses involved with big decisions such as mergers and acquisitions activity. There was a case of the buyer taking a hit during this process after discovering a previously unreported cyber breach. It resulted in an increase in the final purchase price.

There are specific actions needed to be undertaken to achieve progress toward the defined goals. These actions are planned to serve a particular purpose. Tactical are those decisions that detail how to get things done. They support strategic decisions and inform operational ones. Tactical decision examples include *"Should we change vendors?"* or *"Which partner to choose?"*

Those tactics need to be acted upon and executed in the field. The details are worked out in operations. Organizational activities relate to the routine functioning of an organization. This is the operational dimension, which are the day-to-day scenarios we are all subjected to. Embedded into our business processes, projects, and initiatives.

Relating to the routine functioning and activities of a business or organization. Operational are those decisions that relate to the routine functioning and activities of an organization. Operational decisions are at the center of all business activities, in all industries, from determining the appropriate amount of credit to lend, to the hiring process, to onboarding a third-party entity, to deploying a new application, to calculating a customer loyalty discount. Every decision carry risk, and companies can pay a high price for poor decision-making both in terms of money and reputation. Decision rules are therefore defined to manage this risk. However, if only a minority have the expertise to understand and apply these rules, the consequences can be far-reaching. Decisions made without informed consideration are risky. Risks can materialize and costs incurred (such as customers becoming insolvent). Examples include response to emerging threats, onboarding new hires, doing background checks, insider threat monitoring, or leaking intellectual property to competitors. Other examples include the following:

- a loyalty discount may not be awarded because the decision criteria have not been clarified

- phishing (or security awareness training email filter, URL sandboxing, endpoint security)

- holding the door to the person behind you in a secured facility (or security awareness training, security cameras, security guards, clean desk policy, locked screen policy)

Realize consistent and optimal decisions day to day to reduce risk. Operational decision examples include response to emerging threats, exploit code available, onboarding, new hires, background checks, insider threat monitoring, holding door to person behind you in secured facility, clicking on phishing email (most common threat attack); or how to configure access control lists.

What happens after we have identified all our risks, triaged the ones that require immediate attention, and documented them in our risk registry? What's next? It is now time to determine our response. The lifecycle management of risk needs to be managed. The common risk management responses include avoid, accept, transfer, or mitigate. With the identification of risk through scenario analysis, we should have a register of risks specific to our organization. The options to response include avoidance, transference, acceptance, and mitigation.

Risk Response

In our various choices and responding to risk, the most obvious and easiest response is avoidance. To avoid a situation in a business environment, we can simply avoid the risk by avoiding said action. Risk analysis informs the avoidance option as a potential business decision. IT's role is to help enable the business to compete in the global marketplace. Often, avoidance is not a realistic option.

Another risk response option is transference. If in fact the business needs require us to undertake risky activities, then instead of avoiding it we can transfer the risk to a third party. The downside is that the third party cannot absorb or reimburse for all the potential financial losses. Your organization is still accountable to all its stakeholders. There could also be regulatory and legal restrictions on the scope of transference. Buying insurance is a popular example of transference. We do sustained losses that require financial payout, then the premiums on our insurance plan can cover some, much, or potentially all full financial liability.

A viable risk response is to just accept the risk. In this response we acknowledge the potential loss, understand the probability of a lost scenario occurring, and compare the mitigation cost and effort. Based on our risk appetite and risk tolerance we can legitimately make the decision to simply accept the last exposure. As in our everyday lives, we face a lot of uncertainty, yet we still seek new opportunities and take chances. There are a lot of situations that are unknown but nevertheless require us to take action that may lead to a future loss. There will be many scenarios that we have analyzed with this response, and acceptance is the best choice for organization. In the real world, though, rarely are there situations where no risk treatment has been done or no controls deployed, referred to as inherent risk. Some mitigations have already been made in our organization that provide some level of mitigation. Many loss scenarios will already have controls in place from previous investments. The next response is the most popular and most common one.

Mitigation is the most common response in an uncertain world. Mitigate means to lessen, to make less severe, to reduce the frequency, to lessen the blow. This means that we can competently go about the business of business in a competitive marketplace while taking chances with known uncertainties and unknown uncertainties with the knowledge that we have crafted effective responses that would mitigate potential unacceptable future losses. This is what makes it possible for organizations to be confident in their ability to take market chances to thrive. Transfer is a form of mitigation. Avoidance is a form of mitigation.

IT needs to think beyond the traditional thinking of adding a new technology, configuring a new firewall rule, or blocking an email attachment. Think about it from the business standpoint. The answers may look more like the sequence of move the data, change the contract with a supplier, not do work with a certain client-business mitigation.

The importance in considering both impact and likelihood really shows up when we get to the question about what to do with a particular loss scenario. To intelligently make risk-management decisions, we must prioritize mitigation efforts. One way is to annualize the loss scenarios, so the potential losses line up on the same time horizon as the cost of mitigations in the annual budget. Because of that reason, it is helpful to convert likelihood into frequency on an annual basis. So instead of a 40 percent chance of a loss occurring, we state a frequency of that occurring over the next year, such as once or twice. In situations where the scenario is rare, like once every five years, then this approach accounts for that on an annualized basis.

This also allows us to not be misled on a single loss event overriding high-frequency events. High-frequency events can have a larger loss impact than one large event. The quantification process is the true enabler for IT to mitigate business risk.

Mitigation investments can be compared among themselves and with other business-related budget items, all in the familiar dollars and cents in a yearly budget. Managing the risk landscape requires a system of managing the process mitigation at the organizational level.

IT needs to be in sync in addressing risk mitigation, as defined by business parameters, not technical constructs. We should address "alert fatigue" with targeted efforts. You can't manage what you can't see, and if you don't know the business impact and probabilities of occurrence, then you are blinded to what is important. You'll misapply controls and expend your time chasing alerts. You must identify, classify, and manage business assets.

On the infrastructure and controls that enable the defense of assets, you must see weaknesses and vulnerabilities to address the gaps and plan mitigation approaches. You must identify the threat actors pertinent to your industry and company, make current attacks visible, and understand their context in regard to risk to your business's assets. You must also determine business impact and probabilities of occurrence. In circumstances where the risk is likely and undesired, then IT must actively improve controls and defend.

Mitigation requires understanding the organization's risk tolerance and appetite, the probable impacts, and a framework to manage the process of continuous mitigation risk across the enterprise.

On our way to enabling this new business functionality, a large, unforeseen vulnerability opens that has the potential to be exploited by current active adversaries. We estimate a high likelihood that this vulnerability will be exploited in the upcoming holiday season that will open our business to potential brand damage. The challenge is balancing the potential business gains from this new functionality against the impact of damages. It is critical for IT and business to establish the framework ahead of time on how to assess and measure the potential downsides of these tough decisions.

There is a constant balancing act between innovation and control. At any time, from anywhere, all the chaos from unrestrained consumerization of IT must be balanced with the need of the business to mitigate against risk. Some have suggested this consumerization is unstoppable and that BYOD is a differentiation between hiring top talent and losing talent due to a traditional stodgy environment. While this may be true, the business owners who have liability and responsibility for the bottom line need the right information to make informed decisions on how to approach these challenges and potential risks. IT and the technology industry at large need to be more innovative. And business stakeholders need to be aware of the implications that new technology, functionality, and innovations add to the risk scale.

There is an inverse relationship between opportunity and the attack surface. Imagine if we could connect all our fleet vehicles with internet connectivity and pull performance metrics. Also imagine a thousand new endpoints exposed to the internet.

If you look closely, you will see that the attack surface has grown in correlation to the expanded opportunity for business. In its efforts to drive business growth, the organization and its employees look for opportunities to be more innovative. These efforts, accomplished by doing work differently, engaging customers in new ways, or using alternative techniques, often lead to different patterns of technology use that often fall out of scope of existing security controls.

The implications are clear that business owners need to be informed and educated on the changing control set requirements. Businesses will need to invest in modernizing their controls, infrastructure, and organizational structure to maintain pace. This will be critical as we do not want to stifle innovation or the productivity gains of the end user. Therefore, we mitigate unnecessary risk as the vendors and manufacturers work to catch up. IT must be ready to make the business case for the changes in investments needed to maintain pace with innovation and to maintain the minimum control update denominator.

For each identified risk, a response will be agreed upon. There are many mitigation types. Often in IT, we think only in terms of technical controls. Along with the tactical controls from IT, there are upstream administrative and operational mitigations from the business. IT needs to embrace a *"Yes, and"* approach to business requests and needs. IT gets to work on how the business can say yes to opportunity. Advise your business colleagues by informing and providing workable options. Plan to mitigate with approaches like tokenization, transfer portions of possible future losses with cyber insurance, and accept the rest.

A risk response is determined for each of the risks identified in consultation with the applicable risk owners. The specific response is determined based on the activity or condition posing the risk, background facts, and circumstances, including taking into consideration our overall risk tolerances. We must pick the best response for the situation. But to know which is the "best," these decisions must be risk informed. There are usually some controls in place somewhere. Don't limit your controls thinking to just more technology or people.

The name of the game for cybersecurity professionals is risk management. In most cases that will be some form of risk mitigation, and doing it cost effectively. IT must be good stewards of every dollar request. Our risk mitigations need to minimize the operational friction that interferes and slows down the business. Inform and advise stakeholders, in their language, to support their decision-making responsibilities.

Understanding is foundational for transforming our thinking to enable us to elevate our security programs. The skill to intentionally think multi-dimensionally allows us to see our problem space and work clearer. The next thing we need to inform our programs is context. We get that context by alignment with the business, enterprise risk management, and the technology infrastructure.

Part 2 – Align

Inform your security program by integrating with the rest of your organization.

Chapter 4
Business Context

Disruption, the interruption of an existing way of thinking and doing. Disruption interrupts today's current reality. Far from being a negative, disruption can enable new ways of thinking about how we work, live, and play. Disruption is occurring at the societal, market, and individual levels.

As a society, many people have experienced changes in how they live. With those changes has come a change in expectations regarding the speed of delivery. We expect faster service, faster access to data, free data, and the ability to receive value while being connected everywhere, all the time.

The relationship between consumer and seller has greatly changed, with more options to price compare, to switch services, and to pay as you go. Markets have been disrupted by transformational changes in the delivery models of goods and services. The time to get new product and services to market has shrunk significantly.

Every living thing must confront its very survival every day. IT must similarly understand the environment and know why it survives from day to day. The failure to understand both the business environment and market forces has led IT to undervalue its role in an organization.

We will explore three main areas of disruption that IT needs to understand: market landscape, business changes, and information technology landscape. Let's start with the market.

Market Landscape

IT works inside businesses, which operate inside of markets. Most businesses are for-profit organizations that sell value on the market to customers in exchange for compensation—normally money. The market may be physical like a retail outlet where people meet face-to-face, virtual like an online market, or a combination of both.

The disruption that impacts IT emerges from the larger market environment. To work with the changes this causes, we must look at the effect technologies, innovators, and inventions have on the market. IT responds to the business, which responds to the market forces and the players inside it.

Technology is the raw source of market disruption. Humans have used or invented technology from the beginning. With each new tool, people have advanced and improved the capabilities to meet human needs. Because humans have built worldwide infrastructures, the supply chain of goods and services now crosses continents to serve billions daily.

Disruption Engine

The engine of market disruption drives change. The conversion of an idea into reality lies at the heart of global changes. Humans disrupt status quo through ingenuity, innovation, and technology.

Ingenuity drives human progress. When confronted with challenges and constraints, we humans adapt, experiment, find new approaches, and generate new ideas. Otherwise, we do not survive.

Further, this ingenuity applies to more than basic physical needs. Being inventive also applies to higher-order challenges. We can see this through many lenses in our world: an observer turned inventor who notices a problem, then explores, experiments on, and tries to improve the situation; a business that pivots in strategy to correct failing performance by using an unorthodox approach; a professional athlete who outwits their opponent by shifting tactics to win the game; a doctor who alters their treatment regimen to help a sick patient; or an engineer who finds an alternative way of reinforcing a structure. In all of these examples, the necessary adaptions were not necessarily known in advance, nor obvious, nor easy to come by. Ingenuity is all about overcoming obstacles.

Innovation drives human progress. Humans use resources in new ways to solve problems. Innovation builds new things. Innovation changes what's now into what can be. Whether innovating to survive or to be curious, people continually seek that next version. Author Stephen Shapiro says:

> Very simply put, innovation is about staying relevant. We are in a time of unprecedented change. As a result, what may have helped an organization be successful in the past could potentially be the cause of their failure in the future. Companies need to adapt and evolve to meet the ever-changing needs of their constituents.[45]

From inventing electricity that lets us keep being productive after the sun goes down to figuring out ways to preserve food to be consumed across the oceans months later, humans are always introducing new ideas for living. When you combine ingenuity with innovation, you get amazingly improved standards of living. But when you add an accelerator—called technology—everything speeds up.

Technology enables human progress. People are at the center of ingenuity, innovation, and technology. IT provides the support for that technology. Technology can be the knowledge of techniques and processes. It is often embedded in machines.

Human life in the last century has been supercharged with change. We have discovered the capacity to sustain life longer for more people.

We've shrunk the world. We've shrunk space. We've sped up time. All of that happened with technology.

To illustrate the speed of change, Gordon Moore (age ninety-one at the time of this writing and the inventor of the series of microprocessors found in most personal computers) once observed that the number of transistors in an integrated circuit doubles about every two years.[46] His observation, now known as Moore's Law, reminds us that the speed and capability of computers can be expected to double every two years or less. We in IT are responsible for not only keeping up with changing technologies but also teaching our companies how to do so.

Technology is an enabler of human ingenuity and innovation to drive progress. Technology multiplies human abilities.

Global Scale

The scale of all this disruption is global. To get a grasp of the scale of technology impact on humans, let's look at the number of people on this planet and the economies that support us all. The human global population numbers in the billions. It's estimated to have reached 7.7 billion people as of April 2019. It took over 200,000 years of human history for the world's population to reach 1 billion, and only 200 years more to reach 7 billion.[47]

And we are a mobile species. Millions of people travel the globe for business and pleasure. Both people and goods are transported world-wide via air, land, rail, and sea.

The world economy consists of 193 economies. Of these, the United States is the largest. "Gross domestic product" (GDP) is the measurement of the value of economic activity within a country. As per World Bank estimates, the nominal world GDP was around $80 trillion in 2017 and around $84 trillion in 2018.[48] It was approximately $86 trillion in 2019.[49]

Combined, these economies have buyers and sellers that transcend worldwide geographical space. Global supply chains with major transportation infrastructures provide the capacity to serve billions of consumers that are facilitated by millions of suppliers.

Global supply chains seek economies of scale so parts can be put together elsewhere and then shipped anywhere on the planet. Let's look more closely at the US market.

Macro forces impact the very nature of a business's lifespan. Just look at the S&P 500 of today compared to members in the 1950s. Innosight, a growth strategy consulting firm, along with author Richard Foster, conducted research on corporate longevity:

> In 1958, the average tenure of a company on that list was sixty-one years. But by 2016 that number had been reduced to twenty-four years. The data suggests this pattern will continue. At the current rate of churn, about half the list will be replaced in the next decade. And by 2027 the average tenure will shrink to just twelve years.[50]

The average holding time for a stock has gone from eight years to five days. What does someone who holds a stock for five days care about? You guessed it—quick returns.[51] Because the average lifespan of a company is decreasing, business models must change. Fewer workers are needed, less infrastructure is required, less capital is needed, and there are new means of entry into the market.

Over the next decade, half of the companies listed on the S&P 500 will be replaced. In another study by Innosight on creative destruction, more trends of the lifespans of companies are explored; there are some interesting findings:

> In the past seven years alone, many renowned companies have been jettisoned from the S&P list: Eastman Kodak, National Semiconductor, Sprint, US Steel, Dell, and the New York Times.

New companies to the list include Facebook, PayPal, Level 3 Communications, Under Armour, Seagate Technology, and Netflix. In tracking all the comings and goings to the S&P 500 for the last 50 years, the study shows that the duration companies spend on the list fluctuates in cycles mirroring the overall state of the economy and disruption from new technologies, including biotech breakthroughs, social media, and cloud computing.[52]

Companies fall off the list because of bankruptcies, market share loss, mergers, and acquisitions. Also, new start-ups with multibillion-dollar valuations positioned for initial public offerings (IPOs) and eligibility push them out. Long-term survival is not possible without transforming core business models.

International Trade

Humans continue to trade on an international scale. The world is flat. Next door extends around the world. Look at how Investopedia describes international trade:

If you walk into a supermarket and can buy South American bananas, Brazilian coffee, and a bottle of South African wine, you are experiencing the effects of international trade. International trade allows us to expand markets for both goods and services that otherwise may not have been available to us. It is the reason why you can pick between a Japanese, German, or American car. As a result of international trade, the market contains greater competition and therefore more competitive prices, which brings a cheaper product home to the consumer.[53]

Global trade allows people around the world to gain access to non-locally sourced goods. Logistics are handled by publicly traded multinational corporations, which happen to be home to some of the largest and most influential companies of the modern age.

Economic Impact

Economic growth drives an increase in productivity. That productivity is a major factor in GDP growth. Increases in labor productivity have historically been the most important source of real per capita economic growth. That productivity has been tied to technological progress.

Everything and everyone are in flux. Technology, business models, producers, and consumers are all changing. The boundaries between industries are fading as more companies swim in overlapping lanes. New market leaders continue to emerge. Laggards will be left behind. The only truth in today's world is to expect the unexpected and adapt fast.

By itself, disruption isn't enough to account for all of the changes across the marketplaces. Here is where we begin to look at the macro forces that drive the rapid changes in both our personal and professional lives.

When disruptions happen in the global marketplace, we feel the impacts at home. These impacts can be on the price of bread, the state of a national election, or the ability of a worker to make a living wage. Technology drives massive changes in commerce. It impacts every industry and vertical, from brick-and-mortar retail businesses to education, utilities, and manufacturing.

Industry Faces of Disruption

Disruption has many faces. What does disruption look like from the perspective of individual industries? Digitization is transforming the oil and gas industry, including areas like upstream producers of oil and gas. The game has expanded from just big production to better margins and increased efficiencies as oil and gas operators have embraced digitization.

Disruption also shows up in industries such as agriculture, finance, legal, healthcare, entertainment, the news industry, and automotive verticals. New terminology is popping up to describe them: agtech, fintech, legal tech, healthtech, etc. We are on pace to add *tech* to the end of all verticals and industries. Where technology intersects with available capital to be invested, you will continue to see this convergence.

The Walt Disney Company has undertaken major digital transformation efforts. Disney invested about a billion dollars in internet of things (IoT) sensors to be used throughout their parks. Guests who attend Disney World get a wristband that uses RFID technology to store "FastPass" ride choices, act as payment, serve as hotel room keys, and more. Disney collects data as their customers use these bands to find more ways to improve the user experience.[54]

In the automobile industry, companies like Carvana are changing the car buying experience by solving several common frustrations. Carvana's e-commerce platform for buying used cars provides consumers with transparent pricing and a wide selection of options. Consumers can research cars, inspect a car using imaging technology, obtain financing and warranty coverage, purchase the vehicle, and schedule delivery—all before they come to the car lot. In 2019, Carvana became the third-largest used car retailer in the US.[55]

If customers want similar flexibility when buying a home, they can turn to Rocket Mortgage, an online mobile experience to streamline the load application and back-end processing.

Interest in the intelligent use of technology for agtech makes sense. Market potential is limitless because our appetites are, too. Mike Macrie, former CIO of Land O'Lakes, said during their digital transformation drive during the mid-2010s:

> In our IT organization here at Land O'Lakes we are working with our business leaders and everyone out in the field to help our membership—which is farmers and agricultural retailers—

transform the way they think about technology. Everything from operations to the way they trade, and deal with their customer. It [affects] every aspect of everything they do, and many aspects of everything we do here. The one that's the most exciting though, is how technology is transforming what happens on the farm. I think we are just at the beginning of that, but at Land O'Lakes we want to be a leader in that space. We believe we help farmers with decisions in agriculture—in the way they grow, make decisions in planting, and make decisions in environmental questions. We believe that technology is going to radically change the way they make those decisions in the future, and we want to be in the forefront of that.[56]

Other agtech disruptions include cows being monitored with Fitbit watches,[57] farming equipment using GPS satellite photos to help make decisions, and artificial intelligence using large amounts of data to direct where seed is put.

Businesses are looking for market shifts. You're a critical member of the team when you grow the skill to look beyond the horizon and better anticipate when and where shifts will happen. You provide value and a competitive advantage. Team members who affect the bottom line affect the growth rate and outlook of the company. Market shifts just might keep your company in business.

Market Players

There are various players in the market. From your IT perspective, notice what market your business orients around to find leading indicators of new ways to apply new technology to customer needs. In each case, there will be risks that could negatively affect the bottom line and opportunities that provide new possibilities to intervene earlier in your organization's strategic choices.

You can also look at market conditions through two different prisms. The first is the current state, and the second is thinking differently. The first prism, the status quo, maintains the current value proposition and customer service. Before this recent age of rapid disruption, this period of stability could be lengthy. Now it's brief. The second prism is thinking differently, which involves seeing the need for new approaches that add value in the marketplace.

The market has producers and consumers. Producers create the products, services, and experiences, and sell them into the marketplace. Consumers are those who buy them. There are two types of producers: incumbents and challengers.

First, let's look at the incumbent that has established its value to its customers. The opportunities here are for controlling the pace of change with the express purpose of anticipating future competitor pressures, and for looking at transformation, innovation, and change.

The goal for the incumbent is to continually bring value to a customer base while also increasing its market share. The threats for the incumbent are the innovators, those upstarts attracting customers away from your goods and services. Over time, this can lead to loss in market share.

Second, let's take the perspective of a challenger looking to break into an existing or new market. This could be either a start-up or an existing company that has the opportunity to rethink the value proposition and market position. This challenger looks for gaps in the existing product lines and reimagines the core customer needs. The threat for the challenger lies in their inability to break into the market because of the difficulties in taking market share from established brands.

Both the incumbent and the challenger can be innovators and can introduce new methods, ideas, services, and products.

We are in a world that is thinking differently. How we manage business interactions, how we enable business innovation, processes, and services, how we consume new technology, and how we mitigate new risks introduced by technology are all up for rethinking.

In one sense, the challengers may have access to more resources. One opportunity is to create start-ups within our own organizations. Start-up methodologies can be used by both small teams and large enterprises. These methodologies are not limited to the size of the company or the type of industry.

Your business can also look for value gaps. Instead of slogging it out in common areas, your business can create uncontested market space and float to the top of innovation, relevance, and value to your customers. Is what you are working on today doing that? Are you doing okay playing in the same solution and product space as your competitors?

Existing businesses have an immense amount of knowledge, resources, and market access. Does what you produce match that? Are you producing the type of outcomes and experiences the market wants or needs?

We should be listening to see where our organizations stand. Continuous experimentation is a characteristic of start-ups and challengers because they don't limit themselves to just one effort. They try again and again, observe the impact, adjust their assumptions, and see what else is possible.

Private equity, venture capitals, and start-ups are having a large impact on the markets. Injecting new ideas and approaches along with alternative funding mechanisms is accelerating market change. Today, start-ups have some advantages over traditional business models. We live in an era where small firms—as small as one person—can start a new business competing with larger and established companies. The disruptive forces in today's digital economy allow small, nimble groups to experiment, and then take advantage of what works.

The advent of digital technology and other disruptive forces have lowered the barrier to entry from a capital investment and infrastructural standpoint. All the infrastructure one needs to start a business in the digital economy can be used with pay-as-you-go and pay-for-what-you-use consumption models from external providers. This includes everything from accounting to human resources systems, marketing, and sales tools. Many traditional systems needed to operate businesses are available online.

An even greater benefit of the low entry barrier is the ability to start and stop services with little to no hassle, as opposed to traditional businesses that may require large lead times for IT to deploy new systems. Young start-up companies can go out to the cloud, provision a sales campaign, try it out, and tear it down in a relatively short period of time. This is an extreme advantage in seeing what works.

On the other hand, larger, more established companies also can access the same type of services in this disruptive market. It's not large versus small as much as it is attentive versus complacent.

For example, traditional customer relationship management systems have involved large and long IT processes to deliver information to businesses. Long project lead times, lots of customization, decreased integration time, and many failed deployments mean businesses are now looking to cloud services to deploy these types of back-office solutions. The same goes for customer-facing digital engagement tools.

Salesforce, a great success story, allows the sales team of your business, regardless of size, to bypass IT and go straight to an established setup. It is one of the most well-known cloud-based solutions in the world. Others include Dropbox, a file-sharing app; Slack, a collaboration platform; and Google Hangouts, a chat, voice, and video communications solution. Many systems traditionally deployed by IT are now directly available to businesses via the cloud.

Changing Business Models

Business models are being rapidly transformed. Business transformation is about more than outcomes. It's also about the experience. Business models are changing who an organization partners with to deliver their goods and services. Organizations can adapt customer interfaces, payment methods, support interfaces, and speed of responses. They can augment their offerings with more personalized experiences. You can be the one who experiments with more channels to deliver value, who bundles more features, or who separates micro features to target customers' preferences.

Depending on which industry you are in, digital disruption can come in many forms or from many different sectors. The digital economy allows the technology enterprise of the digital world to coexist and interact with the physical world. Many consumers are willing to pay more based on how they feel about a given consumption choice.

Consumers worldwide have embraced the digital storefront, but industries that still require physical labor, such as construction, are heavily influenced on the back end by technology. The leading start-up companies in the tech field, along with traditional marketing firms, law firms, and the medical fields, are changing their revenue streams in areas where traditional models of profiting off sales have been static.

Customer experience is driving companies to be intentional in their value proposition. Changes to the buying experience continue to occur in the new digital world. To purchase a new item, one can go to a website or a traditional brick-and-mortar store. Many industries traditionally immune to rapid technology changes, especially on the front end, are making many changes on the back end to transform business processes.

Customers are also feeling the disruption. Consider the experience of the customer faced with an overwhelming number of choices in food, clothing, music, and more. Companies are competing to capture the attention of the end user. IT teams must choose to vie continually to improve and innovate their companies' digital storefronts.

Amazon is the most obvious online storefront where you can shop for food, music, magazines, electronics, books, spare parts, appliances, toys, office supplies, and more. Walmart now competes with Amazon, having expanded from a traditional brick-and-mortar store to an online storefront that sells many of the same items Amazon offers. Walmart is just one example of a business that has responded effectively to technology-driven disruption. Most businesses across most industries, both large and small, are seeing some dramatic changes in how they do their work.

IT is clearly feeling the effects of this disruption. It is important for IT to understand what these changes mean to the revenue stream and how technology must be best positioned to adapt to the changing environment.

There are roadblocks to success. A common response to market pressures is to leverage technology to drive digital transformation. This initially seems wise. But we're discovering that there are other dimensions to success. Two roadblocks to being successful in changing business models stand out for waste of finite resources, in particular money and time.

The first roadblock is failed strategy execution efforts that miss out on potential revenue. In 2018, enterprises were expected to invest $1.3 trillion in digital transformation initiatives to apply digital capabilities to improve efficiencies, increase customer value, and create new monetization opportunities. Tragically, research tells us that 70 percent of these initiatives will not reach their stated goals. That equates to over $900 billion worth of spend that will miss the mark.[58] This is mismanagement on a colossal scale. That is dangerously close to al-most a trillion-dollar hole in organizational strategy.

Success in managing market transformations is completely dependent on employees working together at all levels and in all units to achieve a program's goals. The whole company must unite to drive success.

This sounds easy and obvious. Unfortunately, most organizations build silos that result in functional areas refusing to, or struggling to, com-municate and collaborate.

A second roadblock is the waste of time on non-value adding tasks, in that much of the day's work is presented in the form of "shadow work," such as administrative tasks, meetings, answering emails, etc. While there is typically some level of value in these functions, we all recognize that shadow work is a prime work type to remove from a worker's plate. How many status meetings would be eliminated by an auto-mated reporting mechanism? How much time could be saved by re-placing email hunting with an interface that has defined fields that cap-ture the needed context?

So, in order to change, we've got to overcome the silos and shadow work with the right mindset. Together—and only together—can we find the organizational practices that bring effective change. These market forces are putting pressure on businesses to change. These changes are in turn having an impact on both the structure of organi-zations and nature of work itself.

Business Changes

Executives seem stuck in their day-to-day operations to pay the bills and meet quarterly targets. The US government seems to desperately lack long-term planning due to the short-term objectives of policymak-ers and special interest groups.

Neither private companies nor governments have to stay caught looking in the short term. They can reinvent themselves and use technology differently. John Chambers, former CEO and chairman of the board for Cisco Systems, noted:

> If you're a leader in today's world, whether you're a government leader or a business leader, you have to focus on the fact that this is the biggest technology transition ever. This digital era will dwarf what's occurred in the information era and the value of the Internet today. As leaders, if you don't transform and use this technology differently—if you don't reinvent yourself, change your organization structure; if you don't talk about speed of innovation—you're going to get disrupted. And it'll be a brutal disruption, where the majority of companies will not exist in a meaningful way 10 to 15 years from now.[59]

The C-suite is under tremendous pressure to deliver bottom-line results: increased revenues, more profit, and lower operating costs. The intelligent use of technology can help, along with updates to business model components.

The market landscape is changing alongside the exponential growth of technology-enabled business models. It is not the technology itself that is disruptive, but rather the business models and market changes.

With these changes come the consumer expectations of near-instant satisfaction and choice. This makes value offerings less sticky, and the pressure to escape commoditization more challenging.

If internal IT is not ready, executives may choose alternative external consumption models. Today, businesses have many options for provisioning services, applications, infrastructure, and end nodes. Consumption models focus on how these resources are procured, paid for, and maintained. It is of great interest to the C-suite, particularly CFOs, to know how procurement of needed services affects cash flow.

Consumption models allow flexibility for both IT and the business. A business might look completely to the cloud for its IT services. Business units have shown a propensity for buying services from external sources. It's tempting to go to the speed and convenience of Amazon or Azure when a developer in a business unit needs to provision new cloud-based capacity.

But the reality is that most consumption models will take a hybrid approach for the foreseeable future. Most companies will continue in the traditional way, while others will be farmed out to multiple cloud providers. These third-party services offer a multitude of service-level agreements, payment types, and contracts.

If the system is mission-critical or contains intellectual property, it may be prudent to keep it in-house. However, a new customer-facing portal could be built in the cloud and connected to the internal back-end systems. Many design approaches are available to meet business needs. These consumption models do allow for agility, but they also have the potential to open the business to increased complexities and risk. Changes tend to create pressure on the internal structure of businesses.

Organization Structure

There are many changes to business's organizational structures. The incumbents are having to adapt. Digital disruption is forcing organizational structure changes such as altering reporting structures, division layouts, cost structures, and compensation packages.

Businesses are changing their structures to improve operational flexibility and their ability to adapt to market conditions.

Because of the decreased time available to make decisions and the resulting decreased time-to-market, the organizational structure of many modern-day companies is becoming flatter, providing fewer middlemen and faster access between the executive team and front-line employees.

Digital disruption also calls for more flexibility in team creation to allow for more innovation.

New roles are being created with titles like chief technology officer, chief innovation officer, and chief risk officer. CIOs and CISOs are interfacing more with their boards and having to speak in more business language. These changes give rise to opportunities for new skill sets and add a warning for those unwilling or unable to make the change.

Increasing reliance on a growing ecosystem of partners and suppliers is another characteristic of digital disruption, along with a reduction in some internal functions and human resource processes, such as provisioning and facility services.

In addition, the ratio of permanent versus as-needed staff is increasing as the freelance market grows. Independent workers make up a large pool of highly skilled professionals available on demand to organizations. A *Fast Company* article titled "6 Ways Work Will Change In 2016" stated that "finding and onboarding talent in the brick-and-mortar world takes an average of 43 days, compared with three days in the virtual world."[60]

You can create or augment your teams with freelancers who can work remotely on an as-needed basis.

Work structures that are adaptable encompass functional job titles, leaner reporting structures, and openness to cooperate with former competitors. Flattening the organizational structure includes organizing in circles (rather than by hierarchical org charts), mixing reporting, and developing communication channels closer to the source of the work.

Workforce Changes

There are changes in the workforce. The demographics are changing in the US and its businesses. The gender, racial, religious, nationality, and age makeup of the workforce is becoming more inclusive and diverse. The next decade will see new faces in the workforce with new skill sets, ideas, norms, and expectations.

Demographic Changes

There are changes in the demographic of the workforce. Consider this from Robert Howell, a senior partner at Howell Group LLC:

> Three major demographics that will significantly influence business in the coming decade: First, the aging population as the "baby boomers" move into super-senior status; second, the increasing proportion of non-whites (African Americans, Hispanics, Asian Americans, and others) in the US census base; and third, the heightened technological competencies of the millennials and their successors. Obviously, business will have to address, and is already doing so, these major demographic shifts.[61]

The aging of the workforce opens the question of organizational knowledge drain. Too often companies create a firm dichotomy that diminishes respect and prejudices workers against differing age or experience (either toward older or younger, newer, or more experienced). Similar to the way businesses need diversity in gender and culture, we need diversity in experience and age. Otherwise, we create discrimination that drains resources from our companies.

When someone with decades of time on the job retires, that intimate knowledge of what makes a company tick may not transfer well to newer workers entering the company. Manuals, wikis, and SharePoint may not capture the know-how and wisdom accumulated over the years by the baby boomers. The ability to troubleshoot problems and create workarounds is too frequently lost. What can IT do to preserve the company's canon of brilliance?

The expectations of the new generation of workers born in the digital age are different. Legacy technology experiences and processes, such as corporate-issued laptops, document sharing via email, or clunky knowledge-sharing portals, can stifle the enthusiasm of new workers and hurt company productivity. On the other hand, established processes can free new workers to pour more energy into innovating rather than expending energy reinventing the wheel. Manager-worker dynamics are also being disrupted by the new generation's worldviews and expectations.

Nature of Work

The nature of work itself is changing. With the sharing economy, the gig economy, consultants, part-timers, and virtual work environments, greater numbers of office workers are on the move than ever before. These factors can result in less face time with coworkers and more delayed responses, or they can result in more nimble face time and responses.

Your ability to stop and intelligently respond to requests is challenged when you are in constant motion, whether you're running down the office hallway or scheduling dozens of virtual meetings per day.

How we work is changing, and that's not necessarily a bad thing. But we in IT do need to meet the needs of these changes. Teams are telecommuting, collaborating over Zoom calls with team members all over the world, and sharing information remotely. This raises significant cybersecurity threats at the same time as it increases revenue-building options.

The location of work is changing, too. People work from places like Starbucks, the airport, or the lobby of an office building.

Workers can give commands from the field in a variety of ways—supervisory control and data acquisition systems for allowing remote operations of infrastructure, remote apps controlling building control systems, or soldiers in US facilities conducting remote aerial drone flights halfway around the globe.

Surgery offers an unexpected remote application. When a surgeon uses a surgical instrument to make a cut during a procedure, they don't always use their own hands. They could be hundreds of miles away from the surgery room, operating the mechanical instruments from a remote console. IT applications for remote surgeries can literally save lives.

No longer restricted to a computer cable in the corporate office, many workers in many industries conduct work on smartphones or connect remotely from laptops while on the road. Such mobilization means the unshackling of the worker from the organization's physical real estate. This in turn allows some companies to downsize and close physical offices. For the fieldworker, it means more face time with clients and less time commuting to the office to fill out paperwork. It means optimizing everyday tasks such as expense reimbursement, timecard submissions, forecast information updates, and customer record reviews in real time. Location is no longer a constraint. We can go to the talent rather than insist the talent come to us.

There are some drawbacks if this is not done correctly. Remote users can become isolated and feel alone. The lack of physical presence with coworkers can lead to excessive back-and-forth emails and a lack of accountability. Work is a human endeavor; and being isolated from others for too long can fragment the experience and decrease creative collaboration.

Some businesses follow the motto of "mobile first" by building more business apps for mobile platforms, leveraging new collaboration tools, and allowing creative freedom in the professional workforce. There are tradeoffs, however. More flexibility in schedules allows for more free-dom in home or work priorities; but this also means the business can reach into workers' personal lives, extending work from morning to night and into weekends.

The massive changes to the market, businesses, and work itself drive changes to IT.

Information Technology Landscape

Market conditions change faster than traditional strategy turnaround times. The time to analyze a situation and respond to both competitor and consumer is shrinking. To keep competitors from launching initia-tives before we make a decision, organizations must detect oncoming changes to manage time-to-market.

Innovations include creative ideas, new ways of engaging customers, or new ways of finding spots to drill for oil. Most new business initia-tives have a technology component. The question for IT is simple: How long will that take? Then, how will we beat that deadline?

As IT professionals, we must be mindful of speed and understand that slow response feeds shadow IT, the unofficial use of technology outside management control. We must be agile enough to adapt quickly while positioning ourselves to help our businesses. IT cannot be the reason time-to-market is delayed. When IT is too slow, we decrease the choices a business has. We decrease its velocity, agility, and flexibility in a highly competitive market. When IT becomes the bottleneck, IT becomes a barrier to business success.

The landscape that IT operates in is different from how it was in the past. The usual places IT turns to for technology are being disrupted. To illustrate this change, look at a 2015 statement from John Cham-bers:

Cisco has changed more in the past year, as we position ourselves for the future, than we have any five years before this.
Over the past six months, we have reorganized the entire company. Almost 70 percent of our engineers are now doing something different for us. We had to do some very painful things like
laying off 7,000 people and hiring back 6,000 with different skill
sets. We have moved from selling boxes to selling outcomes.[62]

Questions for IT to ask based on this new landscape include the following:

- Is the business cherry-picking the healthiest patients and the
  top students?

- What are the challenges of the legacy infrastructure being left
  behind?

- Is IT being left with the heavy lifting, while other lines of businesses take the easier productivity tools and simpler workload
  to the cloud?

- Is IT being short-changed on funds?

IT is often asked to operate existing infrastructure, which includes
maintenance and compliance with regulatory requirements, while also
putting a focus on innovation and growth.

Legacy systems and applications sometimes restrict what IT can do. Often, these legacy systems are mission-critical but run old code that few
modern programmers understand. The systems may even use hardware no longer supported by the manufacturers. In some cases, the
manufacturers have gone out of business. IT can upgrade and migrate
these systems but may be constrained by cost and/or the difficulty to
technically accomplish it.

Traditionally, IT has been held to what today seems like an eternity in
refresh cycles: five, six, maybe even ten years. Some businesses

operating under these systems may believe that if something isn't broken, there is no need to expend the money for major upgrades. This can constrain IT's ability to take advantage of technology capabilities that could help the business solve significant market challenges.

Also, depending on older systems puts enormous strain on getting each new budget request just right, as IT fears the next new thing may be just around the corner when they receive their new gear. We fear getting it wrong, and those fears are compounded by the uncertainty in the technology supply chain.

Technology Supply Chain

The beginning of this century has seen an acceleration in mergers, acquisitions, consolidations, splits, spin-ins, spin-offs, and partnerships in the technology ecosystem. This has involved hardware manufacturers, software developers, service providers, and integrators. Together they comprise a large network of inputs to an organization's technology needs.

IT relies on this network to provide a chain of technology—raw, semi-processed, workforce augmentation, and as-a-service—to get the job done. This technology supply chain network is a system of organizations, people, activities, information, entities, and resources responsible for supplying the components of technology services.

The vendor industry is in transition. Companies that start today grow up in the age of the cloud, requiring less capital expenditure on infrastructure. And this means a direct challenge to existing vendors' on-premises infrastructure products. There is significantly less friction between business's needs and technology buying—because of flexible financing operational expenses, flexible time commitments, faster turnaround on new features, and shorter time to get new functionality into the hands of users.

How organizations view the vendors has also been disrupted. This is leading to massive changes in organizational structures, product mix, maintenance options, licensing options, and service contract structures. These changes result in shorter launch periods for new products and services as well as an increase in software offerings.

Vendor lock-in with companies like Oracle and SAP is expensive, has complicated licensing, and slows infrastructure request fulfillment, which in turn slows software developers.

Foes are entering into arrangements, friends are stepping on each other's toes, outside investors are increasingly merging existing players, and more ecosystems are developing. Many vendors are forced to adapt their business models to market forces and disruptors.

Young upstarts with new ideas may be right. Traditional thinkers may be right. One thing is certain; we all need each other's best.

It is both an exciting and challenging time. Traditionally, business requests for new systems would be vetted through the IT department, who would then go out into the vendor community looking for products and solutions. These vendors and manufacturers of products, hardware, and software traditionally had direct relationships with IT.

Now, buying technology outside of IT has become more common. The term *consumerization of IT* describes the cycle of information technology emerging in the consumer market and then spreading to business and government organizations.[63]

In the age of rapid disruption and the consumerization of IT, vendors are finding they must greatly adapt to the changing environment. Big-name players like Microsoft, Cisco, HP, Oracle, and Dell have in the last few years downsized by cutting tens of thousands of jobs, but at the same time they have created entirely new positions with different job requirements and technical focuses. These new positions have names like data analyst, cloud architect, software developer, and enterprise architect—all attempts to stay relevant and compete in the market-place.

Digital vendors compete hard against cloud providers as internal IT in-frastructure such as storage and computers are on a steady decline. In addition, desktop PC sales are on a decline, eclipsed by laptops, tablets, and smartphones.

Vendors also find the sales process has deftly changed in our new digi-tal economy. Whereas traditionally the vendors' sales forces pitched their *products* to IT, they now focus on systems and business outcomes.

With many IT products becoming commoditized, most information that IT has traditionally relied on the vendor for can now be searched for online. This can happen long before the vendor's salesperson can get on-site to make a pitch. As a result, vendors are adapting by offering more professional services, consulting work, and managed services to their offerings. This comes with options for cloud-assisted services or replacements for on-premises solutions. Some vendors are insourcing and spinning out parts of their company to innovate, while others are aggressively acquiring additional companies to diversify their offerings. Expect to continue to see consolidations, acquisitions, spin-offs, public-to-private moves, and private-to-public changes in the near future.

In today's environment, vendors must partner up to stay relevant. The technology stacks are too complex and varied for one vendor to cover the breadth of customer needs, even in a narrow vertical. As such, ven-dors are continually aligning themselves in strategic and sometimes tactical partnerships to bring a more complete level of service to their customers. To fail to do this invites the risk of being left behind, fol-lowed by market share decline.

If instead a vendor decides to go in a radically different direction with their solutions, they risk cannibalizing their existing revenue stream.

Existing customers may feel like the stability and roadmap they were pitched at initial purchase are being abandoned.

This dilemma helps explain a common business complaint about vendors—that they are not innovating enough, or they are too focused on maintenance with just an incremental improvement. As new upstarts force even more market changes, established vendors will have hard decisions to make about how to confront the innovator's dilemma.

The entire technology ecosystem is being impacted and disrupted: internal IT, third-party contractors, hardware manufacturers, cloud providers, software vendors, consultants, integrators, and value-added resellers (VARs).

All these entities are undergoing significant changes to their business models, requiring changes in go-to-market strategies, service offerings, and revenue models. Some of the largest manufacturers are significantly reducing headcount in some areas, while at the same time staffing up in new, emerging areas.

Partners, who include consultants, technology integrators, and VARs, are also feeling the effects of disruption. Having traditionally implemented vendors' choices with their specialties, many now add consulting services and managed offerings to get higher-margin business deals.

Differently from how they operated in the past, many VARs are adapting their value proposition. First, they now offer more businesses packaged solutions. Second, in response to margin compression because of commoditization, many VARs also add managed services solutions, such as taking care of a business's day-to-day operations. This allows for customized service with many options that have defined contract terms. Third, they are converting traditional in-house services into as-a-service models for customers. This is a fixed service that has a flexible usage model, meaning you can stop using them whenever you want.

Fourth, more VARs are getting into security and other advanced areas, such as big data, automation, and the IoT. Each of these have become very important emerging technology areas desired by its customers. VARs are selling solutions, not services.

Fifth, many VARs are acquiring emerging firms to expand their offerings, making acquisitions to provide a national presence. They also are getting their engineers more training and certifications.

In the partner landscape, many changes are occurring, such as VARs acquiring other firms to bolster their capabilities, customer relations, and reach.

Added to this, private equity has become attracted to the technology sector and is aggressively investing in integration and solution providers. Private equity is making plays to nationalize their reach by buying and consolidating target firms to provide end-to-end technology services.

The entire nature of buying IT has been disrupted by the rise of the cloud. Netflix completed its migration to the cloud in seven years. The cloud provided the scalability needed to grow the business and added the agility needed to keep up with future demand, which powered the end to physical rental stores.

Netflix used Amazon Web Services (AWS), which provided a global infrastructure that could scale on-demand services and provide the required availability of services. A side benefit was that the cost per streaming was significantly reduced compared to on-premises infrastructure. By going cloud native, Netflix was able to rebuild almost all its technology. This type of success story is happening to many companies.

Amazon, Google, Facebook, and others have disrupted the market, ushering in the age of the cloud. Upending the previously common ways of consuming technology via on-premises infrastructure, the cloud allows businesses to get out of the hardware business and reduces the friction of dealing with the plumbing by building a utility service. By off-loading infrastructure, the cloud frees up an organization's attention for the organization-specific work of its business. It appeals to the business's need for more agility and ease of use.

A frequently forgotten fact is that the cloud still uses hardware. It's a network of servers around the globe, each with a unique function. So, when any business calls on this vast network of connected servers (which operates as a pool of compute, storage, and network resources), that business has more resources than it would have had individually. It's no wonder then that cloud-based services increase the perception of internal IT being too slow.

Perception of service delivery speed is colored by cloud providers' specific offerings, similar to next-day delivery increasing the perception that standard mail through the postal service is slow, despite its exponentially lower cost. Also, cloud providers have created multiple flavors of offerings: software as a service (SaaS), platform as a service (PaaS), and infrastructure as a service (IaaS).

SaaS is, at the time of this writing, the most impactful offering. It is a complete solution, from the underlying hardware to the application itself and taking care of all operational tasks of maintenance. It is immediately available for business use. Salesforce, Workday, and Experian illustrate the ready-to-go option. Add to this the fact that your business users can go to well-crafted websites to get their questions answered, get a free trial with no lock-in, and find a convenient payment system. Your business just pulls out the corporate credit card, and they are up and running.

Marc Benioff, CEO of Salesforce, which owns the largest share of the customer relationship management (CRM) market, says, "When I look at the largest transactions...every transaction was done with the CEO.

I think it's really unusual, and that's why we're really selling more enterprise software than Oracle or SAP."[64]

PaaS provides benefits to software programmers looking to dive right into coding who don't want to deal with building the underlying technology stack with all its dependencies for their environment. PaaS also provides flexibility for programmers who don't have a problem with dependencies and just want quick access to virtual environments. More importantly, PaaS allows IT an easy way to scale its infrastructure and reduce capital expenditure requests.

IaaS allows IT to scale its computing power much more quickly and many times more inexpensively than procurement. It also has the benefit of allowing using these resources to be used on an as-needed basis when extra capacity is needed instead of permanently acquiring new infrastructure.

The cloud provides a new consumption model for technology, with ease of use, scalability, and high availability. You pay for only what you use. This provides businesses the flexibility to meet the demands of today's markets.

The cloud is disrupting the traditional path for businesses to procure new technology, as major players like Cisco and HP discovered after they failed to capture cloud market share from the likes of Amazon and Azure.

Hitting this home even further is the time when the CIA chose Amazon to build its private cloud. A traditional, private data center buildout could not compete with the efficiency of the technology Amazon had developed.

The changes caused by the *consumerization of IT* have been profound in expanding who does the technology shopping for organizations. Again, we IT members can become the next innovators. We just need to be mindful that employees are influenced by consumer market technologies at home that they would like to use in the workplace.

Consumerization of IT impacts internal IT by raising the expectations of business end users in several ways.

- End users and stakeholders measure time-to-delivery by IT against their experience with both personal mobile apps and the increasing availability of cloud versions of business-critical services.

- Consumerization presents consumption model differently. IT bills the business with both capital and operational expenses.

- The packaging of the technology use and delivery are expected to be seamless. Allowances are rare for maintenance downtime or for problem-solving.

- The packaging is expected to be more consumer or user friendly. No long meetings, prolonged information gathering efforts, or clunky interfaces. IT is in competition with the best the world has to offer. And that's not necessarily a bad thing.

End users have come to expect that the ease of use of technology in their personal lives should be matched at work by what IT provides. If they can provide a few details online and be using a new app in a few minutes, then they don't understand what the problem is the workplace. That is an interesting question. However, the issues of interoperability, governance, and security are requirements that must be worked through. We can't just wave a magic wand and enable a new feature. All that heavy lifting is left to IT, often without the corresponding upfront budget. This results in increased demands on IT and delivery times. Every new business request goes into the work queue along with requests to build and maintain more intricate and dependent systems.

Getting the organization and its end users what they need is our job in IT. The combination of three realities makes this a daunting challenge: the number of direct and after-the-fact requests, the speed at which the requests come in, and the large number of different types of requests.

Silos

Silos influence we all work. On the surface, *sales team*, *campus*, *organization*, *frontline*, and *partner* are terms that seem natural. They are characterized by being different enough by their context to be understood by most people. They have some form or boundaries for distinction. But look closer, and you'll notice something more fascinating. Dave Gray, founder of XPLANE, says, "Most boundaries are convenient fictions. What divides the people who are 'on' a team from those who are not? What separates one company, department, or division from another, or an employee from a customer? Boundaries give life structure, which makes us comfortable."[65]

But are those boundaries good for businesses and team members?

Silos are everywhere—in the physical world, in the digital world, among groups of people, surrounding processes, and in every aspect of technology.

Focus less on the name *silo* and more on how silos manifest. Don't get hung up on the organizational structures in and of themselves, but focus more on shared goals, fast feedback, and information sharing.

A silo is an entity that functions apart from others. So where did silos come from? They are a byproduct of the way organizations have developed and been managed over the years. The existence of silos has the potential to affect mergers, acquisitions, and reorganizations. Do silos provide any value? Yes, but it's very limited and comes in the form of local optimization.

As with other departments and groups in our organizations, IT falls prey to the problems of silos. Similar to other departments/groups in the rest of the organization, silos have their origins in the division of labor and specialization that were designed to optimize throughput. The internal structure of the IT team can be very compartmentalized. This inhibits the sharing of knowledge, the brainstorming of initiatives, and the joint solving of problems among teams. Compartmentalization also leads to operational friction, where getting things done is bogged down and delayed in a structure not designed for the speed and response of a modern digital world.

Compartmentalization in IT also leads to unnecessary complexity, when instead we need all the streamlining we can get. Processes are opaque, frustrating both the business and the IT service delivery team. Increasing the speed to customer value is of prime importance.

There are three basic types of silos: human silos, process silos, and technical silos.

The first silos are human. Workers stay loyal to their unique groups or departments. Examples include those in development, operations, service desk help, networking, and security. These workers show more professionalism when they share ideas between silos and hear others' ideas. We in IT sometimes show a bit of arrogance about our preferred processes, rather than opening ourselves to learning from others what might work even better.

The second silos are processes. These might be a process used during customer interactions, such as digital business process that leverages existing knowledge in a database or might be a manual workflow that asks a user for the majority of data to be re-captured manually. We in IT might show a preference toward our area of expertise. Learning from others makes us look much smarter and more capable.

The third silos are technical. The layers of systems that IT manages, such as the infrastructure of tiered applications, data storage, or networking stacks, are often made, installed, and managed in isolation from one another. Each component has context that another upstream or downstream component could benefit from to optimize its performance, enhance its capability, or warn operations staff of future potential disruption.

Silos might exist between IT and their preferred partners in the business procurement department, for example. The business's desire to optimize the procurement process and provide governance around it may end up detrimental to the value these partners, vendors, and consultants provide. Onerous processes and time delays are a downside of these silos.

IT can be proud that it has pioneered the breaking down of silos. We have partially addressed the problem on the technology side by consolidating services centrally and sharing them across the enterprise. These shared resources take on service-level agreements of all additional groups. As such, the security and reliability of the shared systems can become exceptionally well designed, maintained, and monitored.

We have further to go, though. IT must build confidence in the systems by marketing them not as servers, databases, and switches, but as services to be consumed by the business.

When an organization's structures don't help it improve, IT can recognize it as an opportunity. We can address the problem. We can let our competitors suffer through market irrelevance in their silos.

Silos' negative effect on the ability of organizations to adapt to changing market conditions is one of the problems with silos. Gail Sessoms, a grant writer and nonprofit consultant, notes, "Organizational silos usually are resistant to change, operating to prevent easy access to the information they hold, and throwing up barriers to change and cooperation. They make it difficult for communication and collaboration to occur across units, while each group works to protect its own interests and data."[66]

Adverse outcomes occur when any person, process, or technology refuses to share knowledge, fixes, insights, or resources. Clues this is happening include comments like:

- "We didn't know."

- "If we knew those guys down the hall had already spent the last six months figuring out the same problem and developing a fix for it, we would not have wasted time and money trying to fix it again."

- "We were unaware there was a better way to do this procedure or task."

For those trying to keep costs down—and that's all of us—these experiences are devastating wastes of finite resources.

The structure of silos is capable of stifling progress. It wastes time and money. Workers in silos can't see over the walls to the big picture to understand their roles and contributions to the company. Valuable data is trapped, cut off from others who could really benefit from it. One team spends more money on something that others won't share, driving up the organization's expenses. Silos continue working with organizational structures built in the past, and teams hope they work well enough to handle consumer demands.

Horizontal teaming is so much more efficient. Let go of the finger pointing, lagging response, and lack of accountability. Manage future disruption rather than create it.

Silos create a misalignment that results in bad experiences for not only the company but also the consumers of the company's services. James Kalbach, author of the book *Mapping Experiences*, believes too many organizations are out of sync with what the people they serve actually experience. He says that misalignment impacts the entire enterprise. Teams lack a common purpose, solutions are detached from reality, technology supplants experience, and strategy is shortsighted.[67]

When systems, processes, departments, and teams stay isolated from one another, they often appear under separate reporting, budget, and requirement structures. In extreme cases, silos represent isolation and individualistic thinking, providing an artificial scope of responsibility— for example, groups celebrating the completion of their tasks while not taking into consideration the fact that work is not actually done until it provides value to upstream customers, be it internal colleagues or external paying ones.

Silos tend to hide upstream and downstream, producing friction in the workflow, limiting visibility in performance, duplicating tasks and resources unnecessarily, and encouraging local optimization at the expense of global performance.

In the presence of silos, getting through multiple steps is rife with friction, slowdowns, and frustration. Silos create suboptimal resource allocation when priorities and incentives of multiple groups are involved.

IT departments must work to break down silos, for their survival as well as for the survival of their businesses. The marketplace demands it since silos cap progress and stop global optimization. In technical parlance, the days of the interconnecting Internet Protocol (IP), Internetwork Packet Exchange (IPX), and AppleTalk networks were challenging. They were islands unto themselves, with systems having to choose sides. But today, global optimization empowers convergence, collaboration, and operational intelligence.

Vertical optimization controls the design of a specific organizational structure, such as a division, group, or department. A manager of one of those structures stays responsible for their direct reports and is concerned with the teams' budget, performance, and mandate. Those outside this group are not the manager's primary concern.

Today's market forces can have a dramatic effect on silos. We in IT can wisely let silos become a relic of the past. Silos trap value, stifle innovation, and put an unnecessary ceiling on getting critical things done. Progress can also be inhibited when dealing with debt.

Technical Debt

For IT, technical debt is a challenge. Debt is used in many aspects of our lives. People recognize it most often when talking about money. Businesses are well versed in financial debt. In IT's case, we know it in the technology aspect. Technical debt is work that is due or owed. When not done in an appropriate time frame, technical debt continues to build up a list of incomplete tasks. This increases the probability of a common mode failure in the future.

Technical debt puts off to tomorrow what would be more beneficial in the long-term if done today. You have been meaning to wrap up those other tasks from the last project, such as writing that documentation, re-cabling the closet, fixing those lines of code, updating the internal portal, updating the script, or reviewing the access control list. But new work keeps coming in, pushing more items onto the to-do list. The backlog becomes your technical debt. You excuse it as long as the lights are on. The imperative to go back and wrap up never comes up until something breaks.

This debt shows in many places. Our infrastructures are haunted by unknown dependencies, poor documentation, unpatched firmware, misconfigured settings, and worse. We always mean to come back and clean all that stuff up when we get some free time. But that free time never comes. *Good enough* rules the day as long as it runs. Tomorrow's cleanup stays away—until there is an incident or system failure caused by the right alignment of conditions to break something.

We must have a tieback from our infrastructure to the business value it provides. Every system we maintain will give us the foundation from which to start asking some tough questions. For instance, why are we still paying for maintenance on this system that is no longer used by the business? Why are we not tracking the usage of the software we pay maintenance on every year? Why are we buying the full version of this software if most end users use only the minimum features?

Maybe we haven't had detailed diagrams, reports, layouts, or documentation for far too long. Maybe we've been afraid to unplug that one cable because we are not exactly sure what will happen.

Are we buying new systems, paying for maintenance on other systems, and testing new systems the business will never use? Can we provide the same service using an external provider at a reduced price? Every time the IT budget includes items that are not used, we increase our level of debt.

Debt is in the code. A critical aspect of debt is that it slows down the delivery of value to the business. In software development, debt can result in struggling to keep pace with your organization's customer needs. Hampering the ability to deliver new functionality as a result of being bogged down by legacy software development practices has market implications.

Technical debt is often used in IT, especially developers, as a term that deals with several issues. These include the accumulation of bug fixes that must be fixed at a later point in the supply chain, as well as all of the software coding work that was not done before, causing delayed access to the software. Another issue is the downstream delays in deploying the code into production by the operations team.

All those little things add up over time and become something big later. Business pressure to deliver code into the field can build up technical debt and reduce IT's ability to move fast in the future. It also makes for buggy code and problems forced upon the end user, who will be frustrated.

Fixing things down the line ends up costing more time and money. The backlog of work just continues to pile up. If the work was done sooner, we would have access to faster feedback that the work is being done correctly. We cannot be nimble with excessive technical debt. Too much technical debt slows down progress!

In data, debt can be found. Being awash in data can be a bad thing when it makes it harder to make sense of it. Big data proves to be both a blessing and a challenge. Not giving enough attention to making it useful can amount to useless noise. We can potentially have too much of it. What we do have can be hard to understand and lead to inconsistent use in decision-making. There can be unpredictable quality in type of data that frontline workers get to influence their daily activity. And once in the field, workers can be slow to leverage the insight gleaned from the data. Data debt has some of the same downsides as technical debt with the added problem of adding noise to the information needed to make good decisions.

The lifecycle management of all this data leads to governance requirements, privacy implications, security exposure, data science skills, and lots of management tools. Letting data hang around past its usefulness means customers will be more likely to know when we allow data debt.

We in IT must stop mounting useless noise by instead keeping only functional data. We keep only crisp, helpful data, and we use it well.

Every time a new data field is added to a database, or a new app produces data, there is potential for data management mishaps. Not everyone who could benefit from that data knows it exists. New translations can spin out of control—losing context—and value can become stale. Bad data jeopardizes decision-making, slows down reporting, and blurs insights.

Every application in production creates data. Organizations must have a framework in place to capture and mine that data to make it useful. The sources of new data continue to grow. Some IT teams are not taking full advantage of the insights that are waiting to be found in that mountain of raw data. As a result, unrealized value sits idle and is denied to the business for use.

Typically, a technology component gives IT an opportunity to make a difference, a chance to lead. Speed is a key factor. If frontline business decisions are taking too long, you could be losing the opportunity to maximize sales. From the back-end operations to the front-end counter, in the grocery line or out in the field, business decisions need to be made at market speeds. In the retail industry, for example, it took companies a while to put data to good use optimizing inventory, and it cost them sales on items that customers wanted to buy that were out of stock at the time. They have gotten much better about using data to help keep the right goods ready for customers' demands.

There has obviously been a lot of progress since then; however, that does not mask the continuing challenges many businesses have with maximizing the value of raw data.

For producers of goods and services, the ability to capture consumer needs and wants relies increasingly on more data and more efficient supply chains. Incumbents who struggle with the amount of data and how to put it to use are leaving money on the table—and a lot of it.

As with financial debt, paying it down is an organization objective. For far too long IT has been deficient in knowledge of what a business needs and how businesses make use of their systems. We can no longer be in the dark about what the systems do and why they're here. So, first, we need to know what we're dealing with.

We must consider everything we're responsible for. What is in the realm of IT from an asset standpoint? What is the infrastructure we are responsible for?

We then must map those responsibilities to all the applications the infrastructure was built to serve. We must understand all our applications infrastructure dependencies and map them to the business services they support.

The more we know, the better position we will be in to help the business compete. Similar to a physical body with a high body mass indicator, we in IT need an inventory of everything we do, produce, and consume: the infrastructure, the code, and the data. Only then can we find where we are managing too much of what we don't need and not enough of what we do need.

We need to know how well business needs are being fed by our technology infrastructure, code, and data. This will allow us to be in a better position to deal with disruption by having the agility to respond to new business needs. And that agility is made possible by paying down our technical debt.

As IT walks in the shoes of the business, more clues to ways for better alignment can be found. The scene has been set for IT to understand and manage the nature of disruption in the markets, the changes a market brings to the organization's work styles, and the way businesses acquire their new technology.

Much has changed in the landscape for IT. The challenges of disruption are clear; technology has provided the means to disrupt the market landscape by introducing new ways of providing value and driving business growth.

IT's business success is rooted in its ability to understand the macro-level market forces at work. That understanding provides the context for the organizational changes that most businesses are dealing with, the pressures today's workers are confronting, and the driving forces behind the new technology consumption models. IT has continually expanded roles, responsibilities, and potential to help.

When an IT team understands its business more intimately—why it exists, how it makes money, and how it plans to compete tomorrow—then it can set the groundwork of what it needs to do to stay relevant and lead.

So as IT, walk in the shoes of your business. When you do this, you increase your understanding of the business, your competitors, and market forces. Discover how other organizations and industries are using technology to address their challenges. What are their business models? How are they improving their collaboration? How are they improving mobile worker productivity?

There are various faces of disruption. These include taking advantage of market conditions to alter customer perceptions of value to draw them your way, as well as interrupting your current way of thinking.

Disruption is neither inherently good nor bad; it is a fact of life. It is the nature of market changes, and it impacts the technological advancements embedded in our way of living. It affects entire markets, individual companies, and individual workers. It can work in favor of the startup as well as the incumbent fending off the upstarts. Change is fundamental to survive, improve, and thrive. Business leaders are tuned into uncertainty. As such, IT professionals need to understand the implications for their organizations, as they will affect everything, including changing requirements, new ways of doing work, and the process budgets are approved. Ultimately, IT can find new opportunities where your organization can disrupt the status quo.

Find out where your organization needs the most help. Is it in increasing speed to market, improving decision-making support, or getting better at talent acquisition and retention? These are the questions that will lead to better alignment between what you do and what the business is trying to do.

Market disruption drives a lot of changes, increases the velocity of new ideas, and increases the need for faster responses. This environment leads to increase in risk as well. IT addresses technology and cyber risks, as well as supports other initiatives that help the business in the market. IT needs to understand that the C-suite has its hands full. The complexity of the risks from different areas beyond technology can be overwhelming to decision-makers if not approached properly. It is the reason that managing risk across the enterprise well is so important.

Chapter 5
ERM Context

Risk never sleeps for the boardroom as cybersecurity adds to the long list of concerns that must be managed. As the continuity list of concerns continues to mount for the board, cyber risks are getting more attention. Directors of boards are trying to grapple with cyber threats. They ask questions such as: Are we doing enough? Will we be next in the headlines? Will regulators and customers be clamoring for our heads? How do we keep up with such a complex and technical area? Or is our management team up to the job? These are some of the questions that generate discussion and concern.

Cybersecurity professionals are charged with leading your organizational efforts in addressing the ever-growing cyber threat landscape. The board looks to their chief information security officers (CISO) or equivalent to defend their organizations.

As new digital initiatives are rolled out to meet business needs, the exposure to risk increases. Sitting at the top of the security team, CISOs are the translators of technical concerns to business relevance. Often at odds with their counterparts in the business, their focus is different than business innovation and the CIO's concern with keeping the lights on.

Organizations at large are facing a growing array of thinking adversaries. Caught up in criminals, hacktivists, and nation-states, security teams have their hands full.

They must be focused on the most relevant threats and cut through all the noise in the cyber threat landscape. They must overcome the brand of "no" or "productivity killers."

CISOs are often pigeonholed as just a technical resource that does not understand the business. In many organizations, they are viewed as a roadblock or obstacles to getting work done. Their C-suite counterparts view them as a technical resource who lack business acumen and inundate them with technical jargon they can't understand. They can't tie back to business needs. They are good for satisfying a compliance checklist but not advancing business objectives. During an incident, they expect them to be down in the SOC in response mode, while they are in the board room managing business risk.

Security would like to be a business partner. They would like to change the dynamics and have your security program be business relevant. We can provide so much more. We can be an enabler of business initiatives. CISOs know they must level up their role: perception, communication skills, presentation skills. CISOs want to be business partners.

We need to align with our organizations' broader management of risk. We must better align our security programs with your organization's ERM programs. The road to making this change lies in aligning the technical security program with ERM.

They do this by first understanding the core principles of ERM. For those organizations without a formal program, this is an opportunity to lead.

Secondly, dive into the workings of an ERM program. How are other risk types handled?

And thirdly, understand the processes of an ERM program. This program can align strategies, process, and reporting approach to a cyber security program and vice versa. That means cyber risk will be measurable just like other business functions and integrated with business decision-making.

ERM is the three-letter word response to risk in the enterprise. It would, however, be a very good question to ask, "What happens when there is no 'formal' ERM program at your organization?" Or if we don't have a chief risk officer (CRO)? What happens when there is no "formal" CISO at your organization? The answer is that the function of ERM is being "handled" in some form or faction at all companies. That does not mean it is being done well, unfortunately. However, we must remember that if your organization is providing value in the marketplace and surviving in a competitive space, then the C-suite is managing well enough to stay alive. It may be done under various other terms, but risk management is critical to a business success. ERM has been evolving over the years, from checkbox exercise to integrated and strategic. ERM should be viewed as a strategic asset, helping the business identify optimal risk-response strategies to preserve value and enable value creation.

ERM Principles

Enterprise Risk Management, also known as ERM, is about helping the business achieve its goals. ERM is a business integrated function for managing risks across the entire organization. As volatility and uncertainty present challenges to all organizations, ERM allows bold action to enter the market, enabling decision makers to adjust and realize more successful business opportunities.

When done poorly, business initiatives fail. When done well, an organization is in the game. Every business will be confronted with threats as it pursues its goals and objectives. Good corporate principles are to manage risk with the most cost-effective means while maximizing the upside of its decisions.

When the management team makes projections about the future performance of the business, it is doing so using the best current information and projections of the future. ERM's goal is to minimize variance of that expected future performance. That variance could come from unexpected expenses or lower revenue performance. Since variance can come from many risk categories and groups, risk management in silo can be limited in efficacy.

What is needed is an aggregated view of risk across all risk domains. That will enable the best opportunity for optimizing risk mitigation and other responses.

ERM empowers both the board and management to make more informed risk/return decisions by addressing fundamental requirements with respect to governance and decision-making at the strategic and operational levels.

While risk is an inherent part of market activities, seeing around the corner and making the best decisions with what is known today is the key to long-term success for all organizations.

The 2008 financial crisis really drove the push for ERM. Adoption of ERM is more heavily concentrated in financial verticals because of the high regulatory visibility and oversight. Companies in other industries are looking at ERM because of its benefits for helping them meet their strategic objectives. The combination of a complex market environment, regulatory scrutiny, and market disruptions are driving the need for mature ERM.

Strategy Integration

The C-suite looks at the big picture. As such they need the big picture of the threats across the organization as well. The implication of this is clear; for enterprise risk management to be successful, it must be fully integrated into the strategy of the organization. Where GRC could be pigeonholed as a standalone function more in the compliance area, ERM is more strategic. It is what keeps the organization surviving and thriving in the long term. From succession planning to dealing with global pandemics to ESG and organizational-killing cyber-attacks such as ransomware, all of this combined with a very tough and competitive global marketplace, with the potential for our business model to be disrupted, it all requires a more forward-looking and proactive approach to business competitiveness. Every organization has a vision, values, and goals in support of its mission.

Its strategy and objectives benefit from effective risk management. ERM encourages seeing around the corner. Unlike too many board audit committees who look back into the past, ERM drives to looking forward on what is next that needs attention. Ultimately it is through effective risk management that organizations can improve their odds of successfully implementing their strategic objectives amidst a challenging and evolving environment. Effective risk management is the cornerstone of long-term business success. Organizations must manage a variety of risks that can significantly affect their financial performance and their ability to meet the expectations from the likes of their shareholders, regulators, and customers. ERM formalizes and embeds sound risk management throughout their organizations.

Risk needs be a part of your organization's business model. Effective risk management enables you to better serve and retain your customers. It helps you maintain and improve your position in the market. And it helps protect the long-term safety, soundness, and reputation of your organization.

A fundamental principle of all long-term business success is the prudent management of risk. Long-term company viability, growth, and profitability rests on great management. And great management looks into the future to plan for a dynamic environment and adapts as needed. When done right, ERM embeds into the strategic planning process to help uncover the most significant challenges to new opportunities and develops strategic options to address them. This allows for structure to the evaluation of the risks/rewards trade-offs of each opportunity.

The other fundamental tenet of ERM is that after strategic planning, those same risk management principles follow into strategic execution. From the board room to the front lines, risk awareness is embedded into daily organizational operations.

Stakeholder Taxonomy

When the Business Roundtable updated their statement of the purpose of a corporation in 2019, it put into words a new perspective on corporate responsibility. Expanding on the previous focus on shareholder primacy, it now acknowledges other stakeholders, like customers, employees, suppliers, and communities. It has a new statement of purpose that specifically includes other stakeholders beyond shareholders. This means delivering value to their customers, investing in their employees, dealing fairly and ethically with their suppliers, supporting the communities in which they work, and generating long-term value for their shareholders.

There are many stakeholders to manage. Every organization has many stakeholders. A stakeholder is a person, entity, or party that has an interest in a company. They can affect the business or be affected by the business. The primary stakeholders in a typical corporation include both external and internal parties, such as management, investors, employees, customers, suppliers, communities, and regulators. A useful way to understand the different stakeholders is to create a classification system, or taxonomy, describing each one and how management will address their unique needs.

Risk Culture

Risk culture is an umbrella term. It encompasses the dominant professional behavior, beliefs, customs, and norms found in groups and organizations. Culture refers to those basic beliefs shared among a group that unconsciously produces collective behaviors. We want to cultivate an environment that expects and promotes robust communication and cooperation among all parts of the organization. Risk management needs everyone to behave in accordance with the desired beliefs when they're not directly told how to act in their roles. The right risk culture is critical to a successful ERM program. A core principle of that culture is that risk management is everyone's responsibility. There are limits to the administrative and technical controls that can be put in place to manage risk at the organizational level. Effective risk management requires that everyone be involved. Fortunately, this is happening in most places every day daily. We normally don't call it risk management. Sometimes it is physical safety, quality, or our best practices. Together it is the expectation on how workers should act. All come together daily to manage risk.

This culture needs the tone to be set at the top of the organization, to have leaders who set the right tone and model the right risk behavior for that right culture to foster. ERM and strong leadership build the conditions, information, training, and guidance for everyone to do their parts in managing risk.

When someone sees something, they are encouraged to say something. They don't want to get their hands slapped for speaking up. Managers, when someone says something, take responsibility. They are adaptable, even when no one is looking. Even when there is no policy written, they don't pass the buck when it comes to doing the right thing. Doing the right thing, even when no one is looking. It means raising your hand when the situation is called for; for example, when someone in our supply chain is using child labor, we are not adequately following safety protocols, or we are careless with customer data.

Good ERM does not work without strong leadership. Management with leadership that does not care or enables bad behavior is dangerous. There are horrible stories of leaders ignoring employees' complaints and not modeling good behavior. In the short run, some stakeholders may be neutral with some of the bad practices like ethical violations if the results mean bigger payouts. Watch out for the regulators, judges, and your customers. The implication for a business to drive revenue, a stated organization goal for most, is the question of how that is accomplished. ERM sets the guardrails from where business objectives can operate confidently in the marketplace, knowing the appropriate levels of risk that are acceptable. That risk level is reinforced by the behavior management rewards. That is the true measure of what the organization values.

ERM programs ensure that effective operational controls exist throughout the company. An overarching objective is in creating a strong risk culture that emphasizes each team member's ownership and understanding of risk.

Management must promote this strong risk culture. Leadership is the art of motivating a group of people to act toward achieving a common goal. In a business setting, this can mean directing workers and colleagues with a strategy to meet the company's needs. Leadership is crucial for culture, due care, and accountability.

Risk culture actualized by having the tone set from above ensures that awareness and understanding of risk management and its value permeate through all levels of an organization down to every team member. This includes engaging executive leadership in risk management workshops, integrating risk management as part of strategic planning and business reviews, conducting risk management education and training at all levels, ensuring proper alignment of team members' incentives and risk taking, communicating, establishing priorities, and engaging stakeholders at all levels.

Risk Appetite

Risk appetite is the level of risk that an organization is prepared to accept in pursuit of its objectives before action is deemed necessary to reduce the risk. It represents a balance between the potential benefits of innovation and the threats that change inevitably brings. According to the ISO 31000:2018 ERM standard, at its most fundamental level, risk appetite is "the level of exposure an organization is willing to take" in pursuit of strategic objectives. CEB/Gartner explains that a well-defined and properly communicated risk appetite statement "creates a set of guardrails for managers to operate within when making strategic decisions. It also provides a tool for communicating the role of guardrails in the decision-making process and for confirming that individual parts of the business are independently and collectively operating within those guardrails." There are various criteria organizations use to establish their risk appetite.

Risk appetite is the amount and types of risk an organization is willing to take to meet strategic objectives. It includes the target level of loss exposure the organization views as acceptable, given business objectives and resources. As part of risk control activities, ERM sets forward how risk appetite is established—management defined and board-approved risk appetite. Risk appetite is the amount of risk that your organization is comfortable taking given its current level situation. That situation includes business conditions, current strategy, market conditions, etc. Risk appetite helps define which risks are acceptable and at what level. It guides business and risk leaders. Risk appetite boundaries are set within the organization's risk capacity.

Management's risk appetite is articulated in risk appetite statements. Management continuously monitors its risk appetite, and the board of directors reviews periodic risk appetite reports and analysis. There are levels of tolerance that demand management's attention. Risk tolerance is what an organization can cope with. It is the degree of variance from the organization's risk appetite that the organization is willing to tolerate. The tolerance can be defined for specific risk domains that, when added up, should not exceed the risk appetite level.

To explore risk appetite and tolerance, we need to take the perspective of the stakeholder. The challenge is that in a business with many stakeholders, individual stakeholders may disagree on what constitutes *bad*, what thresholds equate likelihood, and what loss impacts are relevant.

Stakeholders' context is critical for determining the "so what?" and how much to invest in mitigation. IT also needs to document stakeholders' risk appetite.

Ranges allow IT to avoid fixed numbers that don't communicate the correct uncertainty. IT needs the ability to aggregate risk data across business units and different stakeholders. IT must become an expert at capturing inherent risk, residual risk, appetite, and tolerance.

An example would be a trip to a casino. How much tolerance do you have for losing? What is your absolute cutoff? This approach allows stakeholders the context to put their risk domains into perspective. If the inherent risk is above the combined stakeholders' appetite level, then IT makes recommendations (of new spend) to bring it down.

Stakeholder context accounts for multiple stakeholders who have different loss scenarios they care about most. The estimated loss impact data needs to be aggregate to produce an enterprise view.

Appetite and tolerance have target ranges. Target levels set the upper and lower bounds of acceptable ranges, given business objectives and resources. Challenges with this include problems with averages and the need for ranges to express our level of uncertainty.

ERM programs are guided by risk appetite. How much risk are we willing to take? How much strategic risk? Market risk? Technology risk? How about in aggregate?

Risk tolerance is a range of innovation, freedom inside of tolerance ranges; for example, between 2 and 5 where the appetite of the organization is comfortable operating. Risk capability shows the level of risks at which the viability of the company itself cannot survive. A risk profile includes risk appetite, the tolerance levels, capacity levels, and thresholds for alerting management.

CIOs and CISOs need to work within ERM to ensure they are aligned in cyber risk. If there is no official ERM program, then the existing structure that is in place providing the best enterprise view of risk management will have to do. We need to have the right context for our security programs.

ERM Program

Enterprise risk management is a strategic approach to achieving business objectives in a volatile, uncertain, and complex world. The business strategy aims to identify, assess, and prepare for any threats that may interfere with an organization's operations or objectives. ERM programs define, categorize, and measure risk through understanding the internal and external factors that impact strategic and business objectives. It is critical for understanding your organization's risk-taking capacity, risk tolerances, and risk appetite.

The purpose of ERM is to manage the approach to taking enough chances to compete in the marketplace, while meeting stakeholders' needs. It helps see around the corner to adapt to emerging threats. The goal is to reduce unexpected variance in business performance. ERM does so by having an aggregated view risk from all types to effectively support the comprehensive and efficient management. Management needs to anticipate emerging risks to be better prepared. Aggregate risk from all types helps avoid siloed effects and to optimize risk responses. ERM programs need structure to be successful.

ERM Framework

As with all programs in management, management can leverage various frameworks to help them define the structure of their unique environments. Some examples of ERM frameworks that can be used as references for designing your own unique program are COSO and ISO 31000. COSO: the Committee of Sponsoring Organizations of the Treadway Commission, a joint initiative of five professional organizations. Those include the American Institute of Certified Public Accountants (AICPA), American Accounting Association (AAA), Financial Executives International (FEI), Institute of Internal Auditors (IIA), and Institute of Management Accountants (IMA). It is dedicated to helping organizations improve performance by developing thought leadership that enhances internal control, risk management, governance, and fraud deterrence. ISO 31000 is a family of standards relating to risk management codified by the International Organization for Standardization. ISO 31000:2018 provides principles and generic guidelines on managing risks faced by organizations. ISO 31000 provides principles, framework, and a process for managing risk. It can help organizations increase the likelihood of achieving business.

There are other offshoots and approaches to ERM frameworks. They all have their strengths and weaknesses. Every organization must evaluate their specific needs for their companies. As always, programs should be designed and built from the inside out, with external frameworks complementing your uniqueness. The ERM framework must work for your organization, culture, and risk management strategy. The various frameworks have several components that guide the ERM program. At the top of the list for a functional framework is laying out a vision for the risk management strategy of your organization.

A risk management framework defines how an organization manages risk in a comprehensive, integrated, and consistent manner. When done properly, it is deeply embedded in the internal processes and management structure. Roles and responsibilities are clearly defined. The key elements of your enterprise risk management framework include a formal risk management governance structure, a comprehensive company-wide risk inventory, and a comprehensive set of effective policies, procedures, and controls.

ERM has been evolving over the years, maturing from checkbox exercises to integrated and strategic. There have been attempts to rebrand the ERM and to improve on the existing frameworks. They have their issues and limitations. Your organization needs to make its framework its own. ERM should be treated as a strategic asset, helping your business identify optimal risk-response strategies. Risk management needs a governance structure to operate effectively.

Governance

Corporate governance is the system of rules and practices by which a company is operated and directed. It involves balancing the interests of a company's many stakeholders. Since corporate governance also provides the framework for attaining a company's objectives, it encompasses practically every aspect of management, including strategy development, management structure and roles, performance measurement, financial planning, and internal audit controls. Also included is risk management, which has a governance structure for ERM. There is varied structure to how different businesses name and structure this. As these programs mature, the structure can become more comprehensive. In the early stages of development, ERM programs often see existing personnel fulfilling multiple roles. Organizational structures often see reusing existing reporting and management structures. Risk management governance, a corporate governance, is the system of rules and practices. One common approach to this governance structure is the use of an operating structure that uses a *three lines of defense* (3LOD) model.

The 3LOD model is a risk management capability embedded into the existing business structure, with specific roles and responsibilities for managing risk across the entire organization. When done properly, it should not feel like extra work, but rather part of the day-to-day work of the business. Three lines of defense defines a clear engagement model that promotes challenge to excessive risk and appropriate escalation of actions as needed.

This model has a governance structure that consists of committees structure at the board of director's level. These committees provide comprehensive oversight of the risks the organization faces and ensures that management can effectively respond to and manage risk smartly.

There are specific ERM activities in each of the lines of defense. The third line of defense is the board of directors with support of the audit function.

The board oversees the company's business, which includes its risk management function. The board assesses management's performance, provides credible challenge, and holds management accountable for maintaining an effective risk management program and for adhering to risk management expectations. At this level, there is risk oversight. It allows the full board to meet its due care and fiduciary responsibilities. It is augmented with internal audit support to act as an independent assurance function and validates that the risk management program is adequately designed and functioning effectively. The board carries out its risk oversight responsibilities directly and through its committees.

The chairperson of the board actively manages the board agendas to provide sufficient time for key strategy planning and risk awareness. The strategic planning process is directly connected to the strategic risk appetite and identifies or helps uncover the most significant opportunities and challenges, develops options to address them, evaluates the risks and trade-offs of each, and articulates the resulting mitigation countermeasures. Risk management is integrated into the strategic planning process and provides credible challenge to the line of business with respect to their planned decisions and strategic initiatives to promote the appropriate diligence of the risk/reward balance. The work of the board is divided into multiple committees.

One key committee is the risk committee, which approves the company's risk management framework and oversees its implementation. It monitors the company's adherence to its established risk appetite. This committee oversees the overall ERM program. The purpose of the board's risk committee is to assist the board of directors in fulfilling its responsibilities to oversee the company's corporate risk function.

The risk committee and the full board review and approve the enterprise statement of risk appetite. The board's other standing committees also have primary oversight responsibility for certain specific risk matters. The committee provides the full board reports at its regular meetings.

Another key committee is the audit committee. The primary purpose of a company's audit committee is to provide oversight of the financial reporting process, the audit process, the company's system of internal controls, and compliance with laws and regulations. The role of the audit committee forms the cornerstone for effective corporate governance. Boards rely on their audit committees to offer effective oversight of the annual auditing process. Audit committees also oversee the system of internal controls and ensure that the company is compliant with laws and regulations.

The next line is the second line. In the second line of defense sits the chief risk officer (CRO) and the management of the ERM risk function. The CRO often reports functionally to this committee and administratively to the chief executive officer (CEO). The CRO oversees all aspects of the company's independent corporate risk function and risk oversight activities. This person consolidates all outputs of all the groups who individually are responsible for all the different risk types. When the CEO wants a clear and consolidated picture of risk in their company, the CRO can provide that roll-up. The CRO is expected to communicate with the risk committee chairperson on any significant risk issues that arise between committee meetings, including issues raised or escalated by management's risk committee. In more mature or complicated ERM programs, the CRO will have their own support system in the form of Office of the CRO.

In some structure, there is a working council, i.e., a risk council. The risk council acts as the highest corporate management level governing body to assist with effective management and oversight of risk. It will include members such as the CEO, CFO, HR, line of business, CIO, CTO, etc. The responsibilities and duties of the risk council include risk tolerance and appetite, key indicators, risk level review and risk aggregation, model risk management, products and services, and risk acceptance and change management. ERM establishes and maintains a company's risk management program and provides oversight, including challenge to and independent assessment of the first line's execution of its risk management responsibilities. The risk council acts as the function responsible for monitoring, reporting, and communicating risks, including all risk-related matters to key stakeholders including the board and management. The second line provides oversight and challenges the first line and provides risk management support for both the third and first lines. That support includes tooling, reporting, logistics, technology, processes, and coordination across the organization.

The last line of defense is the first line. The first line of defense is the business lines along with support functions—business units and corporate operating functions. The first line is composed of the business. During its business activities, the first line identifies, assesses, manages, monitors, and reports on risk associated with its business activities and balances risk and reward in decision-making while operating within the company's risk tolerances as defined by the established risk profile. The support functions include activities of enterprise functions such as HR, finance, and IT.

With governance structure in place, let's look at a how management gets an enterprise view of risk.

Risk Taxonomy

An enterprise risk taxonomy provides an aggregate view of risk across the organization. A taxonomy is useful to see the different types of risk at a summarized view. And it can be visualized to reflect risk appetite per risk type as well. A risk taxonomy is a comprehensive, common, and stable set of risk categories used across the enterprise to classify and aggregate risks. Build a robust framework to enable aggregate reporting across the organization that will drive informed decision-making. After a taxonomy is in place, we can then drill down into the individual types and document the scenarios of concern. It is here that we keep track of our concerns. What are we concerned about? Where is our focus? Communicate that across the organization to guide everyone.

The taxonomy can be subdivided into different levels: a higher top level (i.e., Leve1 1: Operations) with several sub-areas below it (i.e., Level 2: third-party risk and technology risk). There are many types of risk across an organization. It is helpful to start with grouping similar types into a taxonomy. This will represent your portfolio of risks your organization faces. It can be coded to reflect risk appetite per risk type as well. There are various ways to categorize the types of risk that an organization must manage. Here we review several, including strategic, reputation, financial, credit, market, liquidity, interest rate, compliance, conduct, operational, third-party/supply chain, legal, model, technology, and cyber.

Strategic risk is the threat to earnings, capital, or liquidity. This can be the result of adverse business decisions, improper implementation of strategic initiatives, or inadequate responses to changes in the external operating environment. If there are insufficient resources allocated to the development and execution of the company's strategic plan, then the successful execution of strategic plans can be at stake.

Innovation risk is the threat that your company is at a competitive market disadvantage because of not investing and executing on new business value to customers. Innovation is at the heart of responding to market pressures. Failure to respond quickly to changing or new customer demands can be financial devasting. There is risk that competitors will leapfrog you and take market share and customers from you. There is risk that your customer retention decreases because of a lack of appropriate focus on your customers' needs and preferences. As your organization engages in mergers, acquisitions, and consolidation, there is the risk that your organization does not adequately integrate new acquisitions in a timely and efficient matter; or that the expected payoffs don't come to fruition because of lackluster performance improvement and/or higher than forecasted costs.

Human capital risk involves the most critical asset for a business, its people. The threat is that you are not able to attract and retain qualified talent that is critical to the success of your business. Failure to do so could adversely affect your business performance, competitive position, and prospects. There is the danger that when an employee leaves the organization, they do so without appropriate transfer of knowledge capital and handover of projects. There is the danger that when that person is in a leadership position, there is not adequate leadership still in place and an appropriate succession plan in place. You need to maintain resources and tools to attract, develop, and retain a diverse talent pool. Be careful that there are processes in place to effectively capture and institutionalize learning across the organization. Organizations that team well perform well. There is the risk that the company fails to recruit qualified employees to ensure optimal staffing levels to support the company's growth strategy. There is the risk that employees don't improve their performance over time because the company fails to create a sufficient support infrastructure that includes resources such as mentorship and training.

Reputation risk is the threat arising from a loss in trust in the organization brand, be it in perceived competence or their ethical integrity. That could negatively affect the organization's ability to establish new relationships or to continue servicing existing ones. The potential negative publicity regarding the company's brand could impact both current and future business. It could degrade positive customer sentiment and result in a decline in the customer base or decrease repeat business. For many organizations, reputation is paramount, and as such, they actively act to avoid engaging in activities that may damage their brand.

Financial risk is the threat to capital, liquidity, or earnings. This may be a result from various internal or external factors. If your company is in a financial vertical, like a bank, they need to maintain capital at an amount commensurate with their risk tolerance objectives. They must take into consideration those needs under both normal and stressed conditions. For all verticals, sound financial planning and analysis is needed to maintain cash flow, forecast operational needs, forecast capital needs, manage expenses, and forecast projected future revenue.

Credit risk is the threat that your customers or other counterparties fail to perform in accordance with agreed upon terms of contractual obligations to your company. Many times, the collateral securing such obligations may be sufficient to recover the amounts due. However, in some cases, the company may experience significant credit losses that could have adverse effects on its operating results or financial condition. If your company provides customers with loans and other credit, there is risk that the threshold for defaults could be exceeded, causing losses. In addition, there is liquidity risk, the threat that the company may not be able to meet its funding needs for customer loan requests, customer deposit maturities, and withdrawals. Financial companies need to manage their liquidity position to ensure that you can meet all their funding requirements (e.g., customer loan requests, customer deposit withdrawals, and cash commitments).

Market risk is the threat of possible economic loss from adverse changes in market risk factors such as interest rates, foreign exchange rates, and commodity prices. This can include volatility in pricing of trading books and mortgage servicing rights. Some trading activities may be needed to accommodate the investment and risk management activities such as hedging to manage the balance sheet.

Interest rate risk is the risk that assets and liabilities may mature or reprice at different times or by different amounts. Short-term and long-term market interest rates may change by different amounts, affecting the shape of the yield curve. Interest rates may also directly or indirectly affect loan demand, collateral values, or credit losses earnings.

Regulatory risk is the threat resulting from the failure to comply with laws, regulations, and rules. The organization's short- and long-term success is contingent upon remaining compliant with the applicable laws and regulations. There is also political risk, the threat of a change in the public sector landscape that changes business conditions that may be detrimental to your organization. These changes could be spurred by an election, new laws, or judicial ruling precedents. The political event could have an impact on the organization's mission, leadership makeup, or business model. The examples include changes in tax law, environmental regulations, healthcare requirements, capital availability, or brand value.

Environmental, social, and governance (ESG) risk is the threat that external stakeholders, in many cases investors, will use a company's adherence to the standards and principles of ESG as a requirement in their investment decisions. Its criteria are a set of standards for a company's operations that socially conscious investors may use to screen potential investments. Failure to do so could result in a competitive disadvantage. That can pressure a company to perform to the core tenets of ESG, along with its reporting requirements and investments in closing the gaps in some of these criteria. These criteria consider a company's social consciousness of protecting the environment, and how well it manages its relationships with other stakeholders beyond shareholders, like employees, customers, and local communities it interacts with. And how a company approaches the diversity of its leadership, executive pay transparency, human rights, and workers' health and safety. Failing to manage ESG risks can lead to loss of future business, reduced investor interest, or diminished customer loyalty. Investors are increasingly emphasizing monitoring, reporting, and disclosure of ESG risks.

Operational risk is the threat resulting from failed or inadequate internal processes, people, and systems. It can also be caused by external events outside your control. These internal failures can be risk factors concerning your conduct exposing yourselves to legal actions, flawed use of models that are relied upon to make decisions, not being diligent with the third parties that you rely on, disruptions caused by technology failures, lagging in innovation, or you being subjected to the effects of cyber-attacks.

Legal risk is the threat to your organization from proceedings, investigations, or enforcement actions concerning matters arising from the conduct of your business activities. These actions can be brought against your organization because of judicial, regulatory, compliance, governmental, statutory, or third-party arbitration. They can also be triggered by internal employees' conduct engaging in inappropriate, unethical, or unlawful behavior, caused by deliberate or unintentional actions or business practices. The resolution of legal investigations or proceedings could materially adversely affect the operations and financial condition of your organization. In addition to imposing monetary penalties and other sanctions, regulatory authorities may require criminal pleas or other admissions of wrongdoing and compliance with other conditions in connection with settling such matters. The effect can lead to restrictions on the inability to engage in certain business activities or offer certain products or services. Other direct and indirect adverse effects might include limiting the ability to access capital markets, limit capital distributions, forcing executive or organizational changes, or putting a stain on the brand, leading to customer losses.

Model risk is a threat that arises from the potential for adverse consequences from business decisions made based on model outputs. It is the potential loss that an organization may incur because of decisions that were influenced by the output of a model. Employees may not fully understand the output of the models and use their output inappropriately in their decision process. Your workers could unwittingly use models in an incorrect way that negatively affects a key decision. In some cases, the models themselves may be flawed, incomplete, or outdated. In other cases, a model may be insufficiently documented in its known weaknesses and underlying assumptions. In addition, the inputs to the model could be flawed, the output could be misinterpreted, or the wrong model could be used. There may not be enough rigor in the process of developing and maintaining these models. The decision-making process must account for the fact that models are driven by data inputs and assumptions whose results are estimates with varying degrees of accuracy. Care needs to be given to over-relying on incorrectly interpreting the output of model results.

Third-party or supply chain risk is the threat of failure or disruption in the operations of external entities such as vendors and service providers that you rely on to run your business. As a result of the growing dependence on external people, process, services, parts, and technology, any operational incident in your supply chain will have some effect on your operations. The reality is that most businesses rely on third parties to enable their business strategy. These include outsourced operations, such as payroll, financial exchanges, cloud services, and security services. Disruption at the external entity could disrupt your businesses, damage your reputation, or increase your costs. From the outside world, your supply chain is a part of you; as such, your organization must meet regulatory requirements and expectations regarding the use of these third-party entities, and any failure by them to meet their obligations to you or to comply with current rules, laws, or regulations could result in penalties, fines, or restrictions on your business. Any failure in your third-party entities that affects your operations is your risk because it could disrupt your business, damage your reputation, increase your costs, and cause losses to your organization's bottom line.

Technology risk is the threat from the failure of the availability of your digital systems or being a laggard on digital transformation initiatives. To achieve strategic goals and objectives, your organization must innovate. That innovation is powered by technology. That requires highly effective IT solutions for both internal use and consumer-facing engagement. This innovation operates in a fast and complex environment. It must happen when it is getting increasingly more difficult to maintain stability and reliability in all our complex systems. IT must continue to deliver relevant technology-enabled services and digital innovations.

Cyber risk is the result of the compromise of the confidentiality, privacy, integrity, safety, and availability of organizational digital assets. All the technology that underpins your business is under constant threat for an ever-growing list of threat actors using evolving tactics. These threats include system compromises, data theft, ransomware, and denial-of-service attacks, as part of an effort to disrupt the operations of financial institutions, commit fraud, or obtain confidential, proprietary, or other information. These attacks have focused on targeting online applications and services, such as online banking, as well as cloud-based services provided by third parties, and have targeted the infrastructure of the internet, causing the widespread unavailability of websites and degrading website performance. It is of critical importance that your digital infrastructure that your business runs on be defended. There are many assets that have value, such as intellectual property, personal information, and sensitive customer data, that need protection. As well as the operations of your systems. In the growing area of privacy, you must reduce your liability by protecting the privacy of your customer data.

Note that cyber risk is one of many risks that your organization must deal with. Wherever business activities could result in the impact on the bottom line, risk management is needed to keep those potential aggregate losses in check.

A good ERM program peers around the corner into the future, looking over the horizon for emerging risk. ERM is responsible for identifying, assessing, and escalating emerging risks. The emerging risk could be the result of a pandemic, groundbreaking new law, or human conflict from warfare. Effective risk management is aligned with an embedded companywide culture driven by the company's vision, strategy, values, and goals. ERM provides that early warning system to management. Risk-informed decision-making makes for a stronger governance culture while being innovative in the market.

After a risk taxonomy is in place, we can then drill down into the individual types and document the scenarios of concern. It is here that we keep track of an organization's concerns while executing on the business strategy. The next step is to identify the relationships and connections among the risk categories. From a taxonomy, the transition to a risk ontology is very useful to see dependencies among different risk types.

The ERM program defines the processes that enable it to accomplish its objectives of managing risk across the enterprise.

ERM Process

Process drives business operations. It is the same for ERM programs. It's how things get done. The ERM framework provides a process approach to operationalize the ERM program. A risk management framework seeks to limit risk and loss to the business. ERM programs establish processes and procedures intended to identify, assess, respond, and monitor all the types of risk to which your company is subject to. That involves the identification, analysis, and assessment of risk. That will help you make the best risk response choices with the proper business context. And those response decisions are continuously monitored to ensure that response intentions are delivering the expected results.

Risk Identification

All risk management begins with the identification of a potential issue, now or in the future. The risk identification process begins when internal or external events or conditions are identified at various points in the business cycle or operations that have the potential to impact your ability to achieve your stated goals and objectives. During the strategic and business planning processes, management assesses the market environment to identify opportunities and any accompanying potential risk. The risk management function is represented on all levels of an organization to enable effective risk identification in strategic, operational, and tactical areas.

This process is supported by an understanding of the enabling assets that are important in achieving your business objectives. It is up to management to ensure ERM has appropriate access to all information necessary to identify risk factors through both top-down and bottom-up approaches. The top-down approach risk identification happens during strategic discussions as potential concerns are identified. The bottom-up approach is identified by frontline workers in the business units and supporting corporate functions. What the identification process looks for is potential downsides to new opportunities and current activities. This can be self-guided inside groups via risk control self-assessments or facilitated by the second line of defense. Internal and external stakeholders who could be impacted are identified, and therefore risk management functions scan the external environment for risk indicators by analyzing applicable business intelligence, including trends in external authority, legislative changes, shifts in market, and payer and consumer models, as well as relationships with external subject matter experts. Finally, risk management functions review the output from internal monitoring and assurance activities to identify gaps and emerging risk areas.

After the identification of a risk, it should be documented in a register that acts as an aggregated single point of truth. This register needs to be standardized to support a global view for management and further analysis. The organizational-wide risk register is accomplished and supported by other artifacts to support deeper understanding and ongoing attention, such as a robust and complete asset management database that identifies critical assets and key risk factors, value stream maps for documenting critical processes and services, and a loss event database to document past losses.

Risk Assessment

Some of the inputs to the enterprise risk register come from the process of analysis and measurement. This includes estimating the range of probable frequency of future losses, the range of probable magnitude of future losses, and a range of mitigation options. In the assessment process, scenario discovery, analysis, and surveys are performed by the business and risk management functions to identify internal and external scenarios that might have potential negative outcomes impacting the achievement of the organization's objectives.

Risks are analyzed, considering likelihood and impact of a given out-come, to determine how they might be best managed. Risk assessment activities are performed for evaluating inherent risk with respect to im-pact on mission, vision, goals, and business objectives; evaluating pri-mary controls to determine level of control effectiveness; determining and quantifying residual risk to strategize further action; determining likelihood and impact to help prioritize risk response; and ranking risks based on organizational priorities in relation to strategic objectives. Measuring the current level of risk or loss exposure can be compared to the established set risk appetite and tolerance levels. The risk assess-ment process can show if you are trending too close to your thresholds. It also gives you a clear indication of how your existing controls invest-ments are performing their job in risk mitigation.

Risk Response

With the results of a risk assessment in hand, the next question is what to do about it. There are many response options. From a management standpoint, the risk could be avoided, accepted, transferred, or miti-gated. That last option is the one IT often deals with; the others are more of a business decision. Often in IT, we think in terms of technical controls for mitigation. But there are administrative, tactical, and op-erational controls as well. There are also many mitigation functions and controls from across the organization that keep loss exposure in check.

Responses happen at strategic, operational, and tactical levels. The ERM processes help decide on a response strategy, a combination of actions across many stakeholders across many different loss scenarios. If the exposure is within acceptable appetite, then management can choose to accept the risk. If the exposure is way above appetite, man-agement can avoid it, by not undertaking in the activity. To get the ex-posure reduced, some of it can be transferred to another party, such as with insurance, derivatives, or hedging. The most common is to mit-igate, reduce the exposure through active means such as increasing controls, strengthening existing controls, or changing some aspect of initiative implementation or use.

The specific response is determined based on the activity or condition posing the risk as well as background facts and circumstances, including taking into consideration your overall risk tolerances. The business can always consider taking on additional risk in areas where it may be prudent to do so to create more value or optimize return on investments. It is all about maximizing opportunities to capture positive outcomes that come with some risks. The context for management's responses is informed by the amount of risk the company is comfortable taking given its current level of resources.

Risk Monitoring

ERM continuously monitors the defined corporate risk appetite and current loss exposure and adapts as needed to capitalize on new business opportunities.

Identified risks need to be tracked over time to make sure the exposure does not change unexpectedly. If a situation begins to deteriorate and loss exposure increases, a change in response may be needed. Organizations must continuously monitor their environment to help support risk management on an ongoing basis. ERM needs to keep all risk factor inputs under systematic observation and monitor the entire risk landscape that interacts with your organization. Using the factors from your risk models, monitor for variance in asset, threat, and control factors. If any of these factors change outside expectations or without notice, then feedback will be provided to management of the need for attention.

Risk monitoring detects changes in the risk landscape and elements of the loss scenario that can be observed and measured. This provides feedback, taking on the form of metrics, reports, and alerts that together help validate that IT's current understanding of its risk state is accurate enough to be useful. They guard against the illusion of good management and help avoid wasted processes and efforts. Management needs measurements to manage, which metrics enable.

To generate these meaningful metrics, you need a platform designed for the volume, velocity, and variety of data types that need to be ingested and analyzed. Leverage both knowledge and machine learning to accelerate value. This is more than security information and event management. You need a data analysis engine designed to serve the business. Use feedback and real-time platforms to track all the factors driving your model. That platform is fed data sources that have been sent to a data repository, such as a data lake, that is processed through various models to formulate relevant context to be consumed by various personnel. This analysis platform provides the engine to power the metrics for the business. Metrics come in various forms.

Key performance indicators (KPI) are metrics that measure the achievement of targets. They are used to evaluate performance over time for an organization, individual, program, project, action, etc. They help to answer the question of how something is performing. A KPI is meant as a measure of how well something is being done. These indicators should link to strategic objectives, direct where to focus resources, and be measured against targets. A common methodology used for developing metrics is the goal-question-metric (GQM) method. For example, a goal could be the reduction of customer default rate. A question could be the percentage of late payments. And a metric could be the number of previous defaults that had over three late payments.

Key risk indicators (KRI) give an early warning to identify a potential event that may harm continuity of the activity. As indicators of the possibility of future adverse impact, they are metrics that provide information on the level of exposure to a given risk that the organization has at a particular point in time. A KRI is a measure used in management to indicate how risky an activity is. They are metrics used to provide an early signal of increasing risk exposures in various areas of the enterprise. They act as an early warning of potential risk. A KRI is a measure used in management to indicate how risky an activity is. KRIs give an early warning to identify a potential event that may harm continuity of the activity or project. It differs from a KPI in that the latter is meant as a measure of how well something is being done while the former is an indicator of the possibility of future adverse impact.

Key control indicators (KCI) are metrics that provide information on the extent to which a given control is meeting its intended objectives (in terms of loss avoidance, prevention, reduction, etc.). They are an even earlier warning system that precedes KRI, keeps track of the controls in place, and allows for monitoring of those things that organizations directly manage. A KCI quantifies how effectively a specific control tool, approach, or methodology is working. KCIs are used to define the company-wide controls to monitor the achievement of the set objectives. An example is an HR awareness program. Managers define the related desired tolerances for controls before measuring.

ERM ensures that strategic planning addresses the risk of the inability to discover, evaluate, and select among alternative decisions. A well-run ERM program provides direction and guardrails to achieve the company's planned strategic objectives.

Cyber Security Program Alignment with ERM

If headline-grabbing cyber-attacks are to be properly addressed, a security program must be in alignment with ERM. Underlying that statement is that the ERM has to achieve some minimal level of effectiveness through its program maturity. The maturing of an ERM program can be measured by its capabilities and ability to scale to meet the needs of the organization's risk management. The large investment in time and money needed to operate a useful ERM program means it will take years for most companies to get there. A maturity scale can be used to measure progress of program improving over time. Qualitative considerations in maturity scales such as five-point references (i.e., initial, basic, established, advanced, and leading practice) can be useful to report improvements over time. More mature programs upgrade to quantitative considerations for higher fidelity in program evaluations.

In the area of cyber risk management, overwhelming technical information needs to be provided to management in business-friendly language. The technical insights of cyber must be translated into business insights. A businessperson must be able to view cyber in comparison to the other risk types. Cybersecurity is greatly enhanced when aligned with ERM.

ERM programs frame the inputs that a cybersecurity program should provide. It can prioritize work efforts, optimize technical control selection, and inspire a mitigation strategy that is business aligned. ERM guides security operations and focuses IT and security teams. You will realize the benefits of understanding ERM when you align your security programs to it.

ERM provides a great reference point for the type of controls that the security team should put in place. When there is a change in the efficacy of the control because of a change in the IT environment, risk management can guide the timing of additional investments and mitigation adjustments. The question can become how well the risk monitoring process is at detecting and escalating to management if the loss exposure is not outside acceptable range. In many cases this type of drop in mitigation efficacy because of the change in the technical environment is not visible or not enough attention is paid to it. It is too technical to make it into business level metrics. It may get buried in future projects that have new funding requests attached.

But this should be considered a serious problem if the basis for your risk tolerance is exceeded and not escalated. If in fact a mitigation response as part of cyber risk management is no longer performing its function, the management should be made aware of this. In many cases they are not. The funding necessary to put the controls in place needs to be made part of the total cost of the business initiative up-front. Through a combination of how the security team makes the funding request and the level of involvement they were in during the initial project planning; business justification becomes masked as stand-alone cost. The visibility that would drive more timely controls change at times is insufficient. A slip in control response missed by management.

Say we were to compare cyber risk to an area such as physical safety for a factory. We can contrast a potential low-loss event frequency of an accident at a physical facility. Many believe it is low frequency be-cause of the safety measures and commitment from the entire organi-zation. Safety is not an accident but a direct result of managing risk through investment of time and money. For those who are watching physical safety and the safety of their employees, the absence of acci-dents by workers in and of itself would not be enough for the business not to approve the acquisition of new safety equipment or training. The implication is stark here. As in safety, the security of a cyber environ-ment is a result of investment in the mitigations. If security mitigations are not funded, then either the approach to the mitigation response was incorrect in the first place or budget request was not framed properly to get approved. Either management is intentional about risk management, or it is left to the best efforts from those on the front lines.

IT can internalize core risk appetite for the business priorities from ERM, along with how the decision-making process works for prioritizing resources. And how the business wants to be informed and the report-ing preferences. The business context for requests for additional secu-rity spend can be properly designed using the framework from ERM, which can make a conscious risk decision to accept the risk as is and sign off on it at the management level, relieving IT of the pressure of assuming a risk they don't own.

The cybersecurity program has outputs that are useful to the ERM program. It organizes cyber loss scenarios of concern in a useful context that can be consumed by the organization's ERM function that supports cost-effective responses to the entire portfolio of risks. In the pursuit of business objectives, this is the value that is at risk. As we operate, the risk factors that drive loss event scenarios change. When those changes affect our loss exposure, security teams inform the business to alert them of the need for attention.

IT's security program provides the first line, relevant and timely risk mitigation; the second line, strategy risk management support; and the third line, the necessary due care and diligence support in support of organization value creation and protection. IT provides the business an acceptable level of loss exposure from the use of technology.

The results are simple, as we need to "show" our risk analysis work. We need to show when an existing control condition is broken, or threat actions have significantly increased. We need to ensure that the second and third lines understand loss exposure from cyber risk. An effective security program delivers an acceptable annual loss exposure.

The complexity in the technology systems that underpin our digital world drive new levels of challenges for IT. IT is now operating under conditions of systemic dependencies, interconnectivity, and activity on a scale too vast and fast to track in our heads—disruption has led to a level of complexity we have never seen before. With better context to align security programs to enterprise risk management programs, now it's time to look closer at the close alignment needed with the actual technical infrastructure that underpins the operation of modern business.

Chapter 6
Technology Context

The world of technology is complex. One in a state of many components woven together. Complexity is many parts, connections, and interactions operating in ways that produce outcomes because of various outputs. No simplicity can happen on the front end without complexity in the back end. IT can understand and manage the fundamental complexity challenges. IT takes on complexity and wins.

Woods' Theorem illustrates the impact of complexity: *"As the complexity of a system increases, the accuracy of any single agent's own model of that system decreases rapidly."*[68]

Every day, people and organizations are working out the details (of technology, pricing, supply chains, process adjustments, legal hurdles, and more) to clear the path for making the products and services the marketplace consumes.

The value your organization provides in the marketplace is the function of navigating complexity. If your systems are not getting more diverse and being enhanced by the expansion of your ecosystem of partners, there is a good chance that you are not driving more customer value.

Complexity is key to front-end success. Simplicity on the front end is a byproduct of your effective work on the back end. And without that simplicity, your organization's value proposition—why it has customers and the resulting revenue streams—can be lost to competitors. Jack Dorsey, CEO of Twitter, said, "It's really complex to make something simple."

The customer/producer relationship is based on the exchange of value. That value can take various forms. A customer can be external or internal. In the case of IT, IT is the producer, and the business is the customer.

IT takes on the challenges of complexity, so others don't have to. For the consumer of the product and/or services, complexity is the enemy. If that complexity makes the buying experience too cumbersome or frustrating, it potentially discourages them from buying what the organization is selling. However, for the producer, complexity is our required friend. Without it, there would be no comfort or advancement in human life. For every simple experience in modern-day life there is a complicated, advanced, and impressive array of people, processes, and technology that brings it to life and runs it every day. Behind the curtains, in the kitchens, in the engine rooms, and in data centers, you can witness the engine that makes everything work. Consider this the next time you push a switch and the lights come on, pull a lever and water comes out, or click a button on your phone and a box arrives at your door the next day.

If simplicity were simple to create, everyone would do it. But true innovation requires lowering the barrier to consumption to be successful in the market. We need to distinguish between the complexity needed to innovate and the complexity that is wasteful.

Let's look at complexity from two perspectives, and from there validate if value is added.

First, from the market and business view, organizations are at the highest risk of disruption from competitors when our value proposition becomes stale. This sometimes happens when our business operations become bogged down in bureaucracy and waste, or we fail to provide customer value. In some cases, no one internally notices it until market share is lost. Non-value-added complexities can slow service, product improvement, and delivery. These complexities often add up over time but are hard to notice when we still are hitting our goals. They accumulate tasks that have been pushed aside for another day that never comes. Even more waste is introduced into the IT processes, making it less efficient. Constraints build over time in the infrastructure, making change progressively harder.

This contrasts with value-*added* complexity, where there exists the opportunity for more competitive value, increased customer retention, and improved experience either as the incumbent or the challenger. Here, complexity is driven from the business meeting customer demand. That demand has very specific technology requirements to make happen.

Value-added complexity results in IT being an enabler, improving governance, enhancing upstream business offerings, and allowing for greater customer value offerings.

Value-added complexity on the back end is needed to innovate, provide differentiated services, enable new features, speed up delivery, and offer more options that the customers require.

So how does IT help? By being aware of the business perspective to guide our strategy.

On the technology side, we run a lean, efficient system. The challenge is in how IT is structured, our workflow, and the way resources are deployed. Success happens by overcoming the organizational and cultural limitations of silos.

Let's look at the drivers of value-added complexity. IT interacts with an increasingly large number of interconnected systems. The scope, scale, and impact of complexity on IT's ability to deliver to the business are driven by many factors. For example, legal may want you to retrieve email for a case, the FBI may be contacting you to let you know data has leaked onto the street, sales teams might be requesting the latest product data on their mobile phones, marketing could want info on their latest campaign, and the board of directors might be worried about the time-to-delivery. IT must manage all of this with the savvy to avoid being bypassed by shadow IT.

A challenge of complexity is higher customer demand and expectations. Customers are accustomed to on-demand services. This manifests on the backend with the challenges of increased systems maintenance needs, fragmentation of vendor solution offerings, and legacy support of mission-critical systems that are difficult and costly to migrate. There is more systems and data to back up, smaller maintenance windows to update systems, more interoperability dependence, more places for complex systems to break. On top of all that, there are usually budget challenges that require IT to perform more analysis and projects justifications.

Add to this list the interoperability headaches due to more moving parts, partners, and vendors. The increased use of non-company-issued devices introduces another variable IT has to account for from a support and security aspect. Variation in endpoint types along with the mobility of the workforce keeps IT on its toes.

Value-added complexity also requires increased levels of activity between silos, and sometimes even the disintegration of the walls themselves. But most times, value is produced by a large number of interactions of multi-directional flows among the silos.

All of this leads to the even more critical nature of systems and the infrastructure that supports them.

Functionality

Technology-enabled capabilities, functions, and services underpin the modern global economy. *Functionality* is all about the ability to do a task capable of serving a purpose. Organizational functionality is the output of all IT work efforts. Functionality provides specific services to the business.

We need hyperawareness in IT. With our new understanding of business transformation and the vital importance of the technology infrastructure, IT must put a laser focus on a higher level of system understanding. Complex systems require systematic responses—the kind that can only come from working in a smarter way, designing an Agile infrastructure, and intelligently implementing the technology.

IT enables the infrastructure, code, and data that feed an organization. It equips the organization with printing, browsing, emailing, saving, opening, copying, downloading, activating, transferring, actuating, operating, and more.

It is not enough for IT to moderate the knowledge of the environment we operate in; IT must have mastery of it. IT must know it inside out.

Functionality requires a lifecycle of multi-level mastery. There are ten capabilities that IT must be skilled in to master the lifecycle of technology use:

- **Design** it: Imagine the components of a system.

- **Build** it: Bring the system to life for others to use.

- **Document** it: Write validation and record its existence.

- **Manage** it: Operate it on an ongoing basis to keep it up. Run it for users to use into the future.

- **Secure** it: Keep it for authorized use only. Maintain its integrity. Protect it from cyber threats. Keep it up and running.

- **Troubleshoot** it: Fix it when it breaks. Figure out what is wrong with it when it does not operate properly.

- **Hack** it: Take the perspective of one who might want to exploit what you have built. Act as an adversary, figuring out how to exploit it, break it, or make it do something it shouldn't.

- **Improve** it: Decide when it requires changes to make it better for its intended use. Make it faster, more scalable, and less prone to breaking.

- **Reimagine** it: See what you have built. See a new use case for it. Change it to match that new use case. Do something that was not imagined before.

- **Retire** it: Recognize when it is time to stop a function and move to another. Gracefully transition it out of operation.

Those ten capabilities are often seen in service providers. There is no room for ambiguity in operating systems that many customers come to rely on daily. This mentality of mastery of understanding is what IT needs to embody. The threefold umbrella of what IT provides to the business are:

- **Capabilities**: the powers or abilities to do something

- **Functions**: activities or purposes natural to or intended for a person or thing

- **Services**: the occupations or functions of serving

These technology-enabled provisions are what the organization sees, benefits from, and relies on day-to-day. IT provides these operations through a digital infrastructure. We know what the business needs. Now, how do we go about executing our part? We need to smooth out and accelerate the flow of our work. A *workflow* is an orchestrated and repeatable pattern of activity, enabled by the systematic organization of resources into processes. These processes create materials, provide services, or disseminate information.

Optimized Flow

It is important for flow to be optimized. Flow is the movement from one step to another, from beginning to end. The best flows happen without undue delay or waste. Eliyahu M. Goldratt, author of *The Goal*—I recommend it for business leaders and IT leaders alike—writes a story about the constraints in any system. In that story, the main character Alex is a plant manager (on his day off) leading a boys troop up a hill. He realizes the pace was too slow for the group to make it before nightfall. Alex came to the realization that while many of the kids had a fast pace, one kid, Herbie, was having trouble keeping pace. As Alex investigated how to correct this, he found Herbie had too much in his backpack. Redistributing the load to others lightened the load for everyone. But more importantly, Alex put Herbie at the front of the line. Alex found and fixed the constraint.[69]

How much more effective was this than accusing Herbie or fussing at the group? Work is required to get anything done. All work is done in some type of linear sequencing, also known as flow. Work from individuals combines into daily activities, which then manifest as workflow.

Without the proper approach and discipline, workflow gets constantly interrupted. The effect is progress that loses its pacing. The result is delayed value creation. Both creativity and production suffer.

IT sees the whole picture to optimize the workflow. It sees the ideas, tasks, collaboration, work, skills, and team members needed to deliver value. IT then pulls in various specialties and interacts with them to create flow that's minimally obstructed by friction, waste, or inefficiencies. In daily work, IT optimizes resources to enhance patterns of activity to enable the production of positive outcomes, services, and experiences.

Optimized flow is systematic and natural for the people involved. Good workflow intelligently provides value, optimizes finite resources, and makes a difference. A well-oiled workflow is tuned for global, end-to-end impacts and highly tuned to the purpose of the activity.

Flow moves from one step in a process to the next step. Flow uses thinking concepts such as Lean. Flow improves the service delivery of everything IT does. Flow uses a model for delivering services to the business—infrastructure, code, security, and data support.

Each service in flow consists of personnel performing certain tasks and following certain principles.

Let's take a step back to discover how this happens in IT. When the business comes to IT and asks for new services, IT looks at every step of every process and comes up with a timeline for delivery based on flow concepts, optimizing the flow from step to step and process to process from a systemic standpoint.

Fast flow is an enabler of getting things done in an efficient manner. It allows for ideation and the rapid iteration of trials. Fast flow gives us the freedom to experiment, try things out, and see what is possible. If we don't like the result, we can adjust or try again, starting at the ideation phase.

Fast flow allows IT to say *yes* more often, and it gives more definitive timelines to business requirements. Fast flow makes IT even more relevant. IT leverages fast flow not only for its own operations but also to help the business with new technology-enabled functionality.

There is planned work and unplanned work. The former is the chance for IT to be strategic, make improvements, and add functionality. Change can come in the form of maintenance operations and tasks. Ideally, we would like to plan these changes throughout the year and not be restricted to particular times, days, or seasons. When IT has Agile architecture and uses the Lean principles, IT can make changes more often, and that improves the stability and security of our applications and infrastructure.

Planned work can be mapped out and anticipated, increasing the chances of success. Secondary projects support general capability and the maintainable systems necessary over the long haul. Projects specifically tied to a business outcome are more strategic in nature.

Unplanned work is what IT calls "firefighting." IT must reduce unplanned work, as it crowds out strategic and operational work. Unplanned work disrupts the flow of personnel and time.

The flow IT creates in work directly affects the impact IT has on the business. The very nature of how work is done needs to be transformed. This transformation is aided by the principles of Lean.

Lean Principles

Lean accelerates the velocity of any process by reducing waste in all its forms. The benefit of this is the ability to see future waste and identify opportunities to reduce lead times where you never saw them before. Process steps thought to be important no longer are. Lean allows IT to see the difference between a task adding value and a task costing time and money.

Little's Law is a theorem that determines the average number of items in a stationary queuing system, based on the average waiting time of an item within a system and the average number of items arriving at the system per unit of time.[70] This law describes the drivers of lead time, the amount of time it takes your organization to deliver your service or products. The equation for lead time is the amount of work in a process divided by the average completion rate.

Businesses have used and discussed Lean principles to dramatically transform business operations. The Toyota Production System (TPS) popularized Lean. TPS used Lean principles to revolutionize the factory floor, dramatically improving performance and speed, and dramatically reducing waste. The Lean Enterprise Institute explains:

> Lean thinking changes the focus of management from optimizing separate technologies, assets, and vertical departments to optimizing the flow of products and services through entire value streams that flow horizontally across technologies, assets, and

departments to customers. Eliminating waste along entire value streams, instead of at isolated points, creates processes that need less human effort, less space, less capital, and less time to make products and services at far less costs and with much fewer defects, compared with traditional business systems.[71]

Many people mistakenly believe Lean only applies to manufacturing. However, Lean principles are also relevant to services, including IT, HR, and customer service. Lean has made its way into law firms and hospitals.

Lean's purpose is to accelerate the velocity of processes that feed the system and deliver business services. The faster IT delivers services, the faster the upstream business can deliver value to its customers. A primary way of increasing velocity is to reduce waste. Lean principles also help us see slowdowns, lags, and reworks where we never saw them before.

IT can use Lean to help discover which process steps we thought were important are not important at all. Value-added tasks will rise out of non-value-added tasks. Time traps—places where work sits idle waiting for human action—will start to stick out. When team members across the system look at the processes from beginning to end, they will find new ways of thinking about the process flow.

Unlike some waste reduction efforts that require capital outlay, revisiting workflows is process related. Often the technology needed to adjust workflow already exists in the environment, so little to no capital outlay is required.

When IT masters workflow optimization, it can branch out and engage other business units about waste. Lean principles lay the foundation for tackling the challenges of organizational silos. It is useful to understand four concepts related to Lean principles: work in progress (WIP), waste, variation, and feedback loops.

The first concept is work in progress. Things waiting on someone or something to complete is *work in progress*. Work has started, but the final product, service, or experience is not yet ready for consumption.

IT must have a firm grasp on the impacts of busy times, idle times, and hand-off times to identify inefficiencies. This allows work to then be optimized by increasing collaboration to accelerate workflow.

Roadblocks and other inhibitors of speed affect WIP. There are three patterns of success. First, identify where work is getting held up. Second, identify ways it can be unstuck. And lastly, identify ways to reduce the probability of work getting stuck again in the future.

How do you recognize a non-Lean WIP? Examples include compliance efforts, manual verification checks, management signoffs, wasteful meetings, budget justification delays, decision paralysis, soliciting multiple bids, and failure to complete preparation work upfront in the design.

One driver of WIP is the mobile workforce. In the traditional cube-bound work environment, as work requests came in, the workers were right there at their desks, ready to manage it. Today, many workers in the approval chain are mobile—in the field, on the road, or on airplanes. A request via email could sit in someone's inbox while they are in between offices. When the request is read, the person may not be in a good position to stop, gather data, think about it, and respond. Some of this happens in office-based interactions as well.

WIP provides opportunities for at least some workflow automation. Could approvals be streamlined, or could decision-supporting data become more readily available?

When a new request comes in from the business to IT and the business needs it fast, IT scrambles to assemble all the parties involved. An example of such a request could be a new system that collects information on the number of trucks transiting the garage or a summary of said truck fuel expenditures. Even as IT manages to produce what's needed in a record-breaking forty hours—an impressive turnaround—the business may scrap that plan and go an entirely different route.

Or three months into the development of the new point-of-sale system that won't integrate with the new rewards program, the marketing department might come back with a decision to change over 50 percent of the scope requirements. This requires major reworks and reallocation of staff.

Or the CIO who has just returned from a convention on new trends now wants to collect 50 terabytes of data from control units onboard tankers and transmit that data back to corporate to analyze in real time.

Every day, IT is required to be agile with providing infrastructure and software, all the while minimizing the potential risks. IT needs the ability to change on the fly, in part because business itself is required to do the same thing in the age of disruption.

But what, truly, does it mean to be agile? Does it mean fulfilling a request from the business when parameters—the scope, pacing, and delivery date—can, and often will, change? Does it mean that as soon as resources have been calculated for the new initiative, everything has been finalized, and new gear is on the way, you have delivered? What if the CIO lets you know something different is needed that requires a different infrastructure—when the gear is already on the way, or the contracts have already been signed? For IT, the frustration is genuine.

The demand and time pressures come from the global marketplace, which in turn leads to pressure inside your organization. This flows down to IT. The impact is felt by both entities. As a result, everyone must become more agile. Agility is the mindset—and action set—you need to affect the overall flow of value through your company into the market.

To create the framework necessary to become more agile, IT must take a hard look at new technologies, shifts, and changes to put in place.

One place agility comes into play is in programmatic infrastructure. This is a principle of both DevOps and workflow automation. Having one hundred steps in multiple processes is not a problem. It is not the number of steps from request to delivery that counts. It's how you can automate the workflow. Leading organizations know that with workflow automation, processes include many steps.

Tightening up the time it takes to execute WIP requires no capital outlay. It is about changing the way work is performed and improving the approach to critical tasks, sequencing, and handoffs. This tightening of time includes eliminating tasks that are wasteful.

As processes occur, we need to know how we are doing. We need to identify changes that might be needed, process feedback that has come in, and determine how we are meeting the needs of both our internal and external customers. We need answers to be successful and relevant.

Slow down to speed up. It seems counterintuitive, but it is often better to not work as fast in order to deliver on time. Each task is part of a flow of other tasks, which together create an outcome.

Are you always asked to do more than you can actually deliver? Or is the problem that you need to create WIP processes? How do you deliver what you should? How do you keep from being sidetracked with one-offs?

It is best to maintain a steady pace to reach your goal. This is more efficient than spreading yourself thin by jumping from one task to another. Avoid the temptation to taking a shortcut to the finish line only to have to go back for rework. The perception of getting things done may be an illusion. There are no shortcuts to reaching your goals. Be consistent in your work.

Get done the things that need to be done in a consistent manner in order to create a sustainable flow of value to the business. Think about consistency of performance over long periods versus being the hero, all knightly for only a portion of what the business needs from IT.

The second concept is waste. Anything that adds no value to the internal or external customer is *waste*. The fact is organizational resources are finite. We cannot afford waste. Two of IT's most valuable resources are time and money, and both are wasted when we don't think and work systematically. Organizations surviving today while still wasting resources will be tomorrow's news.

IT must stop spending valuable time, money, and resources on supporting obsolete systems, processes, and relationships. IT must instead focus on future growth.

In many cases, the business is constrained by these same limits. For everyone in the company, from boards of directors to C-suites to leaders in business units, cost control is important.

Good flow needs velocity, and waste is a major drag on that. Any resources tasked with fighting avoidable fires detract from more strategic work.

Budget cuts increase the challenges. IT then needs even more innovation. No matter what, IT must seek ways to work smarter, eliminate waste in processes, and redirect the resulting savings to fund innovation. All of this should happen while keeping budgets flat.

In reality, many IT departments have already been forced to scale back because of cuts in budgets and manpower. Businesses are pressuring us to streamline expenses and do more with less. Capital expenditures are down, but operations expenditures on third-party firms are up.

When IT is slow to respond to a business request, IT wastes business money. Slow hand-off times also create waste. Requests waiting for a simple change, sitting in the queue, are an opportunity for the automation of certain process flows. The cloud providers have mastered this. We in IT can master it too: the ability to orchestrate and automate multiple routine tasks, allowing higher speeds and giving the illusion of instantaneous service delivery.

Money tied up in an IT project that is way over budget wastes what IT could use elsewhere. This is similar to lacking a part on a plant assembly line. That is one reason for the importance of accurate estimates for projects, not only in money but also in time. IT projects are notorious for coming in late and, at times, failing to be delivered at all.

IT must make good use of our finite resources. We need to rationalize our technology portfolio, which includes applications, hardware, partners, methods of working, and how we spend our time. This means getting rid of things that slow processes, reduce competitive effectiveness, and constrain growth.

IT can do these actions well by leveraging Lean principles to identify and mitigate waste. Patterns of reducing waste include:

- Gaining visibility into workflows and value streams
- Reassessing the number of vendors, partners, and consultants for redundancy and overlap
- Investigating manufacturers' solution stacks
- Trimming the fat of too many vendors, partners, contractors, and tools
- Investigating converged infrastructure
- Investigating cloud partners to off-load functionality
- Making time spent collaborating via meetings more impactful
- Reducing expended time on symptoms by developing a culture of identifying the root causes

Tackling complexity is not a waste; it provides value. Understand it to optimize it.

The third concept is variation. A change or difference in condition or level is a variation. Sometimes variation manifests as inconsistencies. Variation can be normal—the nature of slight changes in processes, things, or flow. Variation can refer to differences in the way we do work, which can depend on who is doing the work and when it is done. But when variation exists without a design reason, it indicates we don't have a standard way of doing a process. Especially in complex environments, this can be problematic, as the level of dependencies dictates a more deterministic and thorough understanding of our environments.

Variation in how different colleagues perform the same work can be the enemy of success. Cloud services minimize variation in the process of provisioning services. This contributes to the speed benefit customers like about the cloud. The next thing we need is feedback.

The fourth lean principal concept is feedback loops. Signals that communicate status back to us are *feedback loops*. It's very important to have a feedback loop to influence how you are doing your work. You don't want to be going down the wrong path for too long. The output of one action produces response(s) to the initial actions. The signal returned is in response to the initial action. Without feedback, we cannot know the effects of our actions; we are limited in knowing which improvement to make and are blind to how we are doing.

Feedback loops are critical to excellence, change, transformation, survival, and thriving. If we take a course of action and don't have a feedback loop, we create a danger of losing and losing big, for when we invest in one of the many options available in business today, we must know how we are doing.

Feedback tells IT to stay the course or to turn and make a change. To go down one path blindly without the feedback loop is too costly in time, money, and effort.

Poor feedback loops in IT and other areas of business have led to inefficiencies and slow operations. Good feedback loops keep timely the response to business needs. Feedback loops keep service desk queues from backing up with chronic performance problems, items from languishing in the queue for weeks and potentially months, and IT from being unable to connect the dots between one issue and another.

If an issue takes too long to resolve, the person working on it needs to know what's going on and what has happened before. This is a feedback loop. When troubleshooting an issue, IT needs to know as soon as possible if they are going down the right path.

The feedback loop is critical to cybersecurity defense. Every second counts, and every second of not detecting a potential intrusion by an adversary can be costly. To deliver solutions and services to the business, we must get feedback to know which attack scenarios we are on the lookout for when considering mitigation options.

We need feedback loops to tell us how well things are operating in the field. Not hearing a complaint back from end users is not the same as good service. We need feedback loops within the company. If a business group in your company is unhappy with your services, you need to know as soon as possible and use the upfront time as the best chance of addressing the complaint. Otherwise, you'll find them working around you, using the corporate credit card to get something done without your input.

Try something different; ideate to see what works. Then use feedback loops to get the fast feedback and discover if that new action does or doesn't work for the business. Without fast feedback, IT loses the ability to try something else.

If we know something doesn't work, we have a better chance to iterate among different options until we can figure out exactly what needs to be changed and, from there, make the change needed. The business needs feedback. We must have feedback loops that are quick. The best example of this is DevOps, which can deliver new capabilities faster in application development.

As IT has fought the friction of organizational silos to keep pace with business demands, a movement called DevOps has developed to bring the principles of Lean and Agile to life, bringing quality code to life faster.

DevOps takes the challenges of IT software developers and of IT infrastructure teams head on. DevOps reduces friction and improves global optimization. The idea behind DevOps is to bring developers closer to the business. In this way, developers properly capture workflow and functionality in both the front end and back end.

DevOps uses the principles of Lean to enable closer integration of software coders and operations. This expands the speed and quality of code delivered, which results in the ability to experiment more frequently and to respond to customer needs at market speed. And this becomes more critical as more standalone products are enhanced with service components powered by software.

The secret to success for anything IT sets out to accomplish is alignment.

Alignment

The arrangement of the team composition, priorities, and workflow into useful positions is *alignment*. Alignment is an agreement of focus between cross-functional teams and working groups. Any time a group or individual works out of alignment, they create friction and drag. Alignment positions elements to optimize their combined utility.

From strategic guidance down to operational priorities on the front lines, IT aligns work efforts. As IT coordinates and aligns these, work efforts are in turn aligned with the larger organizational context, from the boardroom to the service desk. Alignment allows work efforts to be coordinated across the horizontal value chain, so they are not hindered by vertical organizational structures.

Make alignment visible across the workflow, handoffs, and dependencies of multiple teams.

The benefit of alignment is acceleration, a key ingredient in getting from here (the current state) to there (the goal). Increasing the velocity of the workflow meets business demands.

If our competitor is delivering to market more quickly than us, we frequently need to increase the flow of value through our system to match. Almost all business processes can be negatively affected by slow flow.

When more speed is needed, humans can bring in the robots. Robots—not the ones from the movies but rather process automation tools—lend themselves to repetitive or lower-level automation tasks. These augmentations emulate and integrate the actions of a human interacting within digital systems to execute a business process.

IT teams have more than one way to do work. Let's examine the multimodal mode. Multitasking is a popular myth—at least on the personal level. Rather than a human doing several things at once, people actually context-switch very quickly from one task to another, to another, and back again. This happens so quickly it gives the illusion of tasks happening concurrently.

In computing, context switches happen even more rapidly. The processor is interrupted to perform an alternative task. With multiple processors, however, each one can perform at the same time within the system without stress. But when humans multitask, they slow themselves down and put stress on the brain.

To solve this, work in teams. In teams, one person can be processor 1, another person processor 2, and so on. Teams process tasks similar to the way computers process tasks, without stress. When the amount of work overruns the number of processors, aka workers, problems happen.

At one point, after being too slow in responding to new business demands, some IT teams considered restructuring themselves. One part of IT did traditional tasks, while another took care of fast needs. The term *bimodal* arose. Bimodal can change your thinking about your role in IT.

Gartner, a global research firm that provides information and advice to IT leaders, teaches this about bimodal:

> Bimodal is the practice of managing two separate but coherent styles of work: one focused on predictability; the other on exploration. Mode 1 is optimized for areas that are more predictable and well-understood. It focuses on exploiting what is known, while renovating the legacy environment into a state that is fit for a digital world. Mode 2 is exploratory, experimenting to solve new problems and optimized for areas of uncertainty.[72]

Some may view the bimodal approach as a quick fix, fast and flashy, no longer tied down by slower legacy systems. But IT supports more than one or two modes. IT finds modes of workflow that adapt to the needs of functionality. IT embraces the entire team and entire range of approaches, with all team members growing as professionals, becoming more agile and capable of speeding up value delivery.

IT teams operating through multimodality work at different speeds, with many internal customers, on different timelines. Market disruption has added the need for more modes of workflow in IT. IT multitasks its functions as it adjusts to new demands, thereby allowing for the creation of various new functionality across a wide spectrum of use cases in the organization.

Identify your team's approach to servicing the business, paying down technical debt, and categorizing the types of work involved. Consider these four types of work: tactical implementation, strategic implementation, maintenance, and troubleshooting.

Identify the types of work streams, determine how much of the work done is drawing resources from the same teams, and consider if enough attention is being given to each team's current capacity and delivery commitments inside of each work type.

Multimodal workflow delivers value with multiple modes of work styles, speed, and delivery timelines. Each mode shares integrated functionality with the others but focuses on different organizational priorities. Modes enable IT to keep the lights on, continually improve service, and deliver on digital transformation efforts.

Workflow modes are a horizontal alignment approach that allows for speed, efficiency, efficacy, and value creation. All modes are critical to realizing the functionality that IT enables for the business.

IT adapts until it's aligned and ready to build, design, support, and protect technology-enabled functionality. To get there, IT creates infrastructure that adapts to a challenging and ever-changing environment.

Adaptive Infrastructure

Infrastructure needs to be designed and configured well. It needs to be capable of adapting quickly to dynamic requirements. This is an IT requirement for faster delivery.

The scope of adaptive infrastructure includes traditional infrastructure, all support areas for the lifecycle of the code, and all support areas of data.

IT works better when it recognizes that business units may see everything from IT as infrastructure that supports their work. IT approaches this by supporting and scaling infrastructure, code, and data enablement.

Infrastructure should be designed and configured to dynamically adapt to changes in the environment. Common examples include:

- The user changed, the system adapted, and the interface was adjusted.

- The device plugged into that port was exchanged for a different type of device; the switch detected this and adjusted the port settings and quality of service dynamically.

- The researcher left the laboratory and logged in remotely from Starbucks on the way home; the system detected the change in location and altered which files were available.

- The web front end was moved from the data center to AWS, and user traffic was automatically rerouted.

- With one AP down, others adjusted the power and radio signal to compensate.

- A new open-source library was added to the build, and it was automatically checked for errors and scanned for vulnerabilities.

When the environment or situation changes, the infrastructure should automatically adjust.

Moving at the speed of business while at the same time mitigating the risks requires IT to examine whether our infrastructure helps or hinders the needs of end users. The traditional infrastructural design of five to ten years ago may no longer meet our needs. Depending on time and requirements, different components could better mitigate and upgrade in much smaller timespans. Spans as short as eighteen months or two years are now possible. IT has the knowledge and principles to do this smartly.

IT supports the systems that enable users to use data, services, and organizational assets. IT's highest priority is to ensure a highly available, always-on environment that hosts the data and services. IT ensures all components, in coordination with risk mitigation input, are kept up to date to improve functionality, security, and reliability. IT brings adaptive infrastructure into reality for its organization.

Stop designing and configuring *things* and start designing *systems*. Three important system principles are:

- A system's design really matters—do your job every day to create critical design.

- Resources inside of these systems should be virtualized—give each resource the capability to be called upon when needed, independent of location.

- Infrastructure needs to be programmable—IT must be able to create what we need to run. IT must code apps, handle data, and serve up services to users.

Design Matters

Functionality is a key design matter. *"Good design requires good communication, especially from machine to person,"* explains Donald A. Norman, author of *The Design of Everyday Things.*[73] Good design indicates what actions are possible, what is happening, and what is about to happen. Users (internal or external) will overcome the frustrations of poor design of the systems they must use to do their jobs every day. But this should not be necessary. Steve Jobs said, *"Design is not just what it looks like and feels like. Design is how it works."*[74]

The design should be so intuitive that a user knows that a specific button on the interface is a thing to be clicked now. They should recognize which button to push next. They should perceive that the hourglass or arrow that changes on the mouse pointer indicates the system is working on the request. Users should not have to get used to *continue, enter, confirm,* or any other function.

From logging in to finding data to filling out online forms, the process of business means interacting every day with the outcomes of design. If users are constantly doing workarounds, going into the shadows, or altering the customer experience to get things done, a purposeful redesign is needed.

Three dimensions to consider when designing systems are processes, components, and technology. Each is mapped to users, nodes, apps, data, processes, and services.

Stay focused on the stated goals, remembering what IT is trying to accomplish. It is critical that IT locks in on their organization's business purpose, needed usability, and required system reliability.

Follow the answer to those questions as you design across teams and for functionality. Rather than do what you can to simply get through, make sure any design compromises are communicated to stakeholders before you accept them. Even better, accept no design compromises.

Too many times IT lets systems be a result of unintentional design. There is no rhyme or reason for how our systems work. But if we approach design from the standpoint of the user, we in IT will significantly improve the experience and the business's bottom line.

The first step is to remember that users are part of the company's value creation chain. Too often we are guilty of looking down on users for not knowing how to do something or for making mistakes. The fault may instead lie with our own poor design and the constraints from the technology we ourselves have chosen. Or we may have created problems with the way we set up the product or with a lack of integration.

Good design facilitates better experiences and outcomes for users. The same principles that make simple things either work well or poorly also apply to more complex operations, including ones in which human lives are at stake. We in IT have not done our job until our design is good, wise, and safe.

In the case of technology, most accidents that are attributed to human error have poor designs as one of the causation factors. Human-centered design is critical to building safety into our systems.

What kind of design are we talking about? It could be for printing, dialing a number, or logging into a web app. These functions can be provided by systems that run on hybrid infrastructure, on hyper-converged infrastructure, or in cloud.

The answer is rapidly becoming less about options like *this* or *that*, *virtual* or *physical*, *x* or *y*. Today's design must be architected differently from just six months ago—technology advances that quickly. Nice-to-have wireless, virtual desktop infrastructure (VDI), and HTML5 are no longer options.

To make our systems resistant to causing accidents or affecting service, IT must embed design principles into our thinking. These principles must consider safety considerations. We must prevent accidents, knowing they are caused by the confluence of multiple factors. These factors can range from unsafe individual acts to organizational errors. The "Swiss cheese" model of accident causation says many contributing factors to an accident are latent errors lying dormant, waiting to be triggered by any number of active errors. Humans are prone to operational errors, which requires properly designed systems to mitigate the errors humans inevitably commit.

Some design principles include migrating from spinning disks to solid state, abstracting the app from the underlying physical infrastructure, moving to virtual machines, and moving from virtual machines to containers.

Nearly all adverse events involve a combination of active and latent factors. Active failures are the unsafe acts committed by workers. An example of an active failure would be an engineer who chooses not to follow the standard operating process and run a new piece of code through dynamic scanning before deploying to production. Latent conditions are the failures built into the security or operational controls by IT. Latent conditions are failures waiting to be triggered by an active error. An example of a latent condition would be a web application firewall configuration setting that is not set to block. If you combine this latent condition with our example of an active failure—failing to scan for known vulnerabilities—you get a successful exploit of the application from hackers.

The Swiss cheese model, invented by James Reason, will help an IT team's design processes to head off incidents. It's human nature to seek simple answers when catastrophic failure occurs. We try to identify the culprit to receive the blame at the site of the incident. But blame won't fix the damage. Wiser organizations adopt a Swiss cheese model for risk analysis and risk mitigation because it provides a holistic and typically more accurate framework for preventing accidents, rather than blaming afterward. The Swiss cheese model recognizes that culture, organization, and process design are all essential building blocks to prevent human error and system failure.

Complex systems design can be greatly scaled to the point of obscuring the interactions. When systems break or fail, the common thought is to find the one thing that will explain it all. In complex systems, there are multiple interrelated *causes* that interact in certain ways that lead to a failure.

Especially concerning are those technology systems that intersect with physical systems that could impact human safety. That is why IT's designs should build in agility and resiliency to reduce the chance of service failure.

IT must also design our processes and culture to limit the amount of debt we accumulate and to pay down any debt as we go, so we stay agile. We compound the benefits by embedding resiliency into our processes.

This should not come as a surprise, for anything in our economy that matters, such as auto safety, building safety, and medical device safety, is built-in, by design. The result is more resilient systems that do their jobs and prevent pain.

Virtualization Systems

Resiliency is supported by the ability for resources to be virtualized. Reboot nodes, not systems! Migrate away from long uptimes on nodes. Patch, fix, and improve nodes as much as needed. Then reboot them.

Make this entire patching and updating sequence a normal process. But strive for very long system uptimes. The system is what humans and other machines interact with constantly. When systems are down while rebooting, that is not good. Work stops. Customers can't use websites to purchase products. Assembly lines cannot continue.

Embrace the difference between nodes and systems. That is great design. Swap out nodes so users can use another node without service disruption. Don't subject users to unavailability.

Design like you expect to have to update stuff! Do not act like it is your smartphone, which is unavailable to receive phone calls while it is re-starting after an update.

Virtualization is growing quickly. Any service or application should be free to be moved from one infrastructure to another, scale between different providers, and maintain control systems when moved. And at the same time, still maintain performance, corporate governance, and business and customer functionality.

Poor design leads to heartache in operational maintenance. The more your business services are tied to a specific architecture, hardware, and providers, the harder it is to make changes. In those cases, simple maintenance tasks can become quite convoluted. Instead, stop your business services from failing because of dependence on a single un-derlying node or component.

Some network devices have been working and available for a long time. Their three or four years of uptime is great for reliability and availability but not so great for keeping up with code upgrades.

A shift in mindset is needed. So rather than having long uptimes for individual routers, firewalls, and servers, we need long uptimes for ser-vices. It's fine to patch and reboot often; but minimize the time it takes to reboot and disrupt service.

Great design detaches the physical from the digital workload. Good de-sign is time-independent, location independent, agnostic (not tied to a specific device), and identity-based. Key concepts to be aware of are design patterns that are highly available, updateable, easy to trouble-shoot, easy to patch, very resilient to failure, and able to be rebuilt rel-atively quickly.

Containers are the next level of virtualization and isolation because the code is developed separately rather than run in production. Faster and more agile than hypervisors, containers allow us to focus on the code and not the underlying dependencies.

One of the benefits of detachment is removing dependencies and making system and application upgrades easier.

We in IT need to remove the friction around making changes to apps and tools. We must not be afraid to change early in a work stream or project to adapt to changing conditions. We must provide micro-services for computers. We must spin up a server when needed in AWS and spin down when no longer needed.

Every IT department provides basic services as an option that can be scaled as consumption rates increase. For IT, it's not a question of whether we should virtualize, serve up virtual desktops, let users bring their own devices, use cloud apps, or have firewalls cover physical as well as virtual environments. We are at a point where all of these should be considered basic services.

IT should not get caught up in decision paralysis, running endless analyses to determine if cutting-edge technology should be used. Instead, IT should automatically leverage advancements in converged infrastructure, cloud services, and flexible financing, alter how we use partners, and virtualize the front-end user interface. IT can ideate quickly over each new technology to determine if it is a good fit for our businesses.

For example, take the case of virtual desktop infrastructure. This is a service that should be available for all core IT services across all industries. It is the virtualization of the user's desktop, made available remotely anywhere and anytime. By leveraging virtual infrastructure, IT can create a core service from a small block of its infrastructure, optimize it for VDI requirements, and not require too large of an initial budget outlay. IT can intelligently scale infrastructure as needed by building modular blocks on top of converged infrastructure.

Virtualization means accessing the corporate offices via network connectivity—through local or remote access—whether on the road, at a Starbucks, or in an airport. This makes universal and unified access available to everyone. IT consolidates the access methodology to secure this universal access, providing universal visibility, strong device identification, and a service assurance model to meet the needs of business users doing their work.

Let's say an employee named Jose comes into the Houston branch office to prepare for a client meeting. No one is around, and he needs to connect his laptop to the network to access his Outlook calendar. Jose can't find an open port in any of the cubes, so he decides to unplug a little black box on the floor next to the printer to connect his laptop. An intelligent network could handle this scenario without any problem while still ensuring a differentiated experience based on the user, the device, and a required service level. For example, if Jose were to swap the network connection of a printer and IP phone, or an analog fax machine connected via an Analog Telephone Adapter (ATA) and an IP video camera, a smart network should handle it seamlessly while maintaining security, functionality, and quality of service.

Networks IT builds should be adaptive enough to not require human intervention. Depending on the context of the connection, the network should identify the device Jose has plugged in, profile the device type, determine the correct access rights, and then begin profiling the traffic types generated from that wired or wireless virtual port.

If a smart TV is plugged into a jack, it should not have universal access to all the data center resources. Jose should not have to worry about where to plug in his device. If there is an open port in the conference room, the risk level of exposing the entire data center to a guest should not depend on a verbal policy or the manual creation of a Mac-based allow list on a switch. The network should be smart enough to handle a guest, distinguishing the rights and access level of each user. All connection types should be logged, all access attempts should be correlated in near real time and logged historically on the back end, and all network traffic types should be profiled automatically.

This is the nature of a smart network designed for today's business requirements.

To be a high-performing IT organization, we should excel at service operations and provide responsive, reliable service delivery, a low mean time-to-delivery, and a low mean time-to-repair. *Active* should be the new standard. If you want to ensure the backup works, use it to process actual workload. Use it in production.

We wouldn't be here without standards; they matter. Use IT standards to leverage global accumulated knowledge and experience. Building codes, ratings on electrical standards, safety rules, regulations, and other standards guide who can design and build in the physical world. The water we drink from the faucet, food we eat at a restaurant, elevators we step into, and cars we drive on the road—everything we use is rooted in standards, along with checks and balances.

Many standards go into making a building safe, such as guidelines, safety protocols, sprinkler systems, emergency lighting, fences, locks, security guards, and cameras.

Programmable Infrastructure

To scale and speed up functionality, we need programmable infrastructure. Programmable infrastructure allows a combination of direct, intermediary, and indirect means to instruct the provisioning, configuration, and maintenance of its operations. Infrastructure encompasses all computing, virtualization, networking, and storage on the back end. Also included is on-premises gear, cloud services, hybrid cloud, remote sites, mobile users and devices, and more. Infrastructure also manages users, identity governance, user devices, and user entitlements to services. Beyond the normal configuring of gear, infrastructure includes patching and monitoring. Think about configuring with a programmer's mindset: "code once, use often."

Manual configuration is approaching legacy status. This marks the coming end of box-to-box configuration. IT now replaces manual config tasks with programmable configuration. This centralizes policy configuration. We use code to program the environment on the fly.

Physical or virtual? On-premises or off-premises? Outsource or insource? *Yes* to them all.

IT must abstract these questions and their implementations from our organizations' services, applications, and data. IT must build northbound application programming interfaces (APIs) for business and process intelligence. IT must build southbound APIs for the heavy lifting of translating the config commands of the underlying infrastructure.

Connectivity is greatly enhanced when IT builds a platform for APIs. APIs are sets of routines, protocols, and tools for building software applications that specify how software components should interact. APIs are a necessity in the digital world for enabling new services and revenue streams. APIs provide the foundational technology for digital enablement and new service and business opportunities. Behind every smartphone, mobile app, and connected experience is at least one API.

IT has the exciting opportunity to support our businesses' digital efforts by exposing more systems to APIs and by using third-party sources to enrich our own sources. This also allows for greater scalability by reusing what has already been created. The value is not in rebuilding what is there but rather, via API, using other platforms to enhance ours.

Brian Koles of ChallengePost explains, "*A company without APIs is like a computer without internet. You wouldn't want a computer without internet access…. If software developers are the new rock stars, then APIs are the instruments with which they make their music.*"[75]

As software continues its transformation, a lack of connectivity increasingly equates to being broken. Many of the best apps are skillfully interconnected collections of APIs.

Digital interfaces are needed for ecosystem partners to work with any organization. In our digital world, platforms and ecosystems will dominate. Our value will lie in our ability to string all the API accessible services together into a cohesive offering. APIs will help service people-to-people, people-to-machine, and machine-to-machine connectivity. They are foundational for the opportunities of the Internet of Things (IoT).

The impact of APIs are increased partnerships, increased connectivity, and often, longer supply chains.

For IT to speed up workflow and produce faster results for the business, it must possess orchestration, automation, and acceleration.

Orchestration allows for the intelligent staging and sequencing of work tasks. It is critical to optimizing flow. Going faster is great, but we might go faster doing the wrong things and end up consistently producing unwanted outcomes. IT must ensure it maintains tight control over the orchestration process, for we have seen how bad guys have used automated tools and processes to exploit us.

Automation is not about replacing people. Automation is about improving process. In an ideal world, your organization would simply hire more people to do the work. But today, more people are not on the way. You are still on the hook for producing results with what you have. In IT, automation allows processes to accelerate and provides flexibility to experiment—changes can be rolled out quickly and IT efforts can be multiplied. Automation is about taking the knowledge of individual tasks and orchestrating workflow. In this light, a whiteboard full of tasks that number in the hundreds becomes trivial when workflow is automated. Make no mistake; human intuition, know-how, and intelligence are required to design such a system, maintain it, and, ultimately, optimize this process. Automation accelerates our processes and provides for agility. We can use tools like Chef, Puppet, Ansible, and AWS CloudFormation to accomplish this goal.

Acceleration is about speeding up the rate of value delivery. We must do our best to make sure that, as we improve our speed, we add value and reduce waste. We need flow. To confront complexity, IT standardization can reduce the number of moving parts by reusing common processes, tools, and inputs. This can make workflow more predictable and can lead to consistent operation and improvement. Acceleration also lends itself to automation. We can leverage robotic process automation (RPA) to emulate some human tasks and robotic decision automation (RDA) inside security operations centers to tackle the volume of security alerts and decrease the time to detect and investigate.

With the speed and repeatability provided by automation, IT supports the abstraction of infrastructure. We gain agility by virtualizing the infrastructure underneath the business service. We decouple the application from the infrastructure, the service from the application, and the user from the device. Acceleration also means we need to embed user and device identities with security protections into the roaming experience.

Digital Realm

Let's explore three viewpoints of complexity of the digital realm from the perspective of IT. They are infrastructure, code, and data. Business users have changed, from their use of technology to their perceptions, all the way to their expectations of what is possible. IT is in a fierce time battle with the consumer side of technology to satisfy the needs of a user population asking why we are so slow. Let's explore the digital world.

Infrastructure

There is a complex web of infrastructure underneath the hood. The modern economy is a digital world overlaid and integrated with the physical world. The digital space is made up of 0s and 1s, freed of the constraints of physical limitations. These 0s and 1s move at near-instantaneous speed—always on, always connected, and increasingly dependent.

Fast and complex, today's disruptive digital world carries with it perils, challenges, constraints, and risks. A lot of the data generation and processing occurs outside the IT-controlled infrastructure.

Modern networks are borderless. Many network users operate away from the office or do at least part of their work remotely. With this ability to work anytime and anywhere, IT has enabled a mobile workforce no longer tied to the desk.

This anytime-anywhere-on-any-device access has profoundly affected maintenance windows. With the amount of preventive maintenance necessary for applying Microsoft patches to servers, for example, IT knows there are many times systems need to be interrupted. As the number of managed systems grows, more patching and rebooting is needed. With business-critical operations running all the time, it becomes a challenge to isolate individual components, which are heavily interdependent, and third-party systems to get maintenance windows to update. These challenges come into conflict with the business need to keep systems online, all the time. The results are fewer and shorter approved maintenance windows. We'll see an even more pronounced impact later when we discuss convergence.

Digitization has virtualized the physical world. Images, sounds, text, and pictures can be converted into 0s and 1s. Audios, videos, faxes, conversations, and information are all free of physical media now. Aided with high speeds and ubiquitous network access, those bits can be transmitted directly to users on their devices anywhere around the world.

Our digital world has seen amazing and transformative changes over the last few years. With high-speed connectivity becoming pervasive, a wide range of new services is now available—from website browsing and email to voice and high-definition video delivery.

The globe has embraced the internet for business use. One effect of the internet is the consumerism-led mindset of end users. This mindset stretches from the executive suite all the way to edges of the organization, dominating people's expectations and conditioning for what service should look like.

Capacity planning, fault management, and troubleshooting have all become more intricate and more involved.

Factors are in flux when planning for how much storage will be needed over the next year or whether a wide area network (WAN) link is big enough. Design and planning phases are more rapid. The infrastructure elasticity provided from cloud providers influences the design of corporate-owned infrastructures. Troubleshooting from the help desk now involves identifying where the user is and what kind of device and app they are using.

How IT designs, builds, operates, and protects technology for business has changed. We are more than ever dealing with parts working together as parts of an interconnecting network. We are thinking and processing horizontally in a vertical world. The advances in our modern economy have occurred largely due to the interaction of many smaller parts sharing, exchanging, and working together as systems. IT must follow suit and embrace increased connectivity and cooperation in its management of systems.

A system is a regularly interacting set of connected people, parts, or things that functions as a whole. In technology, a system consists of nodes—a network of endpoints, connectivity, and communications.

The internet, e-commerce, software development, and process automation are all systems designed to produce outcomes and services. Many "systems of systems" interact, each with their own constraints and processes. We in IT can manage this noisy, confusing, fast, and seemingly always changing technology environment.

To those outside IT, the initial contact point is all that is seen. IT knows the complexity behind these systems. The most challenging complexities are those not directly controlled by IT. Many third parties interact with our systems in ways that may not be completely understandable. IT influence may decrease while our businesses, partnerships, and dependencies on an ecosystem are normal.

If we zoom in on systems, the basic unit is the node. Objects with electronics run some form of operating system code, process machine instructions locally, and communicate over an IP stack. Nodes come in many forms such as PCs, laptops, tablets, smartphones, IP phones and cameras, thermostats, printers, etc.

What makes systems interesting and useful is communication among them enabled by connectivity. Without connectivity, technology has limited value—there can be no system. Connectivity is fundamental to all systems, living and technical. Systems thrive because of networks—groups or systems of interconnected people, parts, or things.

Vessels carry blood to the brain. Arteries carry oxygen from the heart. In a digital system, networks carry the bits that make local node activity happen. With or without cables, nodes on a networked system can process local code and communicate with other nodes. Wired, wireless, and remote connectivity is underpinned by a worldwide fiber cabling system.

Nodes talk a lot. The internet we know today was built by the US military for connectivity and functionality. It is amazing to look back at the initial need for communication for a handful of nodes in a research environment and see how it could, decades later, lead to global connectivity supporting billions of nodes. The resulting pervasive connectivity is the underlying basis for the astounding explosion of new opportunities for our economy and way of life.

The underlying infrastructure, protocols, and systems of the internet, however, were not designed for security.

Sometimes it is amazing that anything works on the internet. The address space of the fourth version of Internet Protocol (IPv4) was more than large enough to accommodate basic functionality. However, the explosion of connected governments, companies, and individuals and the deluge of diverse IP-enabled devices today will require the sixth version of Internet Protocol (IPv6) and its larger address space in the future.

We are learning to expect to connect with refrigerators, light poles, and tractors. In short, connectivity is pervasive. The infrastructure required to support IP is impressive. It is firmly rooted in the physical world—with most of the traffic traversing physical cabling. However, there is also a diverse set of non-cabling infrastructure that allows users to be untethered. IP is carried via land, air, sea, and space.

Cabling remains key to our digital world. Underground and underwater fiber-optic cables connect the internet's backbone across the world. The global economy is dependent on it, with 99 percent of all intercontinental internet traffic being carried via underwater fiber.[76]

High-speed bandwidth is available to both businesses and homes via nearly ubiquitous broadband access. However, there are still millions of homes in the US that don't have that type of access yet. The branch and home offices are being reimagined. This opens new opportunities for small businesses and teleworkers. Metro Ethernet options are continually being offered at lower rates and higher bandwidths, such as 10 Gbps. In data centers, 10 Gbps is becoming more common, and even 40 Gbps and 100 Gbps connectivity is becoming available. Internet speeds to the home are expanding to up to 1 Gbps.

Both users and their devices have been untethered from the wall jack. This is made possible via several technological advancements. First up are cellular networks, with 3G and 4G currently prominent and 5G right around the corner. These are powered by cell towers and antennas that litter our landscape. The current Wi-Fi standard of 802.11x can get up to gigabit-plus speeds. For hard-to-reach locations with limited physical cabling infrastructure access, we have satellite-based infrastructure. That includes location-based services (LBS) provided by space-based infrastructure for both military and commercial use. We are also near even more coverage via balloons and airplane-based network access to bring connectivity to areas that are difficult to connect by fiber.

The internet is a global, resilient traffic delivery system made possible by IPv4 and in the future IPv6, border gateway protocol (BGP), and autonomous systems (AS) with autonomous system numbers (ASN). The domain name system (DNS), powered by root servers, allows people to easily navigate the web with human-readable names.

Connectivity provides the foundation for all that is possible in a digital economy. In 1995, the year that the first commercial traffic was allowed on the internet, Amazon and eBay were born. When people, processes, and data are connected, the possibilities are limitless. Every business process opens the possibility of participating in a system that allows human interactions to be transformed, which in turn transforms how we live, work, make war, and solve problems.

The impact can be felt everywhere. For those who can remember what the process of an operating system upgrade used to look like, you can appreciate downloading the newest version of the Microsoft operating system via the internet instead of installing it from a compact disc (CD). The existence of a simplified upgrade process that can be set to automatic, combined with high-speed broadband, paved the way for the Microsoft 10 operating system to be streamed in the background to millions of users over the internet.

Given the pervasive locations of high-speed access, such as coffee shops, malls, and airports, we are now location independent. And we may or may not be on secure networks and servers when we do our work.

Along the same lines, consider how you no longer go to a rental store to pick up the latest movie. You stream it, compliments of the digital world. Or how you back up a data center over the wire instead of to removable media tapes.

Some new offices are taking advantage of new speeds to go all-wireless, with LAN-like performance exceeding many wired connections. Some homes have more bandwidth than some businesses. Newer cellular technology also provides high-speed access, allowing bandwidth-heavy apps like video to be delivered to and through phones.

Many people are drifting away from landline phones to instead use cellphones. Integrated TV, voice, and internet services over broadband are available. A wave of new end-user devices is expanding the options beyond the traditional laptop to include smartphones and tablets.

Some new start-up companies are forgoing buying their own infrastructures and instead relying completely on the cloud to operate. Corporations are migrating off traditional, expensive WAN links and going with higher-speed and cheaper internet connections with virtual private networks (VPNs) linked to corporate networks.

Progress builds on existing infrastructures. In a world where machines talk to other machines, the opportunities are abundant. IT has an opportunity to guide the discovery process. The existing infrastructure and processes have constraints that must be confronted.

In the background, IT must also keep today's revenue engine up and running while protecting it from ever-present cyber-attacks.

Both humans and machines talk, in various ways. Connectivity is becoming omnipresent across all domains—machines talking to other machines, machines talking to people, and people finding new ways to talk to other people. People-to-people (P2P) connections include capabilities such as workforce collaboration, instant communications, and expert locators. Machine-to-people (M2P) connections include feedback from technical systems, feedback from dashboards, and location navigation. Machine-to-machine (M2M) connections include sensors, radio-frequency identification (RFID), Wi-Fi or cellular communication links, and autonomic computing software programmed to help a networked device interpret data and make decisions.

The internet and improved standards for wireless technology have expanded the role of telemetry, the collection and automatic transmission of data from remote locations, from pure science, engineering, and manufacturing to everyday use in products like home heating units, electric meters, and internet-connected appliances. Products built with M2M communication capabilities are marketed to end users as being "smart."

When many components come together, we get convergence. It brings together disparate systems to form a whole. It unifies smaller moving parts to make them more dependent, more complex, and more rapid. Convergence is the future of digital infrastructure and operating models.

Consider further these five areas of convergence: protocol convergence, converged infrastructure, hybrid on-premises/cloud, information technology/operational technology convergence (IT/OT), and smart things.

Convergence affects such areas as data, voice, and video, transmitting them on a single wire. It includes information technology and operational technology for smart systems. It happens in team collaboration.

Traditionally the cost to upgrade gear has prevented upgrades. Now convergence offers traditional programmable devices the option to share the same data service fabric as the data network. Convergence also integrates industrial data for remote control and automation of industrial systems.

Protocols will continue to be converged to optimize shared transports resources. Convergence changes the traditional models of support, protection, and maintenance. IT first took advantage of data and voice convergence years ago. In those early years, many thought it was risky to put voice traffic on the network. Traditional private branch exchange (PBX) systems used to run on that PC on the floor in the wiring closet that no one touched. Now systems run multiple applications on a modern unified collaboration platform, making use of available resources on the wire. Voice was added, then video, and then physical video. You now see convergence in the data center with storage traffic.

In protocol convergence, IPv4 is the industry-leading protocol on both private and public networks. Its current available address space is all but exhausted. Through workarounds over the years, including the widespread use of network address translation (NAT), we continue to make it through. Now we have the approaching advantage of IPv6 with its much larger address space. We can expect a long period of dual stack routing.

IP-based networks make up the service backplane. This shared resource is built upon a long history of stable and reliable use. Traditional data now has company of quality of service (QoS), virtual isolation via virtual local area networks (VLANs), and higher bandwidth speeds (up to 100 Gbps). All of these create a platform for integrated data, voice, and video.

The convergence of physical security with IP-based infrastructure is another fascinating use of a share resource. Increasingly, more buildings are installing new IP-enabled, high-resolution cameras with video feeds riding on common networks. And traditional security cameras mounted on the exterior of buildings for security guards to monitor are now being converged onto data networks. These campus and core backbone networks are now transmitting video feeds that protect the exterior gates and the back doors as well as any internal hallways of physical buildings.

Convergence is seen in traditional public switched telephone network (PSTN) analog systems that are steadily migrating over to digital and IP telephony. Video conferencing from one desktop to another, video training, and even interactive video are also migrating.

Convergence has implications for the lifecycle management of an infrastructure, in particular for patching systems. From network switches and routers that process packets to storage and computers that store and process the video, consideration must be given to how the system's design accounts for minimizing or eliminating disruption. What once was just a printer is now also a camera recording activity on the grounds.

Infrastructure that is converged is the new future. Converged infrastructure operates by grouping multiple information technology components into a single, optimized computing package. These components may include servers, data storage devices, networking equipment, and infrastructure management software.

Convergence has taken off in the data center. Convergence began years ago with Internet Small Computer Systems Interface (iSCSI), Network

File System (NFS), and Common Internet File System (CIFS) protocols sharing storage traffic with data traffic. Now we are looking at Fiber Channel (FC). FC is the backbone of traditional storage area networks, with characteristics such as high performance and high security, measured by domain expertise and storage administration. Today, many people see FC as still being off-limits to convergence.

The benefits of FC include fewer moving parts, shared physical devices, lower cabling costs, and lower power and cooling requirements. FC storage is coming under the realm of convergence. That convergence is being made possible with enhancements to the Ethernet protocol to support FC and bigger pipes. Pipes as large as 10 Gbps, 40 Gbps, and even 100 Gbps allow a large enough highway system to handle data, voice, video, and block-level and file-based storage, all differentiated based on logical separation, performance, scalability, and security.

This allows for a converged fabric inside the data center, which has implications for the design of data centers. These implications include how storage is laid out, how the different components integrate, how computers interface with the network, how the network takes input from other networks, and how both physical and virtual computing resources integrate with other networks.

Convergence helps the data fabric become smarter and more agile. This produces the ability to carve out virtual lanes for applications, data, voice, and video types.

The above elements become part of the agility IT needs to keep up with business demands. To equip the business, new applications are brought online, new characteristics for disk I/O come about, and new characteristics for data traffic arise. From bursty to bulky, the data fabric can and must handle all of the different types of services and requirements.

Convergence removes huge constraints IT has had in designing the data center, resulting in isolation, secure connectivity, performance, and service assurance.

Hyperconvergence is a level beyond convergence. It's an infrastructure system with a software-centric architecture that tightly integrates computers, storage, networking, virtualization resources, and other technologies from scratch in a commodity hardware box supported by a single vendor.

A hyperconverged system allows the integrated technologies to be managed as a single system through a common toolset. They can be expanded through the addition of nodes to the base unit. One use case for a hyperconverged system is virtual desktops. Under the converged infrastructure approach, a vendor provides a preconfigured bundle of hardware and software in a single chassis with the goal of minimizing compatibility issues and simplifying management.

Infrastructure can be a combination of on-premises and in the cloud. Infrastructure that lives on-premises, at a co-location, and/or in the cloud is being stitched together to appear as a unified set of resources. Convergence is coming to hybrid architecture. Flexibility in current capacity, cost, and privacy/regulatory requirements allows IT to run workloads where it needs to. Network connectivity, management oversight, and systems visibility bring disparate components and locations together.

Information technology and operational technology is increasingly connected to enable more business functionality. As operational technology continues its convergence with the IT infrastructure side, there are implications across security, performance, and management domains. It can mean software, connectivity, centralized control, feedback loops, and real-time communications.

All this connectivity and localized computing power is enabling things to become smart. We're now seeing the evolution to smart things. Some things that continue to get smarter are planes, trains, automobiles, building control systems, meters, and TVs. Now, let's look at buildings, homes, cars, and cities.

Smart things make the office building smarter. The convergence of information technology infrastructure, software, and programmable controllers allows builders to transform the way buildings operate. Automation systems use the IT service fabric to provide connectivity, isolation, and security.

Building automation systems control fire, heat, water, power, lighting, elevators, HVAC, video surveillance, and physical security. In a new construction, the building's operational control systems change the model of how contractors build from the ground up. These systems use less overall physical infrastructure, leverage a common platform, and lay the foundation for more energy-efficient buildings.

This means that before an owner can take occupancy, IT must install a basic IT switching infrastructure. This IP network is the primary means of connectivity for all the building's systems. Before HVAC systems, heating systems, or lighting systems can be brought online, IT must put into place the infrastructure (the computers, networking, and storage). Software applications then control these systems. Instead of multiple wired infrastructures for each building, one IP service fabric serves all systems, such as overhead pagers, fire sprinklers, security surveillance, building automation, and elevators. Software on the back end now directs different systems across the IP backbone.

This level of automation brings significant cost savings to the business owner. Smart systems not only minimize the total cost of ownership, but they also provide flexibility for operational maintenance and value-added services. All systems communicate over a common platform, on a single IP backbone.

Smart business buildings operate more efficiently. They reduce expenses by using motion detection to be smarter about when lights come on and go off. They sense when the temperature needs to be adjusted based off the number of people in a room. Smart buildings optimize energy efficiency and improve visibility of energy consumption. Even retrofits of existing buildings can become smarter.

Convergence also makes it easier to provide agility in the construction of new buildings. A single converged network allows physical cameras, building system controls, and voice and data traffic to share a single architecture. Convergence provides resilience and flexibility in new constructions and renovations, no longer needing three separate networking infrastructures. Now a single cabling infrastructure is all that is needed.

The smart home provides similar functionality. Existing homes are now installing add-on systems to control indoor and outdoor lights, digital video cameras for security, and devices to open the door when the homeowner comes near the garage.

Smart cars optimize fuel mileage, improve safety, avoid collisions, and assist with parking. Onboard embedded chips and software talk across cellular networks, back to the cloud provider, and over to the service provider, to offer services such as OnStar. These smart features enhance the driving experience.

Smart cities strive to achieve similar efficiencies. Governments can optimize taxpayer money through a smart approach. From lighting and security to traffic routing, movement of vehicles, and the efficient use of parking, the smart city has great potential to reduce governmental costs and enhance municipal services.

The ultimate convergence is when functionality gets blended and becomes something new. Where once you carried a camera, phone, and music player, now you have your smartphone. Where once you logged into three consoles to build a new virtual instance, now you go to one screen and provision all of the elements needed to make it functional. Where once you pulled multiple cables through the walls, now you pull one. And where once you had three teams managing the process of getting a new user up and running, one can do it and handle all the needed requests.

IT is needed to support all this infrastructure and technology that runs atop code—the 0s and 1s that direct activity in the digital world. The storage arrays, core network switching, and three-tiered computer setup all support applications housed and used to service end users. Software drives hardware, infrastructure, and business.

Code

Infrastructure needs something to tell it what to do. It needs code. Everything you see, hear, and read through your screen comes to you as the result of a simple true-or-false choice, made billions of times over. That's made possible by binary code. José Américano N L F de Freitas explains:

> Imagine trying to use words to describe every scene in a film, every note in your favorite song, or every street in your town. Now imagine trying to do it using only the numbers 1 and 0. Every time you use the internet to watch a movie, listen to music, or check directions, that's exactly what your device is doing— using the language of binary code.... The genius of this system is that the binary sequence doesn't have a predetermined meaning on its own. Instead, each type of data is encoded in binary according to a separate set of rules.[77]

Code is the language of the digital world. Marc Andreessen, cofounder of Netscape, famously noted years ago that "software is eating the world."

Software code is the brains of the digital world. Code tells machines what to do, when to do it, and how to do it. There are various types of code, including desktop production suites, apps on your smartphone, instructions running mainframes, the logic inside devices, and multi-tiered hybrid apps powering business processes.

Code can also be made to talk more easily with other machines through the use of application programming interfaces (APIs). APIs are a more accessible way to integrate than continually building from scratch. This is a set of routines, protocols, and tools for building software applications, to guide how software components interact. These computing infrastructure building blocks can reuse definitions coded as infrastructure.

Software directs technological and physical activity. Software is everywhere. It creates the underpinnings of our society, providing an invisible layer of functionality to make technology work for people. Software powers the cars we drive, cash registers, air traffic control centers, and e-commerce purchases.

There are millions of lines of software code in smartphones, printers, automobiles, desktop operating systems, and cloud services. Software code runs elevators, building automation systems, televisions, fighter jets, and traffic lights. Software handles inventory management for retail stores, controls assembly line robots, and powers the check-in systems at hotels.

All these actions in the digital world are powered by code. The application development world is supercharging human innovation.

Machines and code underpin our digital world. And we in IT are responsible for them.

Computing devices need a collection of instructions to tell them what to do. The most important enabler of digital services and digital infrastructure is software code. Infrastructure's purpose is to support software in all its forms. When you understand code, you understand the underpinnings of the digital realm. A business's perspective is shaped by what technology has and can do. And the capabilities of technology are a function of software.

Software code is any set of instructions that directs a computer to perform specific operations. This code executes multiple levels. This includes at the lowest level of machine language giving instructions to the underlying hardware; the software for the base operating system, which includes device drivers and operating utilities; application software that most end users are accustomed to as they interact with it every day; and back-end multi-tiered applications that drive business processes.

Considering the complexity of the software development landscape, many organizations seek to streamline multiple coding efforts, especially those involving integration with both legacy and modern systems. Because of this, developers often make use of APIs.

IT also leverages Infrastructure as Code (IaC) to model an infrastructure end state and ensure consistent configurations across the stack. This is a fast and flexible approach to configuring and maintaining infrastructure. By taking a system-level approach to lifecycle management, we can define how we want system components to behave, and centrally declare the state we want them to operate in, whether they are physical or virtual, on the premises or in the cloud.

Software is also re-defining computing, networks, and the data center itself. In the trend for many IT teams to favor infrastructure configured via code, known as software-defined, we can accelerate the environments themselves needed to run application code. This infrastructure includes computing, storage, network, and common middleware components. This opens the possibilities of faster provisioning, greater visibility, and fewer constraints in the data center. We're no longer tied to racks or specific data centers. We can become more agile and more responsive.

As disruptions force faster responses, we in IT can get in front and proactively create rapid processes. We can equip our companies to stay relevant and to compete. This puts a premium on clever software developers.

Traditional development approaches are characterized by long completion cycles with full functionality testing done at the end of the project. These approaches tended to deliver at what today is deemed too slow. This has given way to smaller functionality goals delivering new value in smaller chunks. Newer development approaches emphasize smaller, faster, and more frequent releases of code to continually add functionality and fixes. And that has the effect of a faster delivery of value. In analyzing the actual workflow of software development, IT has identified opportunities to improve turnaround times on new software functionality for the business by changing how developers and operations teams work.

Fast iteration of code changes is happening hundreds and thousands of times per day to systems already in production. These in-production systems lead to many benefits, including allowing a business to function at a higher speed, fix bugs faster, add new features faster, offer something new on the digital front end, and add new futuristic features to back-end systems integrating multiple software platforms.

Today, billions of people worldwide get notifications on their phones that an update is available for the phone's base operating systems (e.g., iOS, Android) and for its apps. Users download these fixes instantly. These updates are code changes made by software developers to add new features, fix bugs, and patch security vulnerabilities. This represents a faster turnaround compared to previous times when delivery could be measured in years. Now, when you want to change one thing, you can target it, develop it, and get it out into the hands of users relatively quickly.

The sheer amount of code that runs our infrastructure outstrips the ability to do it all in house. It is possible because of a supply chain of code from many places. Code comes from many sources. Commercial off-the-shelf (COTS) software is ready to use upon purchase. Internally developed apps may have been written by your developers. Other components of code have been developed for free use through open source. Both types of code run on hardware mainframes, bare metal, virtual machines, the back end, middleware, the front end, websites, firmware, mobile devices, and smart devices. IT is responsible for governing all code, regardless of source or device.

Thanks to the work of developers around the globe who contribute their time and effort, open-source code is available to the public at no charge. New code often starts as open-source software.

Software developers have responded to the need for speed in business and consequently sped up the development cycle by making use of existing software components and modular software building blocks. The logic behind reusing existing modules is the simple fact that it saves time from rewriting the same process repeatedly. This has the benefit of freeing up valuable developer time to focus on unique features. Developers too often grab a copy of code without checking it for known vulnerabilities. When modules are shared among many different consumers of software application development, we must be wary of components, especially open-source components, that are shared across millions upon millions of systems. Software applications are prone to widespread impact from cyber-attacks that exploit vulnerabilities—like the Heartbleed bug, which resulted in uncounted lost time and distraction.

We must take into consideration what would happen if the digital supply chain were interrupted or compromised. With encryption being at the heart of the digital economy, the assumption for operating commerce is that our communications are safe from external view. When we browse secure sites on the internet, we assume encryption is protecting us. When the Heartbleed bug was discovered, the scope of the potential impact was astounding. Hundreds of thousands of sites were affected, as well as hundreds of major vendors' products, and it struck at the heart of our digital economy.

The digital supply chains must be watched and improved from beginning to end to protect us. In addition, much of the infrastructure that supports mobile apps utilizes the same back end that supports web applications. Developers not familiar with handling this type of environment can introduce vulnerabilities.

IT needs a test environment, ideally identical to that of production. This prevents problems when the code gets into production. Coders are under extreme time pressure to deliver workable code. Don't let this come at the expense of sound sanity checking. Become trained in the best practices of secure coding.

Don't lose security to functionality. Fixing bugs after the fact costs more and is disruptive to operations. The best time is upfront, in the development phase. As more time passes and more defects are coded in, the more time must be spent on fixing the code later.

The digital supply chain is the lifeline of many businesses. IT also has a supply chain—its component pieces and parts move from one station to the next, often without checks. Cyber-attackers know this. The headlines are full of reports of software bugs being exploited by cyber-attackers. Prevent attacks by attending to where our software comes from, including firmware, drivers, infrastructure management platforms, plug-ins, or middleware platforms.

The digital supply chain is a critical aspect of digital infrastructure. IT must be diligent in how we source, consume, develop, deploy, and maintain software for our organizations.

Data

Infrastructure, code, and their functionality generate a lot of data. From the beginning of recorded time until today, we have created exabytes (billions of gigabytes) of data. The amount of data that once took centuries to create is now being created in hours and days.

Some compare data in technology to oil in the physical economy because data is the fuel of the digital economy. Just as oil is refined for multiple uses such as fuel and plastics, data provides the raw material for keeping the work going as well as for innovation.

Data drives everything. It starts out raw, and we process it to make it useful for business purposes. Data informs our decision-making. Data powers the global market, businesses, and IT. There are great opportunities in improving the value refined from data. The goal is to continually produce actionable information and insights for our businesses. To make more use of connected devices and real-time applications. And to make this data more easily available and available more quickly—both in a secure manner. In all these efforts, we give our companies a competitive advantage.

Data is a critical asset in operating a business. However, the traditional means of processing data for organizational consumption has been up-ended. Back-end storage infrastructure has been turned on its head. Cloud storage usage is exploding. Companies want anytime, anywhere access to it. Businesses can't get enough of it. And, IT has been tasked with supporting the infrastructure by handling the large volumes, variety, and velocity of that data.

There is a lot of data in various formats that need to be ingested at different rates. Drilling for data is exemplified in *big data*—that is, the volume, variety, and velocity of data. Previously, the data may have been collected once a day or once a week, but now the data is collected every millisecond, every second of the day. We deal with a variety of different data sources that can number in the hundreds and are in very different formats. Also, we must deal with various physical locations of the data itself and the implications for collection for processing.

Modern data can be described in terms of several characteristics. The first is volume, or how much data there is. The second is variety, or how many different formats or structures the data can be in. And the third is velocity, or how fast the data is being produced.

The volume of data is incredible. In 2012 alone, 2.5 quintillion bytes of data were generated.[78] Data structures include structured, semi-structured, quasi-structured, and unstructured data. Unstructured and semi-structured together account for approximately 80 percent of the data in the world.[79] New sources of data are coming online every day, including data from mobile sensors, social media, video surveillance, smart devices, geographical exploration, medical imaging, and gene sequencing. An IDC white paper described all of the data created, captured, and replicated on our planet as the "global datasphere" and forecasted that by 2025, the datasphere would grow to 163 zettabytes (a zettabyte is equivalent to 1 trillion gigabytes). It noted that this is ten times the 16.1 zettabytes of data generated in 2016.[80]

Data repositories include spreadsheets, databases, data warehouses, tweets, and transactions. Distinct challenges come with this massive amount of data. The format of data warehouses is often too rigid, and traditional data architectures inhibit data exploration. Higher levels of analysis and architecture change based on where data is collected.

Data analytics is another important factor in data. The drivers of analytics are varied:

- Optimizing business operations, which includes sales, pricing, profitability, and efficiency.

- Identifying business risks, which includes customer churn, fraud, and default.

- Predicting new business opportunities, including upsells, cross-sells, and the best new customer prospects.

- Complying with laws, regulatory requirements, and privacy requirements.

Business intelligence and data science have evolved from an explanatory to an exploratory approach. Analytic models are many, including those for clustering, association rules, classification, regression, time series, and text.

Data must be transformed to be useful. Data is truly the new oil. And like oil, raw data must be refined into information, which then powers operational intelligence and insights. Data feeds the day-to-day operations of a business.

Oil must be drilled out of the ground to be useful. Then it must be refined. Then it can be transported all around the world to be put into use in the global economy. Data is similar. Raw, unfiltered data needs to be collected from different sources. Then it must be aggregated, filtered, sorted, and categorized. It then can be presented to a multitude of end-user consumers. All of this may happen in a split second.

This raw material supports decision-making, enables operational intelligence, and provides insights to businesses.

Raw data use cases include those such as assessing risk, understanding decision options, or helping optimize processes.

Several challenges to data can negatively impact a business. If you can't get to the data, it has no value. If you take too long to refine it, it loses value. If the refined data is hard to interpret, the data could become useless. If the insights are delivered too late, they could negatively affect good decision-making. If you are unable to search or retrieve historical data, it could cost your business opportunities. If you are unable to protect it from inappropriate disclosure, your business could end up on the nightly news.

Refining raw data transforms it into the key inputs for operational intelligence. With this being the case, this data must be available in near real time. Someone may need this data within the hour to make a decision. Knowing about it the next day after a batch process would be too late.

IT has the expanded role to play of delivering usable information faster to a business. The traditional schema defined the data structure upfront—the way the data had to be ingested, manipulated, and read back. This had the disadvantage of slowing down the time to value, and potentially making the data irrelevant to the business. New approaches use "schema on read," applying structure to raw data as it is read from storage. This contrasts with "schema on write" in which the structure has to be defined upfront before data can be written to storage. The advantage is allowing the flexibility to define, change, and experiment with the data. This accommodates users' needs while leaving the underlying raw data intact. This flexibility gives freedom to IT when adjusting on the fly to all the different data types being ingested into various analysis platforms.

Data can be used in automatic systems (where applications are aggregated to run and adapted on the fly) and in manual systems. Streaming data acts as input to control systems, such as traffic control systems, systemic control systems, and alerting systems. For example, data can alert a manager to put an extra cashier in the checkout area.

When software uses data as input, it can make the system alert, allow software the opportunity to act on it, and enable the software to respond to changes on the fly. IT can make data available everywhere.

Taking care of data governance and mitigating data leakage are prerequisites for business operations. These are standard operating environment requirements for IT to handle. Data drives business growth, competitive differentiation, and innovation.

One of IT's primary goals is to help its organization win by making the right data available to the right people at the right times.

Data is an asset that must be managed from creation to destruction. IT is custodian to tremendous amounts of data, some of which is sensitive and includes personally identifiable information (PII). We collect more private data today than ever before, and this includes metadata about user behavior. There are many connection points to this data that support value-adding. We must be sensitive to sound governance around all data collected. Issues of privacy are increasingly important as the digital exhaust of unstructured data gives increasingly more insights into the behavior of people.

IT must concern itself with the management of infrastructure over the lifetime of its use. Data often lives on far longer than it should.

The challenges of tagging and destroying data past its usefulness are growing. Information kept too long can end up on the front pages or in a court case. Email is often the dumping ground for unstructured data. The sensitivity of the information is often not easy to surmise, even by the owner of the data.

Every time data is migrated from one system to another, the chance for losing context grows. Users and businesses can become paralyzed by the question of data destruction. IT's understanding opens the doors for businesses to tackle these impacts.

IT must get its arms around complex systems. The challenges of complexity are clear. The rate of organizational change and requests for new business capability can be overwhelming to IT teams. Combined with the need to provide more intricate customer value, you have a situation that requires a higher level of understanding of our systems. Our businesses require technology systems that are larger, more connected, and more complex to manage.

Technology is the engine required for businesses to compete in the marketplace. IT will continue to require even more intimate knowledge of systems thinking to keep pace.

When IT understands technology and manages from a systems approach, we will be in a better position to map these systems to its business value chain. This will allow us to keep up, respond as needed, and be positioned to help lead.

IT needs to think systematically. That means: Break the perils of team silos. Increase your understanding of business services and their process dependencies on specific technology stacks. Find out where complexity is needed to drive frontline simplification. Look to attack complexity with a combination of different thinking, updated platforms, and updated working frameworks. Code the world to meet the needs of the business. Encode business and technology processes. Enhance user experience with more automatic intelligence. And leverage code to better manage and scale system functionality and stability.

The complexities of today's technology infrastructures drive the need for a systems approach. IT is up to the challenge.

As more moving components operate in new and different ways in a dynamic market, the level of risk increases. Market disruption drives changes, increases the velocity of new ideas, and increases the need for faster responses. These factors lead to more risk for businesses, and they must be understood to be properly addressed.

IT will need a new operating model to be successful. Without one, the risks to the business will outstrip the benefits of new technology and thinking. New levels of complexity tend to increase the probability of bad things happening. IT has done an admirable job with dealing with availability of systems. In the areas of the confidentiality and integrity of systems, an active threat force makes IT's job of securing the digital world challenging. Make no mistake, cyber risk management is hard. It is one thing for a business competitor to try to capture your customers, or to be caught up on the wrong side of market disruptions; it is another to be the target of human-driven goals of warfare, espionage, criminality, and activism. Humankind history of conflict and dangers extend from the physical world into the digital realm. There are active humans with activities that threaten the very existence of modern business. From these threats, IT dedicates a cyber security team to support the efforts to keep the digital infrastructure available and safe.

Part 3 – Manage

Establish and maintain an annualized loss exposure below management's risk appetite.

Chapter 7
Security Program

To the outside world it looks easy. Just install the latest security tool to improve security. But it takes more than just installation of technology. It takes more than just the initial installation of tech. Or the configuration of settings. Or the heroic engineer working through the weekend troubleshooting a problem. It must be embedded into our organization's capabilities. The technology is operated by a team as opposed to just one person. The tool continues to run and be maintained even when the person who initially installed it leaves the company. The tools are effective over a long period of time. That timeframe is as long as the organization requires that capability. This is accomplished by designing, building, and operating a cybersecurity program. Enterprise risk management programs need cyber risk to be managed. And it is managed by the security program. Security programs mitigate cyber risk. IT keeps losses in check.

IT's goal is the same as that of every other group within an organization: maximizing value and minimizing cost. This is accomplished with IT's fundamental capability of mastering the complexities of technology. IT explicitly understands how losses occur and properly frames the business context to mitigate risks. IT strives to do all of this cost-effectively.

Stakeholders must confront the potential of bad things happening in all their various forms. These stakeholders can be anyone affected by the organizational structure. Any of them would prefer the lower cost of preventing bad outcomes to the increased cost of cleaning them up afterward or of not being able to fix them at all.

Something bad could happen because threat actors are drawn to the value we create. A *risk*, as defined in Chapter 3, refers to something bad that could happen. In practical terms, the assumption is that some forms of controls are already in place to manage the current level of risk. But are they enough?

Mitigating risks is everyone's responsibility. Mitigation is the most common response to an uncertain world. *Mitigate* means to lessen; to reduce the frequency of, or to lessen the blow of something. Effective mitigation means we can competently go about doing business in a competitive marketplace having identified knowable uncertainties. As we identify knowable risks, we respond diligently by investing in people, processes, technologies, and approaches that can mitigate potential future losses. This is what gives the organization confidence in its ability to take chances, thrive, and compete in the marketplace.

IT strives to default to *yes* to new requests from the business. Our yes is accompanied by mitigation recommendations as needed to support sound business decisions. We process our risks and send them into a "mitigation funnel," a series of controls applied to lessen likelihoods and impacts. In mitigation, we identify potential risks, resulting in a large list collected from all parts of the organization and across all domains. As we apply mitigations to the inherent risks, the amount of risk, size, and severity decreases to a manageable level. After going through the "mitigation funnel," what is left over in terms of frequency and magnitude is termed *residual risk*.

We do not stop there, as mitigation is a dynamic process. Mitigation requires management endeavors for as long as the organization is open for business. *Risk monitoring* is part of the ongoing process of managing risk. Risk monitoring tracks the execution of mitigation strategies and approaches. Similarly, residual risks that remain and are within acceptable stakeholder tolerance levels should be continually monitored to scope out new risk, eliminate controls that are no longer relevant, ensure mitigation measures are working, and get feedback on any changes.

Management of enterprise risk results in various responses, such as mitigation, avoidance, and acceptance. Those are executive management stakeholders' decisions. For IT, we lean into "yes." As such, our focus is on the areas of clarity, context, and mitigation.

Clarity is the quality of being coherent and intelligible. IT seeks to communicate clearly what the risk is, how it arises, and how we prevent it.

Context is the circumstances that form the setting for an event, statement, or idea. The benefit of context is increased understanding and insights of our situation. In what contexts does this risk come?

Mitigation is the end goal—the action of reducing the severity, frequency, or both of potential future losses. By documenting the appetite and tolerance levels of stakeholders, we can strive to keep the aggregated annualized loss exposure of the organization within agreed-upon target ranges. To do this well, IT needs to rise beyond the fog of noise.

Beyond the Fog of Noise

Risk is composed of several risk factors. In an environment where the sights and sounds of those factors are blurry and garbled, IT clarifies. We illuminate the path and amplify the signal.

IT's understanding of how to defend the organization's digital infrastructure helps enterprise risk management efforts. IT clearly and calmly—but firmly—communicates the dangers to stakeholders. IT's help is derived from its ability to see the business goals, identify relevant threats, and receive feedback from all of the factors that comprise digital risks.

IT helps others to see the risk landscape. Why? It is vital to be good stewards of finite resources while minimizing user slowdowns and protecting corporate assets. Impediments to that clarity are what can be imagined as the "fog of noise" that gets in the way of a clear vision of our risk space.

Like real fog that obscures visibility, the fog of noise is problematic, as we need to see our risk environment to prevent accidents. IT perceives meaningful and important elements of our current risk situation by forming mental pictures of risk factors.

Our organizations, our environments, and our coworkers all need visibility into risk factors to do their jobs well. That is why fog causes problems. Fog makes our risk picture less clear. This hinders us all, as it interferes with our ability to be on the same page.

Fog, therefore, is a metaphor for the elements of IT that interfere with clarity. Rather than present elements that are not clearly visible, IT needs to illuminate risk factors to clarify our digital risk space.

There are ways we can do this. We can leverage power tools, as discussed in Chapter 5, to assist with focus. We can stay mindful of conversations with others. We can light a path to guide us toward where we need to go. Like a person in the front of the line carrying a torch to lead the group through the darkness, IT can illuminate a route from the current state of high loss exposure to a satisfactory future state of acceptable exposure.

As with our challenges with sight, we also have challenges with hearing our environment. *Noise* is an unwanted signal or a disturbance that often leads to misunderstanding. It can come from complexity, a high speed of change, changes in the risk landscape, or changes in team roles. Noise contributes to confusion. Driven by chaos, irrelevant and meaningless outputs occur together with the desired information. This noise diverts attention away from the message and leads to distractions that in the end hinder IT from giving full attention to what matters. Noise moves our focus away from an accurate interpretation of risks, thereby diminishing our reception of early warning signals. Noise also increases uncertainty and unnecessary blame.

The fog of noise is a pathway to needless fear. There are reasons people talk about being "paralyzed by fear." Poor communication, doubt, and complex threat environments undermine decision-making and subvert a well-thought-out cyber strategy.

IT has been known to lean on fear to justify budget approvals. For organizations that have recently formed a security team or hired new leadership, multiple security items might appear on the budget wish list. If the pace of funding seems slow, the CISO might become frustrated, putting more pressure on otherwise persuasive business cases. If not adept, they might use worst-case scenarios and substitute fear for a sound business case.

IT might also choose poor language, affectionately known as "technobabble." Rather than help, technobabble injects noise into the lines of communication between the IT security team and stakeholders. The byproduct can be a failure to understand risk factors correctly or the rejection of more important risk actions. This lack of mental clarity about our shared goals can become a downward spiral of unpleasant situations that is hard to escape. It can show up in fighting to get budget approvals, struggling to get business buy-in for a new process, failing to prioritize work efforts, and exasperating control deficiencies.

The negative effects can lead to mistrust, hurt feelings, and frustration in employees who feel powerless to change their environment. The lack of progress toward mitigation goals and that feeling of despair can make IT teammates conclude that what to do doesn't really matter. At this point, it is important to be wary of false ideas and narratives that are likely to be wrongly perceived by others.

For individual team members, despair can lead to feelings of loneliness. Loneliness typically includes anxious feelings about a lack of connection with other teams, both in the present and extending into the future.

Finally, IT's feeling of responsibility for possibly being wrong about a decision or performance can keep it from future accuracy. After a breach, putting blame on one team member or one team is an abandonment of the team concept. Doing so short-circuits the process maturity that would prevent future system failures. The fog of noise leaves a feeling of stressful urgency, the perception that one needs to be doing something and doing it very quickly.

Success lies in focusing on what is influenceable and doable. Success has its foundation in due diligence, in moving beyond the fear of what could happen and instead dealing with what is most likely to happen.

Art of the Probable

We need to understand the *art of the probable*. Many situations and outcomes in life are theoretically possible, but most are not probable. Just because a cyber threat is possible does not mean it will occur. We need to distinguish between probability and possibility. Too often people think the mere chance of something bad happening means that it should become our priority and that we should commit many resources to stopping it. Uncertainty and fear lead us to inefficiently work on possibility.

Instead, choose pragmatism and due diligence to effectively work on probability.

Once again, *probability* is the measurement of the likelihood of an event occurring. The higher the probability, the more certainty we can have that the event will occur. We are concerned with adverse events, e.g., cyber breaches. IT must embrace an environment of rapid disruption and uncertainty. Business leaders are moving with boldness toward opportunities while simultaneously navigating the uncertainties and risks of those opportunities. IT must move with a similar wise boldness. IT must learn new ways of thinking and create new frameworks for safely operating with the speed and attention necessary to be successful.

Flexibility and speed are the key capabilities of our time. Being ready when the business needs us is vital. The technology pervading our personal and professional lives is the language of IT, and this puts us in a position to thrive, to become the leaders our businesses need us to be. In the past, many IT teams have lacked fluency in business language. IT must develop the abilities to properly align goals and priorities and then communicate them to the business. Even if we have previously not successfully focused on the relevant risks, we can begin now to excellently fulfill our advisory role.

Forecasting, at its most basic level, is the process of estimating the likelihood of future events based on past and present data. Based on what the threat landscape looks like and what our business is doing in the market, what risks are most likely to impact us? Uncertainty is a reality. We are not in the prediction business. We are in the business of informing and driving conclusions based on evidence and reasoning.

As cybersecurity has become a primary driver of business risk mitigation, IT must ensure we have the correct mindset to tackle the challenge it presents. Many mitigation methods are available in IT's sphere of control. In addition, business itself has a vast array of mitigation methods at its disposal.

One difficulty in today's landscape is the overflow of risk information from multiple sources. This overflow puts fog, noise, and other masks over critical clues. The battle with cyber threats doesn't really begin until a relevant threat event to our organization comes to fruition.

IT must understand that our focus is on the business's defined concerns. IT then informs mitigation strategies and response plans. Mitigation has been, and always will be, a business-level discussion. This is something IT cannot do for the business; rather, this is something IT can facilitate for the business, and then IT can enact the business's decision.

Businesses are adept at mitigating risk through various mechanisms such as insurance, contracts, and processes. More companies are buying insurance in the form of cyber policies, which means insurance companies will now be assessing defensive postures and maturity levels more often in their underwriting processes.

Clarity is what is needed. *"It was a sophisticated attack by what must have been a nation-state,"* is a common theme when defenders explain to the business what happened. It is also what the business leader says when they get in front of the cameras to explain why they were not able to stop a breach. In some cases that could be accurate, but in others the attacker could have been a much less advanced threat actor using common tools and documented techniques from previous attacks in the same industry. This condemns the organization's commitment to defense and operational efficacy. We know a lot can go wrong. What our businesses need from IT is more clarity on which risk are likely to materialize.

Guiding Principles

We need to be guided by fundamental principles. There is no need to wake up tomorrow and build a mitigation approach out of thin air. There is not an infinite number of new principles IT must create. Other people and nature have provided hints and guiderails for us. The path is well worn.

The laws of security are truths that the security team has experienced for years. Bad guys do what bad guys do in the cyber domain just like they do in the physical domain—no surprise. Over the years, common-alities, trends, and patterns have been observed. From these threat event patterns, the necessary strategies, tactics, and controls have been inferred—a predictable set of conditions that are necessary to implement. If you leave a system unpatched, a bad guy will exploit it. If you are not watching, bad guys will camp out in your environment and recon you. Global IP connectivity allows remote attacks that can be more dangerous than in-person attacks.

Many years ago, Microsoft released a guide on what it had observed in the security landscape titled "Ten Immutable Laws of Security." This guide describes key security principles and approaches to tackling threat actors' methods that have proven effective. Of note is that these principles were not necessarily solved by technology but were long, enduring challenges to the defenders. IT should view some principles as common sense.

If a bad guy can find a way to make money, he will seek your data, whether it is your credit card numbers, health records, or some other juicy bits of personally identifiable information (PII). Keep in mind what bad guys could do when not being watched. Bad guys are aware when others are around. They see the police, security guards, or army. Being seen acts as a deterrence to bad actors.

Attackers, criminals, and hostile nation-states act differently when watched. Also, bad guys take advantage when the cost equation is in their favor. If the cost of conducting the attacks does not increase, they will continue to use the same TTPs. If they can get enough organizations to pay the ransoms, they will keep up their future attacks. Bad guys like operating in the shadows and taking advantage of companies that must defend a large attack surface.

Cyber defenders know what good security looks like because of lessons learned from so many breaches. Factors that surrounded these events often included staff shortages, lack of visibility, incomplete tools implementation, inadequate response plans, and lack of stakeholder accountability.

After-action reports typically show multiple issues as opposed to a single root cause. A failure to patch, static controls, unwatched areas, and slow responses cause threat events to become loss events.

IT must identify and remove blind spots beforehand because we have designed and built this infrastructure, entered into business agreements with third parties, and allowed access and sharing with certain parties. We know the prevalent attack scenarios. We have intimate access to knowledge of the specific loss scenarios of concern to our organizations. Outside forces have codified them for us.

There are countless standards that organizations can leverage. The modern economy is built on widely accepted standards. Without them, chaos would ensue, with every person doing their own thing.

Cybersecurity also uses standards. The National Institute of Standards and Technology (NIST) Cybersecurity Framework is voluntary but offers advances for our industries. The framework is the result of a US presidential executive order. It is also applicable to organizations outside critical infrastructure. Many companies have adopted it for due diligence and benchmarking purposes. It is good mark in the eyes of regulators as well.

Even though IT has industry tribal knowledge that feeds the standards and general practices recommended by many security professionals, there is opportunity in the future for more widespread adoption of industry standards.

When sound design principles, features, and functionality are built in from the ground up, without the organization having to engage in risk analysis, this level of due care and diligence is expected as standard business practice. Encourage your organization to contribute to minimum standards for IT. We cannot win if our identification process of relevant risk only looks inward.

The digital world needs to meet minimum-security standards and to practice foundational security hygiene. This is second nature the technical experts, those who understand the technical underpinning of the infrastructure.

IT must consider basics such as central logging, synchronized time sourcing, multi-factor authentication, and timely patching diligence.

A dynamic inventory should be considered standard, not something that requires a consultant to convince management about. The defender-attacker state will be better known when we put in place the basic preventions that have been proven in real-world application. Make sure you get organizational support for appropriate standards and regulations.

Due diligence and reasonableness are well known in courts of law. What is reasonableness? What is the minimum due diligence your organization should be expected to have done?

Directors of organizations need cybersecurity programs that provide information on appropriate standards. This speaks to the *duty of care*, a legal obligation that requires adherence to a standard that prevents harm to others. Duty of care is the first element that must be investigated if corporate officers are accused of negligence.

One goal of a business is to protect shareholder value. This does not mean adding more mandates and regulations; it means being reasonable. A risk-based approach is more in line with stakeholder needs. Ironically, compliance often results from lag at the macro level of risk mitigation.

Loss exposure for organizations may be higher than stakeholders believe. This leaves governments to mandate minimum standards of due care. Privacy, as seen in the legislative actions of the General Data Protection Regulation (GDPR) and California Consumer Privacy Act (CCPA), opens another threat effect front those businesses must contend with. Privacy requires broad visibility and oversight.

When we put in more controls to address the security and regulatory challenges, we must be mindful not to create excessive friction on the daily lives of workers. We mitigate risk by using controls, but we must also mitigate risk by staying aware of control friction. Friction from controls slows the user or business process. If we present controls that end users perceive as too onerous, they may lean toward shadow IT and bypass safer governance structures.

This control friction could turn users off and color their perception of the value of participating in the program. The level of perceived obstruction, delay, or confusion of a control indicates the likelihood of users circumventing it.

With our focus on what is probable and on foundational principles, it is time to look at the path forward.

The Path Forward

Risk mitigation is a game played by known and unknown players. The rules are not exact, and the length of play is infinite. There is no traditional "win" to this infinite game.

The threats can never be completely defeated, but they can be thwarted repeatedly. The objective is to continue playing the game and continue thwarting bad guys. Examples of infinite games include business, politics, crime, and life itself.

You can tell when stakeholders believe that cybersecurity is a finite game. They expect at some point IT will stop bugging them about it. When they ask when they can stop worrying about cybersecurity, you can answer the same day the police or military is no longer needed due to the end of criminality and nation-state adversaries.

The sign that your organization is playing the long game is when there are sufficient trained personnel in place operating with mature processes. Beyond fear, uncertainty, and doubt (FUD) lies the pathway to opportunity.

IT protects the right assets with the right controls and informs stakeholders when adjustments are needed. IT's goal is to keep future losses from exceeding the appetites and tolerance levels of stakeholders.

Common choices that inhibit IT progress in mitigating risk include fear, ignorance, uncertainty, illusions, doubt, and overconfidence.

IT can reduce the grip FUD has on its organization by focusing on the probable rather than the possible risks, closing the gaps in adherence to the common laws of security, and leveraging cybersecurity standards.

Define material breaches and incidents properly. IT must communicate the actual business loss probability and whether the costs of cleanup could be mitigated with the right cyber insurance.

IT also needs to let management know if there are stock price implications or monthly cash flow impacts. Are there any legal actions against the organization that might result in a payout? IT must communicate the real meaning of loss or leakage when discussed in the context of digital assets.

IT helps management comprehend the difference between everyday embarrassment and embarrassment that could lead to reputation or brand damage. The latter would impact revenue. Businesses and individuals have become very good at mitigating physical crime and its impacts. We must do the same thing for digital crime and attacks. Fear cannot hold the business hostage from operating, nor make it do too much or too little.

Businesses must be careful not to fall into the trap of "if we just had more of *whatever*, the problem would go away." Before a check is written, IT should show a deep understanding of what that purchase will accomplish.

IT's role includes establishing a cybersecurity baseline. Many baseline techniques to reduce both the impact and likelihood of cyber-attacks are not being implemented. As our organizations mitigate risk, we must support broader, industry-wide initiatives. We must support appropriate changes that obey laws and government oversight. We must demonstrate common sense.

Without domain expertise, consultants cannot adequately understand the business environment or make sound judgments. That's what IT is for. Our domain expertise is a requirement, as is our ability to translate techno-speak into clear communication that management can understand and act on.

In the same vein, the quickest way to inefficiencies is to continue to speak different languages. We can translate.

We in IT must also be honest. Overhyping the threats to our organization is wrong. Bad guys are bad, but they are not supervillains. We have ways to stop the bad buys. We deal with bad guys every day in the real world. Their ways can be studied, learned, and adapted to. IT must limit how far the bad guys will be allowed to roam. The digital world still is bound by the physical world. We humans still use physical responses to critical threats.

The uncertainties around the level of sophistication of the attacker and their techniques have provided cover for IT and organizations when they fail in their due diligence. But when IT uses uncertainty as an excuse for a failure, IT loses the opportunity to thwart a larger number of attacks in the future. Thwarting these attacks is critical to preventing financial and brand damage to the business.

We in IT must become and remain proactive rather than default to defense. We don't help our case by using the collective cry of "prevention is dead" heard from businesses, vendors, and consultants. We must guard against using that as a crutch for underperforming. Prevention can only be dead if it has been tried! When we force attackers to work harder to achieve their goals by using preventive methods, then that cry is a more apt description. But when we haven't implemented many of the basic controls and best practices, we have not done our job. We need to get better at protection.

IT cannot limit our thinking of protection to technical terms only. Getting malware on an endpoint does not automatically translate to business risk. In the attack chain are many phases. The biggest breaches have had a continuum of phases to get a business on the nightly news.

IT must help stakeholders answer the "So what?" question to provide the proper context around how much time and money should be invested in further mitigation.

A sophisticated threat actor does not mean unstoppable or even that something is relevant in the business context. Let us also challenge the mantra of "prevention has been taken care of; now move on to detection and response." More preventive controls are available than we currently use. As workload moves to newer infrastructure, security vendors develop new capabilities to address it.

And attackers follow these new surfaces. The time in between the new infrastructure and the availability of new controls is when attackers take advantage. Before attackers attack is prime time for IT to adapt their control posture.

Resiliency is the capacity to recover quickly from difficulties. Every single day across the country and across the world, crime happens. This is a reality, but we cannot devote all of our attention to criminals. Our main objective is to help the business, so we must provide a resilient infrastructure. We must quickly respond to intrusions without negatively impacting the business's daily operations.

The cyber resiliency value chain allows us to remove single points of failure so we can recover quickly from interruptions and make the impacts far less costly to the operation of our businesses. And of course, we continue to prevent attacks with the myriad of available tools.

We need a more certain path forward. The bad guys are resourceful, persistent, and agile. There's no reason the good guys can't be the same.

Beyond the fog of noise lie sound risk mitigation principles and practices. IT can and must actively use them. These principles and practices work and have stood the rigors of time. By building a more accurate and useful model of the risk landscape, IT can realign with sound, cost-effective, and effective risk mitigation. We can use risk-aligned decision-making, a good business practice no matter the risk domain. To be successful, IT needs context. We can get that from modeling risk.

Program Goals

Next, let's talk about program components. A program is a plan or system under which action may be taken toward a goal. A program can be operational, programmatic, and administrative. People are the heart of an organization. We develop policy, a deliberate system of principles to guide decisions and achieve our outcomes. It is a statement of intent and is implemented as a procedure or protocol. Policies are generally adopted by a governance body within our organizations.

From policy, we develop process, a series of actions or steps taken to achieve a particular end, a systematic series of actions directed to some end. It's a continuous action, operation, or series of changes taking place in a definite manner.

Technology is the sum of techniques, skills, methods, and processes used in the production of goods or services or in the accomplishment of objectives, such as scientific investigation. Technology can be the knowledge of techniques, processes, and the like, or it can be embedded in machines to allow for operation without detailed knowledge of their workings. The definition of technology is science or knowledge put into practical use to solve problems or invent useful tools.

In the physical domain, physical security is the protection of personnel, hardware, software, networks, and data from physical actions and events that could cause serious loss or damage to an organization. This includes protection from fire, flood, natural disasters, burglary, theft, vandalism, and terrorism. Physical security is often overlooked—and its importance underestimated—in favor of more technical threats such as hacking, malware, and cyber-espionage. However, breaches of physical security can be carried out with brute force and little or no technical knowledge on the part of an attacker.

Physical security has three important components of access control, surveillance, and testing. Obstacles should be placed in the way of potential attackers, and physical sites should be hardened against accidents, attacks, or environmental disasters. Such hardening measures include fencing, locks, access control cards, biometric access control systems, and fire suppression systems. Second, physical locations should be monitored using surveillance cameras and notification systems, such as intrusion detection sensors, heat sensors, and smoke detectors. Third, disaster recovery policies and procedures should be tested on a regular basis to ensure safety and to reduce the time it takes to recover from disruptive man-made or natural disasters.

Security programs need to govern, enable, and defend.

Govern

Security programs govern the management of cyber risk. IT has governance structures to operate efficiently. Organizations have a governance structure to provide order, consistency, and accountability. To govern is to conduct the policy, actions, and affairs of an organization. Cyber risk management needs a governance structure to be effective. The maturity of a cybersecurity program can be inferred from the effectiveness of its governance structure. Governance serves as the precedent for everything IT does for cyber risk management. Governance encompasses the organization structure by which IT operates its risk mitigation functions. Standalone security teams that do their own things get frustrated when they cannot get other parts of the organization to follow their lead. And other parts of the organization can get frustrated with a security team on how it lobs over the fences requests that are not aligned. Governance defines how IT will approach the design, implementation, support, and defense of technology. It establishes the mechanism by which people will be held accountable.

Now, the administrative domain on controls is operational, relating to the running of an organization. Administrative controls are enhancements and additions to work procedures. They include the policies and processes just discussed. They also include training. All these are for the purpose of lessening the potential future losses by means of reducing the duration, frequency, and/or severity of loss scenarios. Administrative controls typically change the behavior of people rather than removing the actual threats. These administrative controls are at the heart of operations, which encompasses design, provisioning, and governance.

Design is from all dimensions—how it works, looks, and functions. Provision is like firewalls, IDs, passwords, certificates, authentication, roles, sharing repository, vuln scan, patch deployment, etc. Governing is a system of control needs, rules, norms, and actions that are structured, sustained, regulated, and held accountable. This is called governance. Protecting services and data requires that the users interacting with our systems, the code that runs across our infrastructure, the infrastructure, and the data, must all be controlled and maintained under the umbrella of governance. Governance covers the users who interact with our systems for the appropriate assignment of access and authorization.

The concept of systemic governance at the systemic level encompasses identity, code, and data. It also accounts for all people, processes, policies, and technologies that IT puts in play to meet this system of control requirements for risk mitigation for the organization. For example, firewalls, anti-malware defenses, web proxies, and cloud access security brokers are different elements of technology controls. Or a standard operating process for onboarding a new user to give it access to email, different databases, and other IT services is an example of process. Or a rule that states that users must change their passwords every ninety days is an example of policy control. Or awareness training that informs users to report suspicious activities on the network. The amalgamation of these people, processes, policy, and technology must all be identified and documented and work in common harmony. The cybersecurity team, which is a subset of IT that is focused on these controls, has a 360-degree view of all these controls, how they interact with each other, and how they map back to specific threat event scenarios and more general lost event scenarios.

To represent users, identity encompasses the process of identification of authorized users to our systems. We also need to verify that this is the ballot attempt for the user to have the type of access. Technology such as multi-factor authentication (MFA) is a type that is used in that verification process. Sometimes this may be backed up with behavioral or dynamic authentication analysis processes to ensure that the context around the user request for access is proper.

Regarding code, it is imperative to maintain the integrity of code that our organization uses. That is the life cycle of all code, in all its forms.

IT maintains an inventory of all code, identifies steps to make sure code isn't altered, and makes sure all code is legal and that all code is kept up to date.

Regarding data, lifecycle management handles the creation, use, modification, storage, transmission, archiving, and destruction of all forms of data. IT ensures the organization maintains proper integrity, confidentiality, availability, and privacy of all its data.

With today's explosion in data volume, data protection strategy has been disrupted. Backup to tape, currently referred to as legacy, is now considered insufficient as a protection strategy. The first problem is time. The maintenance window for backup to tape is no longer sufficient to cover the volume of data to be protected. With newer storage technologies, storage area networks, and data replication snapshot technology, new strategies are being developed to protect digital assets. Integration into the application stack is allowing snapshot-like technology and protecting critical applications at the application level, making recovery realistic in meeting an organization's recovery point and recovery time objectives.

In addition, today's data protection strategy must count for the risk factors introduced by a cyber-attacker's use of encryption to extort organizations. The ability of today's data protection replication technologies to use DVR-like features to roll back files to previous versions at a particular time has become invaluable as a mitigation resource. The ability of IT to report back to the business with the recovery of unencrypted files from a snapshot two hours ago will limit the loss of work and potentially allow the business to forgo considerations of paying a ransom.

A strategy to tier the level of protection for different types of data allows IT the flexibility to take an Agile approach to protecting data. With a combination of strong user authentication, information rights management, encryption, and data loss prevention, including user behavior analytics combined with ease of user access and reliable performance for access, IT can provide the foundation for minimizing organizational risk.

Enable

Security programs enable the business. To make possible business operations there are both internal and external requirements that must be met. This could be a license, an inspection, or a specific way of building something. If a business wants to sell liquor, it must get a license. If a business wants to do contracts with a government agency, there are certain requirements they must meet to get awarded the bid for that type of work. If your business wants to process credit cards as a payment method, there are specific regulatory requirements that must be met for that to happen. It opens interfaces with these types of requirements in the form of compliance and regulatory requirements. At its essence, compliance is a business requirement. In most forms it is not optional or nice to have. Compliance means if the business wants to perform certain activities or do certain types of work, one must adhere to these requirements. So before one can even talk about cyber defense against bad actors, the business must have certain minimum requirements met to conduct operations that drive revenue and profits. As such, adherence to compliance and regulatory requirements is necessary to enable the business.

The business looks at compliance as the cost of doing business. If you want to measure the value of compliance, you need to look at it through the lens of the cost of doing business, and, as such, as part of the calculation for return on investment. All means to make revenue requires some type of investment, and the cost to meet all the requirements to do the business that you need to do to meet your custom demands is a necessity. From a risk management standpoint, you can actually calculate the cost of not being compliant. It is what you cannot do to generate revenue from your customers. It has a cost to it, and that can be measured. So, if you want to know why there is so much attention paid to compliance, you can just look at the numbers and may find that in many cases the lost business opportunities can far outweigh the ultimate cost of a cyber incident.

Sound and solid security principles address the majority of compliance and regulatory requirements. These requirements are driven by failure of individual organization programs that create real-world impact. Increased visibility drives more oversight. It is a vicious cycle. The result is that even though your organization does everything right, other businesses can do the wrong and end up driving external forces to drive up your compliance costs. Before the requirement, suggestion, or recommendation for the control was made, there was no driver. At micro level, a single or small number of high-impact, high-visibility, real-world impacts can trigger a new need for control. That can drive additional requirements, friction, and cost at the macro level. So, if your classmates, neighbors, or compatriots "mess up," the whole "class" can be caught up in the repercussions. So even if you would have never done that, or you are already diligent, you can still be caught up in other misdeeds. A fact of life.

Do you want to do business with the Department of Defense? Welcome to CMMC, DFARs, and NIST 800-171. Is the solution you offered hosted by SAAS? Welcome to FedRAMP. Want to do credit card processing? Hello, PCI. In the health care field? Hello, HIPAA. Operating in the financial industry? Hello, SEC, Dodd-Frank, GLBA. Do you handle PII? Hello, privacy regulation along with CCPA, GDPR, and NYDFS. You will need to demonstrate proof of diligence. SOC-2 report, pen testing report, etc. There will be a stream of new acronyms to describe new regulations, laws, and requirements to do business. As threat actors cause impact to different sections at increasing frequency and larger magnitudes, more will be added to your plate.

Our organizations will be held accountable for duty of care. External stakeholders will hold us responsible for reasonable efforts to manage all kinds of risk.

Defend

Security programs defend the business. Every day, we actively defend against threat actors that are conducting attacks against our organizations. A combination of direct attacks and attacks of opportunities. An approach and plan for achieving the cyber risk management objectives over a long period of time. Following the guidance of addressing your cyber loss scenarios, your risk register, aligned with your ERM programs register, keeps IT focused. The register provides the higher-level concerns to address. It is in the operation of the security program that the responses at a granular level of those concerns are addressed.

Each entry should be quantitatively measurable. The register should not be a dumping ground for control deficiencies, assets, threats. Threats personas should be in a threat agent library and assets in their own database. Control deficiencies should be tracked separately but can be linked to underlying risks in the register. After checking the boxes on compliance, how do you prioritize your mitigation efforts? What guides where you and your team spend your time, money, and focus? Risk register, done properly, keeps the focus on where it needs to be, the bottom line. The *shift left* principle is simple—it is cheaper to catch problems earlier in the development pipeline compared to when it is in production.

IT puts hands on their keyboards to counter the other side—live, active, thinking adversaries with resources, time, and persistence to attain a multitude of undesirable objectives against our organizations. The goal of the security program is the ongoing active identification and response to cyber-attacks to keep potential future financial losses in check.

A Team Built to Thrive

Steve Jobs said, *"Great things in business are never done by one person; they're done by a team of people."*[81] The hallmark of high-performing organizations is teamwork. It takes a team to succeed. If you stay in a silo, then you, IT, and your organization will struggle. You do not have to go it alone, so assemble a team, and then work as one.

We are built for human, face-to-face interaction among ourselves and with our customers. Years ago, I came back into work 13 hours after signing out to find a coworker still there, plugging away on the same support call with the vendor, trying to crack the cause of a problem. He was burned out. He went at it alone. We later established a new rule at our company: "If you cannot figure something out within two hours, call on your teammates to assist." Don't struggle alone! This is one way to engage the team, avoid individual burnout, and improve problem resolution response time.

Organizations that lead the pack in the marketplace do so by working as a single organism, with many individuals who interact collectively—for the benefit of staying agile—while continually getting better to sustain success. These organizations understand the nature of their work, anticipate outcomes, see problems, get a handle on root causes, fix the problems, and spread new insights organization-wide. They learn from each other and use teamwork to tackle problems.

The structure of the organization needs to support this level of teamwork. Agile organizations manage the structure and dynamics of the process.

IT teams have had a long history of individualism in work efforts. Teams are isolated not only from other departments, but also from the business. Dominica DeGrandis and Kaimar Karu explain the "State of IT" in their paper:

> Many IT operations professionals have grown up in an environment where having more work than capacity was the norm and finding creative solutions to keep the fires under control was part of daily work. While widely acknowledged as an

unattainable model, it has prevailed for a long time and has, among other things, been partially responsible for the emergence of the "hero culture," in which the IT operations specialist saves the day. Again.[82]

There's no heroism in having IT fix a problem that should have been avoided in the first place. This is applicable when we ourselves broke a system or was slow to repair a known fault condition. In operating complex systems, we have to be vigilant in not creating future problems with our repair work.

Be mindful of workers. IT knows it's not a wise idea to run compute nodes at 100 percent utilization. However, the same IT team will run its own people over 100 percent utilization and burn them out in mind, body, and soul.

Knowledge workers are toiling in the back and up front, leading boardroom discussions on business strategy, serving on the front lines of cyber battles, saving lives in healthcare, revolutionizing the entertainment industry, etc.

The great news, IT, is you are not alone. Others in the organization are facing challenges like yours, trying to navigate the complexities and keep their heads above water. We can learn from them. Teamwork is vital when dealing with complex systems, such as those that power our always-on digital world. The team has a common purpose, a shared vision, and a desire to improve. They help each other by regularly going the extra miles.

This contrasts with a group of employees who begrudgingly engage with each other because their manager makes them. Individuals showing up only for the paycheck, who are just trying to make it through the day, or who have mentally checked out to survive poor leadership make the problems of hero culture more acute.

If IT wants to overcome obstacles and improve its condition, then it must operate as a team. The innovators in a startup company based out of a garage are working as a team, and as recent history has shown, their kind of growth and success can be traced directly to the multiplying power of teamwork and shared focus. If you do not want to be relegated to irrelevancy, then team up and get to work.

Teaming

You and your work colleagues need to team. A team is a group of individuals working together to achieve a goal. Teams normally have members with complementary skills and generate synergy through a coordinated effort that allows each member to maximize their strengths and minimize their weaknesses. A group does not necessarily constitute a team. There is a distinction between a team and a group.

A group is a collective of individuals with similar or separate goals who are brought together for work purposes. Even if an individual shares information and resources with other group members, each member is responsible for their own work.

Conversely, a team is an interdependent group of individuals who deliberately share responsibility and common goals. People in a team build mutual understanding with the other members. By working together, they maximize each other's strengths and minimize their weaknesses. Unlike a group, where each member is expected to contribute separately, teams are more synergistic when they function well.

A team is greater than the sum of its individual members. Teams introduce new ways of looking at job titles, team names, skill sets, and roles to alter how work gets done. Naresh Jain, a technology and product development expert, explains:

> Team members need to learn how to help one another, help other team members realize their true potential, and create an

environment that allows everyone to go beyond their limitations. Teams can be broken down from a huge team or one big group of people, even if these smaller secondary teams are temporary.[83]

The hallmark of a team is actual teamwork. There's no other way to succeed in complex goals and projects in the long run in its absence. Teamwork is a basic human function, a force multiplier of human effort. Andrew Carnegie, businessman and philanthropist, remarked, *"Teamwork is the ability to work together toward a common vision. The ability to direct individual accomplishments toward organizational objectives. It is the fuel that allows common people to attain uncommon results."*[84]

Consider a moving day to visualize teamwork in action. Person A is in the truck; person B is outside the truck on the ground; persons C and D collect boxes from person B and carry them to the house; person E is at the door to hand them off to persons F and G; person H takes boxes to individual rooms; and finally, person I unpacks the boxes.

We also see this in sports. The offensive line blocks, receivers go out in patterns, running backs carry the ball, and the quarterback orchestrates the play. Inside IT, we see it in building a new app. The business analyst gathering requirements, developer coding, quality assurance developer performing quality assurance checks, engineer putting operations into production, and service desk technician configuring devices to use the app.

Another key characteristic of teams is temporal variability. Teams can come together for a short-term, immediate need to get something done. An example of a brief teaming effort is a project-based team that builds a new app function. Teams also come together for longer durations to tackle larger and longer-term initiatives. An example would be an architecture firm with permanent resources that's working all the time on new building designs.

There is a wave coming of a new type of work. Embrace the various ways of working. For example, the digital era is priming workers of all ages for different expectations of work. Because we are less tethered to physical offices, teamwork increasingly happens remotely.

Embrace working with those heading into retirement as prime sources of information and insights as consultants. They have the experience and wisdom that younger generations haven't had the time to build.

Embrace digital interfaces, collaboration, information sharing, and process interactions.

Embrace dynamic projects and sprint-based projects, pulling teammates from all over the globe. By working across time zones, languages, and different cultures, teamwork can be global. This flexibility in teaming arrangements can be supercharged by having a culture of disciplined workers.

Jim Collins, author of *Good to Great*, explains a culture of discipline:

> All companies have a culture, some companies have discipline, but few companies have a culture of discipline. When you have disciplined people, you do not need hierarchy. When you have disciplined thought, you do not need bureaucracy. When you have a disciplined action, you do not need excessive controls. When you combine a culture of discipline with an ethic of entrepreneurship, you get the magical alchemy of great performance.[85]

A culture of discipline allows your team to be structured leaner and to be more agile in work itself. Beyond the org structure and titles, who are the individuals who make up your team?

Member Sources

Team membership is more flexible than a list put together in another era of work for a static purpose. Team building can be used to overcome skill set deficiencies. For example, finding a data scientist who happens to have domain expertise in security can be challenging, but we can bring together multiple people with complementary skills to accomplish the work of data science. Teams are composed of people in and outside of the organization. Many individual departments have been managing risk for years. Imagine combining the knowledge and experience of multiple departments. Down the hallway, one of your coworkers has a faster way of accomplishing the same task you are spending too much time on. There are usually people in your building who can share with, teach, and advise you. You may see them in the elevator every morning and not realize they are allies waiting to be called upon.

Like ants, teams survive exactly because of good teamwork. No one ant can accomplish the most basic of survival tasks. Alone, they are limited. As a team, they can move much larger objects. Together they pool their efforts to live and work.

Internal teams are the primary team efforts. Groups like the desktop, server, storage, cloud, security, service desk, and developer teams sync their work efforts for the technology infrastructure needed to meet business needs.

Teamwork makes possible organizational structures that are flatter more open. Communication tools and channels support more collaboration and improved status updates. This reduces the interruptions of individual teammates by providing information to everyone. When the work streams are underway, we can track the overall goals, and adaptations can be made as needed.

Arguably the richest source of human talent in an organization is the underdeveloped worker. One of the most important attributes of future business success is increasing productivity of all its workers.

There is a good chance that there are employees at your organization that you've already met that would be good teammates. Current talent allocation mechanisms may not make effective use of the data available to identify each employee's skill set or recommend where in the organization an employee might be most successful. With so many talent allocation decisions being made in an uninformed manner, internal talent is often underutilized, and teams are sometimes poorly constructed. As a result, companies cannot execute quickly enough. Belinda Rodman, VP of Global Services, explains:

> Most employees have skills that transfer across many different areas, but they're only known for the skills for which they were hired. A new understanding of an employee's value in the organization, how to allocate them to best leverage that value to the organization, is on the horizon.[86]

We must be cognizant of mismatched roles and titles. Excluding those whose degree or past work experience does not exactly match up with the description of a new position is a missed opportunity for improving the team. There is a difference between someone who can do the work and someone who the hiring manager or HR classifies as being qualified. An entire section of existing talent can be overlooked because decision makers overemphasize surface-level requirements.

At the same time, much technology enablement comes from outside the IT group. Consider the quality of your human resources—from the employees on your own team to that guy down the hall who could help break the business into a new market. People are the most important factor for success in business operations, more than process and technology. They are also the most important factor in how well your IT team performs and delivers for the business.

HR is IT's friend when IT performs its end-user education around technologies and threats. Those emails announcing video training for compliance, security awareness, or a new expense system often come from the HR department. Any time the IT team needs to communicate information around processes, changes, and trends in general, HR can be a valuable asset.

When HR completes the process of onboarding a new employee to the company, they normally have a process to request IT set up a new active directory user account, set up home directories, and assign the user to the proper groups.

And on the back end, when an employee departs the organization, HR normally notifies IT of the event, which triggers the process of decommissioning and disabling user accounts as appropriate as well as retrieving corporate equipment.

Now consider legalities because business law matters. Your legal team covers areas like employee rights and privacy. IT could be called on by the business to examine emails or files for evidence in legal cases against the organization. Legal could also come to IT requesting a forensics analysis of a laptop for potential insider data leakage to a competitor. Legal helps IT set the parameters for such processes.

Also, legal can provide guidance on the legal recourses available to the company when IT assesses risks of shadow IT moves by users, such as file shares in the cloud. Intellectual property may need to be retrieved from that user's private files.

If IT would like to make a stronger case to the business that such services should be blocked in the organization, legal provides the needed justification from a business standpoint.

Lawyers often have more impact on stakeholders who have liability. Legal departments also set the guidelines for what the business is required to report in the intervention of a cyber breach. That includes the particulars of who must be notified and when, what types of information must be revealed to potential federal investigators, and what needs to be held back to protect against potential legal consequences.

Think about auditors and their role. Is your organization bound by the Health Insurance Portability and Accountability Act (HIPPA), Sarbanes-Oxley Act (SOX), or Payment Card Industry (PCI)? Do you come under the purview of the Federal Trade Commission (FTC) or North American Electric Reliability Corporation (NERC)? In the case of an audit, one way to maintain positive standing with regulatory and governmental entities is to collaborate with your auditor, who interprets the regulations and laws but may not have the technical knowledge to properly judge your compliance. Using good people skills while working with them can smooth the relationship and give you an open channel to make your case for why and how you are in compliance.

Need to promote a new service or announce a change initiative? Your company probably has a marketing group. It may consist of one person or a whole department. Along with the sales team, your marketing group is out on the front lines to drive revenue. Whatever you sell, someone is branding your business in a noisy marketplace. That is what marketing is there for. Have you had lunch with the director of marketing? You should. Remember that you get paid based on the products or services sold, and marketing has a hand in that. Marketing has experience in branding, message encoding, and persuading.

Do you need to persuade decision makers? Or do you need to get end users to stop doing something? Check in with marketing. Reach out to them for help on your internal messaging challenges. Next time you are struggling to get users to switch to that new system (the one your team spent six months developing and testing), check with marketing to see if they could help persuade them.

When it comes to protecting stuff, you need allies to keep the physical infrastructure safe. An immutable law of cybersecurity is that if you cannot physically secure your assets, you no longer own them. That's why we need to consider physical security. It is critical that your data center is physically secure, and no one except vetted IT teammates is wandering around your server racks. It's also important that your wiring closets are secured, and no one has attached a tap to an edge switch.

Typically, IT finds itself integrating with third-party systems for physical security, like badge scanners and IP video surveillance systems. Within the realm of physical security is a wealth of information that can be leveraged to detect threats. One valuable physical security technique is a clean desk policy, which is a corporate directive that specifies all important documents, confidential letters, binders, and books are removed from a desk and locked away when an employee leaves their workstation. This policy limits what unauthorized people can glean from unsecured documents.

Take advantage of your partners. Teach them how to work better with IT. Consider your technology partners, integrators, vendors, consultants, and the like. As highlighted above, your team is not limited to internal employees.

Think differently about how you use your partners. Are you getting the most out of them? Are they getting the most out of you? Do you have too many? Do you not have enough? Are you in the same domains?

IT wants more than fulfillment and product pitches. IT needs business partnerships that assist with producing outcomes and experiences while reducing risk. We need other business partners to help battle the complexities in system design and lifecycle management.

Provide guidance to your preferred partners on how you want to consume their services and products. This will not only significantly curtail the value-added reseller pricing battle over commodities but will also allow you more design options on the front end. Work together to plan out multisystem and multiyear initiatives to produce a more predictive project scheduling process.

Find opportunities for VARs to develop business relationships beyond fulfillment. They can truly off-load work from your plate by proactively bringing new ideas to the table and partnering on the toughest challenges. IT can begin by raising the standards for VARs on projects, including those in IT design and architecture.

A two-way partnership can be a win-win for both parties. IT should pose several questions in regard to partnering:

- What are the consumption possibilities?

- Can you work out flexible financing?

- How can creative financing make our investments CFO-friendly?

- What can our people off-load to you?

- How are your partners handing off the end-of-project to you?

- How do you handle features not available from the solution at the time of implementation?

- What resources, like labs, can you leverage or practice on?

- Can you beta test the next version?

- What principles does this team embody?

Team Principles

There are key principles that successful teams need. What principles underpin a team built to thrive? Trust, alignment, learning, sharing, expanded decision-making, and agreed-upon arrangements for how we work. The teaming discussed so far has some fundamental principles that make it possible to excel in performance and worker satisfaction.

The first principle is high trust. When we trip and fall, we want to know there will be someone there to catch us. The most critical factor for success is a high level of trust and trustworthiness among team members. We rarely work well in an environment with fears of job loss, loss of credit, or reduced resources. These constrain the contributions and collaboration of talented teammates. In this situation, knowledge is hoarded, existing resources are hidden, and budgets are guarded. This happens because if anyone exposes a gap in skills, it could be turned against him or her down the line.

Teams also need to avoid becoming fractured when things get tough. Competition must take a back seat. No one should accuse others of not pulling their weight or of exploiting workload distribution—nor should anyone do those things.

Good leadership—often from IT—prevents these work wasters.

Our work environment needs to both feel safe and actually be safe. The culture must value employees who engage in their work and work with each other for the goal. The culture must not fixate on individual recognition at expense of team success. The culture must ensure the workload is fairly distributed based on team members' roles, abilities, and availability.

Teammates believe in what the team does. Others in the group do not feel the need to hoard. There is little to no pressure to do everything yourself. Mistakes are allowed; suggestions for improvement are welcome. Instead of blaming one another, all team members work together to fix any problems.

The culture must value the talents of each individual and challenge others in return.

The business case for high trust is stronger financial performance. High trust shows up as higher internal customer satisfaction, lower employee turnover rate, and faster completion times. In contrast, low trust can be expensive. High trust is a prerequisite for great culture.

The second principle is shared alignment. Focus, strategy, and execution need to be in sync across the team. Aligned teams use the same language, follow the same timeline, and hold the same expectations in their work. They all know what success looks like in their project. In a sense, a team is a shared mind. The terminology is the same. Time boundaries are honored. There is accountability for individual contributions.

The third principle is continuous learning. This is a natural progression that sprouts from knowledge sharing (see below). As individual members acquire new skills and learn new things, their knowledge combines to make the team itself smarter. Continuous learning is culturally embedded. A dynamic world requires the team to be always learning. Continuous learning applies to new technology, different business concepts, and interpersonal interactions.

The fourth principle is knowledge sharing. As teammates work locally through new discoveries, insights, or findings, they can share these globally with the rest of the team. If they don't, they constrain team success and waste time. Others then must go through similar experiences to make identical discoveries. Knowledge sharing communicates changes, documents the way something works, shares status updates, and notifies teammates of any systemic change.

The fifth principle is participatory decision-making. In the participatory decision-making process, each team member has an opportunity to share their perspectives, voice their ideas, and tap their skills to improve the team's effectiveness. A great example of this comes from Liberating Structures, which was curated by Henri Lipmanowicz and Keith McCandless. They were also the authors of the book *The Surprising Power of Liberating Structures: Simple Rules to Unleash a Culture of Innovation*. Liberating Structures are simple rules that make it easy to include and unleash everyone in shaping the future. Liberating Structures introduce tiny shifts in the way we hold meetings, make plans, make decisions, and relate to one another. They put the innovative power once reserved for experts in the hands of everyone. As an example of distributing decision-making, General Stanley McChrystal, retired United States Army general, followed this process:

> McChrystal could see that his superb teams were embedded in an authority-based bureaucracy in which communications and decisions flowed slowly and vertically. He knew that he had to do something different. He had to eliminate "the deeply rooted system of secrecy, clearances, and inter-force rivalries." He saw that the ability to adapt to complexity and continuous unpredictable change was more important than authority and carefully prepared plans. Rapid horizontal communications were more important than vertical consultations and approvals. Teams had to be able to take decisions as needed, without seeking approvals higher up the command.[87]

Participatory decision-making works in tandem with the other team principles. Decisions have input from multiple members of the team, who each have unique viewpoints and areas of expertise. Participatory decision-making gives team members a vested interest in the outcome of a decision because each one had a part in making it.

Participatory decision-making by top management teams can ensure the completeness of decision-making. The talent of a large percentage of the organization can be applied to the front lines of work rather than restricted to a few at the top. Participatory decision-making can increase the likelihood that the decision is correct.

The sixth principle is working agreements. These map out the details of how we work. Working agreements answer questions like, *How often will we meet? Who should lead the discussion? Who should take notes during the meeting? How will we make the final decision?* A working agreement establishes a shared understanding and way of working for teams. Sometimes called a *social contract*, working agreements build high-performing teams. They free teams to operate by agreed-upon rules of the road.

Leadership

Leadership is a necessary component of business success. To lead is to take responsibility for inspiring change in your current circumstances. Denis Waitley, motivational speaker and writer, says, *"There are two primary choices in life: to accept conditions as they exist, or accept the responsibility for changing them."*[88]

The act of leading requires individuals to courageously step up. Leadership is a role, not a title. It's a choice, not an assignment. Leadership is the art of mobilizing others to struggle for shared aspirations.

Technology is critical to a business's competitiveness and long-term survival. IT is positioned to influence business strategy. Where it can, IT should lead the way. Leadership pushes getting the important things done.

Leading is a prerequisite for getting things changed. Our world, now digital, is constantly disrupted on multiple fronts. These disruptions require speedy decision-making, feedback, and outcomes never seen before.

IT needs to lead, inspire, and thrive through each disruption. IT's leadership is transformational. It guides, encourages, and inspires others to work toward shared goals with a common vision. IT recognizes the challenges and risks, looks at the possibilities, and sets change in motion down the right path.

As technology dominates the operations and growth of our modern economy, IT is positioned to enable businesses to win. A tour of today's business, technology, and risk landscape trends begins with exploring both the opportunities and the risks. IT will bring new ideas to the table for business leaders. IT will lead in navigating the risk landscape.

IT can't help someone until IT helps itself. We need to put our mask on first before trying to assist others, so to speak. IT is a team that contributes and helps teammates succeed. IT increases the power of technology applied to business use. IT is a part of the larger organization. IT is a team within a larger team.

Leadership can be a broad term. Many people can live like leaders and make positive change in their organizations. In their own ways, individuals can add to the larger group to create something bigger than the sum of its parts. You don't need a title or explicit mandate to lead.

However, you do need to understand your sphere of influence. There are things you can control, things you can influence, and things you can neither influence nor control. Spend your time and energy on what you can affect.

In IT, anyone can lead, regardless of title and position in the org chart. This reality is true throughout the organization. And since challenging and disruptive times affect everyone, everyone can decide to lead and inspire.

There is a special club that those who want to see change can join. When I make the case that IT should lead—that *we* should lead—exactly who am I referring to? This triggers several questions. What do I mean by *leading*? Who is being led? Don't you need a title to lead? Doesn't the boss lead? Won't someone else take care of that? Who are the leaders? Who is in this club?

Leaders are not born, entitled, or granted superpowers. Leaders choose to influence others for the good of the team and the organization. Leaders can be any of us, regardless of our standing in the org chart, time on the job, or assigned roles. Leaders are defined by their actions, influence on others, and ability to help their team get things done.

Anyone can lead or be led. Anyone can imagine new ways of thinking, inspire others, and guide team efforts in the right direction. Anyone can be influenced by another to help their cause. Unfortunately, if no one—including those who technically may have been tagged as leaders—steps forward, the work can linger unfinished for a long time. Problems can grow rather than be repaired, giving victory to the status quo.

Some people will resist you and put up roadblocks. That is normal. That is the nature of the human condition. Though our world is different from how it was in the past, the patterns of change resistance are similar. But true leaders guide the resistant team members as well as the overeager ones. Once we know a new challenge is upon us, we are bound to that cause and are responsible for bringing the team along with us.

The future viability of your organization, the relevance of IT, and the prospects for your future career all depend on leadership through change. If no one else is leading, then it is in your best interest to step forward.

The nature of leadership is changing. We are moving away from a command-and-control leadership style where wisdom comes from an all-powerful, all-knowing, charismatic leader inspiring the masses.

Instead, leadership now needs to be dispersed across the organization. Many processes and innovations exist because someone took it upon themselves to do what was necessary. These individuals—whose names are often not written down or mentioned in a corporate video—brought enough people along to attain a shared goal.

Leadership is courageous, selfless, and inspiring. No one can afford to wait for the next great pronouncement from above about a new transformation initiative. The window for shaping change shrinks the longer you wait to act.

Leaders behave differently. Leadership takes courage and initiative. You need leadership in your everyday work life. Everything is now being left in your hands—your career path, your job future, your financial well-being, and your health. Your quality of life is now, more than ever, in your hands. Determine to embody the change you want in the world. Influence the outcome.

Leaders create action that is intentional, explicit, and focused. Leaders set timelines and milestones to drive daily activities toward meeting the organization's goals. Leaders pay attention to today's realities and ways of financing the business. Leaders carve out time and effort for tomorrow's destinations. Leaders not only keep eyes on the hockey puck today but also anticipate where the hockey puck is heading in the future.

Leaders play the infinite game, practice empathy with others, and tune themselves in to the daily indicators of opportunity. Leaders are open to new ways of solving problems and are agile in their thinking. Leaders embrace the team mentality and focus their intention on the work that needs to be done. Leaders refuse to throw teammates under the bus to save themselves.

For the tough conversations that might need to be had to move things along, leaders take the reins.

Leaders prioritize and then focus people on those priorities. Leaders assist in the flow of ideas and information. Michael Papay, cofounder and CEO of Waggl, says:

> There's a common misunderstanding that leadership needs to have all the answers. But they can't possibly have all the right answers; it's not realistic given the pace of change and the precision of expertise required. Communication, however, is the key

to success: clearly, frequently, authentically, transparently communicating with employees and colleagues who can provide additional perspective and knowledge.[89]

Leaders create an environment conducive to letting all voices be heard, where the smartest one in the room turns out to be the room itself—the collective voice of everyone. Leaders know they can't be everywhere, solve all problems, or process all the issues coming in. In response, they create a collaborative environment to distribute problem sensing and problem-solving to the edges of the organization. All of this is possible because the culture they create focuses on sharing, exploring, listening, and solving.

Leaders know that communication is critical in all efforts. *"The single biggest problem in communication is the illusion that it has taken place."*[90] This unfortunate reality provides leaders a golden opportunity. Encode and transmit your messages in a manner that the receiver understands. Confirm that you have decoded their feedback and find ways to get on the same page. This leads to the very value of IT itself. Enabling the business while mitigating risk through a systemic approach.

Chapter 8
Mitigation System

A control is anything that can influence the probability, frequency, or impact of an unwanted scenario. It can be administrative, physical, or technical in nature for the purpose of avoiding, deterring, resisting, or responding to the threat factors driving the scenario. Controls come in many varieties, serving a wide range of risk management functions. For common technical controls such as firewalls, intrusion prevention systems, and web proxies, the interesting thing about security is to be effective and useful, there must be integrated coordination among the controls. Organizations have a multitude of controls, and the investment of time and money to implement and operate all of them can be daunting for many.

You need a controls model, a representation of the various types of controls, that describes how they interact and work together. That model guides you in the design of a system that coordinates organizational resources to properly defend an organization. Mitigation of digital risk is manifested through the use of controls. The mechanism of that mitigation is a "system of controls," better known as *security*. Security is a collection of people, policies, processes, strategies, approaches, tactics, operations, and technologies working together as a system. The aim is to maintain an acceptable level of organizationally defined risk. IT builds and operates this system to keep the harm from threat actors within a tolerable range.

Today's business needs the next generation of cyber security to better manage cyber risk. That is not possible without a fundamental understanding of the nature of business transformation. Without this, efforts to secure the business from the myriad of threat actors will be a wasted investment of resources. IT will have little chance of success. Security is an embedded system, dependent on the larger IT infrastructure, which itself is dependent on the business at large.

The scope of the security system is larger than in the past. IT now uses digital risk mitigation to encompass traditional IT security, as well as information security, physical security, and operation technology security. IT covers these security areas and the interconnectivity of each.

Businesses are being disrupted and reimagined by digitization. IT must be at the intersection of the value at risk to keep the threat actors from disrupting our organization's attainment of its goal. At the end of the day, all these areas are business risks.

IT advises about potential initiatives. Then follows the green lights our businesses give. IT's main goal is the implementation of new technology and mitigation of risk.

IT creates a state of full capability. Be protective, be defensible, be early, be active, and be quick.

A system is a set of connected things or parts forming a complex whole. A series of controls working together to accomplish the organization's defined risk management objectives. That system needs to be intentionally designed.

The design elements of a security program include its functionality, means of operations, any approach to mitigating risk. You know the real-world impact on how well the system of controls operate. As all controls have some elements of interactions with each other and among each other, there are a lot of options to the types of control, the number of controls, and how we integrate all of them together. It is not possible to look at a single control and evaluate its mitigation efficiency against real-world threats. Rather it is the interaction among multiple controls that was specifically and intentionally designed to maximize the effectiveness of a wide range of threats being targeted towards our organizations.

Security must be an embedded function in enterprise architecture. The security function must be components of the technology architecture informed by real-world TTPs. Its function is to ensure overall and complete coverage of the technology infrastructure that has been designed to meet business needs. In many security programs the design of the program is guided primarily from outside regulatory and compliance requirements, not from internal-based requirements of design that are aligned with business needs. Design happens inside the architectural process, which must be intentional in the selection of controls to meet your specific risk mitigation needs.

The controls that we employ, from administrative to physical to technical controls, along with our own blue team tactics, techniques, and procedures that are informed by our approach to security to mitigate risk, need a centralized focus. We need to be able to map out all our loss scenarios against our digital infrastructure. We need to be able to visually see where our controls are placed how they interact with each other.

The controls system works by using multiple approaches to risk mitigation.

The first is avoidance, which takes care of most of the threat activity in the digital infrastructure. Between automated discovery and manual hunting of vulnerable systems, if we can limit the systems an attacker can see or interact with, we can significantly reduce the amount of attack surface we have to defend. Traditional networks were not designed to limit connectivity; on the contrary they were designed to encourage connectivity as much as possible among all things and people. As such, we must change our approach and re-design of our infrastructure to take a differentiated approach to the connectivity of all the nodes, elements, and people in our systems. The controls system must provide the right access, at the right time, between the right resources. Avoidance controls shield organizations from most of the access from the outside. The practical effects of avoidance controls are what causes the attacker to have to spend more resources. It also limits the number of threat actors willing to put in the effort of a campaign. You can think of avoidance at the top our mitigation funnel.

Next up is deterrence. When a threat actor identifies an asset of interest, the question now becomes is there anything that can deter them from proceeding with an attack. The simplest example is an asset of value to everyone who sits in a room with an open door that has no cameras or guards. In a scenario where there's very little risk of being caught or having any personal repercussion, this would produce a high level of loss events. This would encourage a much larger number of threat actors to target your asset. If someone walking by that room entered, and now there was a security camera, there's a certain number or percentage of the threat out of community that could be swayed to stop their efforts. The security camera as a control to deter infers negative actions against the threat actor if they can be identified. Many attacks happen because criminals and threats believe they will get away with it. You must defer them by having them believe they might be caught, in this case due to a security camera that captures their face and identifies them. If not, there is the potential for delaying the attack activities.

One of the effects of deterrence is the effect of increasing the level effort that needs to be put into the attack. A close relation to deterrent is delay. Once the attacker has started into your infrastructure or environment, the amount of time and effort needed to be successful in their attack could be influenced by the defender interfering in their attack chain. The practical effect of this is to delay the successful completion of the attack campaign. Not all attackers in this scenario will continue. Many criminal campaigns are opportunistic, such as in the case of access to a compromised credential of an externally accessible vulnerable system. That differs from the sophisticated attackers or nation-states willing to persist in their efforts for the long haul. Even for the more sophisticated attackers, the more times they are in the environment potentially gives offenders more opportunity for detection and countermeasures. Delay controls could be honeypots, black hole networks, changed API keys, or reset credentials. The next approach is resistance.

To resist is very familiar in a security space, the most popular ones being patching a vulnerable system, adaptive authentication, stronger encryption, or micro-segmentation. This could also include adjusting security awareness training to address new phishing campaigns to reduce the number of clicks of suspicious emails from end users. This could be resetting network connection settings, blocking specific host connections, or tightening authorization access. If the attacker does gain initial access, we may be able to limit their activities.

We can limit the aspects around the ultimate objective and parts of the attack chain in the campaign. We can limit all users who potentially have access to a certain database to only certain parts, we can put time restrictions on how long the access can be granted, automatically change passwords for admins after every session after checkout. We can limit the locations where the connectivity is allowed, or we can dynamically force reauthentication of a device to validate illegitimate users. Despite all the headlines IT security efforts in general to hardening systems has had an effect. Even though it may seem hard to believe, anytime an attacker changes their established method of attack, they are reacting to defenders' actions. These controls are starting to lead up to ejecting the attacker from the environment.

Ejecting attackers can be accomplished using similar tactics and techniques from the resistance and limitations approaches. In this case we're attempting to force the attackers off our systems and have to start their attacks from scratch, thus driving up the costs on their efforts.

And for those times that the threat attacks are successful through all other controls, we can apply many mitigation tactics to lessen the blow from a loss magnitude standpoint. We could potentially avoid having to make a report to an external stakeholder. A successful threat event or technical attack that leads to malicious cold or compromised credentials, as we have talked about before, does not necessarily mean a loss event. Also, we can lessen the impact in such a state that the financial losses fall within an acceptable range of the business risk appetite. From limiting the number of times an attack is successful, to the impact on a high number of payouts, mitigation controls keep the ultimate impact on the organization, the business bottom line, to such a state that the business continues to operate while taking losses all under an acceptable risk appetite and capacity.

Together the design elements of our controls from this approach means that we are providing an umbrella of protection for our organizations, which allows it to operate inside of an infinite, dynamically constantly changing threat environment, while still allowing the business to meet its objectives. As we say, that is the point of risk management. Now let's talk about the five elements of our system of controls. They are value protection, defendable architecture, early warning system, active threat defense, and rapid response system.

Value Protection

Value at Risk needs protection from harm. Value is the concept of relative worth or importance. Relative is a crucial element here, as it is not static and can be different for everyone. In markets, you can measure it with what people are willing to pay for something. That value can be represented with money. For businesses, value is what it has that it uses for market consumption from others. This value is generated by combining human capital with various types of assets. There are different types of assets, some physical, some digital. These different types of assets can be divided into classes. Some asset types are containers for other assets. It is important to understand the differences. You can have a physical asset such server. You can have an asset such as a database. You can have an asset such as customer data. The data can live in the database with is housed in the server. From a business standpoint, the asset that it primarily seeks to protect is the data. The database is a container for that data. The same as the server is the container for the database.

From a business relevancy standpoint, the data is what provides value in the way it is used to carry out the daily operations of any organization. Management cares about the data asset class. The server is of much lower value to the business. IT cares about and manages the server and database asset classes because those are the containers that are the conduits through which attackers target the data. It serves a purpose by storing and serving up access to the data. So, in this case we have two assets, the file server and the data. IT puts technical controls around the server and database to mitigate compromise of the data. We can't protect data if we don't protect the other asset classes.

So, when we come to the business saying there is a vulnerability against one of our assets, we convey the importance of that message by focusing on asset the care about, the data itself. IT needs to track all assets classes and types. Because of the nature of the relationship between these different asset types, we need to understand intimately the dependency between them. We should map our technology assets over a value and service maps to visualize the asset classes relationships. When IT makes a budget ask for a security control, we should be able to reference the business asset at the heart of the need. Threat attackers' goal is not to steal our servers but our data.

Let's start with an asset portfolio. Value at risk is contained in real physical assets. These real physical assets can be seen and touched. Like a library that contains human knowledge, that knowledge is contained in solid physical books. Assets can be directly owned by an organization, "leased" from a third party, or have some type of legal arrangement where someone else provides the physical assets that their digital value lives on. Organizational assets live in or supported by technical containers. Technical assets outnumber the business assets in numbers, while the financial value of business assets dwarfs the combined technical ones all put together. That is what the C-suite cares about.

In some forms, the asset library can be found in many organizations, partially in a configuration management database, aka a CMDB. Often, though, the CMDB has had limited functionality across the organization. In the context of IT, an asset library is much more because it specifically documents the business context in terms of value. All this information is linked and stored in an asset inventory database. This database should be maintained by dedicated resources that could be thought of as asset librarians, charged with lifecycle management of the inventory of all organizational assets that IT will protect from harm.

Assets can be thought of in at least five different ways. They can be devices, software, services, processes, or data.

A device is a thing, especially a piece of mechanical or electronic equipment, made or adapted for a particular purpose. Devices can be servers, storage array networks, routers, switches, laptops, kiosks, IP cameras, IP phones, etc. They can be internal, purchased directly by the organization, or external, such as IaaS inside a cloud provider. If physical technology gear processes the organizational data or services, it needs to be inventoried as such.

Software ranges from back-end application services to local operating systems, such as Windows on corporate laptops, custom-designed mobile apps, device drivers running on servers, firmware, storage area networks, and networking devices. Any code running inside the organization or on technology running business services or data needs to be inventoried.

Services can be described as technological activity that is intangible, is not stored, and does not result in ownership. Some examples include the ability to print from one place to the next, the ability to bring in multiple people on a single video call, electronic signatures on a document that notifies a user when it's processed, and the intake of new information from a customer. IT must keep a breakdown of the services that have underpinning technology. IT should document these as assets. Service assets covers all the operational matters their business today runs on that has a technology dependency through it. This encompasses everyday tasks that employees perform to do their work with their interact with some element of technology that IT support.

Processes are another form of asset and include the onboarding of new hires, provisioning equipment, and servicing end user technology requests. IT must identify and protect these assets.

Data and all its various forms—raw, semi-processed, or fully processed—should be identified, inventoried, and protected. Data is produced from the exhaust of all the technology infrastructure, covering raw data, tactical information, and insights the drive the day-to-day business.

Value is protected by controlling access to organizational assets. Be protective! Defend your value and protect your assets. Maximize system uptime. Control access on a need-to-know basis. There is the need for both service and data protection. Service protection covers all the technology our businesses run on. This encompasses technology that employees use for everyday tasks, as well as all interactions with any elements of technology that IT supports. Data protection focuses on the outputs of the technology infrastructure. Data protection covers raw data, tactical information, and insights that drive the day-to-day business. IT governs access, availability, integrity, privacy, and safety of assets. Assets can be thought of in several ways, physical, virtual, or intangible. IT will often work with devices, software, services, processes, and data.

Protect your organization's value by protecting its assets. To aid in this effort, the architecture of your technology systems needs to be designed with security in mind.

Defendable Architecture

Our digital infrastructure needs to be designed to aid in cyber defense. IT gives its assets a chance to be defended. We need to create digital infrastructures conducive to defense. Defense principles include several key attributes. Avoidance takes us out of the loss scenario. Concealment obscures value at risk from attackers' view. Deterrence increases the cost or time and/or reduces the incentives for a threat to target you. Resistance is about making it difficult for the attackers' efforts to be successful.

Defendable architecture aids in defense, is built into the overall architecture, uses foundational principles, is updateable and easy to patch without disrupting services, uses secure code, is malware-free, and uses supply chain confirmation. Controls can be inserted, IP traffic can be blocked, node service can be stopped, checks can happen regularly, rights can be restrained, monitoring can be activated, and all traffic can be seen.

Defendable architecture can be protected. It aids, assists, and encourages risk mitigation from cyber-attacks by making it difficult for all components of the attack chain to succeed over time. Attackers fail because defenders detect and counter them.

Defendable architecture reduces the impact of the actions of the attacker, limits the impact of a vulnerability, and decreases the probability of business loss from an unwanted outcome.

To feed continuous improvement in defenses while maintaining business operations, we must take advantage of the design of our infrastructure, the lifecycle management of hosts, and the visibility of the situation.

It is beneficial to design a system that makes it easy to be monitored. This is a prerequisite for the feeds needed to build an early warning system.

A critical secure by design principle is to give your assets a chance to be defended. We need to give digital infrastructure conducive to defense. Defense principles include limiting what attackers can see. For what they can identify, make the costs to successfully attack high in cost and effort. Make it hard at every stage of the attack chain. Design in elements of the architecture that make attackers' TTPs difficult. This architecture needs to be easy to update, patch, and monitor while limiting service disruptions. Make it easy to insert security control as the need arises.

Defendable architecture can be protected. It aids, assists, and encourages mitigation of risk from cyber-attacks by making it difficult for all components of the attack chain to succeed over time without defenders detecting and countering them. Defendable architecture reduces the impact of the actions of the attacker, limits the impact of a vulnerability, and decreases the probability of business loss or an unwanted outcome.

There are some common risk factors widely seen in successful breaches. These factors are exploited by threat actors in the most talked-about breaches, and many challenges have hampered our defense efforts. The last few years have seen advances in technology that give IT more ways to address these gaps. We have also seen changes in how we think about approaching defense strategies. I believe that, in the end, there are some things we need to get better at doing.

Time after time, if you read the details of cyber breaches, you realize that often the exact initial point of compromise is not known.

Obviously, for gaps and determining the entire nature of the attack, and often because of potential legal liabilities, all that is known about the attack is not shared with the larger community. We are left with statements of the sophisticated nature of the attack, suggesting help-lessness of the defenders. After breaches occur, some businesses use that as a cover for something preventable or possibly minimized. As we know, the attacker will take the path of least resistance; therefore, it makes no practical sense for an attacker to use the latest zero-day ex-ploit when the front door is wide open.

Business risk factors in the cyber world are often a function of business processes, which emphasize speed, efficiency, cost control, and profits. Security controls that inhibit the business from doing the job of making money often result in recommended controls being ignored or by-passed. Here, IT must heed the call of the business priorities and realize we must employ more sophisticated security controls and focus on a critical path of attack success. Success in your security program is a function of success in your enterprise risk-management program. The manifestations of success can include larger IT budgets, larger head-counts, and more buy-in from management on needed process changes.

We must take advantage of the design of our infrastructure, the lifecy-cle management of hosts, and the visibility to gain situational aware-ness if we want to feed continuous improvement in defenses while maintaining business operations functionality.

Let's start with a framework that works to help our mitigation efforts. A framework provides the basic structure of how an organization's in-frastructure is designed, how users, services, applications, and data in-terconnect and interact with one another in a systemic way.

When IT thinks about this framework, it should focus on the business's defined assets. Our thinking should be asset-centric, with concern for how users interact with technology. This framework should enable, encourage, and assist with identification, prevention, recoverability, and response against a wide range of threat actors and methods. The focus should be on business risk. We must be careful to watch out for actions that are technically cool but do not have an actual impact on reducing risk. If we want users to "take off their shoes" before logging in, we want to make sure we are gaining some security and not just slowing the business down.

IT has suffered over the years by budget constraints and component isolation. The effect has been designed by cost. Components that don't talk with each other, undersized solutions, single fault features, expensive features activations, complicated maintenance contracts, and fragmentation are the result, producing a management nightmare.

The budget constraint challenge should be attacked by a vision and strategy rollout aligned with business initiatives scheduled in phases. The individual components are configured a certain way on purpose. Architecture makes it easy to make changes, watch user and device activity, enforce service assurances, and isolate the spread of malicious endpoints. Our design should limit which security and operations we should watch and respond to. The greatest gift we can provide them is to limit the noise and the impact of breach.

The cost for new controls should be attached to technology initiatives that are ties to specific business initiatives. If a capability does not exist and there is talk of a new initiative, the design should specify the additional capabilities along with cost, right next to the implementation costs.

IT can really shine by finally documenting how infrastructure is structured and why it is that way. This includes assumptions and workarounds and our expectations for performance and maintenance.

And to the business response that a security product is too expensive, we should respond with a business case presenting our security vision and strategy. We should get out of the business of product pushing.

We must know what mitigation options are available. Perhaps we only need to cover a subset of critical systems. Rethink trying out new services, products, and software. Vendors are responding to market disruption and are altering how they sell their offerings. There are more choices and ways to consume from them. Also, try rolling out new products to systems over shorter periods of time and running tighter evaluation testing. Or perhaps there are compensatory controls that can cover control gaps. Maybe only a subset of systems needs to be covered—for example, point of sale systems or devices used by the executive team, HR, and legal. Map out who would best be helped by it. Proxy the internet connections of internal users, like customer support reps, if you want to try out that new sandboxing technique. Recruit a willing road warrior to try that new secure app via a mobile application security suite.

IT must learn to love and embrace platforms, not individual products. Platforms allow us to plug in other solutions, leveraging that which is already there. We need to stop overbuying, duplicating functionality, and making work for ourselves. Simplicity, transparency, visibility, and recoverability are the key words.

The cyber security defensive prime concept is to design and build infrastructure that is optimized for defense. IT gives its assets a chance to be defended. We need to create digital infrastructure conducive to defense. These defense principles include:

- avoidance, where concealment means attackers can't see assets

- deterrence, where attackers can see your assets, but they determine that the cost or risk to them is too high to continue

- resistance, where that after they attack, your team resists their further attempts

- recovery, where business SLA, RTO, and RPO are all met

Defendable architecture aids in defense, is built into the overall architecture, uses foundational principles, is updateable and easy to patch without disrupting services, uses secure code, is malware free, validates, and uses supply chain confirmation. Controls can be inserted, IP traffic can be blocked, node service can be stopped, checks can happen regularly, rights can be restrained, monitoring can be activated, and all traffic can be seen.

Defendable architecture can be protected. It aids, assists, and encourages mitigation of risk from cyber-attacks by making it difficult for all components of the attack chain to succeed over time. Attackers fail because defenders detect and counter them.

Defendable architecture reduces the impact of the actions of the attacker, limits the impact of a vulnerability, and decreases the probability of business loss through an unwanted outcome.

To feed continuous improvement in defenses while maintaining business operations functionality we must take advantage of the design of our infrastructure, the lifecycle management of hosts, and the visibility to gain situational awareness.

An architecture that lends itself to monitor the system and all its individual components is designed to allow it to be monitored. This is a prerequisite for the feeds needed to build an early warning system.

The design of the architecture makes a big difference in the performance of a security program. A design is a plan and specification for the construction of something. It describes a unifying structure of that thing.

In the beginning of all user activity on your infrastructure, identity is key to who you are. At the most fundamental level, the context of who you are must be established. In a digital world, you are who their systems think you are based on, many times, a username.

You are who the username and password say you are. Impersonation in the digital world is as dangerous as it is in the physical. Cyber criminals are using compromised credentials to log into systems. Also, they are using compromised personal information for identity theft and fraud. This is the problem with single-factor authentication. Also, we need to ensure the level of access to services, applications, and network resources matches the user's role and proper context. IT must master identity.

For users to do their work, they require access to networks, data, services, and applications. The context of access includes who the users are in their roles in the organization, the endpoints they are connecting from, the times of the request, the location of the request, the means, and the business reasons.

We need to ensure we match the role to actual rights. Excessive rights tend to expose larger attack surfaces. From the day the users are hired to the day they leave the organization, our ability to manage differentiated access over the lifetime of the users will be critical to assuring controls are adequate. From the viewpoint of the users, their ability to get their work done often requires access to many applications. For some enterprises, this could number in the hundreds.

Your signals that your system is not user friendly enough is the amount of account lockouts, wrong passwords entered, simplicity of the passwords chosen, use of sticky notes, and reuse of the same passwords. We have an opportunity to simplify with stronger authentication and increased identity factors in conjunction with federated identity management. Shift the complexity to the back end to us and get the user out of the business of managing passwords and getting access instead of focusing on work to help the business succeed.

Privileged account management is useful in decreasing the attack surface by limiting the time accounts have access to systems. This includes tagging and monitoring trust relationships for correct context. Legitimate user access from a legitimate system at legitimate times needs to be flagged for unseen, or indicators of, leakage or persistence. User account rights for administrative purposes should only be set up when needed. Develop processes around auditing service accounts and monitoring for privilege abuse.

Threat agents will often attempt to compromise user credentials to gain access. Our architecture must allow us to identify malicious attempts to move laterally and limit their potential range.

A key principle for all infrastructure defense is managing the attack surface. Once initially compromised, can this host pivot to critical areas of your network? In far too many environments, the answer is yes. We know the TTPs often used by attackers leverage lateral movement to find their target. Past attempts to effectively segment industry and customer networks has proven too burdensome and challenging in practice. Advancements in today's networking and security technology, coupled with tighter integration between vendors, mean it is now possible to create a dynamic, differentiated, secure access control system, one that scales to cover wired, wireless, and remote access. It supports multifactor user authentication, including 2FA and device profiling (to identify the source of the node attempting to connect) to define and apply specific context access to authorized resources. Segmentation limits lateral movement and makes unauthorized access easier to detect.

That makes visibility and monitoring critical. IT needs to continuously monitor context access for pattern detection and adaption of control configuration, anomaly detection, baselining, and machine learning.

The scope includes the core, data center, enterprise edges, re-mote/branch, and endpoint visibility.

In addition to identity management, IT must master keeping track of all the technology the business buys and uses. It must be proficient in in-ventory management. When you know about a thing, you can account for it in your defense strategy.

Controls are applied to known entities, components, and systems. Making sure you know what you have, where it is physically located, or if it is corporately owned. Knowing who uses your systems and how they use it. Audit actual use, get rid of little-used resources, continually look for ways to kill legacy systems or get to more attractive migration price points, and audit for legal software. Ask yourself what your users are trading for all that free stuff and convenience. If you don't know about a system, then you can't apply controls and keep it up to date.

IT must guard the end-to-end software supply chain for the code a busi-ness consumes. Software code runs the world. Know what code you have, where it comes from, and watch over it to make sure it is legit.

IT must have pervasive visibility on all software used in its organization, so it can govern it to reduce risks.

Where software is sourced from, how it is installed and updated, how to audit it to prevent illegal and rogue apps, how to stop malware from being installed, as well as maintenance consistency and licensing ra-tioning (effects of the cloud)—all of these are important for IT to know about. We can't govern what we don't know about. We should be com-mitted to patching software for the systems we manage. This includes operating systems, firmware, appliances, IoT devices, the core operat-ing system, commercial off-the-shelf (COTS) software, in-house devel-opment, and third-party developed services.

A digital software supply chain exists where most of the code is assem-bled from multiple developers and sources. If we are going to be entrusting our cars, elevators, and IV pumps to software, then we should demand accountability, transparency, and agility in every part of the supply chain.

There is hope around using some of the principles of Lean, Agile, and DevOps to assist the efforts of mitigating cybersecurity risks. This means continuous delivery capability, automated testing, and service cataloging for providing repeatable builds for developers.

The benefits to this include faster time to code delivery, higher code quality, more frequent releases, integrated processes (such as ITIL treating automated changes not requiring approval like manual processes), easier to insert security testing, and a safer environment to introduce changes into without breaking functionality. In the software development lifecycle, there is opportunity to more closely integrate security principles, mitigation steps, and code review into the DevOps process. Some are calling this DevSecOps, where the security team meets the DevOps movement, with its commonalities and adjacencies.

Consider the supply chain attack, where one of your vendors is breached for the sole purpose of abusing trust relationships. For example, in what was viewed as a precursor to attacking upstream targets, the vendor RSA was targeted for its proprietary algorithms, which could potentially be leveraged against some of their customers' authentication tokens.

"In that case, the attackers weren't doing it for gain at RSA, as far as anyone's been able to tell, but there were reported attacks shortly after that against defense contractors that had characteristics of someone exploiting what was probably taken from RSA," said Eugene Spafford, professor of computer science at Purdue University. *"Those defense contractors were the real targets, but they were using a very strong security tool—RSA's tokens. So, if you're an attacker and faced with a strong defense, you can try to break straight through, or find ways around that defense."*

In that sense, Spafford said, the Bit9 and RSA attacks can be thought of as "supply chain" hacks. *"Supply chain doesn't necessarily mean the sale of finite items, but it's all along the chain of where things might find their way into your enterprise that can be contaminated, and I suspect we'll continue to see more of these types of attacks."*

Secure coding from birth—application security at the code level, at the earliest stages of the development lifecycle—is important. The costs of fixing code at later stages, or even after it's been released to end users, is much higher. Building quality into the development lifecycle from the beginning makes financial and security sense. DevOps allows for faster delivery times to the business, so you have the time to code more carefully in the innovation stages.

A mature security program is capable of providing differentiated access for different users to different systems based of environmental context. In contrast to the beginning of the Internet when the main goal was connectivity, today sees a far more dangerous landscape that requires all access to be conditionally granted. Zero trust, network access control, zero trust networking, and software-defined networking are some approaches that are being used to address these challenges. The concepts of least privilege and just enough access for the right people to do their jobs are becoming mainstay approaches to security architecture.

Modern architecture needs to support both the system overall and all its individual components to be monitored without too many extra work-rounds. This is a prerequisite for the feeds needed to build an early warning system.

Resiliency means we can sustain degradation to service and continue to service business requests. We can swap out an endpoint in minutes and get the user back on another system, access data that's replicated to another location (should the primary site become unavailable), and restore files encrypted by CryptoLocker—unleashing your own version of Netflix's famous Chaos Monkey tool.

Flex your deployment muscles by trying to deploy a new agent on 10,000 endpoints, gather relevant data, capture end-user input, evaluate, and decide within a month's time. Stop being constrained by technology that is no longer relevant, contracts that have outlived their usefulness, and solution partners who are deploying tech that requires rework after they put it in.

Early Warning System

Be early in detecting threat activity! As security teams stop bad events from impacting our organizations, it builds a business case for "early" by continually shifting left. The cost to address security issues are modest in the earlier stages of development and implementation. Costs go up considerably after a system is in production. Businesses pay more later with longer restore times if we don't guide them to act earlier in the attack chain. Cyber defense needs early warning to give IT sufficient time to respond.

The goal is to stay "left of boom." In the military the term "left of boom" refers to the time before an explosion, such as an improvised explosive device (IED) going off in the battlefield. It is a term that refers to the U.S. military's effort to disrupt insurgent cells before they can build and plant bombs. This means striving to stay one step ahead of the next potential business-impacting event. To accomplish this, IT needs to build an Early Warning System (EWS). An EWS alerts IT early on of a cyber-attack. It can identify relevant indicators through all the operational noise, alerting the right people for a timely response. It should be the default breach notification for the C-suite, not customers, news reporters, or the FBI.

For warnings to be useful, timing is everything, so we need to be early. There must be business relevance known for a warning to be warranted. Early means the detection is happening near the beginning of the attack chain. Factors that change before the bad things happen, such as system disruption or cyber breach. We are looking for patterns or trends that precede the attackers' TTPs. It is possible the earlier indicators of attack can potentially predict the follow-on activities. Early detection is a leading indicator. The earlier the better as it can avoid an incident altogether. And when something does occur, it could be smaller losses, less disruption, and less cleanup.

A warning indicates a possible or impending danger or problem. The detection of these early indicators needs to be communicated to someone who can respond. A warning must interrupt the defenders' daily routine to alert them of a potential future event. The alert must be "heard" or "seen," avoiding the common problem of getting lost in the noise of a ticketing system or email inbox. Since these indicators are early, they are not the high visibility of an outage or encrypted systems that come later in the attack chain. To be useful, the recipient of the warning needs to understand the business significance and is empowered to act.

The EWS is a set of connected things, people, processes, and technology that connects the alerting system together. Its goal is early signal detection. To be effective, it must be operationalized by building this capability with a monitoring program that encompasses the security methodologies and frameworks to scale out across your entire infrastructure.

Some may question, "Don't we already have a network operations center (NOC) and security operations center (SOC) for this? What's the difference?" Liability and responsibility can't be outsourced. Based off what we know from the dwell times of successful publicly reported breaches, attackers are often going undetected for long periods of time with traditional approaches to detection. EWS addresses detection at a systems level, producing key indicators for both leading (drivers of results) and lagging (outcome of results).

There are various approaches to detection logic. Spikes can be detected in a data value as part of time series monitoring. Value detection allows you to identify a new data value. A direct method is just observing a specific log event that tells us of a problem. We can detect the absence of a normal event, as systems often produce pattens of normal operation and a deviation can be flagged. For known malicious activity, its patterns can be detected with correlation rules. Also, previously unseen patterns can be flagged.

There is variance in activity of the components in our infrastructure. These variations can be detected. We have access to more raw data than ever before. Everything generates logs and activities. Variance in this context is a slippage of the desired state of loss exposure for the business, resulting from a change in the factors in the current level of exposure. Detecting change in those factors is critical, thus the need for operational intelligence. When something changes in the environment, IT needs to know about it.

The security team must have access to the data already being captured by the operations team. Data must be correlated with threat, vulnerability, and change information. It is needed to provide an early warning system for response.

An EWS is used in many systems in the physical world. The same need is in the digital world. "In an intrusion case, spotting the difference between abnormal and normal is often the difference between success and failure. Your mission is to quickly identify suspicious artifacts to verify potential intrusions."

Detection is not dead! Ever wonder if something invisible to the naked eye and odorless can be detected? Considering that it can be life-threatening, we should hope so. Think about a carbon monoxide detector.

So, are we helpless to detect cyberattacks? The attackers and their TTPs can be detected. Their entrance into our environments always changes something. We should be good enough to detect that change.

Early warning is a major element of business risk reduction. A change makes the form, nature, content, future course, and the like of something different from what it is now. The challenge in recognizing change is to detect relevant signals from your organization in the ocean of data. Second, when something deviates from what is standard, normal, or expected, we call that an anomaly—and anomalies are inherent in change. Thirdly, when something, especially a trend or fact, indicates the state or level of something, we have an indicator. Lastly, something left behind after an event of intrusion has occurred, like a file or process, is an artifact. Changes are signaled by anomalies, indicators, or artifacts.

A cyber warning system needs the ability to run automatically in near real time. Required features would include scalability, minimization of false positives, the ability to learn or recognize repeating patterns, and the knowledge to discount periodic spikes. Challenges involving the amount of human effort to accomplish this are ongoing, because such an early warning system is not easy to operationalize manually.

Anomalies can take the form of unusual behavior like rogue processes, unknown services, code injection and rootkit behavior, unusual OS artifacts, suspicious network activity, and evidence of persistence. Some examples of general categories of anomalies of interest are deviations in counts, values, and frequency, or presence of rare events or unusual peer population outliers.

It is not enough to use basic statistics, such as Gaussian normal distribution, deviations, and standard deviation, to analyze our data. Our IT does not fit a standard bell curve. Instead, we need something more sophisticated, like probabilistic modeling and analysis. We can use machine learning to best fit the right statistical model to our data in our specific environment and aid the analyst. The development of unsupervised machine learning models can be used to find anomalies in massive data sets. Supervised models required us to know the structure of the problem and feed the model existing data. Supervised models must be trained based on known data, while unsupervised models do not.

Such an approach results in fewer false alarms. Basically, we take our raw data, both historical and real time, and map it into detectors to produce anomaly alerts. We want to change how we are operationalizing the information—for example, with an anomaly dashboard. Then we fold the results into our workflow for investigation.

Use cases for this approach are many. We detect unauthorized login activity. This includes an unusual number of login attempts like brute force attack activity, anomalous login times or geographies, or rare accounts accessing systems.

We can identify data exfiltration. This includes anomalies in byte ratio behavior; rare destination IPs/geographies; pervasive access of rare content categories; and unusual lengths of DNS requests.

We can find compromised endpoints. This includes rare outbound connection attempts, like unusual rates of port/IP scanning; rare destination/port access; rarely occurring event codes; and unusual rates of security events such as event storms.

We can detect snoopers and scrapers. This includes excessive requests to rare URLs; clients generating rare status codes for URLs; and unusual data volume by a client.

These methods need to be put into use. Operationally, integration with organization includes the initiation of new workflows to head off potential problems to the appropriate team. The EWS provides "curated," actionable intelligence for business owners to make informed decisions. It speaks in terms the business can understand. And it provides prioritization framework for IT.

An EWS is a centralized function that deals with indicators of potential negative business impact issues at an organizational, technical, and physical level. A successful investment in detective and response tools requires the development of mature operational processes. An EWS's most valuable work is analysis of all data to produce early warning intelligence. That requires human analysts. An EWS is business's source of truth. It's real-time, relevant, and the most reliable source for informing decision-making. It is an aggregation of many tools, such as a directory service, CMDB, SIEM, UBA/UEBA, threat intelligence, threat and vulnerability management, security orchestration, automation, and response (SOAR), incident response, and ITSM. In addition to threat indicators and alerts, an EWS will bring to the surface organization silos, control gaps, misconfigured settings, controls deficiencies, and design flaws.

How does an organization interact with an EWS? On a modern car, when gas or tire levels get low, you can see a warning on the dashboard, a prompt to stop by a gas station to fuel up or put some air in the tires. Like a low-fuel light, how does an analyst know how to respond to an alert? Playbooks to define the communication workflow—that helps the decision-making process. That would encompass multiple domains. For example, a remote cyber intrusion of a building controls system; a new exploit on a smart pacemaker that a hospital has installed in patient's bodies; an unauthorized alteration to a financial report; or the detection of a message from a disgruntled employee indicating an impending potential active shooting incident. In all these examples, an analyst would need to triage and alert the appropriate teams. It's more than just IT relevant; it's business relevant.

Outside IT, some well-known examples of early warning systems that have integrated functionality that feeds other systems include NORAD and NOAA. The North American Aerospace Defense Command (NORAD) is a combined organization of the United States and Canada that provides aerospace warning, air sovereignty, and protection for

North America. Its job is to provide early warning against military threats. The National Weather Service, headquartered in Silver Spring, Maryland, is a part of the National Oceanic and Atmospheric Administration (NOAA) branch of the Department of Commerce. Its primary objective is to provide weather forecasts and warnings and other weather-related products to the public. The goal is to assist in providing protection, general information, and safety. This includes both life and property. The NOAA and National Weather Service provide an early warning system of upcoming weather storms, including potential impacts, areas affected, and recommendations.

We need something similar in our situation. A cyber EWS allows us to reevaluate, prepare, and make the necessary preparations. We need to identify and use indicators so we can recognize changes and anomalies that indicate potential issues. We also need to know what active threats could impact our environment. As in the case of an impending storm, we need to watch out for fast-moving threats attacking industries like ours, similar systems to ours, and those that are effective against defense like ours.

IT is faced with the challenge of keeping the bad guys at bay to head off service disruptions, cyber breaches, and physical harm. There are increasingly dependent systems, more diverse components, continually caught updating and maintaining while enabling new business functionality. IT wants to be in front of the early indicators of trouble to head off bad things before they happen. EWS supports IT and gives us more time to address our roles of actively defending our organizations against cyber threats.

Active Threat Defense

Our defenses need to be active in thwarting cyber-attacks. Be active! Engage defense against threat actors. IT should be ready for what we know we are facing. There are five things to keep in mind in regard to threats. We need to model them, detect them, identify them, respond quickly to them, and go hunting for them.

Traditional information security employed static controls, architecture, and posture. How a system connected to the network was defended and rarely changed. Access control lists (ACL) at the edge and in the interior changed infrequently, and any changes were performed manually. The scope defined in those ACLs often was not specific. There was no context to the endpoint communicating on the network. Attempts at network control were fraught with operational difficulties and not widely implemented beyond finding an infected host and then remediating.

In addition, the behavior of users of those systems was not known. Where or how they were connecting, to which type of applications, and at what times and durations were not taken into consideration in access requests. All of those needed updating, but in addition today's infrastructures require agility, dynamism, and context awareness to adapt to the environment and current state of use.

The four areas that comprise an Active Threat Defense approach are threat modeling, adversarial review, threat hunting, and active countermeasures.

We can't stop all attacks and their impact on our organization. When we come up short, we must be ready to respond and recover. For that to be viable, we must prepare.

We can't be passive in cyber defense. We must be active against threat actors. Perhaps the most significant action an organization can take to mitigate business risk is preparation. At this very moment, hackers throughout the world are scanning networks and looking for victims. Companies that are prepared can handle these as routine incidents rather than an inevitable series of high-profile crisis events.

The security team needs a clear mandate of its mission, the resources (personnel, training, tools) needed to get the job done, a clear picture of the threats and vulnerabilities, variance controls to detect changes in the state, and well-thought-out response plans. We should be ready for what we know we are facing.

Traditional information security has employed static controls, architecture, and posture. How endpoints connected to the network and the way security defenses were built were well established and rarely changed. Access control lists configured at the network edge were not changed frequently and internal networks often not segmented. The scope defined in those ACLs often were not specific. There was no context to the endpoint communicating on the network. Attempts at network control were fraught with operational difficulties and not widely implemented beyond finding an infected host and then remediating.

In addition, the behavior of users of those systems was not known. Where or how they were connecting, to which type of applications, and at what times and durations were not taken into consideration in access request. Today's infrastructures require agility, dynamism, and context awareness to adapt to the environment and current state of use.

The are several areas that comprise an active threat defense approach. IT needs to be on the watch for threat actors. IT must have resources that watch for the bad guys and what they are up to, identify who they are, and have a good idea of what is relevant for their organization. The security team will have a structured approach to assessing vulnerability disclosures and advisories.

We need to have command visibility over the posture of all our controls. We need a process for evaluating our controls to ensure they are functioning as designed. With input from threat modeling, are the controls configured properly, optimized, and working as they should be? We must know the current state of our controls at any given time.

There is no reason we can't seek out and find most of the weaknesses in the design, configuration, and controls of our environments by using an active process. Some of the common vulnerabilities are weak or default passwords, open ports, unpatched systems, misconfigured access control lists, poor input checks, and excessive rights. New systems that plug in or connect to our network should be identified by automatic processes, especially newer IoT devices brought in by business users. This identification should auto-populate our configuration management databases, be labeled, and assigned to defined access groups. Known vulnerabilities should be identified and incorporated into our patching process. These types of weaknesses often are present upstream and downstream in employees,' partners,' and vendors' systems that connect to our network.

Automatic vulnerability checks should feed results back into our operations process. Known exploit tools should automatically be run against our environment, and any success should auto-alert our operations team. IT should be the first to detect the exploit. The insider threat represents a challenging problem. By their very nature, insiders have been deemed by your organization as trusted. They have rights to systems and data as part of their jobs. We must verify that trust by monitoring behavior, observing patterns in user activity, establishing trends, and looking out for anomalies in behavior (user, endpoint, and network).

We should be able to answer yes to the questions of whether a particular control is up to date, documented, and configured properly per our policy.

For example, we need to verify that our inline intrusion prevention system has a valid certificate to allow it to see encrypted traffic. Expired certs have been in breach news as the control put into place to detect and block attacks was rendered inert because it was not known and corrected so the device would function like it should. You need to verify that blocking is configured to block malicious traffic that is identified.

Check that the doors are locked, the alarm is on, and the cameras are set to record.

We need to be proactive in managing our vulnerabilities in both infrastructure and code. This entails ensuring our systems are up to date, replacing any known vulnerable third-party libraries, hardening our systems before deployment, and actively modeling threats. That was makes hackers so innovative, exploring and experimenting with systems to see if they can be made to do things that others didn't think possible.

The security team can also be proactive by using different lenses to assess the different characteristics of threat actors. There is a need to profile the threats, the threat actors, and their methods. Years ago, Intel created the Threat Agent Library, a listing of the profiles of the threat actors and the characteristics. This enabled a common context for discussing what they were trying to protect their infrastructure from. So, when the board of directors asks you who the bad guys are and why they are doing this, you will be ready to answer. Know thy enemy is an apt mindset for defenders to stay vigilante and prepared.

Threat modeling is a process of using a hypothetical attacker's point of view to approach compromising our systems. Looking for underlying system vulnerabilities and different ways to exploit the current design and configuration, defenders can be equipped with the common tactics and techniques of attackers. It finds probable attacker approaches. Conceptually, most people incorporate some form of threat modeling in their daily life and don't even realize it. Commuters use threat modeling to consider what might go wrong during the morning drive to work and to take preemptive action to avoid possible accidents. Children engage in threat modeling when determining the best path toward an intended goal while avoiding the playground bully. Threat modeling has been used by militaries to prepare for future enemy activity and security teams to harden a facility from physical intrusions.

To help with designing and building such an infrastructure, it is very useful to model your threats. Models are used to assist decision makers and IT responders in making higher-quality business decisions to contain threats and mitigate business risk.

We need a way to visualize the threat actors, tactics, techniques, procedures, and motives and their interaction to our unique organization to inform our security posture, strategies, and operational guidelines.

Threat modeling is a process to identify threats in the earliest stage. Threat modeling is a structured activity for identifying and managing threats. The earlier the better. Who are threat actors, what are their motivations, TTPS, and goals? What is trending, what is in the news, what are industry-sharing organizations? Watch news on the threat environment.

Threat modeling allows us to understand threats and facilitates smart countermeasures. For instance, defenders can go threat hunting to answer the questions: Are we compromised? Are there attackers currently in our environment right now? We can answer that by going hunting. Hunting is defined as "the process of proactively and iteratively searching through networks to detect and isolate advanced threats that evade existing security solutions."

IT teams need to embrace the hunt. An understanding of the various threat communities and their methods allows you to look for them in your environment. With assistance from automation, the real-time activity of endpoints at your fingertips, and better algorithms, malicious activity can be detected. You know what to look for, and you know where to look. Find the threats to your business now.

In our dynamic environment, things are constantly in motion, with them being created, moved, changed, and deleted. We must actively search and test our environment in a similar way to that of the attackers. We need to flip our time and effort distribution to over 80 percent in design and testing and 20 percent in applied time. We need to scale our effort and time by automating security checks on our apps against attacks on our infrastructure and our people.

One goal should be the active, dynamic, and proactive approach of organizations that self-initiate behavior in anticipation of a dynamic threat environment involving acting in advance of negative business impacts. This means taking control and making things happen rather than just adjusting to a situation or waiting for something to happen. Let's look at indicators of attack and compromise, design and control weaknesses, insider threats, threats against the executive suite, and data leakage.

The TTPs of threat actors are observable on the network and endpoints. It is possible for IT to look for these signals. Indicators of attack give an early indication of potential breaches, especially in an era where an attack does not require malware. We also need to have some means to determine the scope and strength of the attack. Without some insight to this, IT will have problems with resource allocation, personnel prioritization, and focus. Is this a nuisance, an automated crime of opportunity, or is this directed by a competitor or a nation-state? Active hunting helps with the process of attribution, helping inform the probability of who is doing the attack. If this is an active campaign, we deal with it differently than we would with a nuisance. For example, on the network, detecting traffic to know command and control (C2) domains or IP addresses is an indicator.

With indicators of compromise (IOC), we are looking for changes, anomalies, and artifacts. The presence of malware is the most obvious. A more sophisticated method is detecting changes in the state of the endpoint that are not normal for our environment. Deviations can be seen in our baselines, snapshots, or changes in start-up registry entries on a Windows system. They could be new or altered processes, files, hashes, or registry entries that can be matched against known IOCs.

Hunting works best by starting with a hypothesis, a supposition or proposed explanation made based on limited evidence as a starting point for further investigation. In this case, develop a theory on how the threat actor is attacking your organization. Taking into consideration the TTPs of a specific threat actor, develop a hypothesis of how the threat scenario will play out and identity potential indicators of their activities.

Also, we need to validate all the systems that we have deployed in our environment. We have the advantage of having designed and built these systems. That gives us great insights on how they operate and when there is unauthorized change or activities. Validation on the security controls on our previously configured systems that run our businesses is a priority for IT. IOCs are the breadcrumbs from an unauthorized intruder. These IOCs can be in the form of IP addresses, port numbers, malware files, PowerShell scripts, hashes, registry entries, or memory fragments. By actively searching our environment for such indicators, we can determine the presence or absence of threat actors.

Threat modeling and hunting are aided with the use of threat intelligence. Threat intelligence is evidence-based knowledge about threat actors and their TTPs that can be used to inform defense response decisions. Your system and organization controls should be able to answer several questions. We need to know what threats our organization cares about and what attacks look like to specific assets. It very helpful to know the different ways hackers might use to access and exfiltrate data or disrupt operations.

From a defense standpoint, know the methods you would use to detect and block such attacks. The response for each attack type must be documented in playbooks. The information included would be regarding severity, response strategy, roles, responsibilities, procedures, and escalation process.

Intelligence collection, analysis, and multidirectional sharing are key aspects of informing our threat models. They keep IT up to date and aware of relevant threats to its organization. A combination of third-party threat intelligence, increasing governmental intel, and the security team's resources feed the variable of credible threats we map out against our current defense controls of our business assets. To assist in understanding the threat potential, we can model relevant threats to any environment.

We need multidirectional threat intelligence collaborating with partners and customers both upstream and downstream. We should be subscribing to several intelligence feeds, using that to quickly make a verdict on their applicability to our environment. We should also be monitoring our network to see if any of the observed IOCs are in our systems. Our personnel should join local and national information sharing and analysis centers. We should actively partner and collaborate with those in our same industry. Also, we should be willing to share intel that can help those in our business ecosystem. Finally, we should be familiar with federal groups that assist.

Today's threat actors are increasingly targeting the executive suite. From spear phishing and whaling techniques, persons with access to sensitive organizational information and power are often coming into the crosshairs of attacks. We can actively check social media sites for our business and its users. For example, the Ashley Madison breach exposed data on its subscribers, many with corporate email accounts. Data dumps like this could include some from our organization, and we want to head off the potential for blackmail. Detecting corporate data leakage in these dumps is also important.

IT also needs to be active in countermeasures. It needs to be active in resisting attack. It can take measures to counter or mitigate attacker activities. It is any technological or tactical solution that is designed to mitigate an undesirable effect. We have options. We can block, resist, distract, limit, contain, and deter. A block puts an obstacle in the way of something attempted. This can be blocking an inbound packet at-tack, C2 communications, or additional tools retrieval. It can be out-bound traffic that could be data exfiltration and/or C2 communica-tions. Limit lateral movement, discovery probes, and malware propa-gation around the network. We block at various points in the technol-ogy stack, including IP blacklist, rate limit, block hosts at the firewall, network, or host levels. Block process from loading, block program from running, kill malicious processes, delete files left behind, block IPs, block emails, and block hashes. We can revoke certificates and change keys.

We can resist the attack. We can patch a known vulnerability that has a fix available. We can re-image the node and rebuild from known good sources. Rotate the keys, move the asset to another segment, or change the service account password.

We can distract the attacker. Set up a honeypot to draw their attention and time, delay their action, learn about their motives and methods, put up false data repository, create phony accounts and phony net-works, use black hole routing, and change contact info.

We can limit the attacker involved with denial of service (DoS/DDoS) with rate limit traffic and third-party scrubbing service. The network architecture can be modified or systems moved to another location to limit this in the future.

We can go with an approach of containment. That includes containing infected nodes, blocking further communication with C2 and other po-tential targets, deploying network access control, blocking switch ports, configuring IP-based or MAC-based access control lists, dissoci-ating device from wireless network, disabling user account, or request-ing endpoint re-imaging. IT can also get assistance by engaging with human resources on an insider threat personnel matter, engaging the FBI on criminal matter, engaging your Internet provider for DoS help, or engaging with legal on action against a competitor following IP theft.

And we can attempt to deter the attacker. We can alert authorities like the FBI, alert our own internal HR and legal, reset the AD golden ticket, and build a red forest.

We can't stop all attacks and their impact on our organization. When we come up short, we must be ready to respond and recover. For that to be viable, we must prepare.

Rapid Response System

We need to respond quickly when our defenses are overcome. Be quick! When defenses fail, threat events can lead to loss events. Be as fast as needed to mitigate the impact of an incident. Fast responses to cyber intrusions range from routine handling with existing resources all the way to material losses requiring massive responses from the business. The faster you respond, contain, and recover, the faster you can give the C-suite help in dealing with the fallout and containing the damage.

When the compromised asset is a laptop, a reimage is possible. When that resource is a mission-critical system production server, it's not so easy or practical to reimage. IT may resort to containing C2 traffic until other actions are possible.

Time is money, and the longer it takes to detect an intrusion, the higher the chance for money damage and losses. The longer it takes to remediate, the costlier the cleanup.

The benefit to stopping more attacks upfront and quickly containing those that make it through our initial defenses is the reduced potential impact of destructive payloads. We must remember that once compromised, the attacker's ability to destroy is massive.

Observe the gap in the breach report. Compromising a host is not necessarily enough for an attacker to gain access to data, but the failure to limit lateral movement may be one of our biggest failings.

Knowing that some attacks will be successful, IT must prepare ahead of time for the needed response actions. If IT fails to prepare, IT must prepare to struggle when the time comes for your stakeholders to take the podium and address the public.

One of the most critical functionalities IT can build along the business is the ability to respond well as a result of preparation. At this very moment, hackers throughout the world are scanning networks and looking for victims. Prepared companies can handle these as routine incidents rather than an inevitable series of high-profile crisis events. The biggest impact IT can have is to contain costs by minimizing potential data leaks, service disruptions, and expenses on cleanups.

IT needs to make recovery trivial. If we respond rapidly enough, there is no cost, and we can minimize the impact to the business—perhaps make it even low enough to be handled by cyber insurance.

We need to make recovery a routine capability if not trivial. If we respond fast enough, there is no cost, and we can minimize the impact to the business—perhaps make it even low enough to be handled by cyber insurance. If it is not possible to prevent the entire attack chain from data exfiltration, we can recover fast enough to limit it to a technical incident rather than a business one. We can rebuild endpoints fast enough to limit loss of productivity to the users. We can transform response with Agile techniques to alter the cost and impact equation. Our goal should be to master automatic response, orchestration, and anticipation where we will need it most.

Response preparation paves the way for confidently taking chances. Incident response will want to know the answers to these common questions around the context of the incident including probable threat actor type, the TTPs, motives, objectives, scope, and timelines. Best effort to determine the extent of any damage.

The implications are clear that business owners need to be informed and educated on the changing control set requirements. Businesses will need to invest in modernizing their controls, strengthening their infrastructures, and updating their organizational structures to not just maintain pace but to prevent attacks. This will be critical, as IT does not want to stifle innovation or the productivity gains of the end user. This is why we mitigate unnecessary risk as the vendors and manufacturers work to catch up.

IT must make the business case for maintaining the right mix of investments in our security programs every year.

The mitigation of the risks associated with economic growth is vital. IT provides value to the business with IT's understanding of what needs to be done, the support of the disruption of the status quo, the simplification of technology for the business, and risk mitigation.

Even more severe is the risk of falling behind in the marketplace. Every day, competitors form a threat to your organization. Mitigation of that comes first.

We all recognize these are not easy tasks to accomplish. The mountains of challenges are rough. It won't be enough to make small changes here and there. What will be needed is the transformation of our businesses.

Speed is paramount in all aspects of the business. IT can't be slow in recovery from the fallout of the inevitable cyber-attack.

Be as fast as needed to mitigate the impact of an incident. When defenses fail, threat events can lead to loss events. Fast responses to cyber intrusions can mean the difference between routine handle with existing resources, all the way to material losses requiring massive responses for a business. The faster you can respond, contain, and recover, the faster you can give the C-suite help in dealing with the fall-out and containing the damage.

When the compromised asset is a laptop, a reimage is possible. When that resource is a production server, a mission-critical system servicing customer request is not so easy or practical to reimage. We may resort to containing C2 traffic until other actions are possible.

Time is money, and the longer it takes to detect an intrusion, the higher the chance for damage and losses. The longer it takes to remediate, the costlier the cleanup. The benefit to stopping more attacks upfront and quickly containing those that make it through our initial defenses is the reduced potential impact of destructive payloads. We must remember that once compromised, the ability to destroy is trivial. Observe the gap in the breach report. Compromising a host is not necessarily enough for gaining access to data, but the failure to limit lateral movement may be one of our biggest failings.

The biggest impact IT can have is to contain costs by minimizing potential data leaks, service disruptions, and expenses on cleanups.

Preparation is the process of being made ready for future use. The entire organization must be involved in preparation if it wants to be ready. We set ourselves up for inefficient, costly, and long responses if we fail to prepare ahead of time. We need to analyze the potential effects of an interruption to critical business operations as a result of an incident. This is an essential phase of an organization's business continuity planning process. Every component of the organization is reliant upon the continued functioning of many other components. Some are more crucial than others and require a greater attention in the recovery process. The development of recovery plans requires practice of the process to ensure it is executable and actionable. Table-top exercises a preparedness activity that takes the relevant participants through the process of dealing with a simulated incident. It is a good way to evaluate the effectiveness of the organization's incident response, disaster recovery, business continuity, and crisis management programs.

Response is a reaction to something. It includes containment, minimization, forensics, cleanup, and lessons learned. Containment is to isolate and limit a compromised system from being able to connect to other assets. This allows the recovery team the breathing room to investigate the host of interest, while stopping the spread of potentially malicious activity. It is critical that all effected hosts be identified and contained, allowing responders to dig in and investigate the systems in question that were the source of the intrusion. This gives IT the context necessary to determine the scope of the intrusion. It also informs IT of the scope of the response in general.

Forensics are techniques used in connection with the detection of the intrusion. Forensics allows IT to gather any potential evidence in potential future legal actions and mitigate the effects of the intruder's actions. Cleanup is the final step in the response phase. If malicious code has been installed on the infected host, then that malware needs to be cleaned up. Any changes to any hosts in the network can also be cleaned up through re-imaging. User and service credentials can be reset. Any other unauthorized changes to the infrastructure configurations can be restored from known good backup if necessary.

Recovery is a return to a normal state. Any incident that disrupts services for the company needs to be returned to a normal state as soon as possible. These days almost any service that is down is noticeable to users. This could be the inability to use a web portal or access files. In cases such as a ransomware attack, the backups could have been targeted by the attackers and destroyed or altered. Both disaster recovery and business continuity planning are the mainstays of IT focus on restoring access to organizational data and systems.

The attack could have damaged equipment. In some cases, for example, laptops or servers might need to be replaced. Once that equipment is replaced, then software can be integrated back into the existing infrastructure. Sometimes it is more than just equipment that needs to be replaced. In some cases, actual personnel may need to be replaced because they may have been involved in the incident. And in other cases, they have been assigned blame for not stopping the incident from occurring and let go. High-profile breach scenarios have caused CIOs and CISOs to be shown the door, prompting a search for replacements for those positions.

The recovery process also involves the organization's interaction with the public. Public relations are critical to incident response. Handling this phase poorly can lead to potential negative secondary effects, like additional regulatory scrutiny or customer backlash.

After the dust settles, the executive team may be required to report to the public and stakeholders. They must have in plain English the explanation of what happened, how the organization responded, the business implications, and recommendations to prevent or minimize such impact in the future.

Closing the loop on the response process is feedback for future improvement. All the recommendations, observations, and suggestions need to be reviewed and consolidated to improve future defenses, detection, response, and recovery efforts. Only by reflecting from the past can we improve our capabilities for the future.

The mitigation of the risk associated with the use of the very engine of economic growth is vital. With the understanding of what needs to be done, the support of the disruption of the status quo, simplifying the technology use for the business, and mitigating risk, IT has provided value to the business. However, these are not easy things to accomplish. The mountains of challenges are rough. It won't be enough to change here and there. No, what will be needed is business transformation.

And to support an organization's efforts, IT must maintain its efforts indefinitely. It is not enough to design and build out the best security program money can buy. A security program has no value if it becomes obsolete or ineffective after it is stood up. Or if a year later the aggregate loss exposure of the organization increases out of control. Like all other business processes, a security program is ongoing. As the risk factors and business environment change, so too must cyber risk management. It must adapt to variance.

Chapter 9
Variance Management

The efficacy of our security efforts will have variance from day to day. Variance is the quality of being different, divergent, or inconsistent. A key aspect of our concern of a variance is whether it was expected. If we know tomorrow that there's going to be a drop-off, then we don't have a problem. Our concern comes when it's unexpected. Nothing stays the same in our environment. The factors that drive risk are dynamic. There are both internal and external factors. IT must stay on top of the changes in the risk landscape and adapt to maintain the efficacy of risk mitigation efforts. Most times, threat events don't overcome our controls. At other times, threats are successful overcoming our controls and a breach occurs. This can be caused by threat actors changing tactics or them exploiting a new vulnerability in our systems.

A security program is a dynamic system of controls that manage cyber risk. Variance in the performance of a security program over a long period of time opens the organization up to more risk than it may realize. The level of risk an organization is willing to accept relies on the expectation that its mitigation efforts are doing its job. IT must be able to detect deviations early and adapt to changes in the risk environment. As the loss scenarios of concern are documented in the risk register, they contain the necessary context to manage a useful security program that is crucial to detecting when risk is getting out of hand. In essence IT is managing variance. This entails monitoring both internal and external risk factors to detect if they change enough to move current loss exposure outside of an acceptable range. IT monitors and adjusts its strategy, approach, and tactics as needed to manage the variance in aggregate loss exposure.

For cyber risk management to work, we must have a mature security program. It is the maturity of that program that allows us to deploy and manage controls over a long period of time up until the control is no longer needed. In many cases, there is no end to the control usage; it is needed infinitely. The specific tooling or process will change over time, but not the core function. Once again, the three variance factors are assets, threats, and controls, all of which need to be decomposed into the component elements to work with.

Most in the security field know that assets are those things that produce value for the organization and are not directly controlled by IT or the security team. The main management function in the asset arena is alignment with the business or progress management.

Variance is the deviation or change in pattern or expected outcome. For example, if I expect the sales numbers to be $1,000,000 next month but the actual outcome is $900,000, that is a deviation from what was expected.

When we invest resources, time or money, into an initiative or project, there are expectations for outcomes. If we believe a certain number of new customers will be signed up every month, and we observe the patterns, we can make projections of future outcome. We can observe and make estimates of expected performance. Often that will be in ranges.

What stands out in that list of examples is the wide variety and types of variation. Some are strategic or operational, while some are very tactical and technical. Because our system of controls is built to handle this variety, we too must also have visibility to be able to manage this variance across all the different elements of multiple systems to interact among themselves.

If we put the effort into reducing and mitigating against a certain loss scenario, we want to know that our efforts are worth it, and we get that investment return year to year. So, when a threat actor capability changes and that increases our loss exposure, it is a goal of our security program and our system of controls to identify that and adapt and bring that back into line to what the expectation is from the exposure level.

The management of variance is the coordination and ongoing administration of activities to execute organizational objectives of loss exposure that fall in an established acceptable range. We monitor the cyber risk factors so we can support the management of variance. To do that we monitor our security programs and their operations to manage cyber risk. The domains of governance, enablement, and cyber defense need full visibility to ensure effective cyber risk management.

Effective monitoring of both risks and controls is essential to the success of any risk management or security program. Risk management functional leadership and business unit management is responsible for providing oversight and governance to help ensure standards are met and risks are mitigated effectively.

Monitoring is used to detect changes in the internal and external environment and alert for potential needed action. Monitoring effectiveness of the overall program is accomplished by periodically reviewing metrics and dashboards, specific incidents, trends in auditing, testing, and assessment results, and reviewing control improvements with relevant stakeholders and operational teams.

Risk monitoring ensures controls and program responses are effective and efficient in purpose and operation. Monitoring key indicators is critical to ensuring that our security programs are efficient. We must ensure that the entire risk management process remains current and relevant. Monitoring provides insight into both critical and emerging risks and trends. It allows us to detect changes in risk criteria and risk itself that requires revision in priority and treatment. From an operational standpoint, all our controls should be onboarded onto a data platform systems bus. All controls need to have telemetry, performance, and logging sent to a data analytics platform via data aggregation tier. Use cases should be logged into controls inventory. All controls should be measured for performance. All controls should be mapped to risk register, loss scenarios, and threat event analysis chains. Metric development solutions should be developed to monitor for changes in loss exposure.

Operational Intelligence

Our security programs need to provide alerts, warnings, and hints to changes in risk factors to support decision-making at all levels of the organization. IT needs to monitor program performance to validate the security program is doing what it is supposed to be doing, and technical conditions to flag threat activity and control failures. We need to provide trend analysis, reporting, dashboards, and alerting. In addition, we have to provide feedback and performance monitor to manage needs of governance, business enablement, and cyber defense.

The operational infrastructure needs to be expanded to accommodate the variety of stakeholders across the organization that needs to process this data. We also need to know the variety of personas that will the info. Identifying the players in play will guide what each persona's monitoring and reporting needs are. The target audience is an important consideration for developing the monitoring output for the relevant insights across the business, IT, and security team. Those considerations help frame the monitoring requirements. Also important are the different lenses to consume the output the various strategic, operational, and tactical areas.

Risk factors that are identified need to be monitored. These include assets value creation, threats TTPs, control efficacy, threat effects, and loss impact. The useful metrics include logistics of how we measure, key performance indicators, key risk indicators, key control indicators, leading indicators, and lagging indicators.

We need to receive feedback on the performance of the security program by observing and checking progress on an ongoing basis. They help us to validate that our risk models are both accurate and useful enough. It guards against fake security controls efficacy, wasted processes, and illusion of progress. Metrics can be constructed to provide clear signals that trigger when there are relevant changes to the state of key risk factors. In contrast, this is not tactical alert fatigue from SIEM noise. Key metrics should provide clarity at a glance with easy-to-consume indications. There should be consensus of what the metric means and the type of actions that should be taken as a response to changes in them.

Risk reporting provides a documented summarization of changes in the risk environment. They should be based on agreed-upon reporting frameworks that align with enterprise risk management. Reporting is a critical component in the communication of risk information across the company. At the company, information and communication channels are in place so business leaders and employees are aware of risks that fall under their purview of responsibilities. Effective internal and external communication should take place to ensure that those accountable for implementing the risk management process and decision makers understand the basis on which decisions are made and the connection to relevant actions. This includes communicating risks with stakeholders, which would include the board, C-suite, and business units. Reporting requirements would include providing status updates on current loss exposure and projected residual levels after security initiatives.

Alerting would detect changes in the risk profile, ensuring communication of risks to appropriate parties, providing information on a need-to-know basis. Alerting brings immediate attention for the need for management to address an issue or problem. Operational intelligence acts as a near real-time early warning system of variance in the risk environment. The intelligence needs to be tied into changes that effect current loss exposure that triggers if it reaches appetite thresholds. All metrics, reports, and alerts are there to support decision-making.

The reason for generating metrics is to inform future decisions. Fundamentally, our scenario analysis is based off current controls and capabilities, measuring their efficacy against current-threat TTPs that increase the probability of an attack causing harm. Variance management requires a detailed pulse on our digital environment. We need intelligence in the operations of our technology systems.

To be successful, we need to be able to observe our complicated and complex systems. We do this for availability and reliability. Before our systems can fail and disrupt our business, we will see the problem, measure it, analyze it, and understand it. This allows us to intervene before the business feels the problem.

Operational intelligence is the ability to acquire and apply knowledge and skills. Operational intelligence includes the capacity for logic, understanding, self-awareness, learning, emotional knowledge, reasoning, planning, creativity, and problem-solving. Operational intelligence is IT's ability to perceive or infer information and apply it toward the goal of resilient and highly available systems.

Keeping track of all components of a system 24/7, 365 days a year is a necessity. Knowing what to look at every morning to ensure service availability is challenging. But bad things happen when we don't initiate certain changes ourselves. We need eyes on everything and a way to comprehend our digital infrastructures.

As technology increasingly becomes easier to set up, the complexity to the end user is hidden. But a third party can't totally remove the challenges and requirements of managing the technology, the services the business relies on, and the data generated. This is where IT comes in. What's easy to start takes more work to operate. That is why IT must build a level of sophistication in visibility to provide a feedback system for ongoing operations, in real time and near real time.

Business, IT, and security operational intelligence are critical to helping organizations operate at market speed. A dynamic environment demands visibility, key performance indicators (KPIs), and data—all in real time—to support decision-making that matters.

IT is uniquely positioned to lead in business innovation and risk mitigation. Business innovation involves disruption, transformation, talent development, and monetary allocations. Business risk management covers brand and reputation, operational resiliency, and business process. Common to both is operational intelligence—the systematic collection, analysis, visualization, and decision support from all sources of available raw data.

Operational intelligence is the secret sauce, so to speak, in establishing organizational cadence and creating that feedback loop discussed earlier. It allows the business to listen to the data and quickly iterate or pivot.

From an operational standpoint, what should you focus on today? What about tomorrow? The answers to those questions can be informed by the insights derived from key data sets analyzed. Insights are found in the ocean of data our technologies contain. Data from our machines clues us in on areas to investigate further.

When potential issues are discovered, IT can swarm to address the problems and perform corrective action. We need to see our environment.

That which we can't sense directly is unknown to us. This blindness leads to missed signals of new opportunities and threats. IT needs full visibility, 360 degrees of both macro and micro focus for service availability, system performance, and preventive maintenance.

Real-time and near real-time deliveries are key characteristics of digital infrastructures. Each time IT considers bringing a new system in-house, IT must also manage it—inventory it, maintain it, keep it up to date, renew support for it, and decommission it when appropriate.

Here are three key patterns of high-functioning systems:

- Know your system better than anyone else, including third parties and attackers
- Know you can't manage what you can't see
- If you can't see it, you can't analyze it
- If you can't see it, you can't defend it

What happens when IT has all this data? What opportunities does that open for your organization? Exploring, questioning, and investigating your environment can be accomplished using *who, what, when, where, how,* and *why.*

- **Who** are the users of interest? Are they the C-suite, board of directors, VPs, or contractors?
- **What** are the nodes of interest? Are they unpatched or newly released from the manufacturer?
- **When** do events occur with users or nodes? The time of interest includes business hours, after hours, and weekends.
- **Where** do events occur in space? The locations of interest include the office, the home, or on the road.
- **How** do events come about? What was the flow of events, and how did it unfold? How do the first three months differ from the last three months of someone's employment?
- **Why** do the events occur? Often, it's a multivariable situation requiring correlation among multiple data areas.

Can you detect an anomaly on your network? How long does it take to detect it? For a machine that has been programmed, this is a trivial task. But for manual human interaction, it's difficult. Know what happens in cases such as unplugging a wireless access point (WAP) on the floor, attempting to log on with a system account, attempting to log on with an account from a fired employee, submitting a patent from a terminated employee for similar work, or seeing an app error in a developer instance that's now showing up in production.

Enjoy the power of metrics, parameters used for comparison or measurement or to track performance or production. They are in use everywhere, every day. Examples include the Dow Jones Industrial Average, runs batted in (RBI), points per game (PPG), and quarterback passing ratings. Simple numbers such as a FICO score for creditworthiness or a body mass index (BMI) as an indicator of health convey a significant amount of information in a small format. In technology, we have key performance and risk indicators. You as the consumer of the metric should understand the context of the metric to get value from it.

To sense your environment, leverage indicators. Leading and lagging indicators provide IT with early signs of both problems and opportunities. Indicators are expressed as metrics. Analysts use metrics to compare the performance of different companies.

Visibility into processes is critical to all aspects of IT operations. This includes process visibility as well. Everything IT does should support the business. Infrastructure, code, and data are support systems for business operations. If you map the process of creating a service, you will see the steps that make the service possible.

Business services in a digital world are composed of many processes that have technology components or dependencies on technology. If IT or the business suspects they are not moving fast enough, IT can look at the underlying input variables that ultimately drive the outcomes. The equation $Y=f(X_1, X_2, X_3...)$ represents this. If Y, the outcome, is too slow, risky, or unexpected, then we need to look at the *X* inputs and how they interact. One potential cause of a disappointing outcome is variability. This is why we need to quantify our current level of uncertainty.

Uncertainty needs to be understood and reduced to a level that can inform our decision-making and allow us to operate our environments at a high level. Measurement reduces the amount of uncertainty. We assign a number to a characteristic of an object or event. This allows us to compare it with other objects or events. IT must continuously measure the following components of our organization's people activities, technology operations, and process operations.

Measurements and metrics both allow organizations to see their current state and inform decision-making. If it is important, it can be measured. It should be measured.

What should you be measuring and collecting now? More than you probably are, but less than you technically can. Know what is useful to measure, including certain data that every IT team should collect.

IT needs to collect the data necessary to run its operations. Data tells you about daily operations that are critical to ensure business service is uninterrupted. IT also gathers data for third parties that need it for assessment or new initiatives.

Looking to move to the cloud? A third party will want data about the current server, network, and storage usage for the type of workflow under consideration.

Thinking about VDI? A third party will want to collect data about a subset of your workstations to understand processor, disk, network, and memory utilization.

Are you still in the process of moving some of your physical machines to virtual ones? If so, a third party will want to collect data on the current utilization of your physical servers to properly size the new hardware to run the virtual workload.

This brings up the importance of centralized logging. In all three examples, third-party vendors looking to do assessments for potential projects request data about IT systems. IT should consider this type of data a core IT service. The data should have already been collected by IT to run normal operations. There is no reason for IT not to have this information readily available. It should be a matter of just pulling the data for third-party vendors to provide an analysis of the existing performance and characteristics of the workloads.

IT must know itself better than anyone else. IT should have an intimate, in-depth knowledge of the systems under its management umbrella. This includes systems that provide the services that underpin a business, as well as the technical operations that support services that are a function of the business itself.

It has long been time for IT to gain a more system-level view of the entire technical infrastructure the business runs on. Third-party service providers thrive on this level of visibility, as it is a requirement for their business model. We have been talking about this for years. For far too long, IT has struggled to procure the proper budget, put in the proper monitoring systems, and find a way to adequately analyze all of the data for systems critical to running a business in the digital world. Far too many tools have been accumulated over the years for the purpose of gaining visibility into the systems IT manages. These individual tools have been trapped in silos, providing just slivers of the picture of the health of these systems. Change is required to operate in today's disruptive environment, and especially to systems.

You should be able to answer these types of questions:

- How many of our systems are currently running production?

- What is the breakdown of operating systems running in the development environment?

- Of all our systems, which ones are current on their Windows updates?

- How many mobile devices are currently accessing our email system?

- Has the amount of wireless traffic in our main headquarters changed in the last three weeks?

- Have any of our critical protected systems with personally identifiable information changed in the last two weeks?

- Are any of our web servers running in the DMZ currently trending up or down in CPU utilization over the last three months?

- Has any host on our internal network attempted to send unusual traffic directly to the internet?

- What is the breakdown of usage by department on the primary storage area network over the last six months?

- Has our build pipeline slowed down as more work has been pushed through?

- How is our AWS workload trending?

These are all common management questions IT should be able to answer in a short amount of time. IT should view each of the individual data elements as the underlying backbone powering its business today. Just as businesses must maintain inventory and visibility of the products and services they provide; IT should be accountable to itself and the business.

Identifying the root cause of an issue or problem is paramount and imperative. Root cause analyses drive smarter decisions and responses to daily operational issues. Know your systems. Until you find the root cause of a problem, you are operating in a state of self-imposed uncertainty. That uncertainty has a habit of coming back at an inconvenient time.

IT needs to be proficient in troubleshooting our systems. That means we need to know intimately how they operate. Make observations about the systems before problems arise. Get under the hood of our systems, taking them apart, seeing how they work, and then testing the components to see how they interact and handle stress. This allows us to know them well and to determine the root causes of trouble quickly.

Baselining is the methodology of observing initialization and operations. Every system has many components. IT must baseline each component as an individual item and, ultimately, as an entire system. IT must put an observation regimen in place to have visibility into normal operations. IT needs to be extremely accurate in what *normal* means. Implied in this is the ability to notice when the system is not running normally to spot anomalies.

On factory floors, manufacturers use statistical process controls to ensure the quality of operations so that it's obvious when the output is out of the norm. Similarly, if we collect data on our systems, we can run analytics across the systems to gain operational intelligence on normal operations. This is the act of mitigating risk. Causal failure paths should be mapped out and analyzed.

Creating baselines and detecting anomalies are not tasks humans are well suited for, especially considering the volume of system data that needs to be analyzed. This is where data science and analytics can be leveraged. Distinguishing the normal from the abnormal allows us to run fast IT. The challenge IT typically faces in troubleshooting is that it does not know what *normal* looks like.

This is even more acute when the configurations and architecture run just well enough on the surface to appear to be working properly. Even more dangerous is when it appears the network is quiet, but our security controls are not providing early warning, giving us a false impression of security. A similar problem in business operations is when our customers continue to make purchases, even though they are on the verge of switching to a competitor. If our business service is declining, and we're slowly turning away customers, trouble may reveal itself at such a slow pace that it's not visible when it does occur.

Raw data's value is in its refinement, so that it's suitable for consumption. The key to making use of data that drives business and IT operations is to extract actionable insights from the raw data. Then IT can make better decisions.

Understanding data comes from a combination of data, people, technology, statistics, and domain knowledge all working together. Gathering meaningful help from data is both a science and an art. Using theories, techniques, mathematics, programming, machine learning, data mining, data visualization, business analytics, accounting, and social sciences, insights come alive. IT can become masters at using data rightly.

The raw data available today has volume, velocity, and variety. These three traits challenge traditional data analytics tools. Volume, velocity, and variety can apply to automated decision-making and can be seen in disruptive business models. Data can help IT solve problems, make better decisions, and do its daily work.

Data science permeates both IT and business operations. New cybersecurity products use data science modeling in solution sets. Businesses use data in their consumer sentiment analyses. Banks use data applications for fraud detection. Security product manufacturers use data processes to detect insider threats. Supply chains use data applications for predictive demand requirements.

There are still more uses of the science and art of data insights such as trend forecasting, A/B testing, root cause analyses, anomaly detection, market segmentation, topic modeling, capacity planning, KPIs, executive dashboards, predictive modeling, sentiment analysis, and conversion funnels.

Data science offers many benefits like trend forecasting of future value or outcomes based on historical data, sentiment analyses, and anomaly detection. Some other examples include transactions that occur faster than human comprehension, such as API call requests for back-end lookup patterns. Data analysis finds statistical outliers, such as non-average outliers (more than two standard deviations from the average) and atypical outliers (more than 1.5 times the interquartile range above 75 percent or below 25 percent). IT must flag these signals for deeper analysis.

There are many examples of data insights for IT operations, such as server CPU and memory metrics, DNS logs, and firewall logs. This information can be distilled down to atomic data elements. Analyses can be performed against the data set, which is how businesses use it for many customer-facing analyses. IT can use it for detecting malware and addressing capability problems, identifying root causes, and understanding customer usage.

Use data to discover your user activity patterns. When do most users log in? How many of them use personal devices? What does the pattern look like for file access? Do users like to stream Final Four games, or are they heavy on social media? What do they like, and how do they like to do it?

Know your systems and how they are used. What does *normal* look like? What does it look like when it works? What happens when an IP phone boots up? When a Windows server reboots, how long does it typically take to come back up?

One of IT's most critical mistakes is its failure to fully understand the systems it supports. Even when it is hard to get under the hood, a system's behavior and effects on other systems must be observed and understood.

Explore the Windows Registry, DNS, DHCP, proxy logs, call logs, badge system, AWS CloudTrail logs, Windows processes, etc. Lay the ground-work for next-generation management of Windows PowerShell and Windows Management Instrumentation (WMI). There is a Linux-like command line in the Windows platform through PowerShell.

IT must know more by leveraging machines to learn for us. Instead of every second manually looking at massive amounts of raw data to see every action, transaction, or external stimulus, IT can use machines to see everything and learn. Machine learning, a subfield of artificial intel-ligence, allows this very capability. Machine learning tasks can be bro-ken into the two broad categories of supervised learning and unsuper-vised learning.

In supervised learning, machines are given patterns and samples that are then compared with known outputs. This training allows the ma-chine to take new inputs and predict the output.

In unsupervised learning, the machines are fed data and left to find pat-terns and structures and to apply labels on their own.

Are business units subsidizing the costs of the cloud and making on-premises solutions look more expensive? Make sure the business is not surprised down the road if its assumptions about the cloud don't match reality in operations, security, and innovation.

As a matter of routine, IT should conduct tabletop exercises in various areas to stay sharp, addressing operational inefficiencies, mapping business priorities to IT concerns, paying down technical debt, plugging IT into the business, making work visible, managing WIP, marketing new services to the business, and informing the business of IT con-straints.

Technology-enabled functionality is what IT provides to the business. By optimizing the flow of work and how we do it, designing adaptive infrastructure, and having operational intelligence over that infrastructure, IT enables the business to make relevant use of technology.

With all this functionality comes value, which attracts the attention of threats. IT must stay proactive to mitigate the growing risks from threat communities operating in the digital realm.

Efficacy Validation

When we can validate that our system of controls is working against the threats most relevant to our organization, then we can have confidence that we are doing our part to protect our organization from future losses.

We need to proactively test the efficacy of our efforts and validate that our controls are working as intended in this dynamic environment. All security programs need to have their performance validated for efficacy. This involves performing *stress tests* of your loss scenarios and risk models using green team exercises, stakeholder tabletop exercises, and simulations. Often gaps and deficiencies in your security program result from flaws in your model—the model that produced the organization's response to a loss scenario. A green team exercise focuses on a risk registry entry, maps a technical attack scenario, and simulates loss scenarios to inform stakeholders of relevant impacts. Have gated translators between the security team, IT, and the business. Begin all models with assets, which are the core of value at risk. Make use of models. They allow for proper visibility into funding mitigation efforts from different internal groups. This visibility to leaders helps funding happen. Funding is embedded in projects and in stakeholders' commitments to pay down both organizational and technical debt.

The lifecycle for the work of a security program is infinite. Risk is defined at the executive business level—not by IT, the government, the auditor, the competitor, or the market. Every organization is a voluntary coming together of people and resources to work toward some goal. Asset owners, those holding liability for the organization, determine which outcomes and experiences are advantageous or unwanted.

No two auditors are the same. They will never make the exact same judgments every time on every individual organization. None of the same rules or regulations will be enforced every time. Interpretation and context vary constantly. The number of legal cases is an indication of how inexact and inconsistent things are. No two CEOs will perceive the same outcomes as the same. No two cyber-attacks will have the same effects on the bottom line.

If the business can't tell IT what the losses or disruptions are from an attack, then is this a risk? And if not, is IT spending too much effort trying to protect the wrong assets? If IT wants to help mitigate risk, it should know what the business leaders view as unwanted, not just in general but especially when disruption and complexity mask the true drivers of risk.

Some outcomes will be positive for your organization, as in the case of an investment proving fruitful. On the other hand, some potential outcomes translate to a loss of money (now or later), more hardships or trouble, or just unwanted outcomes. You and your teams still put in money and time, but this time you lost. Whatever the case, in a world of uncertainty, we must take chances to succeed. We must act without knowing all the information upfront, knowing some of the potential outcomes could be unwanted.

And in our everyday business operations, there is always the risk of unwanted outcomes. This doesn't mean we should do nothing. This means IT should take an ongoing, programmatic approach to understanding and responding to risk. IT must think beyond the traditional thinking of adding new technical controls, more access control lists (ACLs), or more analysts. Think about it from the business standpoint.

Mitigation from a business perspective may look more like discontinuing using the data, changing the contract with a supplier, or terminating a partnership.

We need to know a risk when we see it. We identify a risk after we analyze the loss scenarios of highest relevance to our organization. IT must turn attention to the longer-term organizational process of managing risk on an ongoing basis.

What happens after we have identified our risks, triaged the ones that require immediate attention, and documented each risk in our risk registry? What's next? It is now time to determine our response. We manage the lifecycle of risk. Risk management response options include avoidance, acceptance, transference, and mitigation.

IT should have the default mentality of "yes." It is the responsibility of the business to make any *no* decisions. *No* is not IT's job! Instead, we understand our role of advisement. We inform, make recommendations, and advise. We make mitigation plans, communicate if additional investments are needed, transfer any amount that is possible, avoid some, and accept the rest.

In the real world, though, we rarely accept potential loss. We recognize intellectually the inherent loss exposure. We put in place investments that lessen the impact and reduce the likelihood of occurrence in general. And many loss scenarios are managed by controls already in place from previous investments.

A security program needs methods of validation to ensure it is performing as needed. If a tree falls in the forest, and no one is there to see or hear it, did it really fall? The same can be said of security controls against attack. If an attacker launches a campaign against an organization and there's no discernible loss to the business, was the attack successful? If the attacker has been in the environment for months or years, and there are no discernible laws to the business, is the attack successful? That is a very interesting set of questions, for there are many more actual attacks or threat events than actual loss events or successful disruptions to business. So how should we digest and understand this potential conundrum? We keep saying how dangerous and prevalent cyber-attacks are—we have lots of examples in the news and headlines—but if our CFO sees nothing in this loss event database over the last year or two or three, then how big of a threat, how big of a risk are we really talking about?

The cybersecurity team must be on the lookout for the trees that fall and use that as a signal of the nature of the threat environment and the frequency of threat events. This gives insight into how often and how efficient threat actors are against our organization. It is also needed to answer the question of how well the security controls are performing. We should be able to answer that question using the telemetry insights our controls are producing on the effect that the attacks have on us, the performance of the controls, and hints at potential improvements in our security program overall. There's a lot of data out there for us if we're prepared to collect, analyze, and digest it as every C-suite asks the question of "*how well we are doing*" and IT needs to be able to answer.

At its essence, security program validation is the function of key program indicators, or key performance indicators of cyber risk management—in this case, KPIs for our security program. They are a very great indicator of how well our investments are returning value back to the business. If we have a low loss event frequency on an annualized basis, and we can map that back to the results of our efforts of our teams, investments, process, and tooling, that is a great validation of our security program. But what we don't want to happen is just to say the lower loss events frequency is a function of just luck. The reality is because after a while, luck does not necessarily justify continuingly more security investments year over year. That investment could be used better elsewhere in the organization. Our investments need to have validation that the money is being well spent. We need to proactively test the efficacy of our efforts and validate that our controls are working as intended. There are several areas to validate.

The first area is in risk response control selection process. We need to validate that are we using the right controls for our risk environment. The results from scenario analysis and the risk assessment process will provide the needed guidance on controls selection. How cyber risk is being mitigated by your security program—which was informed by previous scenario and risk analysis along with the business, ERM, and technology contexts of your organization—can be measured against current and projected future loss exposure. The security program is a leading indicator of future loss exposure. If we pay attention to all the signals, we will get hints that we don't have the right team or strategy. Revisiting your scenario analysis and risk models to run more what-if variations can assist with validating that the best controls were chosen. If needed, alternative risk approaches or responses can be taken. How well your response strategies perform are greatly dependent on the maturity of your security program.

You need to assess the maturity of your security program to ensure it is mature enough based on your risk appetite and business strategy to operate the selected tools. We conduct security assessments to identify the maturing of our capabilities. A security program is headed by a CISO and his direct reports, but the capabilities delivered to the business encompass input and help from other parts of IT, organizational support, and the business units. From developers to cloud architects to network engineers, security capabilities are enabled by a cross-section of teams beyond the immediate security team. When we measure the maturing to a program, we evaluate a much larger team. Mature security programs happen at the intersection of inter-team collaboration across the organization. With programmatic foundations in place, tools can be deployed to operationalize risk mitigation.

Assessing how well the tools have been implemented helps to validate that you are implementing your controls correctly for your risk environment. You conduct controls review to make sure everything is configured correctly. There are so many settings and options in technical controls that there can be a wide variation in efficacy. Multiple use cases can be addressed with one control, and as such it is vital that care be given to how they are configured. Once initially deployed, they require care and feeding. Other verification factors are completeness of deployment of the control, making sure there is full coverage, and validating that the support from the vendor on technical controls is satisfactory. Every time a technical control is updated, there is the potential that the mitigation efficacy could be negatively affected. If processes are not strong, then efficacy can decrease over time. The controls need to be fully staffed, with redundancy on the personnel who support it. With the controls fully in place, then it can be tested against real-world conditions.

Efficacy testing validates that are your controls are effective at mitigating risk from real-world threats. Adversarial assessments—i.e., penetration testing and breach simulations—are performed to test what has been built. From the perspective of the threat agent, the testers emulate real-world adversaries, mimicking their TTPs to attack your organization to evaluate your operations and controls. Perform a stress test of your security controls on a regular basis to sharpen the efficacy, identify gaps, and continually get better. This can entail red team-blue team exercises and tabletop exercises. To do this, we often will have various testing engagement done both internally and by third parties. These include vulnerability assessments, penetration testing, which includes social engineering and physical testing, and breach simulations. This feeds the next process, control posture evaluation. We need to validate that the controls are working as intended. When satisfied that they stand up well to adversary TTPs under real-world simulation, the final verification is to make sure it is the best value for the investment. Continuous validation would be on the lookout for alternative controls in the future that meet the same mitigation needs at a better financial return on investment.

Finally, you need to validate that your controls portfolio is returning the best bang for your dollars. There are many choices in types of controls, how they are implemented, and in what combination. We conduct return on mitigation analysis to see the effect of the cost of the control to the monetary reduction in loss exposure. The cost of the control should be total cost, initial implementation plus ongoing annual operations. And the loss exposure reduction should be quantitatively measured, expressing in dollars how much less risk there will be after a specific expenditure. We need to be good stewards of every dollar we request. For example, in the scenario where current loss exposure is measured between $2,000,000 and $10,000,000, you propose a $250,000 investment in a new EDR tool to all endpoints to reduce the chance of ransomware shutting down our operations. You estimate that will reduce the loss exposure down to $25,000 to $150,000.

This can also be done for investments made specifically to comply with a regulation as part of the cost for doing business in a specific area. For example, adhering to PCI allows an organization to process credit cards, which is a popular consumer method of payment for goods sold and services rendered. The revenue generated from that business is the return. You can contrast those controls costs to the cost of not being able to access credit cards. Management understands cost of business.

Could changes in loss exposure factors keep loss exposure within existing ranges? ROI is a very useful and commonly used financial tool. For every control bought or implemented, IT should be able to articulate the ROI. As you model a scenario, run a simulation of the current state, then consider specific investments. You can evaluate the impact on the same scenario. The difference between the loss exposure in the current and future states, minus the cost of the control, is the return on that investment. The effects of any attack expose the organization to potential loss. At the heart of risk in our context is a financial impact. It is vital that IT can express this loss in financial terms.

Given that cyber incidents have the potential to cost an organization significant loss, risk management has the critical role of preserving business value. Value preservation peers into the future and provides due care of threats to value creation.

Cost-effective security program: As you drive a mature security program and maintain risk mitigation, do it cost-effectively. That starts with understanding the necessary context and managing the uncertainties and confusion created by the fog of noise. Safely walk the gauntlet of obstacles to clearly see what actions should be taken to mitigate risks.

How do you handle the avalanche of risk scenarios coming your way? How does the security team, IT, and the business coordinate your inputs to the risk model? The answer is a programmatic approach—a security program. A security program comprises people, process, and technology. A CISO typically leads it to ensure a consistent approach. This security program is a set of related measures and activities with the long-term goal of minimizing the occurrence and severity of undesirable loss scenarios. Its efficacy is based on how much it decreases both the likelihood of the scenario taking place and the impact it has if it does. This in an ongoing effort that has to be managed continually.

You want to do this as cost-effectively as possible while trying to avoid the problems of underspending on essential mitigation resources, or overspending, which could take dollars away from its necessary use in another business initiative. We want that system of controls to be effective against real-world threats.

With these caveats in mind, IT's aim is to protect assets by designing technology infrastructure that lends itself to defense, provides an early warning of potential threats, actively protects the business, and delivers a rapid response to incidents.

Create a dynamic security program that enables a system of controls that keeps potential future losses within the acceptable defined risk appetite ranges set by the board of directors. IT needs to understand, align, and manage to be successful.

All variation requires IT to be agile to respond to obstacles and difficulty in adjusting to a dynamic environment.

Overcoming Obstacles

We need to get past the things that inhibit progress. Obstacles are always present. Rather than be surprised, embrace them. Otherwise, your change efforts will stall out. Michael Jordan, arguably the greatest NBA player, said, *"Obstacles don't have to stop you. If you run into a wall, don't turn around and give up. Figure out how to climb it, go through it, or work around it."*[91]

Change is hard precisely because it requires people to think and act differently. The current state is a known state. As such, those inside it will put up obstacles, most of which are unintentional, subtle, and persistent. You must be equipped to overcome these obstacles.

There is no challenge or situation that a focused team cannot overcome. Every challenge or obstacle has a force behind it, so don't knock your head against the wall trying to oppose it. It is what it is. Inside the problem statements, details, observations, and test feedback lie the clues, hints, guides, and indicators of how to get to the right approach.

If change were easy, everyone would do it. The stated goals would have been achieved already. But transformation requires actual change—getting things done. It means getting from your current situation to a future target one in the real world. A business is special because of its ability to get its special sauce onto millions of burgers served up all over the world while making a profit. Getting things done is successfully convincing millions to come through your doors to buy your goods or enticing people to click on your checkout button on your site.

We can successfully navigate this obstacle course. Obstacles are often a byproduct of complex systems that have reinforcing loops that make the problem seem insurmountable. We should not be stopped from achieving our goals. Our team chooses to be intentional in its focus on what needs to be done. We are agile and resilient as we power through obstacles. This is made possible by three advantages we can have by building a team designed to thrive, developing specific approaches known to work around common team constraints, and leveraging *power tools* to enhance our work efforts.

We all will have to confront constraints in what can be done. But that is normal and to be expected. Michael Jordan once remarked, *"Never say never, because limits, like fears, are often just an illusion."*[92] View constraints as a signal to improvise. Go over, go under, go through, go around, go the other way, go backward, or do not go at all.

A *constraint* is a limitation or restriction that's in the way of what you need to accomplish. You won't be going anywhere if you do not address the constraints obstructing your progress. Constraints are a fact of doing business. Rather than worry about them, manage them.

In the movie *The Martian*, the main character is a stranded astronaut named Mark Watney. He improvises by reusing what he has at hand, from growing food to being resourceful about communicating back home. With limited resources, IT must also improvise to be successful. As IT, you are well-versed in making do with what you have.

You will find you often have what you need close at hand. Make a list of the goals, initiatives, and tasks you want to accomplish, and those you are having difficulties overcoming. Then evaluate your resources.

We will almost always face a variety of constraints in the pursuit of our goals. But we are equally skilled to manage those constraints. Five common constraints you might face are in the areas of people, time, knowledge, technology, and money.

The human aspect is a common area for constraints. This is the domain of human capital development. Investing in the professional development of current employees can reap the reward of new skill sets in the areas you need.

There will still be times when you will not have enough people for the work. You must look at the headcount, the belief systems in play, and the culture.

Seek to have enough team members who work well together. Hire the right people up front. Put people in the right roles. Leverage the vast network of talent. You may think you do not have the headcount necessary to keep pace with business demands, but your people are talented and are readily available as resources.

The belief system of your team, how they think about their work, and whether they are in the right roles for a project are all vital in both making initial assignments and in filling gaps.

The way people on your team think can either dampen or energize their motivation to enact change. This is where your leadership comes in. Team members' thinking may conflict in various areas:

- Newer techniques (e.g., PowerShell scripting versus GUI Scripting)
- Methods (e.g., Agile versus Waterfall)
- Architecture (e.g., hybrid cloud versus on-premises only)
- Design (e.g., converged wired/wireless edge versus autonomous)

Or your team members may be itching to try the newer techniques without appropriate cautions. Bring them back to center.

Your overall organizational culture can be a great aid in how much teams can produce. Or the culture can throw up roadblocks. You may have a group that shuts all the other groups out. You might hear:

- "Our group spent money on this new system."
- "You can't share."
- "We don't trust your way of doing things."
- "We are old school—the age of the mainframe and now the x86 architecture has worked just fine."
- "Why change?"

Incentives and human interactions may or may not be conducive to the kind of collaboration needed to get things done. Groups may be locked into organizational silos, hoarding valuable knowledge, expertise, and budget. Or the problem may simply be a case of "it is mine, not yours—keep out!"

But in all cases, you can be a leader. You can influence the culture as an IT guide.

There are several actions you can undertake:

- Leverage staff augmentation—through partners, vendors, and consultants—and take an ecosystem approach to multiplying human resources for a market-facing value chain.
- Develop leadership skills to inspire a new culture of responsibility, empathy, teamwork, and collaboration.
- Sponsor an internal meetup with the business to explain possible responses to market pressures.
- Develop career roadmaps for team members across silos.

- Look beyond current job titles and dive into the skill sets and aptitudes individuals possess so they can grow into new roles and take on new responsibilities. This will scale the capabilities of the existing team and its size, allowing it to focus on more important endeavors.

The people constraint may be real, but our responses can be more focused.

Humans do the work against the backdrop of time constraints. The most important time constraint solution is to not let the important get drowned out by the urgent. Time is life's most valuable resource. In some environments, you have the right people and culture, but your people just do not have the time to keep up.

Days are time-boxed. You will often hear, "If we had another week, we could get to it." "Our time is eaten up by redundant requests." "We have a way and system to correct it—if only if we had the time to deploy it."

This is the epitome of a downward spiral of overwhelming time pressure eating away at the ability to get things done. You need to somehow multiply your time. Rory Vaden, author of *Take the Stairs*, says, *"Automation is to time what compounding interest is to money."*[93]

Realize you cannot manage time because it is finite and consistent. There is a limit to borrowing time. You need to multiply your time by spending it on things today that will give you more time tomorrow. That is why, every day, IT should be paying down technical debt.

Rather than try to manage time, think differently about it. Creating next-level results requires next-level thinking. The amount of busywork always expands to fill the amount of time we allow for it. Time thinking is not about prioritization or merely working faster or harder. The amount of time in the day is fixed. You cannot add a twenty-fifth hour to the day.

Time thinking is about efficacy—leveraging the right types of work efforts to produce an intended result. Too many times we focus on the things we did instead of the results of what we did. Too many times we convince ourselves that if we are doing something, then we are working. Too many times we soothe ourselves with a false sense of satisfaction from all the thought and time we put into something, even when it did not produce any significant results.

We may need to reduce customization and increase the things that can be reused. Reduce meetings, conference calls, cross-country flights, overly long emails, and circular email threads. Understand the power of compounding interest in terms of time. The investment in effort everyday makes tomorrow successes possible. That can't be taken for granted.

We also may need to see mistakes with a different lens—as opportunities rather than time wasted. Kiichiro Toyoda, founder of Toyota, said, *"Every defect is a treasure, if the company can uncover its cause and work to prevent it across the corporation."*[94]

Also find approaches that pay off tomorrow. Consider the end user on the front lines. Teach users how to perform a task today so they can do it themselves tomorrow. Fixing symptoms is an infinite task, but fixing root causes is finite. The time invested today to teach someone else pays off tomorrow when that person can now deal with similar issues that might appear. You've saved future time.

Other actions that manage time constraints include:

- Carving out time to enact future time savings, such as cleaning up that wiring or fixing some of those application bugs. Perform those updates on that documentation and get it posted on the internal knowledge share.

- Off-loading work or tasks to a third party, such as up/down monitoring systems, performing backups, or handling account resets.

- Giving better visibility into IT, with total resource commitments broken down by business priorities and owners, as well as a list of available vetted third parties capable of picking up the work-load (along with their cost structures).

- Optimizing work task flows such as virtual computing environments, policy-based security access, or rights entitlement with orchestration and automation.

- Implementing more self-service for end users, such as password management and equipment requests.

- Getting earlier indications of future technology needs to reduce the lead time on requests by embedding it in the process.

- Learning to say no to requests for your time. Time is a finite and precious resource. Limit your work in progress. And reserve capacity for true future emergencies.

The accumulation and application of knowledge for workers is critical to productivity and getting the important things done. Stop rediscovering old things and learn about new technology you can share globally. For example, if a specific system installed years ago needs to be updated, but the people who worked on it have long since left the company and there was virtually no documentation created, this is out of your control. What technology would do the same tasks more efficiently than updating the older system? That's a knowledge constraint solution.

Another knowledge constraint solution is to encourage continuous learning in your teams. Are you leveraging even a fraction of the talent on your team? Sharing acquired knowledge and insights among your coworkers saves everyone valuable time in the day.

The are several actions you can take to help with knowledge constraints:

- Encourage continuous learning in your team on new and emerging skills. Every month, your overall team knowledge will improve, and they'll know how to do more. Discover, highlight, and share this improvement.

- Identify remediation plans to address documentation deficiencies.

- Address new systems you are responsible for.

- Do not repeat bad documentation.

- Hire outsiders who already have the knowledge.

- Don't be shy about sharing fixes and workarounds.

IT gets to work with some fantastic and exciting technology, but it's not always easy to operate. Technology could be a constraint. The rate of tech enhancements grows exponentially.

To manage technology constraints, focus on creating technology domains and getting the rest from third parties. A myriad of these problems will arise over time, such as out-of-support systems, out-of-business suppliers, capacity limitations, or shortages of licenses.

As-a-service consumption flexibility allows you to use the technology you need. It allows for a great expansion of capability to be leveraged without the upfront and long-term acquisition of people and technology.

Choose actions like these to drive future benefits for your company:

- Develop a remediation plan.

- Develop a roadmap and budget.

- Sell management on the vision of the next-generation infrastructure needed to compete in the market. Highlight current technical constraints and communicate the effect they have on business value creation.

- Develop a software and hardware rationalization strategy to trim your vendor mix.

- Begin the process of transitioning to platforms that have good enough functionality in lieu of best of breed individual point solutions.

- Build out a more agile infrastructure and replace legacy systems as soon as possible.

- Spend some time today preparing to handle tomorrow's challenges.

In some sense, all the other constraints could be caused or exacerbated by a shortage of money. This constraint can be the most impactful, as this resource is the fail-safe for the lack of people, time, technology, and knowledge. If workaround strategies fail to address those four previous constraints, a lack of money can constrain your efforts.

Waste less and value the dollar. Money is a time-honored constraint, and every dollar should be fought for, especially when looking to address other constraints.

Invest wisely to get better returns on your organization's investments. Spend money to buy the most effective combination of people, knowledge, and technical capabilities.

Is your organization getting the most out of its investments? Maximizing every dollar approved for technology spend will demonstrate good stewardship on what is given. For example, when a second firewall is proposed in the design of a new network, IT might inform the partner that the budget is already tight, so it will do without.

The firewall example could have been many other things such as another piece of equipment, another software module, more time for a programmer to do quality testing, or more time for testing the new wireless before implementing the RF tags to be used for inventory tracking in the warehouse. And yet at other times, giving that programmer more time for quality testing would save money down the road.

From equipment to contractor time to project management time, a cursory look at the bottom number can distort the IT design process and set a course for the downward spiral of accumulated technical debt. More workarounds and gaps in redundancy, proper testing, and scalability put the system architecture supporting business operations in future jeopardy.

Every shortcut can eventually interact and cause the system failure that you never expected when you were doing the continuity, disaster, and cyber response planning. And every day that our systems go unmonitored because of a lack of infrastructure to capture, monitor, and analyze data is another day of lost historical and contextual insights that could help us improve our systems and lessens the chances of service disruptions.

There are several actions you can take:

- Learn how decision makers make decisions.
- Learn how those in the business who successfully get budget approval do it.
- Learn how to communicate at the level of the C-suite, board members, and other stakeholders.
- Demonstrate your value for the budget that has been approved.
- Demonstrate business and financial literacy specific to your organization (e.g., speaking in terms of risk mitigation versus the new cool technology).

- Learn how to visualize and communicate the current state, threats, and opportunities to a nontechnical audience, from the C-suite to the workers on the line.

- Learn how to assemble multiple group leaders on common outcomes, experiences, and functions to leverage existing common technology platforms.

- Counter the argument when a group says that the solution is too expensive. And make a larger business case that resonates with how spending now will save money later.

- Value and communicate with those who must make tough decisions every day. If this really is important enough for the business, our ability to intelligently educate them on the given issue gives them the opportunity to reprioritize and fund the need.

Here are some things to think about. What constraints are you subject to today? Do you know how you will work around them? If you could work around them, what would that allow you to accomplish?

Rethink the downsides of constraints. View constraints from the perspective of the half-empty glass. Then try the half-full perspective. The upside of constraints comes through narrowing the range of possibilities and putting guardrails around what we come up with. In essence, constraints help us utilize well the number of people, amount of knowledge, and amount of time we have. To overcome our constraints and obstacles, we are going to need some tools.

Agility helps with constant nature of change. All security programs must be adept at change in all its form. Successful risk management demands adapting to change. That is what IT does, adapt as needed to deliver for its organization.

Notes

1. Eleanor Roosevelt, quoted in "Purpose Sayings and Quotes," Wise Old Sayings, accessed October 23, 2020, https://www.wiseoldsayings.com/purpose-quotes/#ixzz6IE99ohLh.

2. Peter Drucker, quoted in "Learning Organizations Quotes," Goodreads, accessed October 23, 2020, https://www.goodreads.com/quotes/tag/learning-organizations.

3. T.D. Jakes, quoted in "15 Quotes to Inspire You to Never Stop Learning," *SUCCESS*, November 16, 2017, https://www.success.com/15-quotes-to-inspire-you-to-never-stop-learning/.

4. Les Brown, quoted in "100 Inspirational Les Brown Quotes," *Raise Your Beast* (blog), accessed October 23, 2020, https://www.raiseyourbeast.com/post/100-inspirational-les-brown-quotes.

5. Michael Jordan, quoted in Steve Agyei, "'Some people want it to happen, some wish it would happen, others make it happen,'" *Steve Agyei* (blog), Medium, February 11, 2017, https://medium.com/@steveagyei65/some-people-want-it-to-happen-some-wish-it-would-happen-others-make-it-happen-aac51d4d35ad.

6. John Chambers and Rik Kirkland, "Cisco's John Chambers on the Digital Era," McKinsey & Company, March 18, 2016, http://www.mckinsey.com/industries/high-tech/our-insights/ciscos-john-chambers-on-the-digital-era.

7. Adi Ignatius, "'They Burned the House Down': An Interview with Michael Lynton," *Harvard Business Review*, July-August 2015, https://hbr.org/2015/07/they-burned-the-house-down.

8. "Opportunity is most often missed...," *Philosiblog* (blog), June 15, 2011, http://philosiblog.com/2011/06/15/opportunity-is-most-often-missed.

9. "Opportunity Is Missed Because It Is Dressed in Overalls and Looks Like Work," Quote Investigator, August 13, 2012, https://quoteinvestigator.com/2012/08/13/overalls-work/.

10. H. Jackson Brown, Jr., quoted in "H. Jackson Brown, Jr. Quotes," BrainyQuote, accessed November 5, 2020, https://www.brainyquote.com/quotes/h_jackson_brown_jr_379375.

11. Keith Alexander, quoted in Brian Wood, "Fat Stacks: $500B Stolen from US Companies — Every Year," NFINIT, October 31, 2013, https://www.nfinit.com/fat-stacks-500b-stolen-us-companies-every-year/.

12. Casey Fleming, quoted in Brian Wood, "Fat Stacks: $500B Stolen from US Companies — Every Year," NFINIT, October 31, 2013, https://www.nfinit.com/fat-stacks-500b-stolen-us-companies-every-year/.

13. Hugo Sarrazin and Andy West, "Understanding the strategic value of IT in M&A," McKinsey & Company, January 1, 2011, http://www.mckinsey.com/business-functions/strategy-and-corporate-finance/our-insights/understanding-the-strategic-value-of-it-in-m-and-38a.

14. Charisse Jones and Elizabeth Weise, "Travel trouble? Here's why your airline flight is delayed," *USA Today*, published August 11, 2016, last modified August 15, 2016, http://www.usatoday.com/story/money/2016/08/11/airlines-complex-aging-systems-lead-to-flight-delaying-computer-glitches/88539190/.

15. Bill Hethcock, "Router at root of Southwest Airlines' computer systems outage; delays, cancellations persist," *Dallas Business Journal*, July 21, 2016, http://www.bizjournals.com/dallas/news/2016/07/21/router-at-root-of-southwest-airlines-computer.html.

16. Bradley Hope, "NYSE Says Wednesday Outage Caused by Software Update," *Wall Street Journal*, July 10, 2015, http://www.wsj.com/articles/stocks-trade-on-nyse-at-open-1436450975.

17. Scott Moritz, "Verizon Reaches Deal for Lowered Yahoo Price After Hacks," Bloomberg Technology, *Bloomberg*, February 21, 2017, https://www.bloomberg.com/news/articles/2017-02-21/verizon-said-to-reach-deal-for-lowered-yahoo-price-after-hacks.

18. Lisa Lambert and Suzanne Barlyn, "SEC says cybersecurity biggest risk to financial system," Reuters, May 17, 2016, http://www.reuters.com/article/us-finance-summit-sec-idUSKCN0Y82K4.

19. Max Fisher, "Syrian hackers claim AP hack that tipped stock

market by $136 billion. Is it terrorism?" *Washington Post*, April 23, 2013, https://www.washing-tonpost.com/news/worldviews/wp/2013/04/23/syrian-hackers-claim-ap-hack-that-tipped-stock-market-by-136-billion-is-it-terrorism.

20. Tero Karppi and Kate Crawford, "Social Media, Financial Algorithms and the Hack Crash," *Theory, Culture & Society* 33, no.1 (2016), May 4, 2015, https://doi.org/10.1177/0263276415583139.

21. Taylor Armerding, "Chinese spies target US intellectual property," CSO, IDG, August 24, 2015, http://www.csoonline.com/article/2973542/security-industry/chinese-spies-target-us-intellectual-property.html.

22. "Supporting Policy and Doctrine," Infrastructure Security, Cybersecurity & Infrastructure Security Agency, accessed November 15, 2020, https://www.cisa.gov/supporting-policy-and-doctrine.

23. "The Adversary Manifesto: A Q&A with CrowdStrike's VP of Threat Intelligence," CrowdStrike, October 15, 2014, https://www.crowdstrike.com/blog/adversary-manifesto-qa-crowdstrikes-adam-meyers/.

24. Albert Einstein, quoted in "Quotable Quote," Goodreads, accessed November 5, 2020, https://www.goodreads.com/quotes/320600-we-can-not-solve-our-problems-with-the-same-level.

25. "5 Whys: Getting to the Root of a Problem Quickly," MindTools, Emerald Works, accessed August 27, 2018, https://www.mindtools.com/pages/article/newTMC_5W.htm.

26. Daniel Kahneman, *Thinking, Fast and Slow* (New York: Farrar, Straus and Giroux, 2011), 20.

27. Ann Pietrangelo, "Left Brain vs. Right Brain: What Does This Mean for Me?" ed. Deborah Weatherspoon, Healthline, last modified March 7, 2019, https://www.healthline.com/health/left-brain-vs-right-brain.

28. Jeff B.R. Gaspersz, "Three Dimensional Thinking," JeffGaspersz.com, July 15, 2011, https://www.jeffgaspersz.com/content/25338/download/clnt/32427_three-dimensional-thinking.pdf.

29. "Defining Critical Thinking," The Foundation for Critical Thinking, accessed November 5, 2020,

https://www.criticalthinking.org/pages/defining-critical-thinking/766.

30. Gray, *Liminal Thinking*, xx.

31. Gray, *Liminal Thinking*, xxiii

32. Gray, *Liminal Thinking*, xxi

33. Gray, *Liminal Thinking*, ix.

34. Theodore Levitt, quoted in Clayton M. Christensen, Scott Cook, and Taddy Hall, "Marketing Malpractice: The Cause and the Cure," Financial Management, *Harvard Business Review*, December 2005, https://hbr.org/2005/12/marketing-malpractice-the-cause-and-the-cure.

35. Sam Grier, "Why Management Should Go to Gemba," IT Managers Inbox, accessed August 27, 2018, http://itmanagersinbox.com/245/why-management-should-go-to-gemba.

36. "Attack tree," Wikipedia, last modified October 21, 2017, https://en.wikipedia.org/wiki/Attack_tree.

37. "The Industry's First Hierarchical Taxonomy of IT Services, Towers, and Cost Sources," TBM Council, accessed November 5, 2020, https://www.tbmcouncil.org/learn-tbm/tbm-taxonomy/.

38 World Economic Forum, *Partnering for Cyber Resilience: Towards the Quantification of Cyber Threats*, January 2015, http://www3.weforum.org/docs/WEFUSA_QuantificationofCyberThreats_Report2015.pdf.

39. "Monte Carlo Simulation," Palisade Corporation, accessed August 27, 2018, http://www.palisade.com/risk/monte_carlo_simulation.asp.

40. Jeff Loucks, James Macaulay, Andy Noronha, and Michael Wade, *Digital Vortex: How Today's Market Leaders Can Beat Disruptive Competitors at Their Own Game* (Lausanne, Switzerland: DBT Center, 2016), 178.

41. Henry Ford, quoted in Erik Flowers, "No one said they wanted faster horses, they wanted less horseshit," *Erik Flowers* (blog), Medium, February 12, 2015, https://medium.com/@erik_flowers/no-one-said-they-wanted-faster-horses-they-wanted-less-horseshit-e5951666f18c.

42. Alexander Osterwalder and Yves Pigneur, *Business Model Generation: A Handbook for Visionaries, Game Changers, and Challengers* (New Jersey: John Wiley & Sons, 2010), 20 – 41.

43. "Mark Zuckerberg: How do you generate innovation?" 30 Second MBA, *Fast Company*, March 2, 2012, https://www.fastcompany.com/3011634/mark-zuckerberg-how-do-you-generate-innovation.

44. Joseph Bradley, Jeff Loucks, James Macaulay, Andy Noronha, and Michael Wade, *Digital Vortex: How Digital Disruption Is Redefining Industries* (Lausanne, Switzerland: IMD, 2015), accessed November 19, 2020, https://www.cisco.com/c/dam/en/us/solutions/collateral/industry-solutions/digital-vortex-report.pdf, 1.

45. Nick Skillicorn, "What is innovation? 15 experts share their innovation definition," *Idea to Value* (blog), March 18, 2016, https://www.ideatovalue.com/inno/nickskillicorn/2016/03/innovation-15-experts-share-innovation-definition/.

46. *Encyclopædia Brittanica Online*, s.v. "Gordon Moore," published January 1, 2020, accessed November 10, 2020, https://www.britannica.com/biography/Gordon-Moore.

47. "World population," Wikipedia, last modified October 22, 2020, https://en.wikipedia.org/wiki/World_population#Global_demographics.

48. "GDP Ranked by Country 2020," World Population Review, accessed October 23, 2020, http://worldpopulationreview.com/countries/countries-by-gdp/.

49. "Projected GDP Ranking," Statistics Times, February 20, 2020, http://statisticstimes.com/economy/projected-world-gdp-ranking.php.

50. Aaron Dignan, *Brave New Work: Are You Ready to Reinvent Your Organization?* (New York: Portfolio, 2019), 29.

51. Aaron Dignan, "The U.S. Economy Is Suffering From 'Graceful Degradation,'" *Barron's*, March 7, 2019, https://www.barrons.com/articles/the-u-s-economy-is-suffering-from-graceful-degradation-51551963636.

52. Ilan Mochari, "Why Half of the S&P 500 Companies Will Be Replaced in the Next Decade," *Inc.*, March 23, 2016. https://www.inc.com/ilan-mochari/innosight-sp-500-new-companies.html.

53. Reem Heakal, "The Investor's Guide to Global Trade," *Investopedia*, last modified August 24, 2020, https://www.investopedia.com/insights/what-is-international-trade.

54. Jason Albanese, "These 4 Companies Have Been Saved by Digital Transformation," *Inc.*, May 24, 2018, https://www.inc.com/jason-albanese/these-4-companies-have-been-saved-by-digital-transformation.html.

55. Brian Deagon, "Cloudera, Carvana IPOs Debut: One Up, One Down," *Investor's Business Daily*, April 28, 2017, https://www.investors.com/news/technology/cloudera-carvana-complete-ipos-with-one-up-one-down/.

56. Peter High, "Land O'Lakes CIO Mike Macrie Enables The Digital Farm," *Forbes*, July 11, 2016, https://www.forbes.com/sites/peterhigh/2016/07/11/land-olakes-cio-mike-macrie-enables-the-digital-farm/#599af6f327f0.

57. Lesley Stahl, "Land O'Lakes CEO Beth Ford and the Changing Landscape of America's Farms," 60 Minutes, *CBS News*, October 6, 2019, https://www.cbsnews.com/news/land-olakes-ceo-beth-ford-and-the-changing-landscape-of-america-farms-60-minutes-2019-10-06/.

58. Steven ZoBell, "Why Digital Transformations Fail: Closing The $900 Billion Hole In Enterprise Strategy," *Forbes*, March 13, 2018, https://www.forbes.com/sites/forbestechcouncil/2018/03/13/why-digital-transformations-fail-closing-the-900-billion-hole-in-enterprise-strategy/#4905a1287b8b.

59. See note 6 above.

60. Jared Lindzon, "6 Ways Work Will Change In 2016," *Fast Company*, November 2, 2015, https://www.fastcompany.com/3052836/6-ways-work-will-change-in-2016.

61. Robert Howell, "How Will Changing Demographics in the U.S. Influence Business in the Coming Decade?" *Wall Street Journal*,

November 29, 2013, http://www.wsj.com/arti-cles/SB10001424052702303562904579228000262387472.

62. Tom Spring, "Cisco's Chambers: 'Disrupt Yourself, Or Be Dis-rupted,'" CRN, January 7, 2015, http://www.crn.com/news/network-ing/300075285/ciscos-chambers-disrupt-yourself-or-be-dis-rupted.htm.

63. Vangie Beal, "Consumerization of IT," Webopedia, accessed Octo-ber 23, 2020, https://www.webopedia.com/TERM/C/consumeriza-tion_of_it.html

64. Eugene Kim, "Salesforce CEO Marc Benioff says his company is outselling Oracle because of this huge change in sales," *Business In-sider*, February 24, 2016, http://www.businessinsider.com/salesforce-ceo-marc-benioff-sells-directly-to-ceos-2016-2.

65. Dave Gray, *Liminal Thinking: Create the Change You Want by Changing the Way You Think* (New York: Two Waves Books, 2016), xxi.

66. Gail Sessoms, "What Are Organizational Silos?" AZCentral, ac-cessed August 28, 2018, http://yourbusiness.azcentral.com/organiza-tional-silos-8237.html.

67. James Kalbach, preface to *Mapping Experiences: A Complete Guide to Creating Value through Journeys, Blueprints, and Diagrams* (Sebastopol, CA: O'Reilly, 2016), Preface, xii.

68. D.D. Woods, "STELLA: Report from the SNAFUcatchers Workshop on Coping with Complexity," accessed October 23, 2020, https://sna-fucatchers.github.io/.

69. Eliyahu M. Goldratt and Jeff Cox, *The Goal: A Process of Ongoing Improvement* (Great Barrington, MA: North River Press, 2004), 94 - 119.

70. "Little's Law," CFI, accessed November 19, 2020, https://corpo-ratefinanceinstitute.com/resources/knowledge/other/littles-law/.

71. "What is Lean?" Lean Enterprise Institute, accessed August 27, 2018, http://www.lean.org/WhatsLean.

72. "Bimodal," Gartner, accessed November 19, 2020, https://www.gartner.com/en/information-technology/glossary/bi-modal.

73. Donald A. Norman, *The Design of Everyday Things* (New York: Basic Books, 2002), 8.

74. Steve Jobs, quoted in Raajan, "'The design is not just what it looks like and feels like. The design is how it works' — Steve Jobs," *Raajan* (blog), Medium, June 26, 2018, https://medium.com/@oraajan/the-design-is-not-just-what-it-looks-like-and-feels-like-the-design-is-how-it-works-steve-jobs-9b79674126bb.

75. Brian Koles, "A Company Without APIs Is Like A Computer Without Internet," ReadWrite, November 29, 2013, http://read-write.com/2013/11/29/company-without-api-computer-without-internet.

76. Klint Finley, "How Google Is Cramming More Data Into Its Atlantic Cable," *Wired*, April 5, 2019, https://www.wired.com/story/google-cramming-more-data-new-atlantic-cable/.

77. José Américano N L F de Freitas, "How exactly does binary code work?" TED, filmed July 2018, video, 0:06, https://www.ted.com/talks/jose_ameri-cano_n_l_f_de_freitas_how_exactly_does_binary_code_work.

78. Joshua Phillip, "The Staggering Cost of Economic Espionage Against the US," *Epoch Times*, October 22, 2013, http://www.theepochtimes.com/n3/326002-the-staggering-cost-of-economic-espionage-against-the-us.

79. Sumit Pal, "SQL On Big Data: Why, How and the Road Ahead," AFCOM, accessed August 27, 2018, https://www.afcom.com/Pub-lic/Resource_Center/Articles_Pub-lic/SQL_On_Big_Data_Why_How_and_the_Road_Ahead.aspx.

80. Marcia Conner, "Data on Big Data," *Marcia Conner* (blog), July 18, 2012, http://marciaconner.com/blog/data-on-big-data.

81. Steve Jobs, quoted in "Steve Jobs Biography," *Business News Daily*, January 22, 2019, https://www.businessnewsdaily.com/4195-business-profile-steve-jobs.html.

82. Dominica DeGrandis and Kaimar Karu, *Using Kanban in IT Operations* (London: AXELOS, 2016), accessed October 30, 2020,

https://www.axelos.com/Corporate/media/Files/Campaigns/ITIL_Guidance_Kanban_website.pdf.

83. Naresh Jain, "Build Teams to Run Marathons, Not Sprints," in *97 Things Every Project Manager Should Know: Collective Wisdom from the Experts*, ed. Barbee Davis (Sebastopol, CA: O'Reilly, 2009), 96.

84. Andrew Carnegie, quoted in "Andrew Carnegie Quote on Teamwork: Working Together Toward a Common Vision," Goalcast, accessed November 5, 2020, https://www.goalcast.com/2018/05/28/20-teamwork-quotes/carnegie2-1/.

85. Jim Collins, *Good to Great: Why Some Companies Make the Leap...And Others Don't* (New York: Harper Business, 2001), 13.

86. Jeff Loucks, James Macaulay, Andy Noronha, and Michael Wade, *Workforce Transformation in the Digital Vortex: Reimagining Work for Digital Business Agility* (Lausanne, Switzerland: IMD, 2016), accessed April 19, 2016, https://www.imd.org/contentassets/0e53bead1660441e9a4c9317dc30cf67/workforce-transformation, 23.

87. Steve Denning, "How Fake Agile At DoD Risks National Security," *Forbes*, September 22, 2019, https://www.forbes.com/sites/stevedenning/2019/09/22/how-fake-agile-at-dod-risks-national-security/#16571e5a8fa8.

88. Denis Waitley, quoted in "Denis Waitley Quotes," BrainyQuote, accessed November 19, 2020, https://www.brainyquote.com/quotes/denis_waitley_146912.

89. Loucks, Macaulay, Noronha, and Wade, *Workforce Transformation*, 5.

90. George Bernard Shaw, quoted in "George Bernard Shaw Quotes," BrainyQuote, accessed November 19, 2020, https://www.brainyquote.com/quotes/george_bernard_shaw_385438.

91. Michael Jordan, quoted in "Michael Jordan Quotes," BrainyQuote, accessed November 5, 2020, https://www.brainyquote.com/quotes/michael_jordan_165967

92. Michael Jordan, quoted in "Limits and Illusions: Michael Jordan in

the NBA at 50," TrueHoop, *ESPN*, September 22, 2009, https://www.espn.com/blog/truehoop/post/_/id/6982/limits-and-il-lusions-michael-jordan-in-the-nba-at-50.

93. Rory Vaden, quoted in "Quote," QuoteNova.net, accessed November 5, 2020, https://www.quotenova.net/authors/rory-va-den/qa42km.

94. Kiichiro Toyoda, quoted in John Reeve, "Defect Elimination," Relia-bilityweb.com, accessed November 5, 2020, https://reliabil-ityweb.com/articles/entry/defect-elimination-from-a-cmms-perspec-tive.

CPSIA information can be obtained
at www.ICGtesting.com
Printed in the USA
BVHW061057111022
649153BV00021B/717/J